Contents at a Glance

Contents

Routers and Routing Basics
CCNA 2 Labs and Study Guide

Allan Johnson

Cisco Press
800 East 96th Street
Indianapolis, Indiana 46240 USA

Routers and Routing Basics
CCNA 2 Labs and Study Guide

Allan Johnson

Copyright © 2007 Cisco Systems, Inc.

Published by:
Cisco Press
800 East 96th Street
Indianapolis, IN 46240 USA

Printed in the United States of America 12 V0N4

Fifteenth Printing, May 2012

Library of Congress Cataloging-in-Publication Number: 2006920176

ISBN: 1-58713-167-6

Publisher
Paul Boger

Cisco Representative
Anthony Wolfenden

Cisco Press Program Manager
Jeff Brady

Executive Editor
Mary Beth Ray

Production Manager
Patrick Kanouse

Senior Development Editor
Christopher Cleveland

Senior Project Editor
San Dee Phillips

Copy Editor
John Edwards

Technical Editor
Tom Knott

Team Coordinator
Vanessa Williams

Book and Cover Designer
Louisa Adair

Composition
Louisa Adair

Proofreader
Gayle Johnson

Warning and Disclaimer

This book is designed to provide information about the labs for the Routers and Routing Basics CCNA 2 course of the Cisco Networking Academy Program. Every effort has been made to make this book as complete and as accurate as possible, but no warranty or fitness is implied.

The information is provided on an "as is" basis. The author, Cisco Press, and Cisco Systems, Inc. shall have neither liability nor responsibility to any person or entity with respect to any loss or damages arising from the information contained in this book or from the use of the discs or programs that may accompany it.

The opinions expressed in this book belong to the author and are not necessarily those of Cisco Systems, Inc.

Feedback Information

At Cisco Press, our goal is to create in-depth technical books of the highest quality and value. Each book is crafted with care and precision, undergoing rigorous development that involves the unique expertise of members from the professional technical community.

Readers' feedback is a natural continuation of this process. If you have any comments regarding how we could improve the quality of this book, or otherwise alter it to better suit your needs, you can contact us through e-mail at feedback@ciscopress.com. Please make sure to include the book title and ISBN in your message.

We greatly appreciate your assistance.

CISCO SYSTEMS

Corporate Headquarters
Cisco Systems, Inc.
170 West Tasman Drive
San Jose, CA 95134-1706
USA
www.cisco.com
Tel: 408 526-4000
800 553-NETS (6387)
Fax: 408 526-4100

European Headquarters
Cisco Systems International BV
Haarlerbergpark
Haarlerbergweg 13-19
1101 CH Amsterdam
The Netherlands
www-europe.cisco.com
Tel: 31 0 20 357 1000
Fax: 31 0 20 357 1100

Americas Headquarters
Cisco Systems, Inc.
170 West Tasman Drive
San Jose, CA 95134-1706
USA
www.cisco.com
Tel: 408 526-7660
Fax: 408 527-0883

Asia Pacific Headquarters
Cisco Systems, Inc.
Capital Tower
168 Robinson Road
#22-01 to #29-01
Singapore 068912
www.cisco.com
Tel: +65 6317 7777
Fax: +65 6317 7799

Cisco Systems has more than 200 offices in the following countries and regions. Addresses, phone numbers, and fax numbers are listed on the **Cisco.com Web site at www.cisco.com/go/offices.**

Argentina • Australia • Austria • Belgium • Brazil • Bulgaria • Canada • Chile • China PRC • Colombia • Costa Rica • Croatia • Czech Republic Denmark • Dubai, UAE • Finland • France • Germany • Greece • Hong Kong SAR • Hungary • India • Indonesia • Ireland • Israel • Italy Japan • Korea • Luxembourg • Malaysia • Mexico • The Netherlands • New Zealand • Norway • Peru • Philippines • Poland • Portugal Puerto Rico • Romania • Russia • Saudi Arabia • Scotland • Singapore • Slovakia • Slovenia • South Africa • Spain • Sweden Switzerland • Taiwan • Thailand • Turkey • Ukraine • United Kingdom • United States • Venezuela • Vietnam • Zimbabwe

Printed in the USA

Trademark Acknowledgments

All terms mentioned in this book that are known to be trademarks or service marks have been appropriately capitalized. Cisco Press or Cisco Systems, Inc., cannot attest to the accuracy of this information. Use of a term in this book should not be regarded as affecting the validity of any trademark or service mark.

About the Author

Allan Johnson entered the academic world in 1999 after ten years as a business owner/operator to dedicate his efforts to his passion for teaching. He has an M.B.A. and an M.Ed. in occupational training and development. Allan is currently pursuing an M.S. in information security. He is an information technology instructor at Mary Carroll High School and Del Mar College in Corpus Christi, Texas. Since 2003, Allan has committed much of his time and energy to the CCNA Instructional Support Team, providing services for instructors worldwide and creating training materials. He is a familiar voice on the Cisco Networking Academy Community forum "Ask the Experts" series. He currently holds CCNA and CCAI certifications.

About the Technical Reviewer

Tom Knott is a Networking Academy instructor and IT career–focused learning community director in the Career and Technical Education department at Southeast Raleigh Magnet High School, Raleigh, N. C. Tom has taught all versions of the CCNA curriculum since v1.1. He coauthored *Networking Basics CCNA 1 Companion Guide* (ISBN: 1-58713-164-1), the only authorized Companion Guide for the Cisco Networking Academy Program.

Jim Lorenz is a curriculum developer for the Cisco Networking Academy Program who co-authored the third editions of the *Lab Companions* for the CCNA courses. He has over 20 years experience in information systems and has held various IT positions in several Fortune 500 companies, including Allied-Signal, Honeywell, and Motorola. Jim has developed and taught computer and networking courses for both public and private institutions for more than 15 years.

Dedication

To my wife, Becky, and my daughter, Christina. Thank you both for your love and patience.

Acknowledgments

As technical editor, Tom Knott served admirably as my second pair of eyes, finding and correcting technical inaccuracies as well as grammatical errors, helping to make this project a first-class production.

Mary Beth Ray, executive editor, did an outstanding job steering this project from beginning to end. I can always count on Mary Beth to make the tough decisions.

Christopher Cleveland, development editor, has a dedication to perfection that pays dividends in countless, unseen ways. Thank you for providing me with much-needed guidance and support. This book could not be a reality without your persistence.

Last, I cannot forget to thank all my students—past and present—who have helped me over the years to create engaging and exciting activities and labs. There is no better way to test the effectiveness of an activity than to give it to a team of dedicated students. They excel at finding the obscurest of errors! I could have never done this without all your support.

Icons Used in This Book

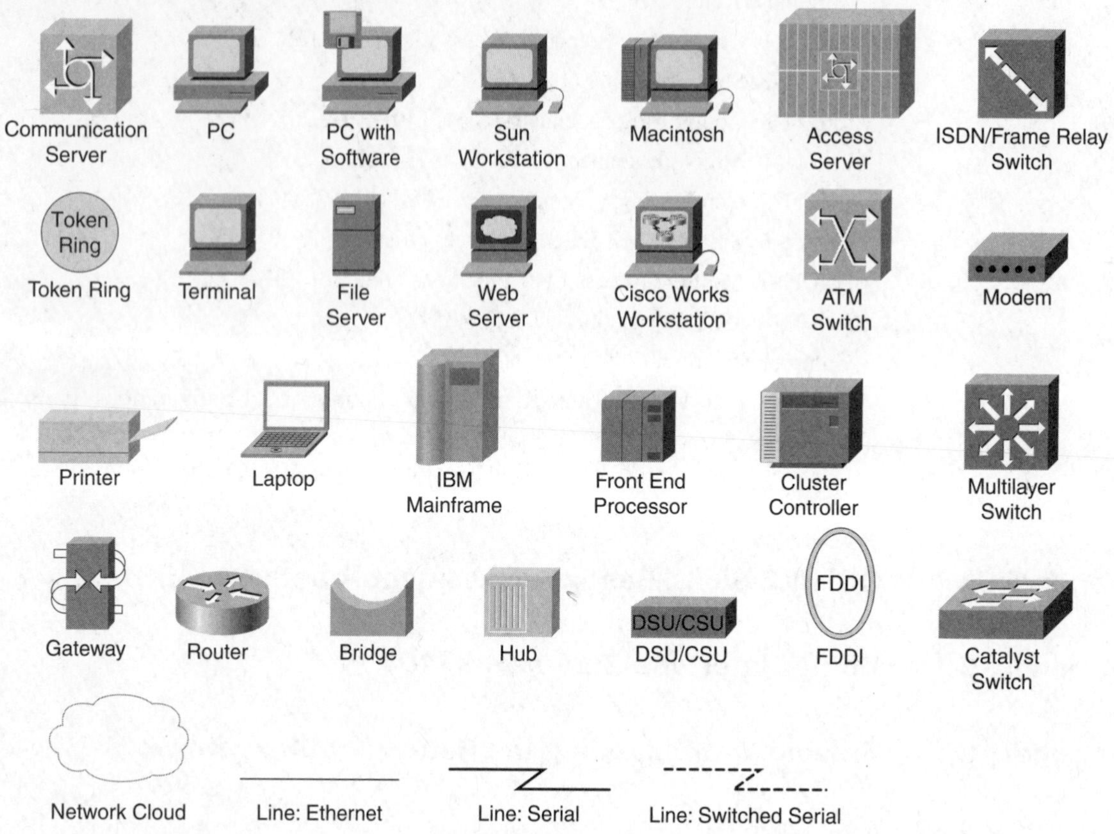

Command Syntax Conventions

The conventions that present command syntax in this book are the same conventions used in the IOS Command Reference. The Command Reference describes these conventions as follows:

- **Bold** indicates commands and keywords that are entered literally as shown. In actual configuration examples and output (not general command syntax), bold indicates commands that are manually input by the user (such as a **show** command).
- *Italic* indicates arguments for which you supply actual values.
- Vertical bars (|) separate alternative, mutually exclusive elements.
- Square brackets ([ ]) indicate optional elements.
- Braces ({ }) indicate a required choice.
- Braces within brackets ([{ }]) indicate a required choice within an optional element.

Introduction

Routers and Routing Basics CCNA 2 Labs and Study Guide is a supplement to your classroom and laboratory experience with the Cisco Networking Academy Program (CNAP). Specifically, this book covers the second of four courses. To be successful on the exam and achieve your CCNA certification, you should do everything possible to arm yourself with a variety of tools and training materials to support your learning efforts. This book is just such a collection of tools. Used to its fullest extent, it can help you gain the knowledge as well as practice the skills associated with the content area of the CCNA 2 Routers and Routing Basics course. Specifically, this book can help you work on these main areas of CCNA 2:

- Configuring a router
- Managing the Cisco IOS
- Selecting a routing protocol
- Verifying and troubleshooting a network
- Implementing basic security with access control lists

Books similar to this one are also available for the other three courses: *Networking Basics CCNA 1 Labs and Study Guide, Switching Basics and Intermediate Routing CCNA 3 Labs and Study Guide,* and *WAN Technologies CCNA 4 Labs and Study Guide.*

Goals and Methods

The most important goal of this book is to help you pass either the CCNA exam (640-801) or the INTRO exam (640-821). Whether you are studying for the full exam or the first part of your CCNA, passing either of these exams means that you not only have the required knowledge of the technologies covered by the exam, but that you can also plan, design, implement, operate, and troubleshoot these technologies. In other words, these exams are rigorously application-based. In fact, if you view the main objectives for the CCNA exam at **http://www.cisco.com/go/certifications**, you can see the following four categories of objectives:

- Planning & Design
- Implementation & Operation
- Troubleshooting
- Technology

Although Technology is listed last, a CCNA student cannot possibly plan, design, implement, operate, and troubleshoot networks without first fully grasping the technology. So you must devote large amounts of time and effort in the Study Guide section of each chapter, learning the concepts and theories before applying them in the Lab Exercises.

The Study Guide section offers exercises that help you learn the concepts and configurations that are crucial to your success as a CCNA exam candidate. Each chapter is slightly different and includes some or all of the following types of exercises:

- Vocabulary Matching and Completion
- Skill-Building Activities and Scenarios
- Configuration Scenarios
- Concept Questions
- Journal Entries
- Internet Research

The Lab Exercises section includes a Command Reference table, all the online Curriculum Labs, and new Comprehensive Labs and Challenge Labs. The Curriculum Labs typically walk you through the configuration tasks step by step. The Comprehensive Labs include many, if not all, of the configuration tasks of the Curriculum Labs without actually providing you with the commands. The Challenge Labs take this a step further, often giving you only a general requirement that you must implement fully without the details of each small step. In other words, you must use the knowledge and skills you gained in the Curriculum Labs to successfully complete the Comprehensive and Challenge Labs. In fact, you should not attempt the Comprehensive or Challenge labs until you have worked through all the Study Guide activities and the Curriculum Labs. Avoid the temptation to work through the Comprehensive and Challenge Labs by flipping back through the Curriculum Labs when you are unsure of a command. Do not try to short-change your CCNA training. You need a deep understanding of CCNA knowledge and skills to ultimately be successful on the CCNA exam.

How This Book Is Organized

Because the content of *Routers and Routing Basics CCNA 2 Companion Guide* and the online curriculum is sequential, you should work through this book in order, beginning with Chapter 1.

Chapters 1 through 11 cover the following topics:

Chapter 1, "WANs and Routers"—After presenting a few vocabulary exercises covering the topic of WANs, this chapter delves into the internal and external components of routers. Understanding how a router works and how you connect to a router are important concepts and skills you need throughout the rest of your CCNA studies. The three Curriculum Labs focus your attention on connecting LANs and WANs using routers. An additional Challenge Lab helps you review the skills learned in the Curriculum labs.

Chapter 2, "Introduction to Routers"—This chapter discusses the basics of using the command-line interface (CLI). Several exercises help you solidify your skills with using the CLI. In addition, you work through exercises that focus on understanding the router boot sequence and interpreting output from the **show version** command. The three Curriculum Labs focus your attention on the configuration tasks covered in the chapter. Two additional labs, a Comprehensive Lab and Challenge Lab, help you review the commands and skills learned in the Curriculum Labs.

Chapter 3, "Configuring a Router"—This chapter first focuses on basic router configuraion, including learning the commands that every router uses as well as activating interfaces and setting up basic routing. Then your attention turns to file-management issues: backing up the configuration and the IOS. The ten Curriculum Labs focus your attention on the router configuration and file-management tasks covered in the chapter. Two additional labs, a Comprehensive Lab and Challenge Lab, help you review the commands and skills learned in the Curriculum Labs.

Chapter 4, "Learning About Other Devices"—The Cisco IOS software offers a powerful tool for gathering information about other directly connected devices through its Cisco Discovery Protocol (CDP). This chapter's exercises center your attention on the benefits of using CDP as a network engineer. Other commands, including **telnet** and **traceroute**, are also part of your tool kit for learning about other network devices. So you spend some time on these as well. The eight Curriculum Labs focus your attention on the configuration tasks covered in the chapter. Two additional Comprehensive Labs help you review the commands and skills learned in the Curriculum Labs.

Chapter 5, "Managing Cisco IOS Software"—This chapter examines in detail how a router boots and loads the IOS. Knowing the default boot sequence as well as how to change the sequence is an important part of your network engineer's skill set. Exercises focus on the boot sequence, the boot system commands, the configuration register, the IOS naming convention, and methods for uploading and downloading an IOS. The six Curriculum Labs focus your attention on the configuration tasks covered in the chapter. An additional Challenge Lab helps you review the commands and skills learned in the Curriculum Labs.

Chapter 6, "Routing and Routing Protocols"—This chapter covers a crucial topic for any CCNA candidate: routing. Exercises focus on reading routing table output from the **show ip route** command, using static routing, choosing a routing protocol, understanding dynamic routing, and learning basic Routing Information Protocol (RIP) configuration. The Curriculum Lab focuses your attention on configuring static routes. Two additional labs, a Comprehensive Lab and Challenge Lab, help you review the commands and skills learned in the chapter.

Chapter 7, "Distance Vector Routing Protocols"—This chapter covers how distance vector routing avoids loops. In addition, you extend your skills in configuring RIP and you learn some valuable troubleshooting tools. The seven Curriculum Labs focus your attention on the configuration tasks covered in the chapter. Two additional labs, a Comprehensive Lab and Challenge Lab, help you review the commands and skills learned in the chapter.

Chapter 8, "TCP/IP Suite Error and Control Messages"—This chapter takes a brief look at the Internet Control Message Protocol (ICMP). A basic understanding of the IP packet header and the most important ICMP messages are covered. There are no labs in this chapter.

Chapter 9, "Basic Router Troubleshooting"—This chapter focuses exclusively on your troubleshooting skills. As a major part of the CCNA exam, you must be proficient at troubleshooting a simple internetwork. Exercises include dissecting a routing table entry, knowing troubleshooting steps, matching a problem to the correct layer, and reviewing the most powerful **show** and **debug** commands. The seven Curriculum Labs focus your attention on the configuration tasks covered in the chapter. An additional Challenge Lab helps you review the commands and skills learned in the Curriculum Labs.

Chapter 10, "Intermediate TCP/IP"—This chapter is mostly a review of material covered in your CCNA 1 studies. Exercises include learning vocabulary, reviewing TCP and User Datagram Protocol (UDP) segments, understanding port numbers, and comparing Layers 2, 3 and 4. The two Curriculum Labs focus your attention on how port numbers work to allow multiple sessions for the same host or application.

Chapter 11, "Access Control Lists (ACLs)"—This chapter covers the fundamentals of access control lists. Having a basic understanding of ACLs and knowing how to implement them are crucial to your success on the CCNA exam and in the networking field. Therefore, the exercises in this chapter are extensive. First, you work through some exercises that help you understand what ACLs are and how they operate. Then you work through eight ACL configuration exercises and scenarios that focus on CCNA-level security implementations. The eight Curriculum Labs focus your attention on the configuration tasks covered in the chapter. An additional Challenge Lab helps you review the commands and skills learned in the Curriculum Labs.

Appendix A, "CCNA 2 Skills-Based Assessment Practice"—This appendix contains a practice lab for the Skills-Based Assessment in which you are required to demonstrate all the skills covered in the CCNA 2 course.

Appendix B, "Router Interface Summary"—This appendix provides a chart of the router interface identifiers that you need for the curriculum-based labs in each chapter.

Appendix C, "Erasing and Reloading the Router"—This appendix guides you through the procedure for clearing out previous configurations and starting with an unconfigured router for use in the Curriculum Labs in each chapter.

CHAPTER 1

WANs and Routers

The Study Guide portion of this chapter uses a combination of multiple-choice, matching, and open-ended question exercises to test your knowledge of the theory of routers in a WAN environment.

The Lab Exercises portion of this chapter includes all the online curriculum labs as well as a challenge lab to ensure that you have mastered the practical, hands-on skills needed to use routers in a WAN environment.

Study Guide

WANs

A wide-area network (WAN) is a data communications network that connects user networks over a large geographical area. WANs have several important characteristics that distinguish them from local-area networks (LAN). In CCNA 1, you spent much of your time studying the Ethernet technology and learning how Ethernet operates at the Data Link layer. WANs use different technologies and protocols. However, much of what you learned in CCNA 1 still applies to WANs. For example, the Internet Protocol at Layer 3 is still relevant. This section of the Study Guide focuses on terms and concepts that relate to WANs.

Vocabulary Exercise: Matching

Match the definition on the left with a term on the right.

Definitions

- **a.** When referring to clocking, the CSU/DSU is this piece of equipment.
- **b.** The software used by a router.
- **c.** Dialup and ISDN are examples of these types of networks.
- **d.** Describes the timing between the router and the CSU/DSU.
- **e.** Lost when a device is powered down or rebooted.
- **f.** Wires or other media through which data is transmitted from one place to another.
- **g.** Connects LANs to WANs.
- **h.** The physical connection point on networking devices where signals enter and exit.
- **i.** A smaller, more compact physical interface specification.
- **j.** A WAN link contracted for use by the customer.
- **k.** Frame Relay and ATM are examples of these types of networks.
- **l.** When referring to clocking the customer's router, this piece of equipment is used.
- **m.** A communications link that is outside the normal IP network, like a console cable or a phone call between two modems and the aux port.
- **n.** A network that spans a large geographic area.
- **o.** A telecommunications path that sends 1 bit at a time.
- **p.** The router port that connects a WAN link.
- **q.** A WAN service provider.
- **r.** Connects a router to the CSU/DSU.
- **s.** The management port on a router.
- **t.** Equipment that is located in the customer's wiring closet and provides a clocking signal to the router.
- **u.** A general term that describes the measurement of a route.
- **v.** If a device does not know how to get to a destination, it sends data to this device.
- **w.** The number of bits per second that the service provider can accept and send to the customer.
- **x.** What the WAN service provider calls your collection of equipment, including the router and CSU/DSU.

Terms

___ wide-area network (WAN)

___ router

___ default gateway

___ leased line

___ telephone company (telco)

___ serial cable

___ channel service unit/data service unit (CSU/DSU)

___ data circuit–terminating equipment (DCE)

___ data terminal equipment (DTE)

___ clocking/clock rate

___ synchronous

___ serial link

___ serial interface

___ customer premises equipment (CPE)

___ metric

___ Cisco IOS

___ contents of RAM

___ bus

___ interface

___ smart serial interface

___ circuit-switching

___ packet-switching

___ console port

___ out-of-band management

Vocabulary Exercise: Completion

Complete the paragraphs that follow by filling in the appropriate words and phrases.

When only two devices are connected across a WAN link, it's called a __________ link or __________ line or __________ circuit, or simply a WAN link. To create a __________ WAN link, a company must use the services of a __________ or an Internet service provider (ISP) that sells WAN services. The router uses a __________ cable to attach to a __________. This device then accepts the line coming in from the provider.

The router interface that attaches to the provider is normally the __________ side of the link, whereas the __________ serves as the __________ side of the link. This distinction is important, because the __________ side of the link provides the clocking or synchronization between the two sides of the link, specifying how fast the router can send data. The router and the CSU/DSU are physically located at the customer's location. Therefore, these devices collectively are called the __________.

Each new advance in WAN speed and technology has required a new set of standards. Most WAN standards are created by one of the following organizations:

- __________, which creates a wide range of standards, not just those for networking
- __________, which develops and maintains the protocols for TCP/IP
- __________, which works closely with the Telecommunications Industry Association (TIA) to develop the electrical specifications necessary to communications
- __________, which is under the control of the United Nations and exists for the purpose of developing worldwide telecommunication standards

Concept Questions

1. What is the most important function of a router?

2. Define *default gateway.* You can use any source at your disposal.

3. In three or four sentences, explain the purpose of DCE and DTE in WAN links.

4. Explain what a router is and what it does.

____

- ____
- ____
- ____

Routers

Routers are specialized computers for networking services using hardware and software. The hardware includes a processor, memory, specialized chips, and a selection of interfaces or ports. The software provides an operating environment for the hardware. This section of the Study Guide focuses on the terminology and concepts relating to routers. You reinforce your understanding of the internal components of a router by working through some exercises. Other exercises ask you to identify external interfaces and choose the right cable to use to connect devices.

Vocabulary Exercise: Completion

Complete the paragraphs that follow by filling in the appropriate words and phrases.

The main purpose of a router is to ______ packets. A router, like a typical PC, has a CPU and memory components. It also has specialized software, which in Cisco routers is called the __________. The ___ provides the basic routing logic. The router also has _____, just like PCs, which holds basic diagnostic software that runs when the router is first booted. All of these basic components (CPU, RAM, ROM, and an OS) are found in PCs.

In addition, just like PCs have an interface to connect to networks (usually called a ________________, or ____), routers also have interfaces. Instead of using a hard drive, routers use two types of memory to permanently store data: ______ and ________.

The main internal router components are as follows:

- _____, which stores _______ tables and the _________ file while the router is powered. It loses content when a router is powered down or restarted.
- ________, which provides storage for the startup _____________ file and retains content when a router is powered down or restarted.
- __________, which is a type of EEPROM. It holds the ____ image and retains content when a router is powered down or restarted.
- ______, which maintains instructions for ________________ diagnostics and stores bootstrap program and basic operating system software.
- ______, which connect routers to a network for packet entry and exit.

Flash memory is used for storage of the __________ software image. The router normally acquires the default IOS from flash. These images can be upgraded by loading a new image into flash. The IOS can be in uncompressed or compressed form. In most routers, an executable copy of the IOS is transferred to ____ during the boot process.

The three basic types of connections on a router are ____ interfaces, ____ interfaces, and __________ ports. The term *interface* specifically refers to physical connectors that forward packets. In contrast, the term *port* refers to a physical connector that manages and controls a router.

The LAN and WAN connections provide network connections through which frame packets are passed. To connect to LAN interfaces, routers use a ____________ cable to connect to a switch, just like a ____________ cable should be used to connect a PC NIC to a switch. If you connect a router directly to a PC NIC without an intermediate device, like a hub or a switch, you must use a ________ cable. This type of connection is common in many of the labs you will configure. To connect to WAN interfaces, the router uses a ________ or ________ cable to attach to a CSU/DSU or when directly connecting two WAN interfaces in a lab environment.

The function of management ports is different from that of the other connections. The management port provides a text-based connection for the configuration and troubleshooting of the router. The common management "interfaces" are the ________ and ________ ports. The console port and the auxiliary (AUX) port are EIA-232 ____________ serial ports and are not designed as networking ports.

Internal Components of a Router

Knowing the function of the main internal components of a router is more important than knowing the locations of the physical components inside a particular model. Therefore, in the following table, provide a sufficiently detailed description of each component.

Component	Description
CPU	
RAM	
Flash	
NVRAM	
Buses	

Component	Description
ROM	______________________________
Power supply	______________________________

Another way to learn the internal components of a router is to list each component's function. For each of the following functions, indicate which of the following components performs the function:

A. RAM

B. NVRAM

C. Flash

D. ROM

E. Interfaces

Answer	Function
_____	Provides temporary memory for the configuration file of the router while the router is powered on
_____	Allows software to be updated without removing and replacing chips on the processor
_____	Stores routing tables
_____	Maintains instructions for POST diagnostics
_____	Connect the router to the network for frame entry and exit
_____	Can be on the motherboard or on a separate module
_____	Is a type of EEPROM
_____	Retains content when router is powered down or restarted
_____	Stores bootstrap program and basic operating system software
_____	Holds Address Resolution Protocol (ARP) cache
_____	Loses content when router is powered down or restarted
_____	Retains content when router is powered down or restarted
_____	Holds the operating system image (IOS)
_____	Provides storage for the startup configuration file
_____	Can store multiple versions of IOS software

Label the External Components of a Router

Choose the correct label description for each number shown in Figure 1-1. Some labels can be used more than once.

Figure 1-1 Rear View of a 1721 Cisco Router

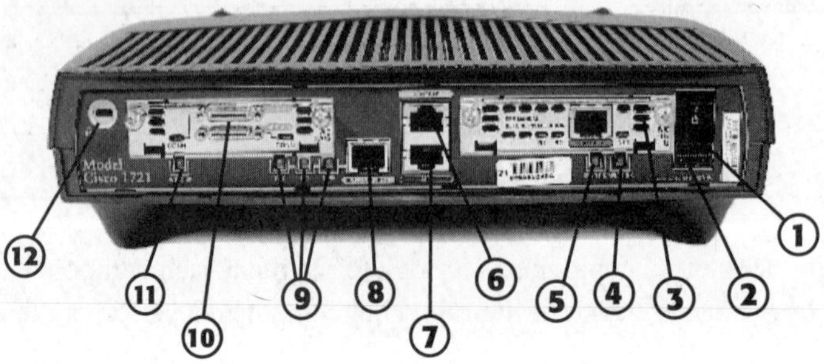

Figure 1-1 Label Description:

___ MOD OK LED, which is on when the Virtual Private Network (VPN) hardware encryption module is installed and recognized by the IOS.

___ Full duplex, 100 Mbps, and Link LEDs. The Link LED illuminates when a good physical connection exists on the Fast Ethernet port.

___ Illuminates when the WAN interface card (WIC) is okay and in use.

___ Power socket that connects to either a 120- or 220-volt AC outlet.

___ WAN interface card that provides access to a specific type of WAN technology.

___ A Kensington-compatible locking socket that allows this device to be padlocked to a secure object, like a rack mount.

___ Allows local configuration of the device.

___ Power switch.

___ Allows remote out-of-bandwidth configuration of the device.

___ LAN interface, which allows connections to hubs or switches through a patch or straight-through cable.

Choose the correct label description for each number shown in Figure 1-2. Some labels can be used more than once.

Figure 1-2 Rear View of a 2621 Cisco Router

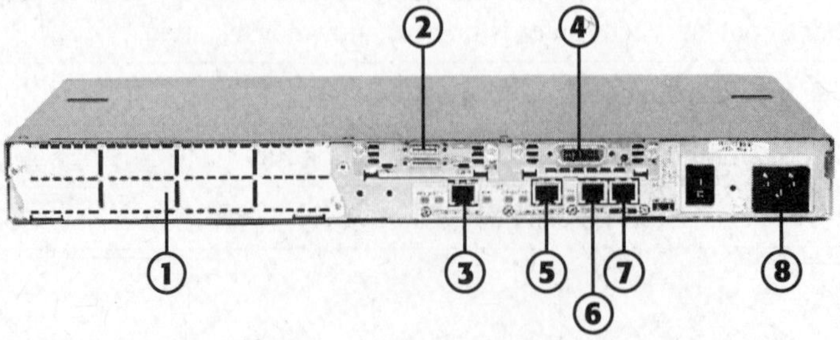

Figure 1-2 Label Description:

6-7 LAN interface, which allows connections to hubs or switches through a patch or straight-through cable.

4 WIC with two smart serial interfaces.

8 Power cord connection.

5 Allows remote configuration of the device.

1 Expansion slot.

3 Allows local configuration of the device.

2 WIC with one DB-60 serial interface.

Label the Topology Components Exercise

In Figure 1-3, the PC is attached to the router, which is providing a packet-routing service to the PC. In other words, the PC is part of the in-band network of the router. Label the interfaces and cable type used.

Figure 1-3 Label the Topology Components 1

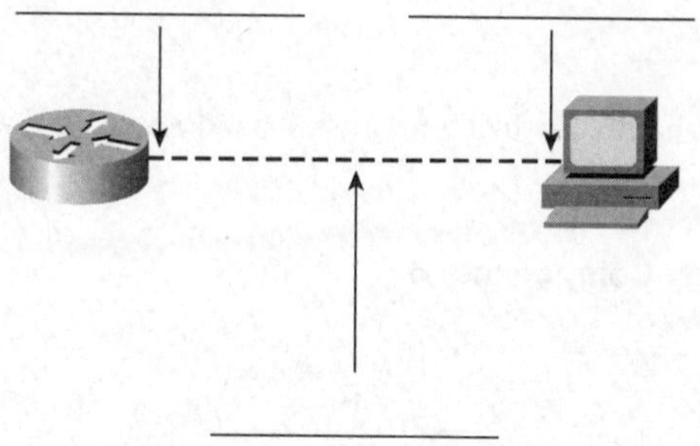

In Figure 1-4, the PC is part of an in-band network and can also manage the router. Label the interfaces and cable types used.

Figure 1-4 Label the Topology Components 2

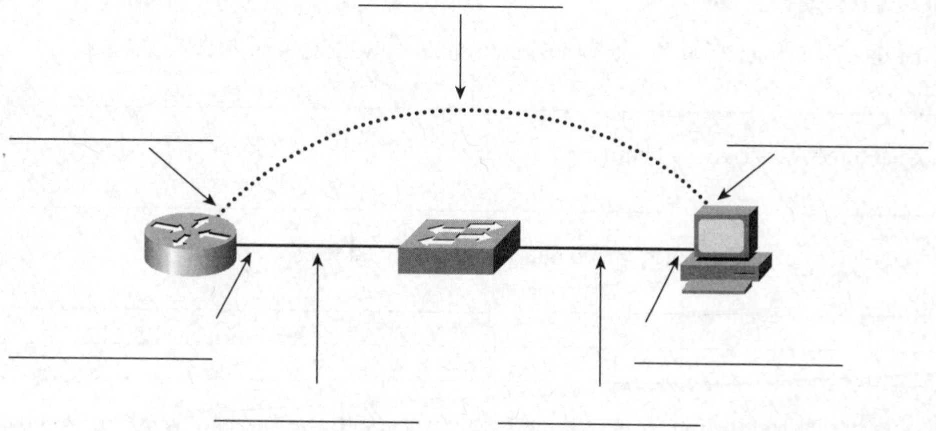

In Figure 1-5, the two routers are directly connected in a lab environment. Label the interfaces and cable types used. Also, choose a side that can provide the clocking, and label it.

Figure 1-5 Label the Topology Components 3

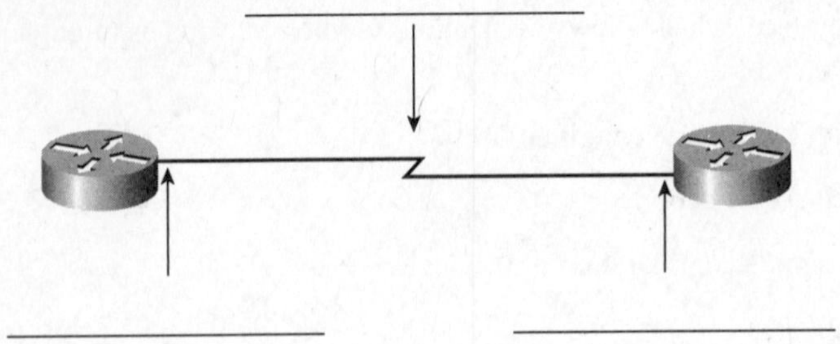

In Figure 1-6, the two routers are connected through a WAN service provider across a dedicated link. Label the interfaces.

Figure 1-6 Label the Topology Components 4

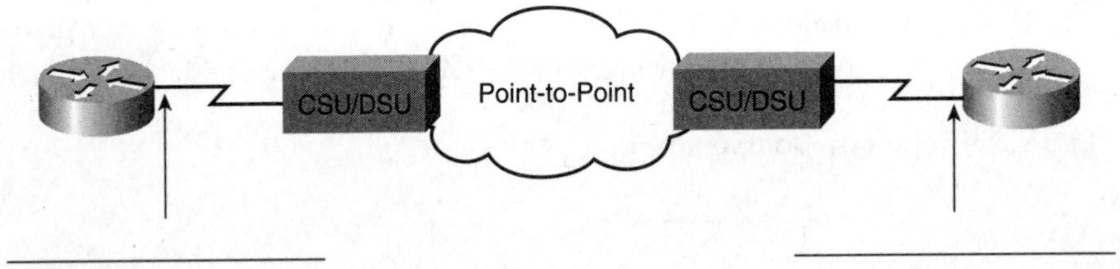

In Figure 1-7, the router and the PC are using an out-of-band network for device management purposes. Label the interfaces.

Figure 1-7 Label the Topology Components 5

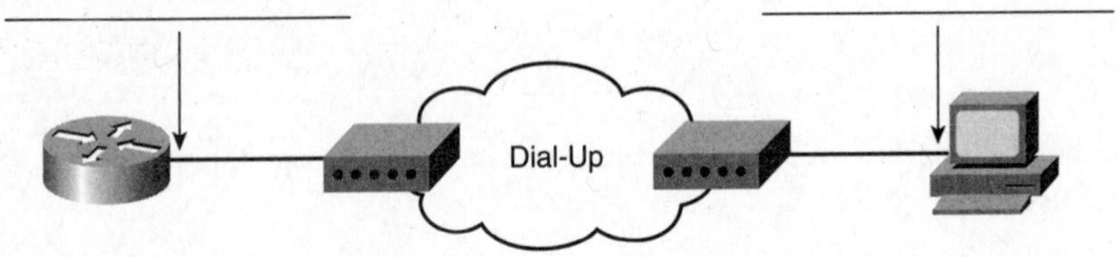

Concept Questions

1. What three components of a router retain their memory when power is not present?

____

2. In what three ways can you configure a router?

____

3. Of the two management ports, which one is preferred, and why?

____

____

____

4. Besides the PC and the router, what three components (software and hardware) are required to connect a PC to a router's management port?

____

____

Lab Exercises

Curriculum Lab 1-1: Connecting Console Interfaces (1.2.5)

Figure 1-8 Topology for Lab 1-1

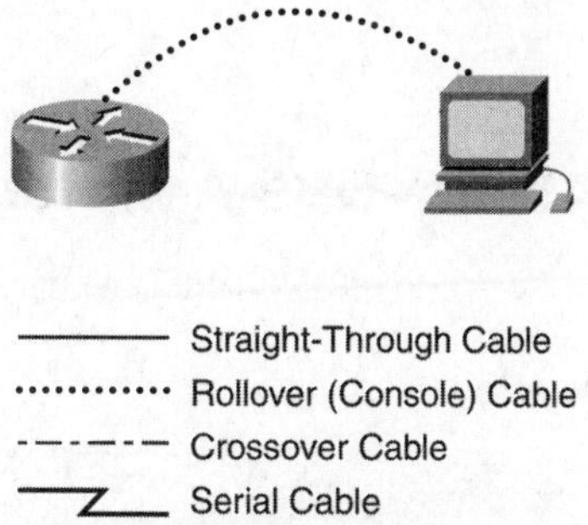

Objective:

Connect a PC to a router using a console or rollover cable.

Background/preparation:

A console cable is necessary to establish a console session so that you can check or change the configuration of the router. You need the following resources:

- Workstation with a serial interface
- Cisco router
- Console rollover cable for connecting the workstation to the router

Task 1: Identify Connectors and Components

Examine the router and locate the RJ-45 connector labeled "Console," as shown in Figure 1-9.

Figure 1-9 Locating the RJ-45 Console Connector on a Router

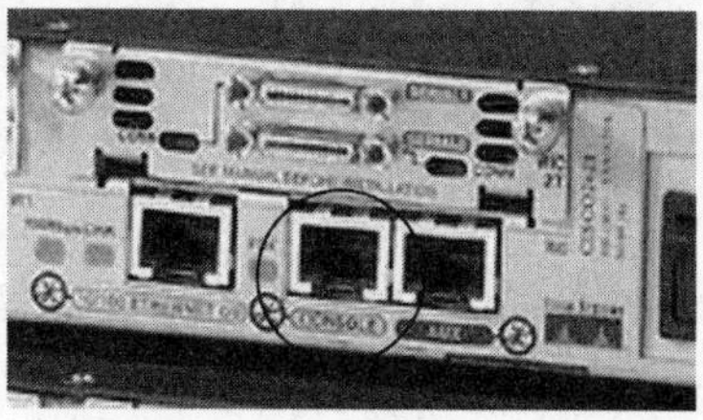

Task 2: Identify the Computer Serial Interface (COM 1 or 2)

Examine the computer and locate a 9- or 25-pin male connector labeled "Serial," as shown in Figure 1-10. (It might not have a label.)

Figure 1-10 Locating the COM Port on a PC

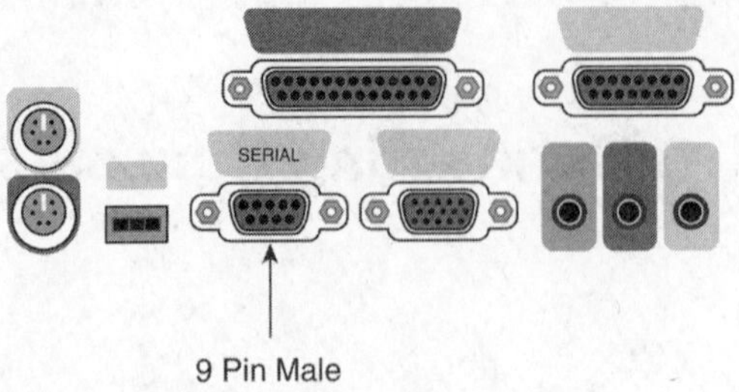

Task 3: Locate the RJ-45–to–DB9 Adapter

This task calls for you to locate the RJ-45–to–DB9 adapter, which is shown in Figure 1-11.

Figure 1-11 RJ-45–to–DB9 Female Adapter

Task 4: Locate or Build a Rollover Cable

Use a console or rollover cable of adequate length (see Figure 1-12), making one if necessary, to connect the router to one of the workstations.

Figure 1-12 Using a Rollover Cable

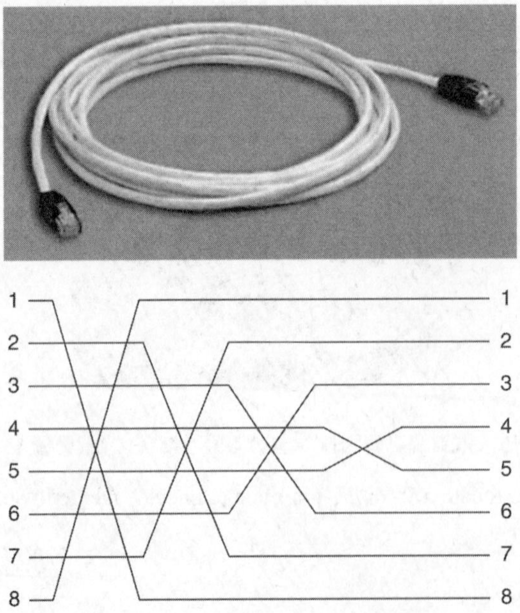

Task 5: Connect Cabling Components

Step 1. Connect the console or rollover cable to the router console port using an RJ-45 connector. Next, connect the other end of the console or rollover cable to the RJ-45–to–DB9 or the RJ-45–to–DB25 adapter, depending on the available PC serial port.

Step 2. Attach the adapter to a PC serial port, either DB9 or DB25, depending on the computer. Figure 1-13 illustrates the necessary connections.

Figure 1-13 Connecting the Router to the PC

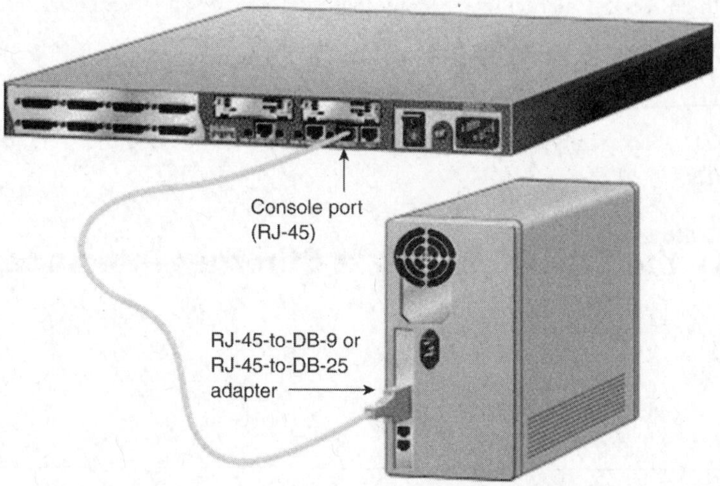

Curriculum Lab 1-2: Connecting Router LAN Interfaces (1.2.6)

Figure 1-14 Topology for Lab 1.2.6

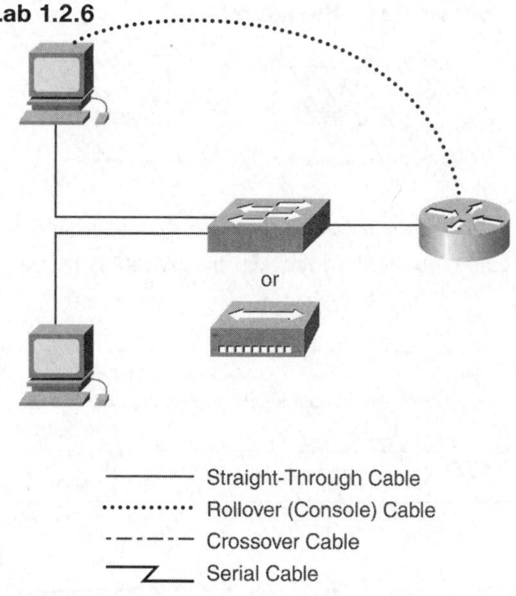

Objectives:

This lab contains the following objectives:

- Identify the Ethernet or Fast Ethernet interfaces on the router.
- Identify and locate the proper cables to connect the router and PC to a hub or switch.
- Use the cables to connect the router and PC to the hub or switch.

Background/Preparation:

This lab focuses on the ability to connect the physical cabling between Ethernet LAN devices, such as hubs and switches, and the appropriate Ethernet interface on a router. The computers and router should already have the correct IP network settings. Start this lab with the computers, router, and hub or switch turned off and unplugged. You need the following resources:

- At least one workstation with an Ethernet 10/100 NIC installed
- One Ethernet switch or hub
- One router with an RJ-45 Ethernet or Fast Ethernet interface (or an attachment unit interface [AUI])
- One 10BASE-T AUI transceiver (DB15–to–RJ-45) for a router with an AUI Ethernet interface (2500 series)
- Several Ethernet cables (straight-through and crossover) for connecting the workstation and router to the hub or switch

Task 1: Identify the Ethernet or Fast Ethernet Interfaces on the Router

Step 1. Examine the router.

What is the model number of the router?

____

Step 2. Locate one or more RJ-45 connectors on the router labeled "10/100 Ethernet" (see Figure 1-15). This identifier can vary depending on the type of router. A 2500 Series router has an AUI DB15 Ethernet port labeled AUI 0. This port requires a 10BASE-T transceiver to connect to the RJ-45 cable.

Figure 1-15 RJ-45 Ethernet Connectors on the Router

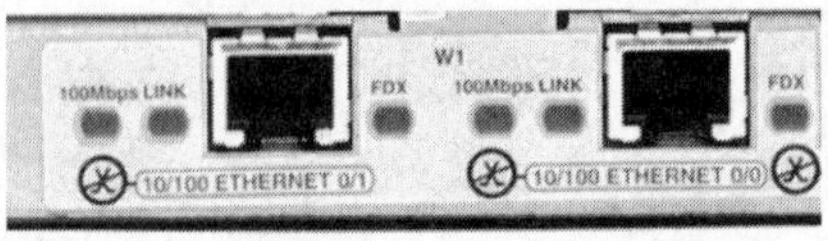

Step 3. Identify the Ethernet ports that you could use for connecting the routers. Record the information in the following table. Record the AUI port numbers if you are working with a Cisco 2500 Series router.

Router	Port	Port

Task 2: Identify the Proper Cables and Connect the Router to a Hub or Switch

Step 1. You can make the connection between the router and the hub using a Category 5 (CAT 5) or better straight-through patch cable. Locate a patch cable that is long enough to reach from the router to the hub. Be sure to examine the cable ends carefully and select only straight-through cables.

Step 2. Use a cable to connect the Ethernet interface that uses the 0 (zero) designation on the router to a port on the hub or switch. Also use the 10BASE-T AUI transceiver for the 2500 Series.

Task 3: Connect the Workstation Ethernet Cabling

The computers can also connect to the hub using a straight-through patch cable. Run CAT 5 patch cables from each PC to where the switch or hub is located. Connect one end of these cables to the RJ-45 connector on the computer NIC, and connect the other end to a port on the hub or switch. Be sure to examine the cable ends carefully and select only straight-through cables.

Task 4: Verify the Connection

Step 1. Plug in and turn on the routers, computers, and hub or switch.

Step 2. To verify the router connections, ensure that the link lights on the router interface and the hub or switch interface are both illuminated.

Step 3. To verify the computer connections, ensure that the link lights on the NIC and the hub interface are both illuminated.

Curriculum Lab 1-3: Connecting WAN Interfaces (1.2.7)

Figure 1-16 Topology for Lab 1.2.7

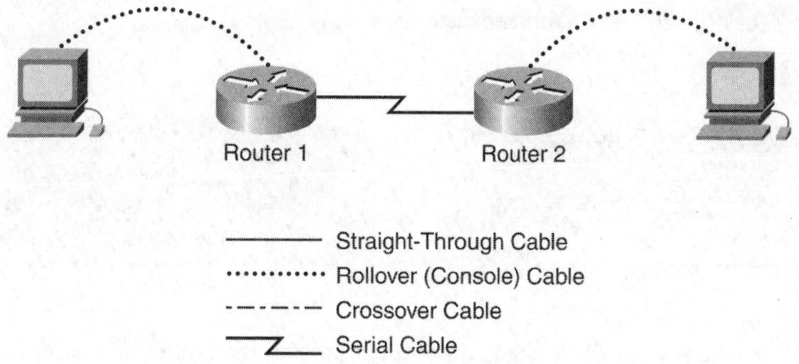

Objectives:

This lab contains the following objectives:

- Identify the serial interfaces on the router.
- Identify and locate the proper cables to connect the routers.
- Use the cables to connect the routers.

Background/Preparation:

This lab connects two routers using directly attached cables to simulate a WAN link. This setup lets you configure and test the routers as though they were geographically separated. You can consider this simulated WAN link, which takes the place of the service provider's network, a CSU/DSU eliminator. The first steps involve finding out the kinds of connections on the router and the kinds of cables you need.

Task 1: Identify the Serial Interfaces on the Router

Step 1. Examine the routers.

What is the model number of the first router?

____

What is the model number of the second router?

____

How many serial ports on each router could be used for connecting the routers? Record the information in the table that follows.

Router Name	Serial Port	Serial Port
Router 1		
Router 2		

Task 2: Identify and Locate the Proper Cables

Step 1. Inspect the serial cables available in the lab. Depending on the type of router and serial card, the router might have different connectors. The two most common types are the DB60 and the smart serial connectors, as shown in Figure 1-17.

Figure 1-17 Smart Serial and DB60 Connectors

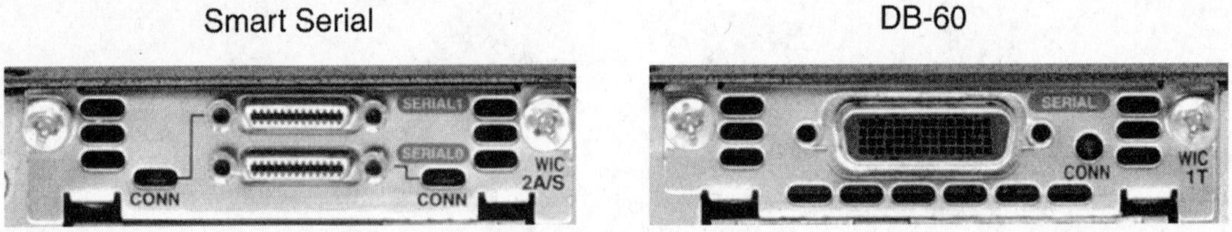

Indicate which type of interfaces the routers have in the table that follows.

Router	Smart Serial	DB60
1		
2		

Step 2. Because this lab is not connected to a live leased line, one of the routers must provide the clocking for the circuit. The service provider normally provides the clocking signal to each of the routers. To provide this clocking signal in the lab, one of the routers needs a DCE cable instead of the DTE cable used on the other router.

In this lab, the connection between routers uses one DCE cable and one DTE cable. The DCE-DTE connection between routers is a *null serial cable.* This lab uses one V.35 DCE cable and one V.35 DTE cable to simulate the WAN connection.

The V.35 DCE connector is usually a female V.35 (34-pin) connector. The DTE cable has a male V.35 connector. Figure 1-18 shows the male and female V.35 connectors. The cables are also labeled as DCE or DTE on the router end.

Figure 1-18 V.35 Male and Female Connectors

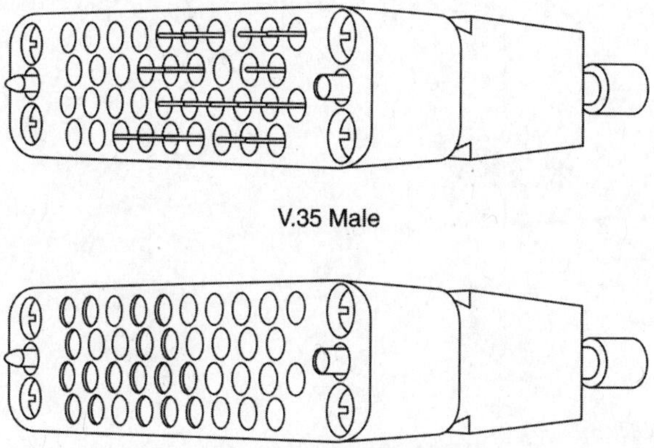

Using the chart in the table that follows, identify the V.35 cable that you can use on each router by placing a check mark in the appropriate column.

Router	DTE (V.35 Male)	DCE (V.35 Female)
Router 1		
Router 2		

Step 3. After indicating the cables required to interconnect the router, locate them in the equipment inventory.

Task 3: Cable the Routers

Step 1. You must now join the DTE and DCE V.35 cables. Holding the V.35 ends in each hand, examine the pins and sockets as well as the threaded connectors. Note that the cables can fit together only one proper way. Align the pins on the male cable with the sockets on the female cable and gently couple them; this should require little effort. Turn the thumbscrews (clockwise) and secure the connectors.

Step 2. Before making the connection to one of the routers, examine the connector on the router and the cable. Note that the connectors are tapered to help prevent improper connection. Holding the connector in one hand, orient the cable and router connecters so that the tapers match. Now, push the cable connector partially into the router connector. It probably will not go on all the way because you must tighten the threaded connectors to completely insert the cable. While holding the cable in one hand and gently pushing the cable toward the router, turn one of the thumbscrews clockwise three or four rounds to start the screws. Now, turn the other thumbscrew clockwise three or four rounds to get it started. At this point, the cable should be attached enough that you can use both hands to advance each thumbscrew at the same rate until the cable is fully inserted. Do not overtighten these connectors.

Challenge Lab 1-4: Build a Two-Router Topology

Figure 1-19 Two-Router Topology with PCs

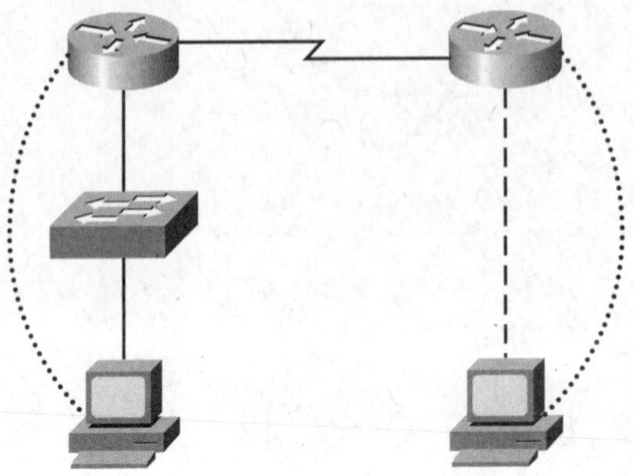

Objectives:

This lab contains the following objectives:

- Choose correct devices, connectors, and cables to build a two-router topology with two PCs.
- Connect the devices.
- Verify connectivity.

Equipment:

The topology shown in Figure 1-8 can use any routers that have at least one serial interface and one LAN interface.

NetLab Compatibility Notes:

Because this lab evaluates your ability to physically connect a topology, it cannot be completed on NetLab.

Task 1: Choose the Devices

From what you have available, choose the devices that you can use. In the following table, document the router models, switch model, and type of PCs you are going to use.

Device	Model

Task 2: Choose the Cables

Now choose the cables that you need to correctly connect the device. Notice that one router is connected to a switch, while the other router is directly attached to a PC. List the cable types that you need.

Connection	Cable Type
Router to router	
Router to PC (in-band)	
Router to switch	
Switch to PC	
Router to PC (out-of-band)	

What other software or hardware would you need to connect and configure this network?

____

Task 3: Connect the Devices

Using what you have learned so far, connect the devices with the cables according to the topology.

Task 4: Verify Connectivity

The devices should all have link lights on the interfaces you have used for your connections. Check and make sure that they are illuminated. This is a good way to verify that, at least physically, you have correctly connected the devices. Also, have someone more experienced check your work. In future labs, your connectivity problems can many times be found at the physical layer. Correctly connecting devices is the first step in successfully completing all labs.

You can check your console connectivity by opening a terminal session with the routers. If the router responds to the **Enter** key, your console connection is ready for management configuration.

CHAPTER 2

Introduction to Routers

The Study Guide portion of this chapter uses a combination of multiple-choice, matching, and open-ended question exercises to test your knowledge of the basic operation of Cisco IOS software and the IOS command-line interface (CLI).

The Lab Exercises portion of this chapter includes all the online curriculum labs as well as a comprehensive lab and challenge lab to ensure that you have mastered the practical, hands-on skills needed for the basic operation of Cisco IOS software and the IOS CLI.

Study Guide

Cisco IOS and the IOS Command-Line Interface

Cisco technology is based on the Cisco IOS, which is the software that controls the routing and switching functions of network devices. A solid understanding of the IOS is essential for a CCNA candidate and future network administrator. You spend some time studying the basic operation of the IOS as well as beginning your journey into the CLI.

Vocabulary Exercise: Matching

Match the definition on the left with a term on the right.

Definitions

a. Signified by a router prompt ending in "(config-if)#".

b. List of various functions provided by an IOS.

c. Rudimentary OS that provides a basic interface; used for password recovery.

d. Verifies hardware functionality during the boot process.

e. Text entered to access privileged EXEC mode.

f. Command that changes the prompt from "Router" to another name.

g. Looks for and loads the IOS into RAM.

h. Found inside the configuration file and tells the router the order in which to look for an IOS to boot.

i. Allows a limited number of commands and no ability to enter configuration mode.

j. Among other things, tells the router where to locate the IOS.

k. Keeps you from having to type the same command repeatedly.

l. Text-based interface that gives the user the ability to type commands on a keyboard.

m. Provides a series of questions that allow the user to build a basic running configuration.

n. Signified by a router prompt ending in "(config-router)#".

o. Software that runs a Cisco router.

p. Text entered to access user EXEC mode.

q. File that contains the entire operating system for a router.

r. Allows full access to the IOS command set as well as the ability to configure the router.

s. Commands entered here affect the entire router.

t. Basic IOS that can be loaded if no IOS exists in flash.

u. The last hex digit of the config register.

Terms

__ IOS

__ command-line interface (CLI)

__ user EXEC mode

__ privileged EXEC mode

__ global configuration mode

__ interface configuration mode

__ routing protocol configuration mode

__ IOS image

__ feature set

__ ROM monitor/ROMMON

__ boot ROM

__ power-on self test (POST)

__ bootstrap

__ configuration register

__ boot field

__ **boot system** command

__ setup mode

__ host name

__ console password

__ enable password

__ command recall

Vocabulary Exercise: Completion

Complete the paragraphs that follow by filling in the appropriate words and phrases.

CLI stands for ______________________. The CLI is not graphical; instead, it is a text-based user interface. The CLI can be accessed through the ______ and _________ ports, with no specific configuration in the router.

The IOS provides a command interpreter service known as the command executive (EXEC), which is separated into two access levels. These levels are ____ EXEC mode and _________ EXEC mode. The main difference between the two is that _________ EXEC mode allows commands that can disrupt router operations.

The following command accesses _________ EXEC mode:

```
Router>enable
```

Now record the new router prompt and the command to exit this mode:

____

From the prompt "Router#", the user can enter global configuration mode, which allows the user to configure commands that affect the entire router. The router prompt and command to enter global configuration mode is as follows:

____

After entering the preceding command, the router prompt is as follows:

____

From global configuration mode, the user can configure specific parts of the router, including all the physical interfaces and management ports as well as routing. The router prompt and command to enter interface configuration mode for Fast Ethernet 0/0 are as follows:

____

After entering the preceding command, the router prompt is as follows:

____

To enter routing protocol configuration mode for Routing Information Protocol (RIP), enter the following command:

```
Router(config)#router rip
```

After entering the preceding command, the router prompt is as follows:

____

Although Cisco IOS software appears to be one OS, from some perspectives, it contains many different IOS _____. An IOS _____ is a file that contains the entire IOS. Cisco creates different IOS _____ for a variety of reasons.

Routers, like computers, need a permanent place to keep their operating system. Computers use _____ _____ to store the OS, but routers use ____ memory to store the OS. To check the amount of this memory in a router, you can use the ________ command. Also like other computers, routers copy all or part of the IOS into RAM when the router is powered on. To determine whether a router has enough RAM to hold the IOS, use the _________ command.

Cisco routers can operate in three distinct environments. ___________ recovers from system failures and recovers a lost password. __________ modifies the Cisco IOS image in flash. A limited subset of features exists in this mode. Normal operation of a router requires a full ____ image.

Concept Questions

1. List and describe three ways to access the CLI.

____

____

____

____

____

2. Explain the difference between user EXEC and privileged EXEC modes.

____

____

____

____

____

____

____

____

3. The naming convention for Cisco IOS releases contains three parts (for example, c2500-js-l). What does each part mean?

____

- ____
- ____
- ____

4. List and briefly describe the purpose of each of the three operating environments available in Cisco routers.

____

____

____

____

____

____

____

____

____

____

____

Internet Research

Follow the web link "Cisco IOS Basic Skills" on page 2.1.3 of the online curriculum. Read the article and fill in the table that follows. You can also type the following URL into your web browser:

http://www.cisco.com/univercd/cc/td/doc/product/access/acs_mod/1600/1600swcf/swskills.htm

Mode	Access Method	Prompt	Exit Method	About This Mode

continues

Mode	Access Method	Prompt	Exit Method	About This Mode

Starting, Configuring, Accessing, and Using a Router CLI

In this section of the Study Guide, you continue your introduction to routers by focusing on the following concepts and skills:

- Understanding the sequence of events that occur as the router boots up
- Using the CLI, including navigation keys
- Interpreting the **show version** command output
- Reviewing the process of accessing the CLI with a terminal emulator

Router Boot Sequence Exercise

Figure 2-1 displays an incomplete diagram of the default boot sequence of a router. Provide detail where information is missing.

Figure 2-1 Diagram of the Router Boot Sequence

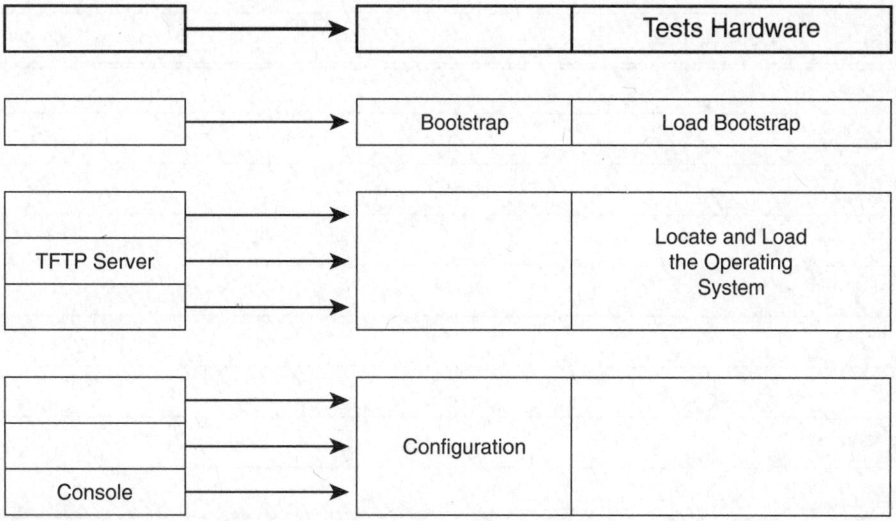

Using the Router CLI Exercise

1. You are at the router prompt that follows. What command or key combination immediately returns you to the privileged EXEC prompt, as shown?

   ```
   Router(config-if)#____________
   Router#
   ```

2. Whenever a "-- More --" prompt appears, the next available screen can be viewed by pressing the __________. To display just the next line, press the _______ key. Press any other key to return to the prompt.

3. Press the __ key to get help with a particular command or to get a list of all commands available at the current prompt.

4. The key combination _______ repeats the previous command.

5. What does the carat symbol (^) in the following output indicate?

   ```
   Router(config)#access list 1 permit 192.168.1.0 0.0.0.255
                         ^
   ```

   ____

6. What does the dollar sign ($) in the following output indicate?

   ```
   Router(config)#$0.0.255 172.16.0.0 0.0.255.255 eq 80 established
   ```

   ____

   ____

7. By default, IOS maintains the last __ commands in its history buffer. This can be changed to a maximum of ____ commands with the __________________ command.

8. Fill in the table that follows.

Key(s)	Description
Ctrl-A	
Ctrl-E	
Ctrl-B	
Ctrl-F	
Esc-B	
Esc-F	
Ctrl-P	
Ctrl-N	
Ctrl-Z	
Ctrl-C	
Tab	

Interpreting Command Output Exercise

From the **show version** command output shown here, fill in the missing information in the questions that follow.

```
Router# show version
Cisco Internetwork Operating System Software
IOS (tm) 2500 Software (C2500-JS-L), Version 12.2(13b), RELEASE SOFTWARE (fc1)
Copyright (c) 1986-2003 by Cisco Systems, Inc.
Compiled Thu 20-Feb-03 14:09 by pwade
Image text-base: 0x0307C780, data-base: 0x00001000

ROM: System Bootstrap, Version 11.0(10c), SOFTWARE
BOOTLDR: 3000 Bootstrap Software (IGS-BOOT-R), Version 11.0(10c), RELEASE SOFTWARE (fc1)

Router uptime is 1 day, 1 hour, 16 minutes
System returned to ROM by reload
System image file is "flash:/c2500-js-l.122-13b.bin"

cisco 2500 (68030) processor (revision N) with 14336K/2048K bytes of memory.
Processor board ID 18423268, with hardware revision 00000000
Bridging software.
X.25 software, Version 3.0.0.
SuperLAT software (copyright 1990 by Meridian Technology Corp).
```

```
TN3270 Emulation software.
1 Ethernet/IEEE 802.3 interface(s)
2 Serial network interface(s)
32K bytes of non-volatile configuration memory.
16384K bytes of processor board System flash (Read ONLY)

Configuration register is 0x2102
```

1. The command that displays the output is Router# __________.
2. The Cisco platform is _____.
3. The name of the flash IOS is ___________________.
4. The name and version of the ROM bootstrap are __________________________.
5. How long has the router been up? ___________________________.
6. The CPU is a _______, and there are __ MB of RAM.
7. What are the number and types of interfaces?

8. The amount of NVRAM is __ KB.
9. The amount of flash is __ MB.
10. The register is set to ________.

Concept Questions

1. List at least five important pieces of information that are contained in a router's boot messages.

   -
   -
   -
   -
   -

2. Describe the default boot sequence from a cold boot to a fully-functioning router. Use the previous Router Boot Sequence Exercise as a guide.

3. List the two ways that a user can enter setup mode as well as how a user can exit setup mode.

4. In setup mode, what do the square brackets [ ] mean?

5. Explain a situation in which setup mode would be a preferred way to begin the router's configuration.

6. Fill in the correct HyperTerminal settings in Figure 2-2.

Figure 2-2 HyperTerminal Settings Dialog Box

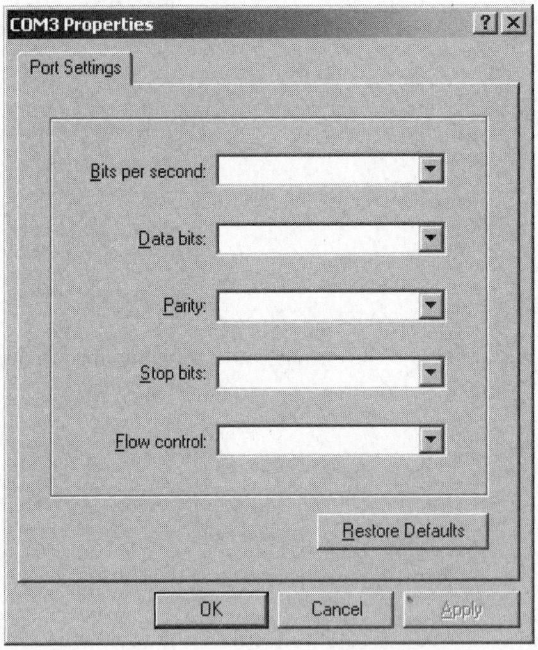

7. Explain the three user passwords that should be configured on every router. In addition, explain how a user can enter privileged mode.

Lab Exercises

Command Reference

In the table that follows, record the command, *including the correct router prompt,* that fits the description. Fill in any blanks with the appropriate missing information.

Command	Description
	Moves you from user mode to privileged mode.
	Moves you from privileged mode back to user mode.
	Logs a user off.
	Enters setup mode from the command line.
	Moves you into global configuration mode.
	The router will now remember the last 25 commands instead of the default, which is the last __ commands. You can set this buffer to up to ___.
	Displays information about the router and the current IOS installed.
	Displays the contents of flash memory.
	Lists all commands in the history buffer.

Curriculum Lab 2-1: Router Configuration Using Setup (2.2.1)

Figure 2-3 **Topology for Lab 2-1**

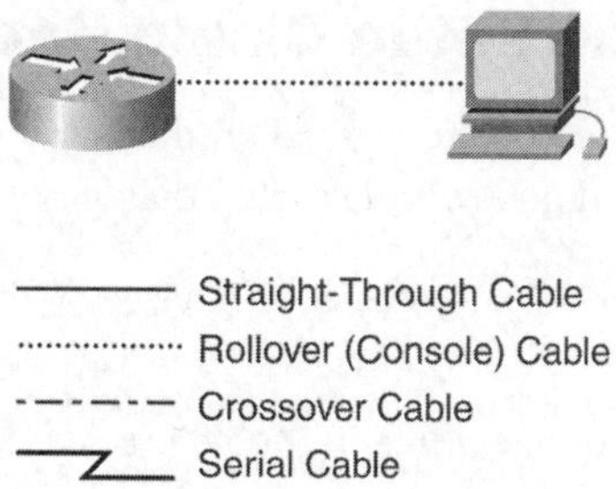

Objectives:

This lab contains the following objectives:

- Use the system configuration dialog box (**setup** command)
- Establish some basic router configuration parameters

Background/Preparation:

A new router cannot find its configuration file when started, so it should automatically enter the setup dialog box. If the router has already been configured, you can use the **setup** command at the command line while in privileged mode. The setup dialog box prompts you for basic setup options, such as protocols and the IP address and subnet mask for each interface. The setup dialog box provides default values for most of the configurable options. You can either accept them or enter your own. If setup does not provide a prompted entry for specific interface information, you must enter it manually at a later time. (In this lab, you run the setup utility but do not save the configuration.)

Cable a network as shown in Figure 2-3. You can use any router that meets the interface requirements (that is, 800, 1600, 1700, 2500, or 2600 routers, or a combination).

This lab assumes that the HyperTerminal console session to the router has already been established by the instructor. You need the following resources:

- A PC with HyperTerminal configured
- One console (rollover) cable and DB9–to–RJ-45 adapter
- A Cisco router

Task 1: Start the Router and Begin Setup Mode

- **Option 1**—If the router starts without a configuration file, it automatically enters setup mode without requiring a password. A new router starts in this way.
- **Option 2**—If the router was previously configured but you want to see and change existing settings, you must log in and provide the password **cisco**. Type **enable** at the command prompt to enter privileged mode, and enter the password **class**. Enter **setup** at the router prompt to open the system configuration dialog box.
- **Option 3**—If the router was previously configured, you can simulate a new router setup by removing the configuration file from NVRAM using the **erase startup-config** command in privileged mode. Use the **reload** command to restart the router and enter setup mode.

Note: The order of the messages displayed during setup can vary depending on the Cisco IOS software release and feature set on the router. Therefore, the prompts that follow might not exactly reflect the messages on your screen.

Task 2: Continue with the Setup Dialog Box

Step 1. The router prompts, "Would you like to enter the initial configuration _______? [yes/no]:". Enter **yes** _______ to continue with the setup dialog box.

Step 2. The router prompts, "Would you like to enter basic management setup? [yes/no]:". Enter **no** and press **Enter**.

What is the importance of the words in square brackets?

____

Task 3: Show the Current Interface Summary

Step 1. The router prompts, "First, would you like to see the current interface summary? _______". Type **yes** or press **Enter** to accept the default answer.

Step 2. Fill in the following table with the information displayed.

Interface	IP Address	OK	Method	Status	Protocol

Task 4: Configure the Global Parameters

Step 1. Configure the router using the default settings for any questions the router asks if it has already been configured. Enter parameters such as router name, privileged-level passwords, and virtual terminal password. Answer the prompts as follows: Router name = **Central**, enable secret password = **class**, enable password = **cisco**, virtual password = **cisco**.

Note: At any point in the setup dialog box process, press Ctrl-C to abort and start over.

Step 2. You are now prompted to enter various parameters, including Simple Network Management Protocol (SNMP) settings and routed and routing protocol settings. Answer **no** to these prompts, except for the "Configure IP?" prompt.

Task 5: Configure the Interface Parameters

From this point on, the prompts vary depending on the available router interfaces. Complete the setup steps as appropriate.

Task 6: Specifying Whether to Use the Configuration Command Script

The router displays the configuration command script that you created and then asks whether you want to save this configuration.

Answer **no** to the question, "Use this configuration?" If prompted with the following selection menu, select __.

```
[0] Go to the IOS command prompt without saving this config.
[1] Return to the setup without saving this config.
[2] Save this configuration to nvram and exit.
```

If you had opted to save the configuration, where would the router save this information? _______

Note: Remember that setup does not let you enter key information such as clock rate for data circuit–terminating equipment (DCE) interfaces. You must enter it later.

When you finish this task, log off (by typing **exit** and pressing **Enter**) and turn off the router.

Curriculum Lab 2-2: Establishing a Console Session with HyperTerminal (2.2.4)

Figure 2-4 **Topology for Lab 2-2**

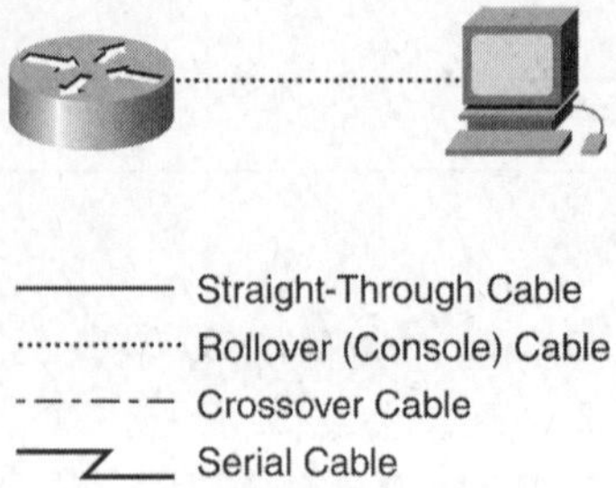

Objectives:

This lab contains the following objectives:

- Connect a router and workstation using a console cable
- Configure HyperTerminal to establish a console session with the router

Background/Preparation:

HyperTerminal is a simple Windows terminal-emulation program that you can use to connect to the router's Console port. A PC with HyperTerminal provides a keyboard and monitor for the router. Connecting to the Console port with a rollover cable and using HyperTerminal is the most basic way to access a router to check or change its configuration.

Cable a network as shown in Figure 2-4. You can use any router that meets the interface requirements (that is, 800, 1600, 1700, 2500, or 2600 routers, or a combination). You need the following resources:

- Workstation with a serial interface and HyperTerminal
- Cisco router
- Console (rollover) cable for connecting the workstation to the router

Task 1: Connect a Rollover Cable to the Console Port

Connect one end of the rollover cable to the Console port on the router and the other end to the PC COM1 port (or COM2 if COM1 is not available) using a DB9 or DB25 adapter. Perform this step before you turn on any of the devices.

Task 2: Start HyperTerminal

Step 1. Turn on the computer and router.

Step 2. From the Windows taskbar, locate the HyperTerminal program (choose **Start** > **Programs** > **Accessories** > **Communications** > **HyperTerminal**).

Task 3: Name the HyperTerminal Session

In the Connection Description dialog box, enter a name in the **Name** field and click the **OK** button, as shown in Figure 2-5.

Figure 2-5 Entering a Connection Description in HyperTerminal

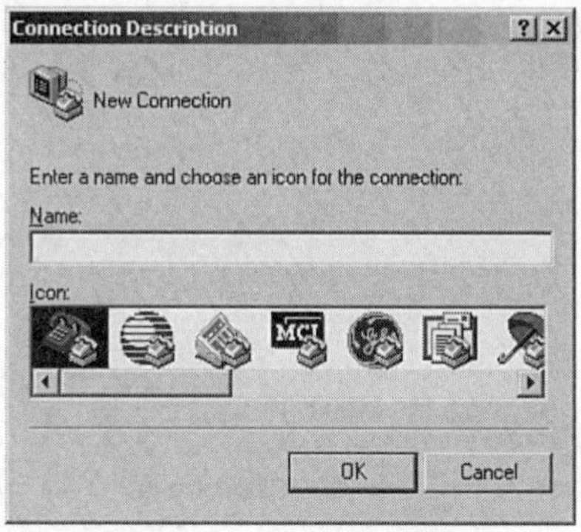

Task 4: Specify the Computer's Connecting Interface

In the Connect To dialog box (see Figure 2-6), use the drop-down arrow in the **Connect using** field to select **COM1**, and click the **OK** button.

Figure 2-6 Selecting the Port to Connect to in HyperTerminal

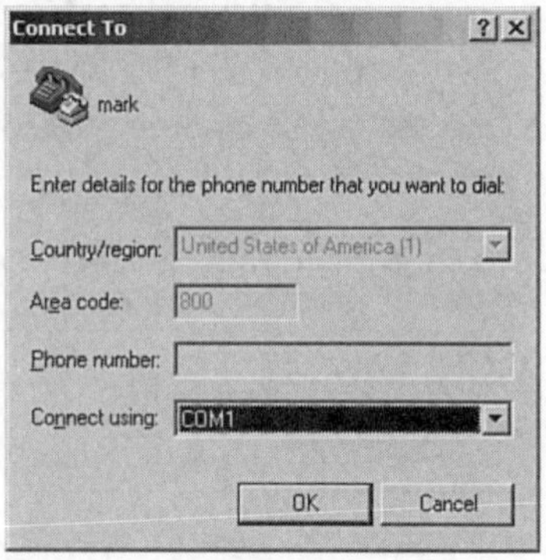

Task 5: Specify the Interface Connection Properties

Step 1. In the COM1 Properties dialog box (see Figure 2-7), use the drop-down arrows to select the following properties and then click the **OK** button:

- Bits per second = **9600**
- Data bits = **8**
- Parity = **None**
- Stop bits = **1**
- Flow control = **None**

Figure 2-7 Specifying the Interface Connection Properties in HyperTerminal

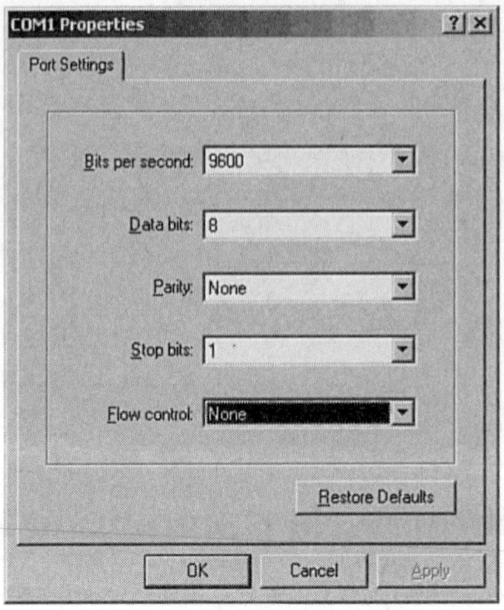

Step 2. When the HyperTerminal session window opens, turn on the router; if router is already on, press **Enter**. You should see a response from the router.

If you do, the connection was successfully completed. If no connection exists, troubleshoot as necessary. For example, verify that the router has power and that you are connected to the correct COM port on the PC and the Console port on the router. If you still cannot connect, ask your instructor for assistance.

Step 3. Record the correct procedure for establishing a console session with the router.

____

____

____

____

____

____

____

____

Task 6: Close the Session

Step 1. To end the console session from HyperTerminal, select **File** > **Exit**.

Step 2. When the HyperTerminal disconnect warning window appears (see Figure 2-8), click the **Yes** button.

Figure 2-8 HyperTerminal Disconnect Warning

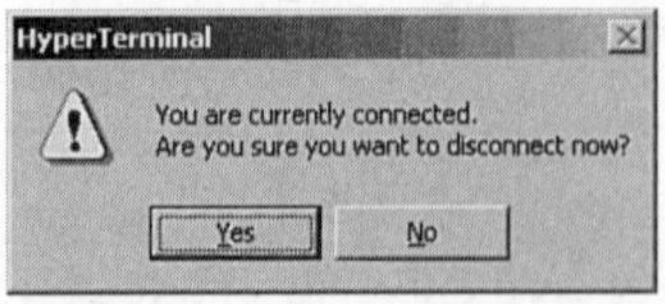

Step 3. As Figure 2-9 shows, HyperTerminal then asks whether you want to save the __________. Click the **Yes** button.

Figure 2-9 Saving a HyperTerminal Session

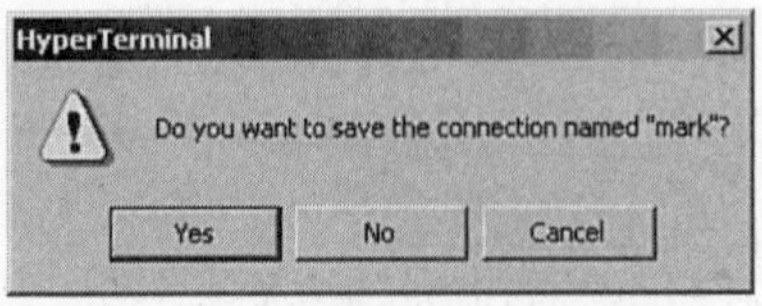

Task 7: Reopen the HyperTerminal Connection, as Shown in Task 2

Step 1. In the Connection Description window (see Figure 2-10), click the **Cancel** button.

Figure 2-10 Canceling the Connection in HyperTerminal

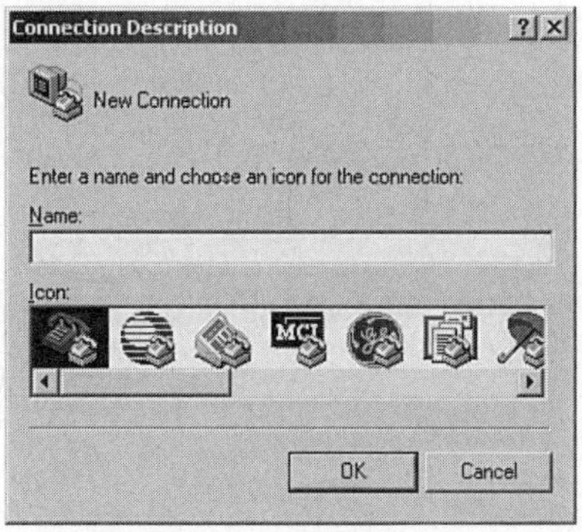

Step 2. To open the saved console session from HyperTerminal, select **File** > **Open**.

The saved session appears. When you double-click the name, the connection opens; you do not have to reconfigure it each time.

Task 8: Terminate the HyperTerminal Session

Close HyperTerminal and shut down the router.

Curriculum Lab 2-3: Command-Line Fundamentals (2.2.9)

Figure 2-11 Topology for Lab 2-3

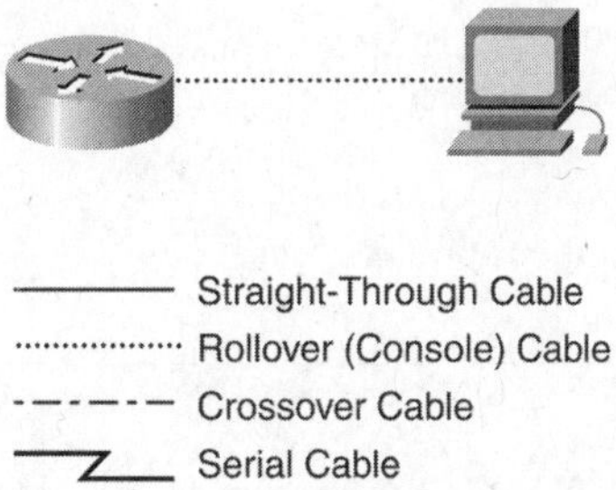

Objectives:

This lab contains the following objectives:

- Log in to a router in both user and privileged modes
- Use several basic router commands to determine how the router is configured
- Use the router Help facility
- Use the command history and editing features
- Log off of the router

Background/Preparation:

This lab focuses on basic command-line skills and the use of IOS help and command history features.

Cable a network as shown in Figure 2-11. You can use any router that meets the interface requirements (that is, 800, 1600, 1700, 2500, or 2600 routers, or a combination). You should perform the tasks described in the sections that follow on each router unless specifically instructed otherwise. You need the following resources:

- Workstation with a serial interface and HyperTerminal
- Cisco router
- Crossover (console) cable for connecting the workstation to the router

Task 1: Start HyperTerminal

Start a HyperTerminal session as you did in Lab 2-2.

Task 2: Log In to the Router

Log in to the router. If prompted to enter the initial setup mode, answer **no**. If prompted for a password, enter **cisco**.

By default, the prompt shows "Router." Something different might appear if this router has a name. What prompt did the router display?

____

What does the prompt symbol following a router name mean?

____

Task 3: Use the Help Feature

Enter the help command by typing a question mark (**?**) at the EXEC router prompt, as follows:

```
Router>?
```

List eight available commands from the router response.

____

Task 4: Enter Privileged EXEC Mode

Enter enable mode by using the **enable** command, as follows. If the router asks for a password, enter **class**.

```
Router>enable
```

Was **enable** one of the commands available from Task 3? ___

What changed in the router prompt display, and what does it mean?

____

____

Task 5: Use the Help Feature

Enter help mode by typing a question mark (**?**) at the router privileged EXEC prompt, as follows:

```
Router#?
```

List ten available commands from the router response.

____

Task 6: List the show Commands

List all **show** commands by entering **show ?** at the router privileged EXEC prompt, as follows:

```
Router#show ?
```

Is **running-config** one of the available commands in this mode? ___

Task 7: Examine the Running Configuration

Display the running router configuration by using the command **show running-config** at the privileged EXEC router prompt, as follows:

```
Router#show running-config
```

List six key pieces of information that are displayed in the output of this command.

____

____

Task 8: Examine the Configuration in More Detail

Continue looking at the configuration. When the word *more* appears, press the spacebar. The router displays the next page of information.

What happened when you pressed the spacebar?

____

____

Task 9: Use the Command History Feature

Use the command history to see and reuse the previously entered commands. Press the **up arrow** key or **Ctrl-P** to see the last command you entered. Press it again to go to the command before that. Press the down arrow (or **Ctrl-N**) to go back through the list. This function lets you view the command history.

What appeared at the router prompt as you pressed **up arrow**?

____

Task 10: Log Off and Turn Off the Router

Close HyperTerminal and shut down the router.

Comprehensive Lab 2-4: Exploring the Router and IOS

Figure 2-12 Exploring the Router and IOS Topology

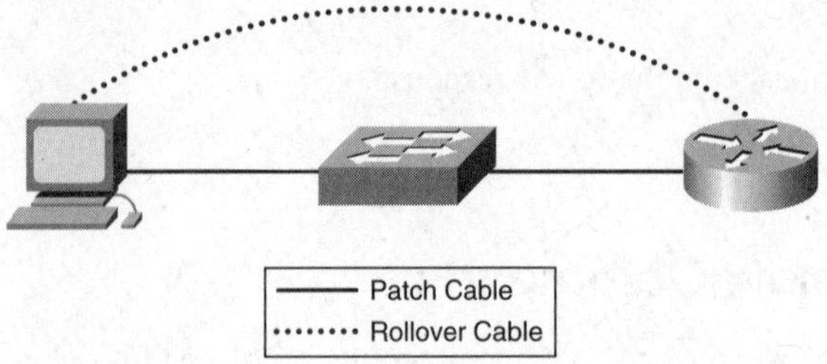

Objectives:

This lab contains the following objectives:

- Connect a router and workstation using a rollover cable
- Configure HyperTerminal to establish a console session with the router
- Briefly explore setup mode (System Configuration dialog box)
- Log in to a router and go to the user and privileged modes
- Use several basic router commands to determine how the router is configured
- Use the router Help facility
- Use command history and editing features
- Attach a workstation to the router's LAN network
- Configure the workstation with addressing compatible with the router's LAN
- Test workstation connectivity to the default gateway and troubleshoot if necessary
- Restore equipment configurations

Equipment:

You need a DB9–to–RJ-45 terminal adapter, a rollover cable, a patch cable, a PC with HyperTerminal, and a router. This lab can be done with any combination of 1700, 2500, and 2600 Series routers. A switch or hub can be used between the router and the host, as shown in _________.

NetLab Compatibility Notes:

This lab can be completed on a standard NetLab three-router pod.

Task 1: Physically Connect to a Router and Start a HyperTerminal Session

Step 1. Connect one end of a rollover cable to the Console port on the router and the other end to the PC with a DB9 adapter to a COM port.

Step 2. Connect one end of a patch cable to the hub or switch attached to the router and the other end to the PC's network interface card (NIC).

Step 3. Locate the HyperTerminal program by choosing **Start** > **Programs** > **Accessories** > **Communications** > **HyperTerminal**.

Step 4. In the Connection Description dialog box, as shown in Figure 2-13, enter your name in the **Name** field and click the **OK** button.

Figure 2-13 Connection Description Dialog Box

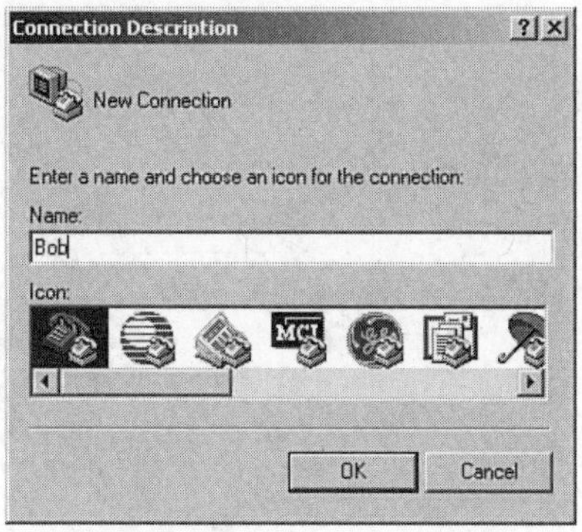

Step 5. In the Connect To dialog box, as shown in Figure 2-14, use the drop-down arrow in the **Connect using** field to select the COM port to which you connect the DB9–to–RJ-45 adapter and click the **OK** button.

Figure 2-14 Connect To Dialog Box

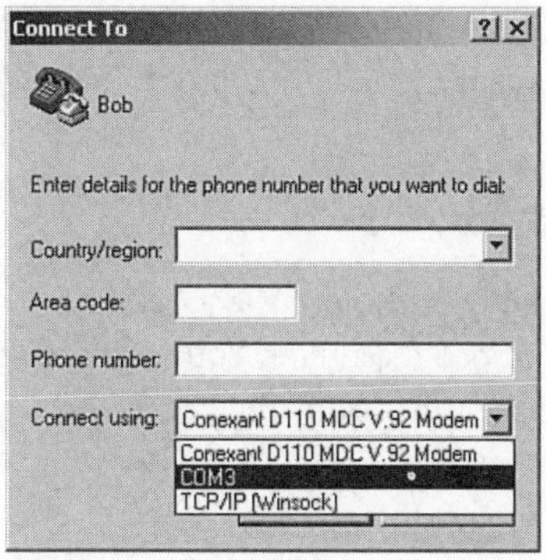

Step 6. In the COM Properties dialog box, as shown in Figure 2-15, use the drop-down arrows to make the following selections:

- Bits per second: **9600**
- Data bits: **8**
- Parity: **None**
- Stop bits: **1**
- Flow control: **None**

Then click the **OK** button.

Figure 2-15 COM Properties Dialog Box

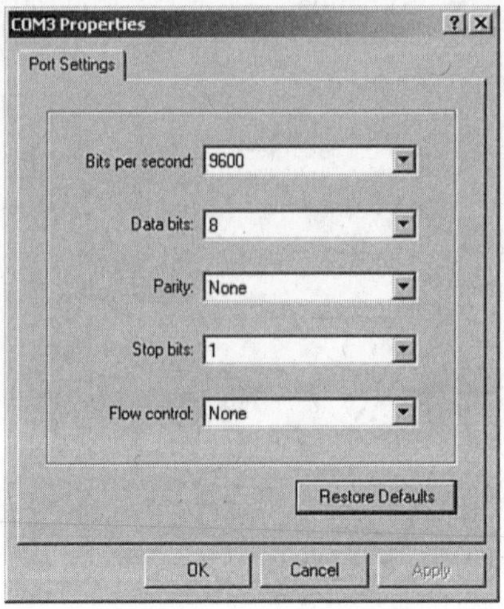

Step 7. When the HyperTerminal session window opens, press **Enter**. You should get a response from the router. If this occurs, the connection has been successfully completed. If not, check your physical connectivity. Make sure that the router is powered on.

Step 8. You can save your connection settings so that you do not have to enter them each time you start HyperTerminal. Choose **File** > **Save As** and save the session to a convenient place for future use. You could save it to the Desktop or to another place specified by your instructor.

Task 2: Exploring Setup Mode

Step 1. To make sure that the router does not have a configuration, erase any potential configurations stored in NVRAM and reload the router. You might have to enter the password **class** to get into privileged EXEC mode. Use the following code:

```
Router>enable
Router#erase startup-config
Erasing the nvram filesystem will remove all configuration files! Continue?
[confirm]<Enter>
[OK]
Erase of nvram: complete
Router#reload

System configuration has been modified. Save? [yes/no]: no
Proceed with reload? [confirm]<Enter>
00:18:30: %SYS-5-RELOAD: Reload requested by console.
```

What would happen if you answered yes to the question "System configuration has been modified. Save?"

____

____

____

Step 2. Depending on the router model and IOS version, the router might take some time to reload. You should see output similar to the following:

```
System Bootstrap, Version 11.0(10c), SOFTWARE
Copyright (c) 1986-1996 by Cisco Systems
2500 processor with 14336 Kbytes of main memory
```

```
Notice: NVRAM invalid, possibly due to write erase.

F3: 14929480+965496+931460 at 0x3000060

               Restricted Rights Legend

Use, duplication, or disclosure by the Government is
subject to restrictions as set forth in subparagraph
(c) of the Commercial Computer Software - Restricted
Rights clause at FAR sec. 52.227-19 and subparagraph
(c) (1) (ii) of the Rights in Technical Data and Computer
Software clause at DFARS sec. 252.227-7013.

            Cisco Systems, Inc.
            170 West Tasman Drive
            San Jose, California 95134-1706



Cisco Internetwork Operating System Software
IOS (tm) 2500 Software (C2500-JS-L), Version 12.2(13b), RELEASE SOFTWARE (fc1)
Copyright (c) 1986-2003 by Cisco Systems, Inc.
Compiled Thu 20-Feb-03 14:09 by pwade
Image text-base: 0x0307C780, data-base: 0x00001000

cisco 2500 (68030) processor (revision N) with 14336K/2048K bytes of memory.
Processor board ID 18423268, with hardware revision 00000000
Bridging software.
X.25 software, Version 3.0.0.
SuperLAT software (copyright 1990 by Meridian Technology Corp).
TN3270 Emulation software.
1 Ethernet/IEEE 802.3 interface(s)
2 Serial network interface(s)
32K bytes of non-volatile configuration memory.
16384K bytes of processor board System flash (Read ONLY)

         --- System Configuration Dialog ---

Would you like to enter the initial configuration dialog? [yes/no]:
```

Because you are exploring setup mode, answer **yes**.

Step 3. Read the output displayed by the router, and answer the following questions.

What key do you type to get help?

____

What key combination do you use to abort setup (configuration dialog box)?

____

What do the square brackets [ ] mean?

____

Step 4. Because you are only configuring one interface, answer **yes** to the following question:

```
Would you like to enter basic management setup? [yes/no]: yes
```

Step 5. Give the router an appropriate name, as follows:

```
Configuring global parameters:

  Enter host name [Router]:Ch2_Lab
```

Step 6. Enter **class** as the secret password. This password is encrypted and accesses privileged EXEC mode.

```
  The enable secret is a password used to protect access to
  privileged EXEC and configuration modes. This password, after
  entered, becomes encrypted in the configuration.
  Enter enable secret: class
```

Step 7. Enter **cisco** as the enable password. This password is not encrypted and can be used to access privileged EXEC mode if an enable secret password is *not* configured.

```
The enable password is used when you do not specify an
  enable secret password, with some older software versions, and
  some boot images.
  Enter enable password:cisco
```

Step 8. Enter **cisco** as the password for Telnet lines:

```
The virtual terminal password is used to protect
  access to the router over a network interface.
  Enter virtual terminal password:cisco
```

Step 9. You are not going to configure SNMP, so enter **no**, as follows:

```
  The virtual terminal password is used to protect
  access to the router over a network interface.
  Enter virtual terminal password: cisco
  Configure SNMP Network Management? [yes]: no
```

Step 10. You are going to configure the Ethernet interface, so enter its name at the prompt. If you are using a 1700 or 2600 router, configure the Fast Ethernet interface to which you attached the switch.

```
Current interface summary

Any interface listed with OK? value "NO" does not have a valid configuration

Interface                IP-Address         OK? Method Status          Protocol
Ethernet0                unassigned         NO  unset  up              up

Serial0                  unassigned         NO  unset  down            down

Serial1                  unassigned         NO  unset  down            down


Enter interface name used to connect to the
management network from the above interface summary:Ethernet0
```

Step 11. Configure the Ethernet interface as shown in the configuration that follows. After accepting the default subnet mask of 255.255.255.0, the router displays the current running configuration. Select _ to save this configuration to NVRAM and exit.

```
Configuring interface Ethernet0:
  Configure IP on this interface? [yes]:<Enter>
    IP address for this interface: 192.168.1.1
    Subnet mask for this interface [255.255.255.0] :<Enter>
    Class C network is 192.168.1.0, 24 subnet bits; mask is /24

The following configuration command script was created:

hostname Ch2_Lab
<output omitted>
interface Ethernet0
no shutdown
ip address 192.168.1.1 255.255.255.0
!
<output omitted>
!
end


[0] Go to the IOS command prompt without saving this config.
[1] Return back to the setup without saving this config.
[2] Save this configuration to nvram and exit.

Enter your selection [2]:2
Building configuration...
Use the enabled mode 'configure' command to modify this configuration.


Press ______ to get started!
```

Task 3: Use the Help Feature

Step 1. Press **Enter** until you get a router prompt. What router prompt is displayed?

____

Step 2. To get information on how to use the Help feature, enter **help** at the prompt.

How do you get help?

____

What is the difference between full help and partial help?

____

____

____

____

Step 3. At the user EXEC prompt, enter **?** to get a full list of available commands. At the bottom of the screen, you see "-- More --".

Press the ________ to scroll to the next screen of output.

Press _______ to scroll one line at a time.

Press any other key to escape from the output and return to the prompt.

List at least six commands that you recognize from previous experience with command-line interfaces. (If you do not recognize any commands, list six random commands.)

____

Step 4. Enter the command **logout** or **exit** (both have the same effect). What happened?

____

Step 5. Press **Enter** to return to user EXEC mode and enter privileged EXEC mode. What command do you use to enter privileged EXEC mode?

____

Step 6. Enter the required password. What password do you use?

____

If you don't remember, refer to the passwords you entered in the section "Task 2: Exploring Setup Mode," earlier in this chapter.

Step 7. At the privileged EXEC prompt, enter **?** to get a full list of available commands. Notice that the privileged EXEC list is much longer than the user EXEC list.

Step 8. Enter **c?** to see a list of all commands that begin with *c*. List all the *c* commands available.

____

____

____

____

____

____

Step 9. Enter **clo** and the press the **Tab** key. What happens?

____

Step 10. Use the Help feature to get help with the **clock** command by entering a **?**. (You must enter a space between the command **clock** and the **?**.) Your output should look like the following:

```
Ch2_Lab#clock ?
  set   Set the time and date

Ch2_Lab#clock
```

Notice that the Help feature gives you a list of available arguments for the **clock** command and a brief description of what the argument does. In this case, only one argument is available. Many times, you will have multiple arguments to choose from, depending on the command you are using.

Add the argument **set** to the **clock** command and use Help to get the next available argument.

```
Ch2_Lab#clock set ?
  hh:mm:ss  Current Time

Ch2_Lab#clock set
```

In this case, the argument is not **hh:mm:ss** but is the format you should use for the hour, minutes, and seconds argument. Enter the current hour, minutes, and seconds using military time (a 24-hour clock). After you enter the correct time, press **Enter**. What happens?

____

Instead of retyping the command, what key combination can you use to recall the most recent command used?

____

Continue using the Help feature to find out each required argument for the **clock** command. When the Help feature finally displays "<cr>", which means carriage return, you are done. There are no more arguments. Simply press **Enter**.

Use the **show clock** command to see the current time displayed, as follows:

```
Ch2_Lab#show clock
16:54:33.511 UTC Fri Jan 23 2006
```

Note: UTC stands for Coordinated Universal Time, which usually should correspond with Greenwich Mean Time, or GMT. In production environments where the network is global or crosses multiple time zones, it is good practice to use GMT as your clock setting so that all networking devices are using the same time.

Task 4: Examining the Router

You can use numerous commands to view and verify a router's current state. Most of these commands start with **show**. At the command prompt, enter **show ?** to get a list of available arguments.

Scroll through all the available **show** commands. This **show** feature of the IOS is a powerful tool for examining the router and troubleshooting problems. Over the course of your study, you will become very familiar with numerous **show** commands. Here are a few to try (the full command is shown first, followed by its abbreviated or unambiguous form):

```
show running-config (sh run)
show startup-config (sh start)
show interfaces (sh int)
show ip interface brief (sh ip int brief)
show ip route (sh ip route)
show version (sh ver)
show flash (sh flash)
show history (sh his)
show protocols (sh proto)
```

Task 5: Configure a Workstation on the Router's LAN

Step 1. Attach a workstation to the LAN. Make sure that you have physical connectivity.

Step 2. Configure the workstation with the correct IP address. Use any available IP address from the 192.168.1.0/24 network. Make sure that you use the router's Ethernet interface as the workstation's default gateway.

Depending on your operating system, you might have to use a different method than shown as follows for changing your workstation's IP address. Figure 2-16 shows Windows 2000/XP.

Figure 2-16 Manually Configure IP Addressing

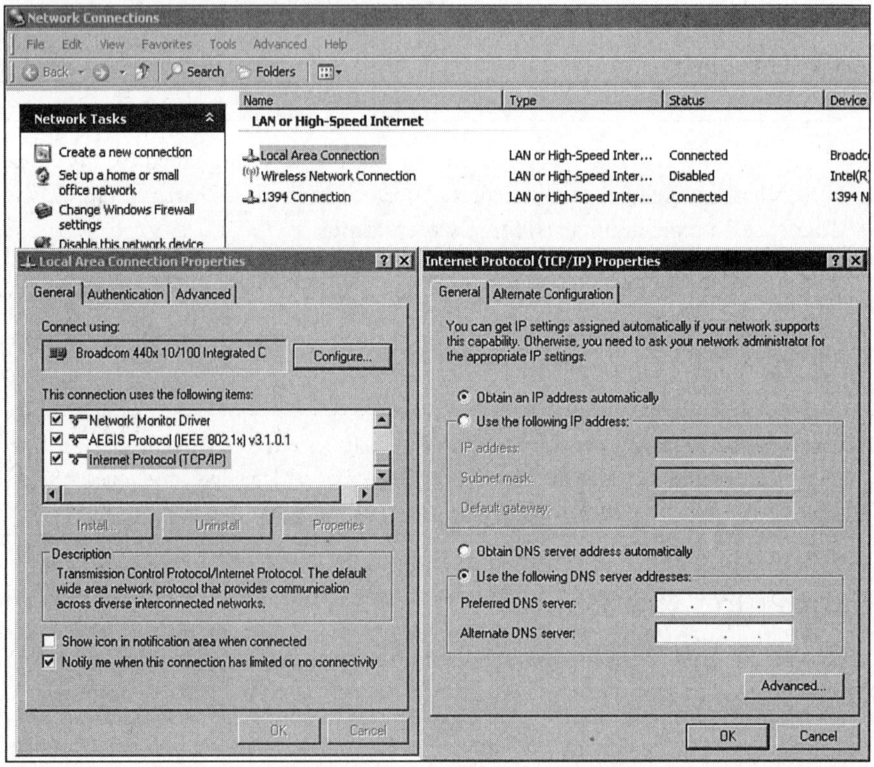

Step 3. Right-click **My Network Places** and choose **Properties**. Right-click your current LAN connection and choose **Properties**. Scroll down and find **Internet Protocol (TCP/IP)** and select it. Then click **Properties**. Choose the **Use the following IP address** option and enter the workstation's IP address, subnet mask, and default gateway. ______________________ to apply your settings. This might take a few seconds.

Step 4. Open a DOS window (choose **Start** > **Run** and then type **cmd**). At the command prompt, type **ipconfig** to verify that your IP address settings have been applied. If they have not, repeat Step 3.

Step 5. Test connectivity to the router by pinging the router's Ethernet interface. You should get output similar to the following:

```
C:\>ping 192.168.1.1

Pinging 192.168.1.1 with 32 bytes of data:

Reply from 192.168.1.1: bytes=32 time<10ms TTL=255
Reply from 192.168.1.1: bytes=32 time=10ms TTL=255
Reply from 192.168.1.1: bytes=32 time<10ms TTL=255
```

```
Reply from 192.168.1.1: bytes=32 time<10ms TTL=255

Ping statistics for 192.168.1.1:
    Packets: Sent = 4, Received = 4, Lost = 0 (0% loss),
Approximate round trip times in milli-seconds:
    Minimum = 0ms, Maximum =  10ms, Average =  2ms

C:\>
```

Task 6: Troubleshooting Connectivity

Step 1. If your ping was successful, you can skip this section of the lab. However, you should be familiar with how to troubleshoot a problem with a PC's connection to a router's LAN.

Step 2. If the ping failed, first check the physical connectivity to the router. Is the NIC's link light on or blinking? If it is not, check the connection to the switch or hub. You might have the cable plugged into an uplink port, or the device might not be powered. You might also be using a faulty or wrong cable.

Step 3. Check the connection between the switch or hub and the router's Ethernet interface. Are the link lights on or blinking? If they are not, check for a secure physical connection. You might also be using a faulty or wrong cable.

Step 4. If the connection from the PC to the router is physically operational, you might need to check your router's configuration. Return to your HyperTerminal session, and check to see whether the Ethernet interface is active. You should see both "Status" and "Protocol" as **up** for the Ethernet interface, as follows:

```
Ch2_Lab>show ip interface brief
Interface            IP-Address      OK? Method Status                Protocol
Ethernet0            192.168.1.1     YES manual up                    up

Serial0              unassigned      YES manual administratively down down

Serial1              unassigned      YES manual administratively down down
```

Step 5. If the interface is down, follow these steps to bring it up:

```
Ch2_Lab>enable
Password:
Ch2_Lab#config t
Enter configuration commands, one per line.  End with CNTL/Z.
Ch2_Lab(config)#interface Ethernet0
!Depending on your platform, you may need to enter
!interface FastEthernet 0 or interface FastEthernet 0/0
!Use the show ip interface brief command output to determine the correct name
!to use.
Ch2_Lab(config-if)#no shutdown
Ch2_Lab(config-if)#
2d18h: %LINK-3-UPDOWN: Interface Ethernet0, changed state to up
2d18h: %LINEPROTO-5-UPDOWN: Line protocol on Interface Ethernet0, changed state
to up
Ch2_Lab(config-if)#end
Ch2_Lab#
```

Step 6. Now test connectivity between the router and the PC again by pinging the default gateway. The ping should be successful.

Task 7: Restore Equipment Configurations

Step 1. Disconnect your workstation from the router. Restore your workstation to its previous IP configuration. For workstations that need to reconnect to a production network or the Internet, you must set the TCP/IP settings to **Obtain an IP address automatically**, as illustrated in Figure 2-17.

Figure 2-17 Dynamically Configure IP Addressing

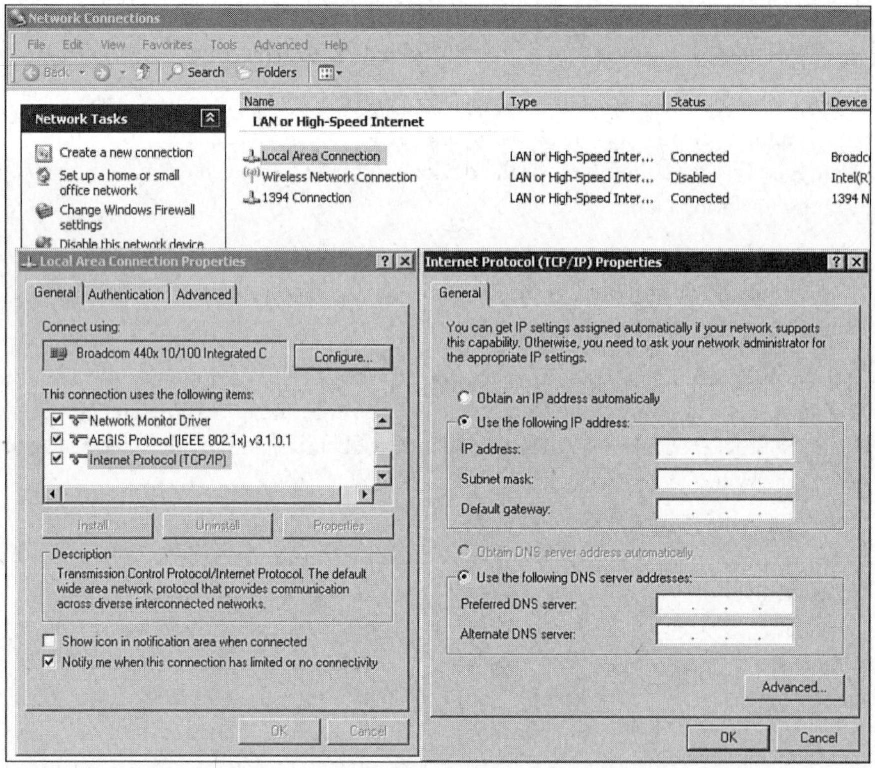

Step 2. From HyperTerminal, erase and reload the router by following these steps. If you are asked, "System configuration has been modified. Save?", type **no** and press **Enter**.

```
Ch2_Lab#erase startup-config
Erasing the nvram file system will remove all configuration files! Continue?
[con
firm]<Enter>
[OK]
Erase of nvram: complete
Ch2_Lab#
Ch2_Lab#reload

System configuration has been modified. Save? [yes/no]: no
Proceed with reload? [confirm]<Enter>
```

Step 3. Disconnect the rollover cable from the router and close HyperTerminal.

Challenge Lab 2-5: Configure a Two-Router Topology

Figure 2-18 Two-Router Topology with PCs

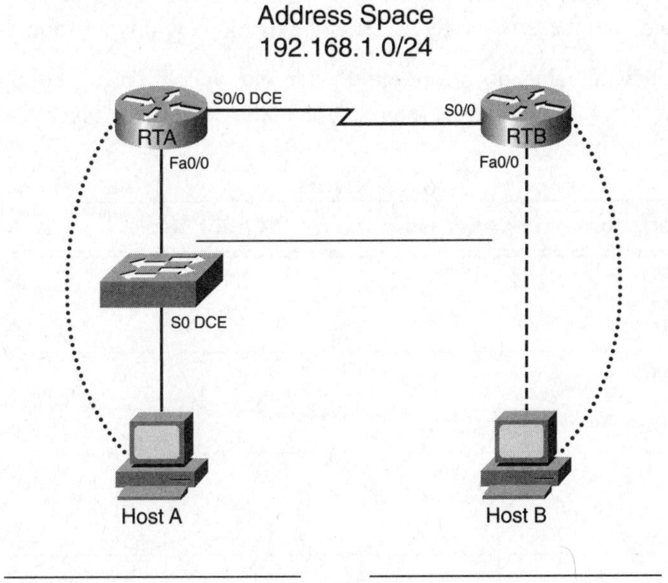

Objectives:

This lab contains the following objectives:

- Cable the topology
- Design and document an addressing scheme
- Configure IP addressing on the two routers
- Configure static routing between the two routers
- Configure IP addressing on the two PCs
- Test connectivity and troubleshoot

Equipment:

The topology shown in Figure 2-18 can use any two routers that have at least one serial interface and one LAN interface. Notice that RTA connects to a workstation directly while RTB is connected to a switch.

NetLab Compatibility Notes:

Because this lab evaluates your ability to physically connect a topology, it cannot be completed on NetLab.

Task 1: Cable the Topology

By now, you should be able to choose the correct devices and cables to set up the topology shown in Figure 2-18. Make sure that all link lights are on to verify that you have physical connectivity.

Task 2: Design and Document Addressing Scheme

Step 1. You are given the address space 192.168.1.0/24. Subnet this address space to provide addresses for 30 hosts. Assign subnet 1 to the LAN on RTA, subnet 2 to the link between RTA and RTB, and subnet 3 to the LAN on RTB. Label the topology with your subnets.

Step 2. In the following table, document the IP addresses you will use to configure your routers and PCs. If you are using different interfaces than those shown in Figure 2-18 and the table, change the labels accordingly.

Device	Interface	IP Address	Subnet Mask	Default Gateway
RTA	Fa0/0			N/A
	S0/0			N/A
RTB	Fa0/0			N/A
	S0/0			N/A
Host A	NIC			
Host B	NIC			

Task 3: Configure IP Addressing on the Two Routers

Step 1. To better identify the routers, configure each router with the name shown in Figure 2-18 and the preceding table. To do so, enter global configuration mode and use the **hostname** command.

Step 2. Configure the interfaces for RTA with the IP addresses you assigned in the previous section. The command syntax follows:

```
Router(config)#interface fa0/0
Router(config-if)#ip address address subnet_mask
Router(config-if)#no shutdown
Router(config-if)#interface serial 0/0
Router(config-if)#ip address address subnet_mask
Router(config-if)#clock rate 64000 <-- on DCE side only
Router(config-if)#no shutdown
```

Step 3. At this point, RTA should be able to ping the serial interface on RTB. Likewise, RTB should be able to ping the serial interface on RTA. Use the command **ping** at the privileged or user mode prompt where *remote_ip* is the address of the serial interface of the other router.

```
Router#ping remote_ip
```

Were your pings successful? If not, you must troubleshoot.

Task 4: Configure Static Routing Between the Two Routers

Step 1. Use the following command syntax to configure a static route on RTA and RTB so that each router has a route to the other router's LAN:

```
Router(config)#ip route network_address subnet_mask outbound_interface
```

The *network_address* and *subnet_mask* arguments are for the destination network. On RTA, the destination network is the subnet for the LAN on RTB. On RTB, the destination network is the subnet for the LAN on RTA. The *outbound_interface* argument is the interface the router will use to send traffic to the destination network. In Figure 2-18, the outbound interface is S0/0 for both routers. Document your commands in the space provided here:

Step 2. After configuring the static route correctly on both RTA and RTB, each router should be able to ping the other router's Fast Ethernet interface. Use the **ping** command to verify your static routing.

Step 3. Were your pings successful? If not, you must troubleshoot. You might need help from a more advanced student or your instructor. However, try to solve this problem on your own.

Task 5: Configure IP Addressing on the Two PCs

You should be able to complete this step without any help. If you are having difficulty, refer to previous labs you have completed. Configure the PCs with the IP addresses you assigned in the section "Task 2: Design and Document Addressing Scheme," earlier in this chapter.

Task 6: Test Connectivity and Troubleshoot

Pings from host A to host B should be successful. If not, make sure that each PC can ping its own default gateway.

Were your pings successful? If so, congratulations! You have just cabled, designed, and configured your first network. If not, carefully review all the steps in this lab. If you found this lab to be difficult, try reworking previous labs.

CHAPTER 3

Configuring a Router

The Study Guide portion of this chapter uses a combination of fill-in-the-blank, open-ended questions, and unique custom exercises to test your knowledge of how to configure a router.

The Lab Exercises portion of this chapter includes all the online curriculum labs as well as a comprehensive lab and a challenge lab to ensure that you have mastered the practical, hands-on skills needed to properly configure a router.

Study Guide

Configuring a Router for Basic Routing

This section of the chapter introduces the core skills that you will use each time you build a configuration for a Cisco device running Cisco IOS software. You should spend a significant amount of time studying the exercises in this section and completing all the labs. In addition, take full advantage of the online curriculum eLabs. Future lessons on Cisco device configuration will build on the basic concepts and commands in this section.

Router Prompt Exercise

Fill in the chart shown in Figure 3-1 with the correct router prompts for the configuration mode.

Figure 3-1 Router Prompt Exercise

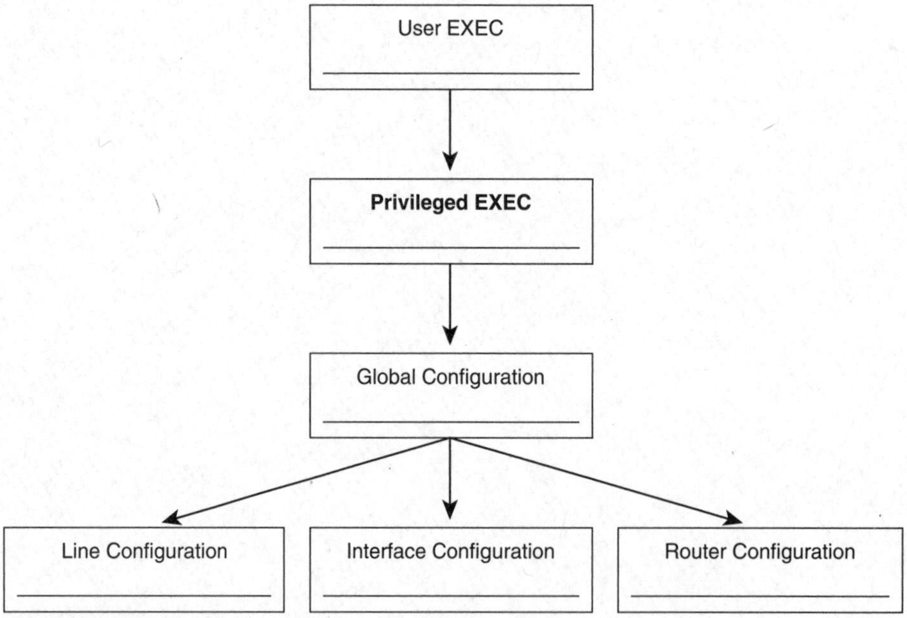

Basic Configuration Exercise

Using the topology shown in Figure 3-2, answer the next series of questions and determine the correct commands to use in each instance.

Figure 3-2 Basic Configuration Exercise

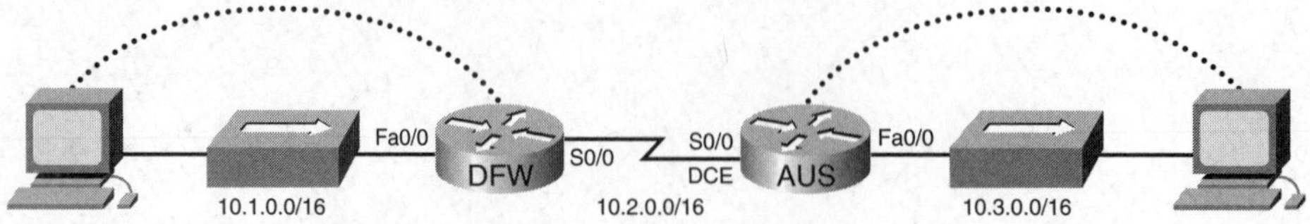

1. Document the router prompt and full command to change the name of Austin's router to **AUS**.

____

2. Document the router prompt and full commands to configure AUS with the two global passwords that can be used to enter privileged EXEC mode. Use **class** as the password.

3. If both are configured, which can serve as the password, and do you need to configure both?

4. Document the router prompt and full commands to configure the console port on AUS. Use the password **cisco**.

Note: These commands should also be used on the Auxiliary port.

5. Document the router prompt and full commands to configure the Telnet lines on AUS. Use the password **cisco**.

6. What global configuration command would you use if you wanted *all* passwords to be encrypted?

7. What is the difference between the encryption used with this command and the encryption used with the **enable secret** command?

8. Starting from the global configuration router prompt, list the four commands, including the router prompt, necessary to configure and fully activate the serial interface on AUS.

9. Starting from the global configuration router prompt, list the three commands, including the router prompt, necessary to configure and fully activate the Fast Ethernet interface on AUS.

10. **Challenge**: What are the two commands you must enter to configure AUS with Routing Information Protocol (RIP) routing and advertise the 10.0.0.0 networks to DFW?

____

____

11. At this point in the configuration of AUS, it is a good idea to save the running configuration to ______________. What command, including router prompt, should you use?

____

____

____

12. What command shows you how much memory the startup configuration is using? (It is not **show version** or **show flash**.)

____

13. **Challenge**: In the following space provided, document the equivalent commands needed to configure DFW with a basic configuration to match AUS.

____

____

____

____

____

____

____

____

____

____

____

____

____

____

____

____

____

____

____

____

____

____

____

____

____

____

____

____

____

____

14. After they have been configured, both DFW and AUS have full connectivity to each other. What tools would you use to test connectivity?

____

____

____

____

show Commands Exercise

1. What command lists the interfaces, their IP addresses, and the interface status, with only one line of output per interface, as shown in the following output?

____

```
AUS#______________________________________________
Interface          IP-Address     OK?   Method   Status                   Protocol
FastEthernet0/0    10.3.0.1       YES   manual   up                       up
Serial0/0          10.2.0.2       YES   manual   up                       up
Serial0/1          unassigned     YES   unset    administratively down    down
```

2. What command shows a lot more detail about the interfaces, as shown in the following output?

____

```
AUS#______________________________________________
FastEthernet0/0 is up, line protocol is up
  Hardware is AmdFE, address is 0002.fd75.2920 (bia 0002.fd75.2920)
  Description: AUS LAN
  Internet address is 10.3.0.1/16
  MTU 1500 bytes, BW 100000 Kbit, DLY 100 usec,
     reliability 255/255, txload 1/255, rxload 1/255
  Encapsulation ARPA, loopback not set
  Keepalive set (10 sec)
  Full-duplex, 100Mb/s, 100BaseTX/FX
  ARP type: ARPA, ARP Timeout 04:00:00
  Last input never, output 00:00:04, output hang never
  Last clearing of "show interface" counters never
  Input queue: 0/75/0/0 (size/max/drops/flushes); Total output drops: 0
  Queueing strategy: fifo
  Output queue :0/40 (size/max)
  5 minute input rate 0 bits/sec, 0 packets/sec
  5 minute output rate 0 bits/sec, 0 packets/sec
     0 packets input, 0 bytes
     Received 0 broadcasts, 0 runts, 0 giants, 0 throttles
     0 input errors, 0 CRC, 0 frame, 0 overrun, 0 ignored
     0 watchdog
     0 input packets with dribble condition detected
     1771 packets output, 170911 bytes, 0 underruns
     0 output errors, 0 collisions, 2 interface resets
     0 babbles, 0 late collision, 0 deferred
```

```
    0 lost carrier, 0 no carrier
    0 output buffer failures, 0 output buffers swapped out
Serial0/0 is up, line protocol is up
  Hardware is PowerQUICC Serial
  Description: WAN link to DFW
<output omitted for brevity>
```

3. What command lists the contents of the routing table, as shown in the following output?

____

```
AUS#__________________________________________
Codes: C - connected, S - static, I - IGRP, R - RIP, M - mobile, B - BGP
       D - EIGRP, EX - EIGRP external, O - OSPF, IA - OSPF inter area
       N1 - OSPF NSSA external type 1, N2 - OSPF NSSA external type 2
       E1 - OSPF external type 1, E2 - OSPF external type 2, E - EGP
       i - IS-IS, L1 - IS-IS level-1, L2 - IS-IS level-2, ia - IS-IS inter area
       * - candidate default, U - per-user static route, o - ODR
       P - periodic downloaded static route

Gateway of last resort is not set

     10.0.0.0/16 is subnetted, 3 subnets
C       10.2.0.0 is directly connected, Serial0/0
C       10.3.0.0 is directly connected, FastEthernet0/0
R       10.1.0.0 [120/1] via 10.2.0.1, 00:00:09, Serial0/0
```

4. What command displays the current configuration stored in RAM, as shown in the following output?

____

```
AUS#__________________________________________
Building configuration...

Current configuration : 1030 bytes
!
version 12.1
no service single-slot-reload-enable
service timestamps debug uptime
service timestamps log uptime
no service password-encryption
!
hostname AUS
!
enable secret 5 $1$0Gxl$h0WM8BRyepUZILCzdJOSe/
!
<output omitted for brevity>
!
!
interface FastEthernet0/0
 ip address 10.3.0.1 255.255.0.0
```

```
!
interface Serial0/0
 ip address 10.2.0.2 255.255.0.0
 clockrate 64000
!
<output omitted for brevity>
!
line con 0
 exec-timeout 30 0
 password cisco
 logging synchronous
 login
line aux 0
 exec-timeout 30 0
 password cisco
 logging synchronous
 login
line vty 0 4
 exec-timeout 30 0
 password cisco
 logging synchronous
 login
!
end
```

5. What command displays the configuration stored in NVRAM?

____

6. What is the difference between the configuration stored in RAM and the configuration stored in NVRAM?

____

____

____

____

____

Note: For more practice with **show** commands, refer to the section "Command Reference" under Lab Exercises, later in this chapter.

7. You entered a command and need to change it. What do you do? For example, you enter 10.4.0.1 as the IP address for the Fast Ethernet interface on AUS.

____

____

8. You entered a command and need to remove it. What do you do? For example, you entered network 11.0.0.0 in the RIP routing process for AUS.

____

____

Documenting the Router Configuration

In this section, you learn how to document your configurations as well as make backup copies. You learn how to reapply a backup copy of your configuration to a router that has no configuration. This skill is particularly helpful when your lab work is interrupted and you must finish it at another time. You can paste the backup configuration into the router and continue the lab from where you left off.

Finishing the Configuration Exercise

1. What is the purpose of the **description** command, and how does it affect the operation of the router?

____

____

____

____

____

2. What two commands can you use to view the documentation of the **description** command?

____

3. Document the router prompt and full command you would use to appropriately describe the Fast Ethernet interface on AUS, which you can assume is attached to the Accounting department.

```
AUS(config)#interface fa0/0
```

____

____

4. According to the online curriculum, what is *not* an appropriate use for your banner?

____

____

____

5. Document the router prompt and full command to configure an appropriate, multiline message of the day on AUS.

____

____

____

____

____

6. Document the command syntax, including the router prompt, that configures the router with the IP address of a Domain Name System (DNS) server to use for name resolutions.

____

7. What is the purpose of a host table, and how does it differ from DNS?

____

____

____

8. Document the router prompt and full command to configure a host table entry on AUS for the serial interface on DFW.

____

Managing the Configuration File Exercise

Fill in the following table with the correct command for the description shown.

Command	Description
	Loads configuration information from a network TFTP server into RAM.
	Copies a configuration file's commands from NVRAM into the running configuration in RAM. It does not necessarily replace the contents.
	Stores the current configuration from RAM into NVRAM.
	Stores the current configuration from RAM on a network TFTP server.
	Erases the contents of NVRAM.
	Displays the saved configuration, which is the contents of NVRAM.
	Displays the current configuration in RAM.

Lab Exercises

Command Reference

In the table that follows, record the command, *including the correct router prompt,* that fits the description. Fill in any blanks with the appropriate missing information.

Command	Description
	Moves into global configuration mode.
	Names the router with the name **CISCO**. You can use any name.
	Sets the enable password to **class**; no encryption.
	Sets the enable password to **class** and encrypts it.
	Enters console line configuration mode.
	Sets the console password to **cisco**.
	Enables password checking when users log in.
	Enters vty line configuration mode for five vty lines.
	Enters auxiliary line configuration mode.
	Applies a weak encryption to passwords.
	Lists all the **show** commands available in privileged EXEC mode.
	Displays detailed information and statistics about all interfaces.
	Displays a summary of all interfaces, including status and IP address assigned.
	Displays statistics for the serial 0 interface's hardware; particularly useful for determining whether a data circuit–terminating equipment (DCE) or data terminal equipment (DTE) cable is attached to the interface.
	Displays the local host-to-IP address cache. These are the names and addresses of hosts on the network to which you can connect.
	Shows the most recent commands used.
	Displays a directory of flash.
	Displays the version of software currently running on the router.
	Configures an interface with the text "Link to ISP", which describes the purpose of the link.

Command	Description
	Sets an interface address as 192.168.1.1/24.
	Configures the _____ side of the link to clock bits at 64000 bps.
	Activates an interface.
	Configures a message-of-the-day banner that uses # as the delimiting character and displays the following when users attempt to log in: This is a secure system. Authorized Personnel Only!
	Configures a host table entry for **LONDON** with the IP address **172.16.1.3**.
	Turns off trying to automatically resolve an unrecognized command by broadcasting for a DNS server.
	This command, entered on the console line, prevents messages from the router sent to the console from interrupting the command you are typing.
	This command sets the timeout for sessions to **0** minutes and **0** seconds, which is the same as never timing out. This is helpful in a lab environment, but should not be configured on production devices.

Curriculum Lab 3-1: Command Modes and Router Identification (3.1.2)

Figure 3-3 Topology for Lab 3.1.2

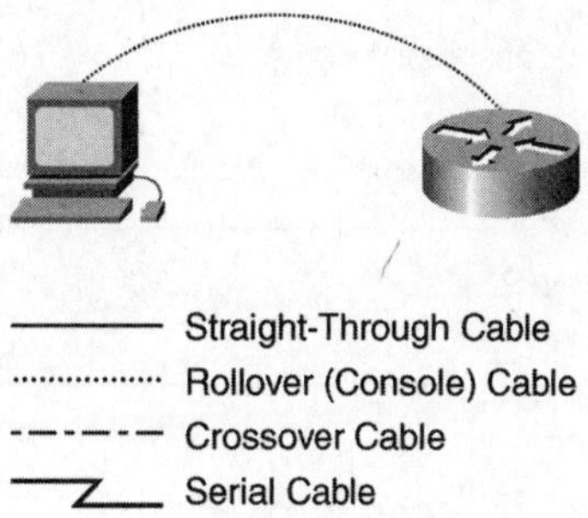

Objectives:

This lab contains the following objectives:

- Identify basic router modes of user EXEC and privileged EXEC
- Use commands to enter specific modes
- Become familiar with the router prompt for each mode
- Assign a name to the router

Background/Preparation:

Cable a network similar to the topology shown in Figure 3-3. You can use any router that meets the interface requirements in Figure 3-3 (that is, 800, 1600, 1700, 2500, or 2600 routers, or a combination). Refer to the information in Appendix B, "Router Interface Summary," to correctly specify the interface identifiers to be used based on the equipment in your lab.

The 1721 Series routers produced the configuration output in this lab. Any other router might produce slightly different output. You should execute the following steps on each router unless specifically instructed otherwise. Start a HyperTerminal session as you did in Lab 2-2, "Establishing a Console Session with HyperTerminal."

Refer to and implement the procedure documented in Appendix C, "Erasing and Reloading the Router," before continuing with this lab.

Task 1: Log in to the Router in User Mode

Connect to the router and log in.

What prompt did the router display?

____

What does this prompt mean?

____

Task 2: Log in to the Router in Privileged Mode

Enter **enable** at the user mode prompt:

```
Router>enable
```

If prompted for a password, enter the password **class**.

What prompt did the router display?

____

What does this prompt mean?

____

Task 3: Enter Global Configuration Mode

Enter **configure terminal** at the privileged mode prompt:

```
Router#configure terminal
```

What prompt did the router display?

____

What does this prompt mean?

___

Task 4: Enter Router Configuration Mode

Enter **router rip** at the global configuration mode prompt:

`Router(config)#router rip`

What prompt did the router display?

___

What does this prompt mean?

___

Task 5: Exit from Router Mode and Enter Interface Configuration Mode

Step 1. Enter **exit** at the prompt to return to global configuration mode:

`Router(config-router)#exit`

Step 2. Enter **interface serial 0** (see chart for your interface identifier) at the global configuration mode prompt:

`Router(config)#interface  serial 0`

What prompt did the router display?

___

What does this prompt mean?

___

Step 3. Enter **exit** at the prompt to return to global configuration mode:

`Router(config-if)#exit`

Task 6: Assign a Name to the Router

Enter **hostname GAD** at the prompt:

`Router(config)#hostname GAD`

What prompt did the router display?

___

What does this prompt mean?

___

What change occurred in the prompt?

___

Task 7: Exit the Router and Global Configuration Mode

To exit the router and global configuration mode, enter the following command:

```
GAD(config)#exit
```

After you exit the router and global configuration mode, log off (by typing **exit**) and turn the router off.

Curriculum Lab 3-2: Configuring Router Passwords (3.1.3)

Figure 3-4 Topology for Lab 3-2

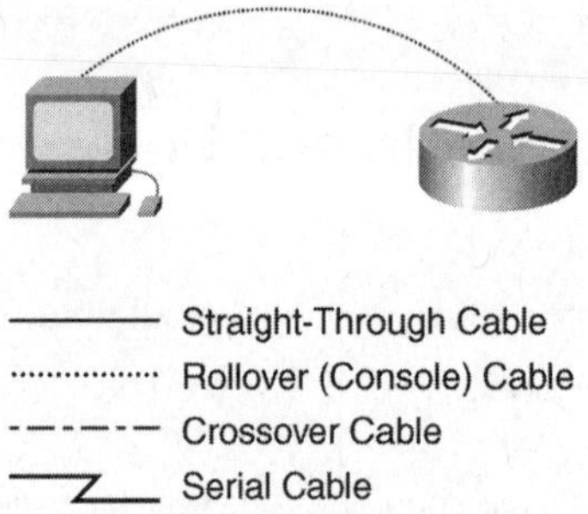

Objectives:

This lab contains the following objectives:

- Configure a password for console login to user mode
- Configure a password for virtual terminal (Telnet) sessions
- Configure a secret password for privileged mode

Background/Preparation:

Cable a network similar to the one shown in Figure 3-4. You can use any router that meets the interface requirements in Figure 3-4 (that is, 800, 1600, 1700, 2500, or 2600 routers, or a combination). Refer to the information in Appendix B to correctly specify the interface identifiers to be used based on the equipment in your lab. The 1721 Series routers produced the configuration output in this lab. Any other router might produce slightly different output. You should execute the following steps on each router unless specifically instructed otherwise.

Start a HyperTerminal session as you did in Lab 2-2.

Refer to and implement the procedure documented in Appendix C before continuing with this lab.

Task 1: Log in to the Router in User EXEC Mode

Connect to the router and log in.

What prompt did the router display?

____

What does this prompt mean?

____

Task 2: Log in to the Router in Privileged EXEC Mode

Enter **enable** at the user mode prompt:

```
Router>enable
```

What prompt did the router display?

____

What does this prompt mean?

____

Task 3: Enter Global Configuration Mode

Enter **configure terminal** at the privileged mode prompt:

```
Router#configure terminal
```

What prompt did the router display?

____

What does this prompt mean?

____

Task 4: Enter a Hostname of GAD for This Router

Enter **hostname GAD** at the prompt:

```
Router(config)#hostname GAD
```

What prompt did the router display?

____

What does this prompt mean?

____

Task 5: Configure the Console Password on the Router and Exit Line Mode

To configure the console password on the router and exit line mode, enter the following commands:

```
GAD(config)#line console 0
GAD(config-line)#password cisco
GAD(config-line)#login
GAD(config-line)#exit
GAD(config)#
```

Task 6: Configure the Password on the Virtual Terminal Lines and Exit Line Mode

To configure the password on the virtual terminal lines and exit line mode, enter the following commands:

```
GAD(config)#line vty 0 4
GAD(config-line)#password  cisco
GAD(config-line)#login
GAD(config-line)#exit
GAD(config)#
```

Task 7: Configure the Enable Password and Exit

To configure the enable password and exit, enter the following commands:

```
GAD(config)#enable password cisco
GAD(config)#exit
```

Task 8: Return to User EXEC Mode

To return to user EXEC mode, enter the **disable** command:

```
GAD#disable
```

Task 9: Enter Privileged EXEC Mode Again

This time, a prompt for a password will appear. Enter the password **cisco**, but you will not see the characters on the line:

```
GAD>enable
Password:cisco
```

Task 10: Return to Configuration Mode

To return to configuration mode, enter the **configure terminal** command:

```
GAD#configure terminal
```

Task 11: Configure the Enable Secret Password and Exit Global Configuration Mode

To configure the enable secret password and exit global configuration mode, enter the following commands:

```
GAD(config)#enable secret class
GAD(config)#exit
```

Note: Remember that the enable secret password is encrypted in the configuration view. Do not type **enable secret password class**, or your secret password will be **password**, not **class**.

Task 12: Return to User EXEC Mode

To return to user EXEC mode, enter the **disable** command:

```
GAD#disable
GAD>
```

Task 13: Enter Privileged EXEC Mode Again

This time, a prompt for a password will appear. Enter **cisco**, but you will not see the characters on the line. If it fails, keep trying until you see the **% Bad secrets** message:

```
GAD>enable
Password:cisco
Password:cisco
Password:cisco
% Bad secrets
```

Task 14: Enter Privileged EXEC Mode Again

A prompt for a password will appear. Enter **class**, but you will not see the characters on the line:

```
GAD>enable
Password:class
GAD#
```

Note: The enable secret password takes precedence over the enable password. After you enter an enable secret password, the router no longer accepts the enable password.

Task 15: Show the Router's Running Configuration

To show the router's running configuration, enter the following command:

```
GAD#show running-config
```

Do you see an encrypted password? ______________________________

Do you see any other passwords? ______________________________

Are any others encrypted? ______________________________

After you finish, log off (by typing **exit**) and turn the router off.

Curriculum Lab 3-3: Using Router show Commands (3.1.4)

Figure 3-5 Topology for Lab 3-3

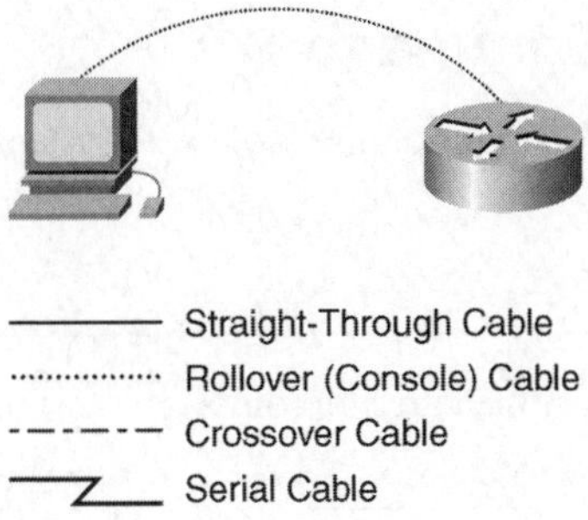

Objectives:

This lab contains the following objectives:

- Become familiar with the basic router **show** commands
- Retrieve the current running configuration from RAM using **show running-config**
- View the backup configuration file in NVRAM using **show startup-config**
- View the IOS file information using **show flash** and **show version**
- View the current status of the router interfaces using **show interface**
- View the status of any configured Layer 3 protocol using **show protocols**

Background/Preparation:

This lab helps you become familiar with the router **show** commands. The **show** commands, described as follows, are the most important information-gathering commands available for the router:

- **show running-config** (or **show run**) is probably the single most valuable command to help determine the current status of a router because it displays the active configuration file running in RAM.
- **show startup-config** (or **show start**) displays the backup configuration file that is stored in NVRAM. You use this file to configure the router when you first start it or reboot it with the **reload** command. This file contains all the detailed router interface settings.
- **show flash** displays the available flash memory and the amount used. Flash memory is where the router stores the Cisco IOS software file or image.
- **show arp** displays the router's address resolution table.
- **show interfaces** displays statistics for all interfaces configured on the router.
- **show protocols** displays global and interface-specific status of configured Layer 3 protocols (IP, Internetwork Packet Exchange [IPX], and so on).

Cable a network similar to one shown in Figure 3-5. You can use any router that meets the interface requirements in the figure (that is, 800, 1600, 1700, 2500, or 2600 routers, or a combination). The 1721 Series routers produced the configuration output in this lab. Any other router might produce slightly different output. Refer to the information in Appendix B to correctly specify the interface identifiers to be used based on the equipment in your lab. You should execute the following steps on each router unless specifically instructed otherwise.

Start a HyperTerminal session as you did in Lab 2-2.

Task 1: Log in to the Router

Connect to the router and log in. If prompted, enter the password **cisco**.

Task 2: Enter the help Command

Enter the **help** command by typing a question mark (**?**) at the router prompt.

What did the router reply with?

___

Are all router commands available at the current prompt?

___

Is **show** one of the options available?

___

Task 3: Display Help for the show Command

Enter the **show ?** command. The router responds with the **show** subcommands that are available in user mode.

List three user-mode **show** subcommands in the following table.

show Subcommand	Description

Task 4: Display the IOS Software Version and Other Important Information

Enter the **show version** command. The router returns information about the IOS that is running in RAM.

What is the IOS software version?

___

What is the name of the system image (IOS) file?

___

Where was the router IOS image booted from?

___

What type of processor (CPU) and how much RAM does this router have?

___

How many Ethernet interfaces does this router have?

___

How many serial interfaces?

___

The router backup configuration file is stored in NVRAM. How much NVRAM does this router have?

____

The router operating system (IOS) is stored in flash memory. How much flash memory does this router have?

____

What is the configuration register set to?

____

Task 5: Display the Router's Time and Date

Enter the **show clock** command. What information is displayed?

____

Task 6: Display a Cached List of Hostnames and Addresses

Enter the **show hosts** command. What information is displayed?

____

Task 7: Display Users Who Are Connected to the Router

Enter the **show users** command. What information is displayed?

____

Task 8: Display the Command Buffer

Enter the **show history** command. What information is displayed?

____

Task 9: Enter Privileged Mode

Step 1. From user EXEC mode, enter privileged EXEC mode using the **enable** command.

Step 2. Enter the enable password **class**.

What command did you use to enter privileged mode?

____

How do you know whether you are in privileged mode?

____

Task 10: Enter the help Command

Enter the **show ?** command at the router prompt.

What did the router reply with?

____

How is this output different from the one you got in user mode in Task 3?

____

Task 11: Display the Router Address Resolution Protocol (ARP) Table

Enter the **show arp** command at the router prompt. What is the ARP table?

____

Task 12: Display Information About the Flash Memory Device

Enter **show flash** at the router prompt.

How much flash memory is available and used?

____

What is the file that is stored in flash memory?

____

What is the size in bytes of the flash memory?

____

Task 13: Show Information About the Active Configuration File

Enter **show running-config** (or **show run**) at the router prompt. What important information is displayed?

____

Task 14: Display Information About the Backup Configuration File

Enter **show startup-config** (or **show start**) at the router prompt. What important information is displayed, and where is this information kept?

____

____

Task 15: Display Statistics for All Interfaces Configured on the Router

Enter **show interfaces** at the router prompt.

Step 1. Find the following information for interface FastEthernet 0. (Refer to Appendix B to correctly identify the interface based on your equipment.)

What is MTU?

____

What is rely?

____

What is load?

____

Step 2. Find the following information for interface Serial 0.

What is the IP address and subnet mask?

____

What data link layer encapsulation does the interface use?

____

Task 16: Display the Protocols Configured on the Router

Step 1. Enter **show protocols** at the router prompt. What important information is displayed?

____

Step 2. After you finish, log off (by typing **exit**) and turn the router off.

Curriculum Lab 3-4: Configuring a Serial Interface (3.1.5)

Figure 3-6 Topology for Lab 3-4

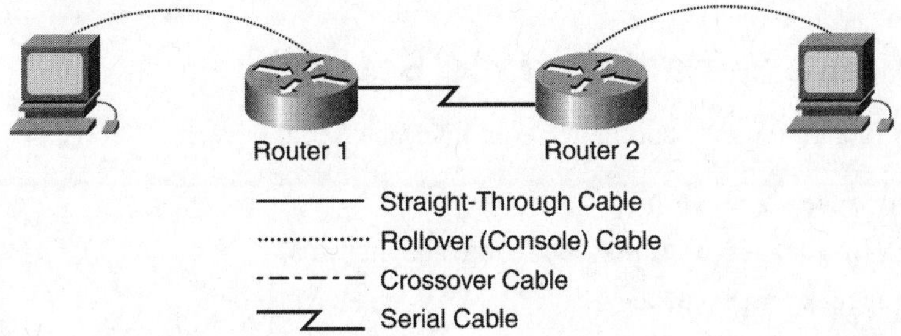

Use the information in Table 3-1 to configure the equipment for this lab.

Table 3-1 Lab Equipment Configuration

Router Designation	Router Name	Interface Type	Serial 0 Address	Subnet Mask	Enable Secret Password	Enable/vty/ Console Passwords
Router 1	GAD	DCE	192.168.15.1	255.255.255.0	class	cisco
Router 2	BHM	DTE	192.168.15.2	255.255.255.0	class	cisco

Objective:

The objective of this lab is to configure a serial interface on each of two routers so that they can communicate.

Background/Preparation:

Cable a network similar to the one shown in Figure 3-6. You can use any router that meets the interface requirements on this diagram (that is, 800, 1600, 1700, 2500, or 2600 routers, or a combination). Refer to the information in Appendix B to correctly specify the interface identifiers to be used based on the equipment in your lab. The 1721 Series routers produced the configuration output in this lab. Any other router might produce slightly different output. You should execute the following steps on each router unless specifically instructed otherwise. Start a HyperTerminal session as you did in Lab 2-2.

Refer to and implement the procedure documented in Appendix C before continuing with this lab.

Task 1: Connect the Router and Workstation Cabling

Connect the routers as shown in Figure 3-6. This lab requires a null serial cable (a DTE and DCE cable connected to each other) and two rollover (console) cables.

Task 2: Configure the Name and Passwords for Router 1

Step 1. On Router 1, enter global configuration mode and configure the hostname as shown in Table 3-1.

Step 2. Configure the console, virtual terminal, and enable passwords. If you have trouble doing this, refer to Lab 3-2, "Configuring Router Passwords," earlier in this chapter.

Task 3: Configure Serial Interface Serial 0

From global configuration mode, configure serial interface Serial 0 (refer to Appendix B) on Router GAD:

```
GAD(config)#interface serial 0
GAD(config-if)#ip address 192.168.15.1 255.255.255.0
GAD(config-if)#clock rate 56000
GAD(config-if)#no shutdown
GAD(config-if)#exit
GAD(config)#exit
```

Note: After you enter interface configuration mode, you must enter the IP address of the interface as well as the subnet mask. You enter the clock rate only on the DCE interface side of the WAN link. The **no shutdown** command turns on the interface. Shutdown is the name of the state when the interface is off.

Task 4: Save the Running Configuration to the Startup Configuration in Privileged EXEC Mode

To save the running configuration to the startup configuration in privileged EXEC mode, enter the following command:

```
GAD#copy running-config startup-config
```

Note: If you do not save the running configuration, the next time that you restart the router, either with a software **reload** command or a power recycle, the running configuration will be lost. The router uses the startup configuration when the router is started.

Task 5: Display Information About Serial Interface 0 on GAD

Enter the command **show interface serial 0** (refer to Appendix B) on GAD:

```
GAD#show interface serial 0
```

This command shows the details of interface serial 0.

List the following details you discovered from issuing this command:

- Serial0 is ______________________________
- Line protocol is ______________________________

- Internet address is ______________________________
- Encapsulation is ______________________________

To what OSI layer is *Encapsulation* referring?

____

If the serial interface was configured, why did the **show interface serial 0** output say that the interface is down?

____

Task 6: Configure the Name and Passwords for Router 2

On the BHM router, enter global configuration mode and configure the router name, console, virtual terminal, and enable passwords, as shown in Table 3-1.

Task 7: Configure Serial Interface Serial 0

From global configuration mode, configure serial interface Serial 0 (refer to Appendix B) on Router BHM:

```
BHM(config)#interface serial 0
BHM(config-if)#ip address 192.168.15.2  255.255.255.0
BHM(config-if)#no shutdown
BHM(config-if)#exit
BHM(config)#exit
```

Task 8: Save the Running Configuration to the Startup Configuration in Privileged EXEC Mode

To save the running configuration to the startup configuration in privileged EXEC mode, enter the following command:

```
BHM#copy running-config startup-config
```

Task 9: Display Information About Serial Interface 0 on BHM

Enter the command **show interface serial 0** (refer to Appendix B) on Router BHM:

```
BHM#show interface serial 0
```

This command shows the details of interface Serial 0.

List the details you discovered from issuing this command:

- Serial 0 is ______________________________
- Line protocol is ______________________________
- Internet address is ______________________________
- Encapsulation is ______________________________

What is the difference in the Line Protocol Status recorded on GAD earlier? Why?

____

____

Task 10: Verify That the Serial Connection Is Functioning

Step 1. Ping the serial interface of the other router:

```
BHM#ping 192.168.15.1
GAD#ping 192.168.15.2
```

From GAD, can you ping the BHM router's serial interface? ____________________

From BHM, can you ping the GAD router's serial interface? ____________________

Step 2. If the answer is no for either of the preceding questions, troubleshoot the router configurations to find the error. Then, do the pings again until the answer to both questions is yes.

Step 3. When you finish the preceding steps, log off (by typing **exit**) and turn the router off. Remove and store the cables and adapter.

Curriculum Lab 3-5: Making Configuration Changes (3.1.6)

Figure 3-7 Topology for Lab 3-5

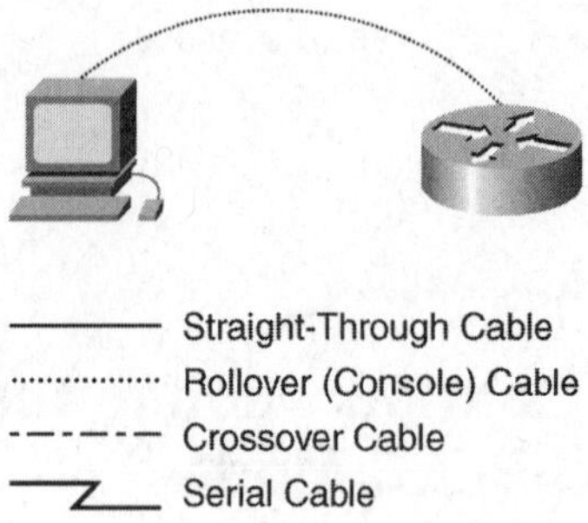

Table 3-2 Lab Equipment Configuration

Router Name	Router Type	Serial 0 Address	Subnet Mask
GAD	192.168.14.1	255.255.255.0	

The enable secret password is **class**.

The enable/vty/console password is **cisco**.

Objectives:

This lab contains the following objectives:

- Configure some basic router settings
- Bring interfaces up and down
- Make changes to the router configuration

Background/Preparation:

Cable a network similar to the one shown in Figure 3-7. You can use any router that meets the interface requirements in the diagram (that is, 800, 1600, 1700, 2500, or 2600 routers, or a combination). Refer to the information in Appendix B to correctly specify the interface identifiers to be used based on the equipment in your lab. The 1721 Series routers produced the configuration output in this lab. Any other router might produce slightly different output. You should execute the following steps on each router unless specifically instructed otherwise.

Start a HyperTerminal session as you did in Lab 2-2.

Refer to and implement the procedure documented in Appendix C before continuing with this lab.

Task 1: Connect the Router and Workstation Cabling

Connect the router as shown in Figure 3-7. This lab requires a console (rollover) cable.

Task 2: Configure Hostname and Passwords

On the GAD router, enter global configuration mode and configure the router name as shown in Table 3-2. Then, configure the console, virtual terminal, and enable passwords.

Task 3: Configure the Serial 0 Interface

From global configuration mode, configure interface serial 0 (refer to Table 3-2) on Router GAD:

```
GAD(config)#interface Serial 0
GAD(config-if)#ip address 192.168.14.1 255.255.255.0
GAD(config-if)#no shutdown
GAD(config-if)#description Connection to the host
GAD(config-if)#exit
GAD(config)#exit
```

Task 4: Save the Configuration

Save the running configuration to the startup configuration in privileged EXEC mode:

```
GAD#copy running-config startup-config
```

Caution: If you do not save the running configuration, the next time that you restart the router, either with a software reload command or a power recycle, the running configuration will be lost. The router uses the startup configuration when the router is started.

Task 5: Verify the Configuration

Step 1. Enter the **show running-config** command from privileged EXEC mode.

Step 2. If the configuration is not correct, reenter any incorrect commands.

Task 6: Modify the Configuration

Based on the information in Table 3-3, reconfigure the GAD router. This step includes changing the router hostname, changing the enable/vty/console passwords, and removing the secret password and interface description. You also need to change the interface address and subnet mask.

Table 3-3 Lab Equipment Configuration: Modified

Router Name	Serial 0 Address	Subnet Mask	Enable Secret Password	Enable/vty/Console Passwords
Gadsden	172.16.0.1	255.255.0.0	Cisco1	

To change the information, go to the proper command mode and retype the command with the new information. To remove an old command, go to the proper command mode and retype the command exactly as it was entered with the word **no** in front of it:

```
GAD(config-if)#description Connection to location XYZ
GAD(config-if)#no description Connection to location XYZ
```

Note: Before making changes to the interface IP address and subnet mask, bring the interface down, as shown in Task 7.

Task 7: Bring Down Serial Interface 0

Step 1. Bring the interface down for maintenance by entering the following commands:

```
Gadsden(config)#interface Serial 0
Gadsden(config-if)#shutdown
Gadsden(config-if)#exit
Gadsden(config)#exit
Gadsden#
```

Step 2. Enter the command **show interface Serial 0** and note the interface status:

Serial 0 is ______________________________

Line protocol is ______________________________

Step 3. Issue the **show running-config** command and note the status of interface Serial 0:

____

Task 8: Bring Up the Serial 0 Interface

Step 1. To make the interface operational, enable the interface by entering the following commands:

```
Gadsden(config)#interface Serial 0
Gadsden(config-if)#no shutdown
Gadsden(config-if)#exit Gadsden
(config)#exit
```

Step 2. Enter the command **show interface Serial 0**, note the interface status, and explain the reason for the status:

Serial 0 is ______________________________

Line protocol is ______________________________

____

____

Note: If the serial interface has been brought down with the **shutdown** command, it shows a status of "Administratively Down." Because no cable is attached, it shows a status of "Down" even if brought up with the **no shutdown** command.

Task 9: Verify the Configuration

Step 1. Enter a **show running-config** command from privileged EXEC mode to see whether the modifications took effect.

Step 2. If the configuration is not correct, reenter any incorrect commands and verify again.

Step 3. When you finish the preceding steps, log off (by typing **exit**) and turn the router off.

Curriculum Lab 3-6: Configuring an Ethernet Interface (3.1.7)

Figure 3-8 Topology for Lab 3-6

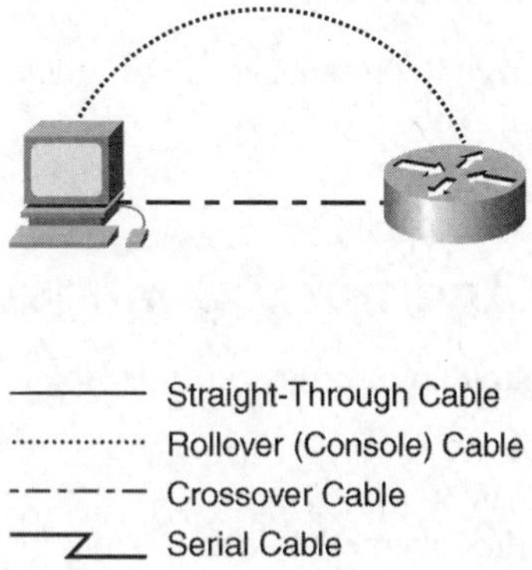

Table 3-4 Lab Equipment Configuration

Router Designation	Router Name	Ethernet 0 Address	Subnet Mask
Router 1	GAD	192.168.14.1	255.255.255.0

The enable secret password is **class**.

The enable/vty/console password is **cisco**.

Objective:

The objective of this lab is to configure an Ethernet interface on the router with an IP address and a subnet mask.

Background/Preparation:

In this lab, you configure an Ethernet interface on the router with an IP address and a subnet mask. Cable a network similar to the one shown in Figure 3-8. You can use any router that meets the interface requirements in the diagram (that is, 800, 1600, 1700, 2500, or 2600 routers, or a combination). Refer to the information in Appendix B to correctly specify the interface identifiers to be used based on the equipment in your lab. The 1721 Series routers produced the configuration output in this lab. Any other router might produce slightly different output. You should execute the following steps on each router unless specifically instructed otherwise.

Start a HyperTerminal session as you did in Lab 2-2.

Refer to and implement the procedure documented in Appendix C before continuing with this lab.

Task 1: Configure the Hostname and Passwords on the GAD Router

On the GAD router, enter global configuration mode and configure the router name as shown in Table 3-4. Then, configure the console, virtual terminal, and enable passwords.

Task 2: Configure the FastEthernet 0 Interface

The designation for the first Ethernet interface on the router can vary. It might be ethernet 0, fastethernet 0, or fastethernet 0/0, depending on the type of router:

```
GAD(config)#interface fastethernet 0
GAD(config-if)#ip address 192.168.14.1 255.255.255.0
GAD(config-if)#no shutdown
GAD(config-if)#exit
GAD(config)#exit
```

Task 3: Save the Configuration

Save the configuration information from the privileged EXEC command mode:

```
GAD#copy running-config startup-config
```

Task 4: Display the FastEthernet 0 Configuration Information

To display the FastEthernet 0 configuration information, enter the following command:

```
GAD#show interface fastethernet 0
```

This command shows the details of the Ethernet interface.

List the following details discovered from issuing this command:

- FastEthernet0 is ______________________________
- Line protocol is ______________________________
- Internet address is ______________________________
- Encapsulation is ______________________________
- To what OSI layer is *Encapsulation* referring? ______________________________

When you finish the preceding steps, log off (by typing **exit**) and turn the router off.

Curriculum Lab 3-7: Configuring Interface Descriptions (3.2.3)

Figure 3-9 Topology for Lab 3-7

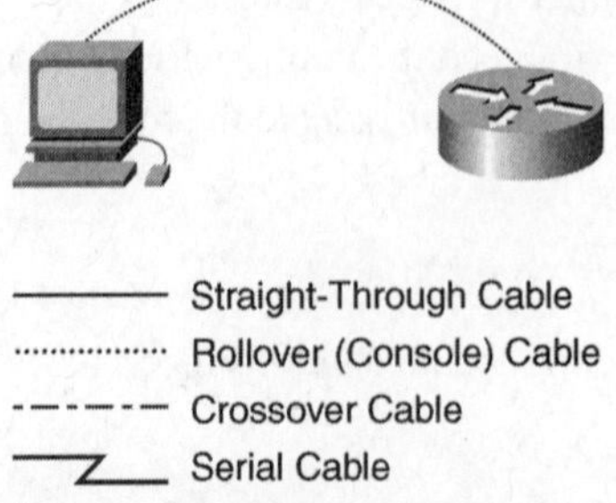

Table 3-5 Lab Equipment Configuration

Router Designation	Router Name	FastEthernet0 Address	Serial 0 Address	Subnet Mask for Both Interfaces
Router 1	GAD	192.168.14.1	192.168.15.1	255.255.255.0

The enable secret password is **class**.

The enable/vty/console password is **cisco**.

Objective:

The objective of this lab is to choose a description for an interface and use interface configuration mode to enter that description.

Background/Preparation:

Interface descriptions are an important part of network documentation. They help you understand how a network is built and provide information for troubleshooting purposes.

Cable a network similar to the one shown in Figure 3-9. You can use any router that meets the interface requirements in the diagram (that is, 800, 1600, 1700, 2500, or 2600 routers, or a combination). Refer to the information in Appendix B to correctly specify the interface identifiers to be used based on the equipment in your lab. The 1721 Series routers produced the configuration output in this lab. Any other router might produce slightly different output. You should execute the following steps on each router unless specifically instructed otherwise.

Start a HyperTerminal session as you did in Lab 2-2.

Refer to and implement the procedure documented in Appendix C before continuing with this lab.

Task 1: Configure the Hostname and Passwords on the Router

Step 1. On the router, enter global configuration mode and configure the hostname as shown in Table 3-5. Then, configure the console, virtual terminal, and enable passwords. If you have trouble doing this, refer to Lab 3-2.

What router command is used to view the current running configuration? ____________________

What command mode must you use to enter the command in the last question?

____

Step 2. Enter the command that verifies the configuration that you just entered. If the configuration is not correct, fix the errors and verify it again until it is correct.

Task 2: Enter Global Configuration Mode

Enter **configure terminal** at the router prompt. Notice the change in the router prompt.

What did the router prompt change to? ____

Task 3: Enter Interface Configuration Mode

Enter **interface serial 0** (refer to Appendix B) at the global configuration prompt.

What does the router prompt look like in interface configuration mode? ____________________

Task 4: Display Help for the description Command

Enter **description ?** at the router prompt.

What is the maximum number of characters in an interface description? ______________________

Task 5: Choose a Description for the Interface

An interface description includes the purpose and location of the interface, other devices or locations connected to the interface, and circuit identifiers. Descriptions help the support personnel better understand the problems related to an interface and allow a faster resolution to those problems.

Given the following circuit information, choose a description for the Serial 0 interfaces for both GAD and BHM. Use the following form to document your choice.

Link	Carrier	Circuit ID	Speed
GAD to BHM	BellSouth	10DHDG551170	1.544 Mbps

Task 6: Enter a Description for Interface Serial 0

From interface configuration mode for Serial 0, enter **description** *text*, where *text* is the description from the previous step. Then, press **Ctrl-Z** or type **end** to return to privileged EXEC mode.

Note: Pressing **Ctrl-Z** is the same as typing **exit** to leave interface configuration mode and typing **exit** again to leave global configuration mode. It is a keyboard shortcut.

Task 7: Examine the Active Configuration File

From enable mode (another name for privileged EXEC mode), enter the command that shows the running configuration. The router displays information on how it is currently configured.

What command did you enter? ____

What is the description for interface Serial 0?

____

Task 8: Confirm That the Interface Description Is Correct

From enable mode, enter the **show interfaces serial 0** command. The router displays information about the interface. Examine this output to confirm that the description you entered is the correct description.

When you finish the preceding steps, log off (by typing **exit**) and turn the router off.

Curriculum Lab 3-8: Configuring Message of the Day (MOTD) (3.2.5)

Figure 3-10 Topology for Lab 3-8

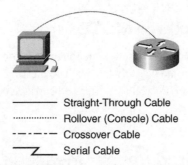

Table 3-6 Lab Equipment Configuration

Router Name	Fa0	S0 Address	Subnet Mask
GAD	172.16.0.1	192.168.15.1	255.255.255.0

The enable secret password is **class**.

The enable/vty/console password is **cisco**.

Objective:

The objective of this lab is to enter a message of the day (MOTD) on the router, which allows all users to view the message upon entering the router.

Background/Preparation:

In this lab, an MOTD banner is configured. A message of the day, or "login banner," can be useful as a warning to unauthorized users and can assist with security measures.

Cable a network similar to the one shown in Figure 3-10. You can use any router that meets the interface requirements in the diagram (that is, 800, 1600, 1700, 2500, or 2600 routers, or a combination). Refer to the information in Appendix B to correctly specify the interface identifiers to be used based on the equipment in your lab. The 1721 Series routers produced the configuration output in this lab. Any other router might produce slightly different output. You should execute the following steps on each router unless specifically instructed otherwise.

Start a HyperTerminal session as you did in Lab 2-2.

Refer to and implement the procedure documented in Appendix C before continuing with this lab.

Task 1: Configure Basic Router Information

Step 1. On the router, enter global configuration mode and configure the router name as shown in Table 3-6. Then, configure the console, virtual terminal, and enable passwords. If you have trouble doing this, refer to Lab 3-2.

Step 2. Enter the **show running-config** command to verify the configuration that you just entered.

Step 3. Save the configuration information in privileged EXEC mode:

```
GAD#copy running-config startup-config
```

Task 2: Enter Global Configuration Mode

Enter **configure terminal** at the router prompt. Notice the change in the router prompt.

Task 3: Display Help for the banner motd Command

Enter **banner motd ?** at the router prompt.

What is the character called that indicates the beginning and end of the banner? ____________________

Task 4: Choose the Text for MOTD

The login banner should be a warning to users to not attempt to log in unless they are authorized. In the following space, enter an appropriate warning banner. The message can contain any printable character, other than the delimiting character, as well as spaces and carriage returns.

____

Task 5: Enter the Desired Banner Message

From global configuration mode, enter **banner motd** # *message* #, where # are the delimiters and *message* is the banner message from the previous task.

Task 6: Test the MOTD Display

Exit the console session. Reenter the router to display the message of the day by pressing **Enter**.

Task 7: Verify the MOTD by Looking at the Router Configuration

Step 1. Enter the **show running-config** command.

How does the banner MOTD appear in the configuration listing?

____

Step 2. Save the configuration information in privileged EXEC mode. When finished, log off (by typing **exit**) and turn the router off.

Curriculum Lab 3-9: Configuring Host Tables (3.2.7)

Figure 3-11 Topology for Lab 3-9

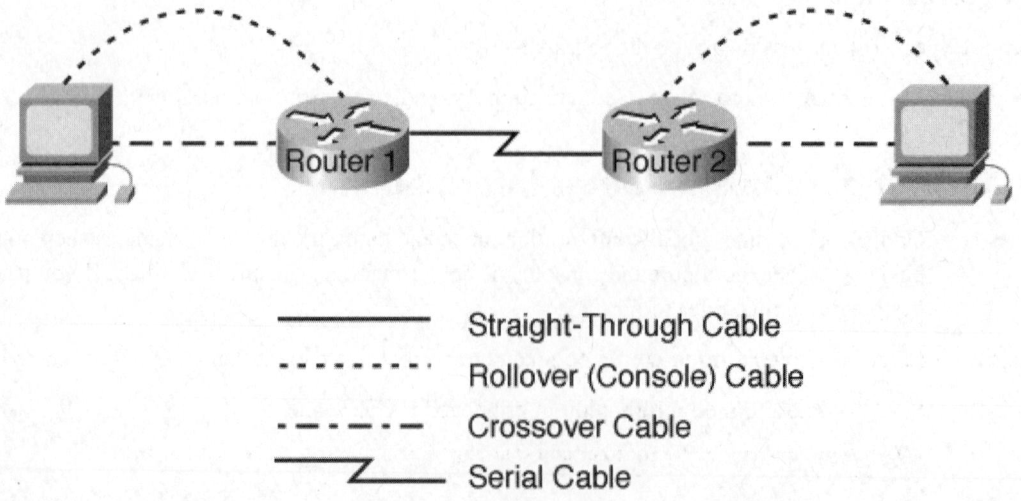

Table 3-7 Lab Equipment Configuration

Router Designation	Router Name	FastEthernet 0 Address	Interface Type	Serial 0 Address
Router 1	GAD	172.16.0.1	DCE	172.17.0.1
Router 2	BHM	172.18.0.1	DTE	172.17.0.2

The enable secret password for both routers is **class**.

The enable/vty/console password for both routers is **cisco**.

The subnet mask for both interfaces on both routers is 255.255.0.0.

Objective:

The objective of this lab is to create IP host tables associating router names with IP addresses.

Background/Preparation:

IP host tables allow a router to use names to identify all the attached interfaces on that router. You can use these names in place of IP addresses in commands that use IP addresses to identify a location such as ping or Telnet.

Cable a network similar to the one shown in Figure 3-11. You can use any router that meets the interface requirements in the diagram (that is, 800, 1600, 1700, 2500, or 2600 routers, or a combination). Refer to the information in Appendix B to correctly specify the interface identifiers to be used based on the equipment in your lab. The 1721 Series routers produced the configuration output in this lab. Any other router might produce slightly different output. You should execute the following steps on each router unless specifically instructed otherwise.

Start a HyperTerminal session as you did in Lab 2-2.

Refer to and implement the procedure documented in Appendix C before continuing with this lab.

Task 1: Configure the Hostname and Passwords on the GAD Router

On the GAD router, enter global configuration mode and configure the router name as shown in Table 3-7. Then, configure the console, virtual terminal, and enable passwords. If you have trouble doing this, refer to Lab 3-2.

Task 2: Configure the Interfaces and Routing Protocol on the GAD Router

Go to the proper command mode and enter the following:

```
GAD(config)#interface fastethernet 0
GAD(config-if)#ip address 172.16.0.1 255.255.0.0
GAD(config-if)#no shutdown
GAD(config-if)#exit
GAD(config)#interface serial 0
GAD(config-if)#ip address 172.17.0.1 255.255.0.0
GAD(config-if)#clock rate 56000
GAD(config-if)#no shutdown
GAD(config-if)#exit
```

```
GAD(config)#router rip
GAD(config-router)#network 172.16.0.0
GAD(config-router)#network 172.17.0.0
GAD(config-router)#exit
GAD(config)#exit
```

Task 3: Save the GAD Router Configuration

To save the configuration for the GAD router, enter the following command:

```
GAD#copy running-config startup-config
```

Task 4: Configure the Hostname and Passwords on the BHM Router

On the BHM router, enter global configuration mode and configure the router name as shown in Table 3-7. Then, configure the console, virtual terminal, and enable passwords. If you have trouble doing this, refer to Lab 3-2.

Task 5: Configure the Interfaces and Routing Protocol on the BHM Router

Go to the proper command mode and enter the following:

```
BHM(config)#interface fastethernet 0
BHM(config-if)#ip address 172.18.0.1 255.255.0.0
BHM(config-if)#no shutdown
BHM(config-if)#exit
BHM(config)#interface serial 0
BHM(config-if)#ip address 172.17.0.2 255.255.0.0
BHM(config-if)#no shutdown
BHM(config-if)#exit
BHM(config)#router rip
BHM(config-router)#network 172.17.0.0
BHM(config-router)#network 172.18.0.0
BHM(config-router)#exit
BHM(config)#exit
```

Task 6: Save the BHM Router Configuration

To save the configuration for the BHM router, enter the following command:

```
BHM#copy running-config startup-config
```

Task 7: Verify That the Internetwork Is Functioning

To verify that the interface is functioning properly, you need to ping the Fast Ethernet interface of the other router.

From GAD, can you ping the BHM router's Fast Ethernet interface? ______________________________

From BHM, can you ping the GAD router's Fast Ethernet interface? ______________________________

If the answer is no for either question, troubleshoot the router configurations to find the error. Then, do the pings again until the answer to both questions is yes.

Task 8: Configure the IP Host Table for the Network

Step 1. Create a name for each router in the network lab. Enter that name along with the IP addresses of the router's interfaces in the table that follows. This local name can be anything that you want. Although the name does not have to match the configured hostname of the router, that is a logical choice.

Router Name	IP Address Ethernet 0	IP Address Interface Serial 0

Step 2. From global configuration mode, enter the command **ip host** followed by the name of each router in the network and all the IP addresses of the interfaces for each router.

For example, to name the GAD router accessible from BHM with the name G, enter the following:

```
BHM(config)#ip host G 172.16.0.1 172.17.0.1
```

What commands did you enter on GAD?

___

What commands did you enter on BHM?

___

Task 9: Exit Configuration Mode and Test

Step 1. From enable (privileged EXEC) mode, examine the host table entries using the **show hosts** command on each router.
Do you see the host entries that were configured in the previous tasks?

GAD: ___

BHM: ___

Step 2. If no IP host entries exist, repeat Task 8.

Step 3. Ping the other router by hostname. From the enable prompt, type **ping** *host*, where *host* is the IP hostname that you configured in the previous steps. For example, for a hostname G, enter the following:

```
BHM#ping G
```

Was the ping successful? ___

If not, check the accuracy of the IP host table entries.

Step 4. From the enable prompt, enter the hostname and press **Enter**. For example, for a hostname G, enter the following:

```
BHM#G
```

What happened?

____

Step 5. When you finish, log off (by typing **exit**) and turn the router off.

Curriculum Lab 3-10: Backing Up Configuration Files (3.2.9)

Figure 3-12 Topology for Lab 3-10

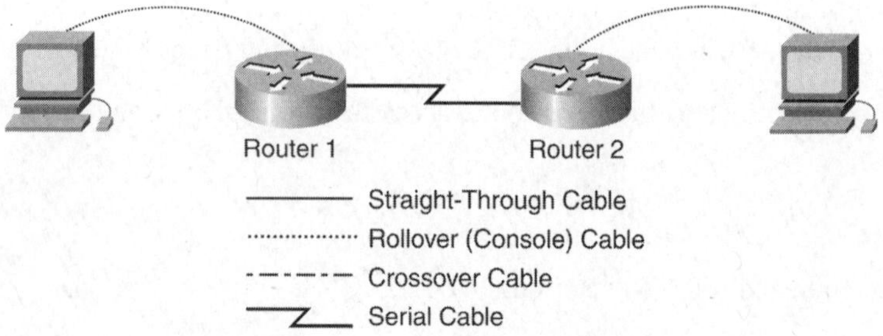

Table 3-8 Lab Equipment Configuration

Router Designation	Router Name	FastEthernet 0 Address	Interface Type	Serial 0 Address
Router 1	GAD	172.16.0.1	DCE	172.17.0.1
Router 2	BHM	172.18.0.1	DTE	172.17.0.2

The enable secret password for this router is **class**.

The enable/vty/console password for this router is **cisco**. The subnet mask for all addresses is 255.255.0.0.

Objectives:

This lab contains the following objectives:

- Capture the running configuration of a router to an ASCII text file with HyperTerminal
- Edit the configuration with a text editor such as Notepad
- Use the edited text file to configure another router using HyperTerminal

Background/Preparation:

The HyperTerminal capture option can be useful not only for saving configuration files but also for capturing command output and for documenting changes. It provides a simple way to save whatever is displayed on the screen of the PC acting as a console to the router.

Cable a network similar to the one shown in Figure 3-12. You can use any router that meets the interface requirements in Figure 3-12 (that is, 800, 1600, 1700, 2500, or 2600 routers, or a combination). Refer to the information in Appendix B to correctly specify the interface identifiers based on the equipment in your lab.

The 1721 Series routers produced the configuration output in this lab. Any other router might produce slightly different output. You should execute the following steps on each router unless specifically instructed otherwise.

Start a HyperTerminal session as you did in Lab 2-2.

Implement the procedure documented in Appendix C before continuing with this lab.

Task 1: Configure the Hostname and Passwords on the GAD Router

On the GAD router, enter global configuration mode and configure the router name as shown in Table 3-8. Then configure the console, vty, and enable passwords.

Task 2: Configure the Interfaces and Routing Protocol on the GAD Router

Go to the proper command mode and enter the following:

```
GAD(config)#interface fastethernet 0
GAD(config-if)#ip address 172.16.0.1 255.255.0.0
GAD(config-if)#no shutdown
GAD(config-if)#exit
GAD(config)#interface serial 0
GAD(config-if)#ip address 172.17.0.1 255.255.0.0
GAD(config-if)#clock rate 56000
GAD(config-if)#no shutdown
GAD(config-if)#exit
GAD(config)#router rip
GAD(config-router)#network 172.16.0.0
GAD(config-router)#network 172.17.0.0
GAD(config-router)#exit
GAD(config)#exit
```

Task 3: Save the GAD Router Configuration

To save the configuration on the GAD router, enter the following command:

```
GAD#copy running-config startup-config
Destination filename [startup-config]?  [Enter]
```

Task 4: Configure the Hostname and Passwords on the BHM Router

On the BHM router, enter global configuration mode and configure the router name as shown in Table 3-8. Then, configure the console, vty, and enable passwords.

Task 5: Configure the Interfaces and Routing Protocol on the BHM Router

Go to the proper command mode and enter the following:

```
BHM(config)#interface fastethernet 0
BHM(config-if)#ip address 172.18.0.1 255.255.0.0
BHM(config-if)#no shutdown
BHM(config-if)#exit
BHM(config)#interface serial 0
BHM(config-if)#ip address 172.17.0.2 255.255.0.0
BHM(config-if)#no shutdown
BHM(config-if)#exit
BHM(config)#router rip
BHM(config-router)#network 172.17.0.0
BHM(config-router)#network 172.18.0.0
BHM(config-router)#exit
BHM(config)#exit
```

Task 6: Save the BHM Router Configuration

To save the configuration on the BHM router, enter the following command:

```
BHM#copy running-config startup-config
Destination filename [startup-config]?  [Enter]
```

Task 7: Verify That the Internetwork Is Functioning

To verify that the internetwork is functioning properly, you need to ping the Fast Ethernet interface of the other router.

From GAD, can you reach the BHM router Fast Ethernet interface? ______________________________

From BHM, can you reach the GAD router Fast Ethernet interface? ______________________________

If the answer is no for either question, troubleshoot the router configurations to find the error. Then, do the pings again until the answer to both questions is yes.

Task 8: Start Capturing the Configuration File

Start the process of copying the router configuration to a text file.

Use HyperTerminal to capture all the text displayed on its screen to a text file.

Step 1. In HyperTerminal, click the **Transfer** button.

Step 2. Specify the name of the router for the filename, and use .txt for the extension. Browse to find a location to store the text file on the computer. This file will be edited and used in later steps of this lab.

Step 3. Click the **Start** button to start capturing text.

Write down the name and location of this file:______________________________________

Step 4. Enter the **show running-config** command. Press the spacebar when the "--More--" prompt is displayed. You use the **show running-config** command to display the active configuration file for the router that is stored in RAM.

Task 9: Stop Capturing the Configuration File

To discontinue capturing the output of the router configuration to a text file, do the following: On the HyperTerminal menu bar, select the following, in this order:

1. Transfer
2. Capture Text
3. Stop

Task 10: Clean Up the Captured Configuration File

Step 1. The captured text file has information that is not required for configuring a router, such as the "--More--" prompts. To put this text in a form to be "pasted" back in the router, remove any unnecessary information from the captured configuration.

Step 2. You might also want to add comments in the configuration to explain the various parts. You do so using the exclamation mark (!). Starting a line with **!** creates a comment; the router ignores this line. You can therefore write any comment that helps you or other network associates understand the configuration.

Step 3. Start Notepad as follows:

1. Choose **Start** > **Run**.
2. Type **Notepad**.
3. Press **Enter**.

Step 4. In Notepad, choose **File** > **Open**. Find the file you created and click the **Open** button.

Step 5. Delete the lines that contain the following:

- **show running-config**
- Building configuration
- Version
- Current configuration:
- --More--
- Any lines that appear after the word *End*

Step 6. At the end of each interface section, add the following line:

no shutdown

The following is an example:

interface Serial 0
ip address 199.6.13.1 255.255.255.0
no shutdown

The next step is very important!

Step 7. The last line to edit is as follows:

enable secret 5 1prts$Rbf8hxlss.ZrufvI7rMVy/

Change this line to the following:

enable secret class

You must enter this password in clear text. If you don't, the encryption algorithm reencrypts the current password, and entry from the user prompt is impossible.

Step 8. Save the clean version of the configuration by choosing **File** > **Save** and exit Notepad.

Task 11: Test Your Backup Configuration

Step 1. Any form of backup that you do not test could be a liability in a failure situation. This rule includes backup configurations. You must test the backup configuration. Put your router out of service for a while. You should schedule the test during low network usage periods because you must take the router offline. You should notify all users who might be affected well in advance to ensure that the downtime will not be an inconvenience.

Step 2. Before testing the backup configuration, erase the startup configuration. From the HyperTerminal session, enter the command **erase startup-config** at the enable router prompt. This command deletes the configuration file from NVRAM.

Step 3. Confirm that the startup configuration was deleted. Enter **show startup-config** at the router prompt.

What does the router show after you enter this command?

____

Task 12: Restart the Router to Remove the Running Configuration

Enter **reload** at the privileged EXEC mode prompt to reboot the router.

Step 1. If prompted that the configuration has been modified, choose **Save**, type **N**, and press **Enter**.

Step 2. When you are asked to proceed with the reload, enter **Y** and press **Enter** (or just press **Enter**) to confirm.

Step 3. When the router restarts, note that the router might display the following message:

```
"Notice: NVRAM invalid, possibly due to write erase."
```

Step 4. When you are prompted to enter the initial configuration dialog, type **N** and press **Enter**.

Step 5. When you are prompted to terminate autoinstall, type **Y** and press **Enter**.

Step 6. Press **Enter** an additional time.

What does the prompt look like? ____

Task 13: Reconfigure the Router from the Saved Text File

Step 1. Use the **send text file** command in HyperTerminal to restore the new configuration. The edited version of the router configuration file from the previous step is copied into the area of memory known as the Clipboard.

Step 2. Change to privileged EXEC mode.

Why did you not need a password?

____

Step 3. Enter global configuration mode by entering the command **configure terminal**.

Step 4. In HyperTerminal, do the following:

1. Click the **Transfer/Send Text** File button.
2. Select the file.
3. Each line of the text file can be entered at the router prompt.

Step 5. Observe any errors on the router as commands are transferred.

What is the most obvious indication that the router was restored?

____

Step 6. Press **Ctrl-Z** to exit global configuration mode.

Step 7. Save the new configuration file as the startup configuration (in NVRAM).

Step 8. Use the command **copy running-config startup-config** (abbreviated **copy run start**) to save the newly created router configuration. This command copies the active router configuration from RAM into NVRAM.

Step 9. Verify that the running configuration is correct by using the **show running-config** command (abbreviated **show run**).

Task 14: Verify That the Internetwork Is Functioning Again

You can verify that the internetwork is functioning again by pinging the Fast Ethernet interface of the other router.

Step 1. Use the **reload** command to restart the router. Verify that the new configuration was saved to NVRAM by restarting the router.

When prompted to confirm, press **Y** to restart the router.

Step 2. When the router restarts, press **Enter** again.

From GAD, can you ping the BHM Fast Ethernet interface? _______________

From BHM, can you ping the GAD Fast Ethernet interface? _______________

Step 3. If the answer is no for either question, troubleshoot the router configurations to find the error. Then, perform the pings again until the answer to both questions is yes.

Step 4. When you finish, log off (by typing **exit**) and turn off the router.

Comprehensive Lab 3-11: Basic Router Configuration and File Management

Figure 3-13 Basic Router Configuration and File-Management Topology

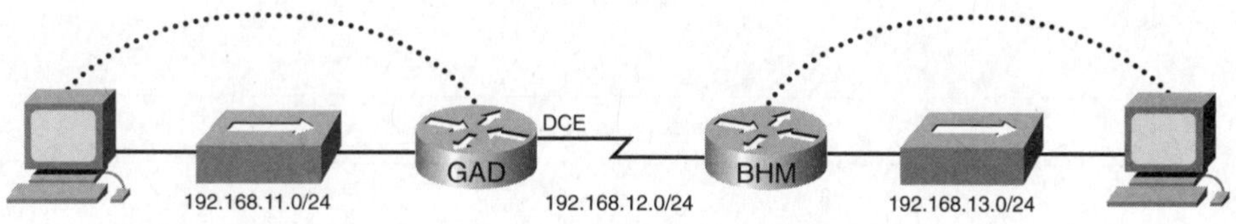

Objectives:

This lab contains the following objectives:

- Configure two routers with basic router configurations
- Verify routing and test connectivity
- Capture scripts, erase/reload routers, and reapply configuration scripts

Task 1: Set Up Lab Equipment and Document

Step 1. Cable the lab as shown in the topology in Figure 3-13.

Step 2. Document the lab by filling in the following table with appropriate configuration information.

Router	Interface Type	IP Address	Subnet Mask	Clock Rate? (Yes/No)
GAD				
BHM				

Task 2: Document Interface Descriptions and Banner

Step 1. Following is information from the contract with BellSouth. Use this information to determine an appropriate description for the WAN link between GAD and BHM.

Circuit ID: C15C0734M; Bandwidth: 1.544 Mbps

What is the WAN link description to be used with the **description** command?

____

What is the LAN link description for GAD?

____

What is the LAN link description for BHM?

____

Step 2. Determine an appropriate banner to warn against unauthorized access to GAD and BHM. Use the guidelines provided by your instructor. Use a simple statement that includes "authorized access only."

____

____

____

____

____

____

Task 3: Basic Router Configurations

Step 1. Make sure that GAD and BHM have empty startup or running configurations. If necessary, what must you do to carry out this instruction?

____

____

Step 2. Configure both GAD and BHM with the following basic router configurations:

- Hostname
- Line configurations
- Global passwords
- Host tables
- Banner
- Other instructor-required global configurations

Step 3. Check your configurations. What command did you use?

____

Task 4: Interface Configurations

Step 1. Configure the GAD and BHM interfaces with IP addresses according to the table created in Task 1.

Step 2. Use the **show ip interface brief** command to verify that interfaces on both routers are operational at the physical and data link layers.

Are GAD's interfaces fully operational? ___________. If not, troubleshoot.

Are BHM's interfaces fully operational? ___________. If not, troubleshoot.

Task 5: Routing Configurations

Step 1. Use the **router** command to configure RIP as the routing protocol, and use the **network** command to configure both GAD and BHM with directly connected networks. Document your commands in the following table. If necessary, refer to the section "Curriculum Lab 3-9: Configuring Host Tables (3.2.7)," earlier in this chapter, for help with the commands.

GAD Routing Configuration	BHM Routing Configuration

Step 2. Use the **show ip route** command to verify that both routers have three routes: two directly connected (**C**) and one learned through RIP (**R**).

Task 6: Configure Hosts and Verify Full Network Connectivity

Step 1. Attach hosts to GAD and BHM. Configure each with an appropriate IP address, subnet mask, and default gateway.

Configuration	GAD Host	BHM Host
IP address	192.168.11.2	192.168.13.2
Subnet mask	255.255.255.0	255.255.255.0
Default gateway	192.168.11.1	192.168.13.1

Test connectivity between the workstations.

Ping the BHM workstation from the GAD workstation. Successful? _______. If not, troubleshoot.

Ping the GAD workstation from the BHM workstation. Successful? _______. If not, troubleshoot.

Step 2. Telnet from the workstation to the default gateway.

From the BHM workstation, Telnet into the BHM router. Successful? ______. If not, troubleshoot.

From the GAD workstation, Telnet into the GAD router. Successful? ______. If not, troubleshoot.

Task 7: Capture Configurations and Clean Up .txt Scripts

Step 1. Use HyperTerminal to capture two .txt scripts: one named GAD.txt for the GAD configuration and one named BHM.txt for the BHM configuration. Save the scripts in a location specified by your instructor or a location of your choice.

Step 2. Open the .txt files and clean them up so that they can be easily loaded into a blank router.

Task 8: Erase Routers and Reload with .txt Files

Step 1. Erase the startup configurations for both GAD and BHM. Reload the routers without saving the changes.

Step 2. Apply the configurations from GAD.txt to the GAD router.

Step 3. Apply the configurations from BHM.txt to the BHM router.

Step 4. Test connectivity by sending pings between the workstations.

Ping the BHM workstation from the GAD workstation. Successful? _______. If not, troubleshoot.

Ping the GAD workstation from the BHM workstation. Successful? _______. If not, troubleshoot.

Task 9: Return Equipment to Former State

Step 1. Erase and reload both routers.

Step 2. Reconfigure and reattach workstations.

Challenge Lab 3-12: Basic Router Configuration Challenge

Figure 3-14 Basic Router Configuration Challenge

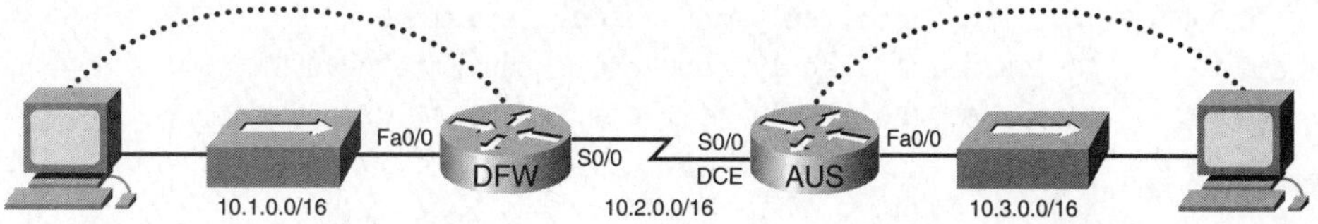

Objectives:

This lab contains the following objectives:

- Edit saved scripts with a new configurations
- Load scripts into routers
- Attach and configure workstations
- Verify routing and test connectivity

Task 1: Edit Script with a New Configuration

Step 1. Fill in the following table with the appropriate addressing information based on the topology shown in Figure 3-14.

Router	Interface Type	IP Address	Subnet Mask	Clock Rate? (Yes/No)
DFW				
AUS				

Step 2. Use the scripts for GAD and BHM that you created in the section "Comprehensive Lab 3-11: Basic Router Configuration and File Management," earlier in this chapter, as a starting point. Save them with new names and then change them according to the topology shown in Figure 3-14 and the addressing table you completed in Step 1.

Task 2: Load Scripts into the Routers

Step 1. Load the scripts for DFW and AUS into the routers. Watch for any errors.

Step 2. Test the connectivity between DFW and AUS, and verify that both routing tables have three routes. Your routing tables should look like the ones shown here:

```
The routing table for DFW

     10.0.0.0/16 is subnetted, 3 subnets
C       10.2.0.0 is directly connected, Serial0/0
```

```
R       10.3.0.0 [120/1] via 10.2.0.2, 00:00:07, Serial0/0
C       10.1.0.0 is directly connected, FastEthernet0/0
```

```
The routing table for AUS

     10.0.0.0/16 is subnetted, 3 subnets
C       10.2.0.0 is directly connected, Serial0/0
C       10.3.0.0 is directly connected, FastEthernet0/0
R       10.1.0.0 [120/1] via 10.2.0.1, 00:00:17, Serial0/0
```

Task 3: Attach and Configure Hosts

Record the configuration information that you will use for the hosts in the following table. Then attach and configure the hosts.

Configuration	DFW Host	AUS Host
IP address		
Subnet mask		
Default gateway		

Task 4: Verify Routing and Test Connectivity

The host attached to DFW should now be able to ping the host attached to AUS. If not, troubleshoot.

CHAPTER 4

Learning About Other Devices

The Study Guide portion of this chapter uses a combination of fill-in-the-blank, open-ended questions and unique custom exercises to test your knowledge of the Cisco Discovery Protocol (CDP) and how network devices learn about neighboring devices.

The Lab Exercises portion of this chapter includes all the online curriculum labs as well as a comprehensive lab and a challenge lab to ensure that you have mastered the practical, hands-on skills needed for acquiring information about neighboring network devices. .

Study Guide

Discovering Neighbors Using CDP

The exercises in this first section demonstrate how CDP acquires information about neighboring routers. First, you work through an exercise that focuses on the concepts and commands of CDP. Then, two topology discovery exercises drive home the power of CDP as you use CDP command output to draw the topology and discover the addressing scheme.

CDP Concepts and Commands Exercise

Answer the questions or fill in the blanks for the items that follow.

1. At what layer of the OSI model does CDP operate?

____

2. What is the primary use for CDP?

____

3. What network layer protocols can CDP provide information for?

____

4. When CDP is enabled on an interface, a router (or switch) sends CDP ______________ on a regular basis, which list information about the sending router. Included in the packets are a series of ________________, or TLV, data structures.

5. The **show cdp neighbors** command can be used to display one line of information about each directly connected CDP-enabled device. List the six pieces of information displayed.

____

6. In the topology of all Cisco devices shown in Figure 4-1, you are on Host A and consoled in to RTA. What devices can you see in the output from CDP commands?

Figure 4-1 Cisco Discovery Protocol Example

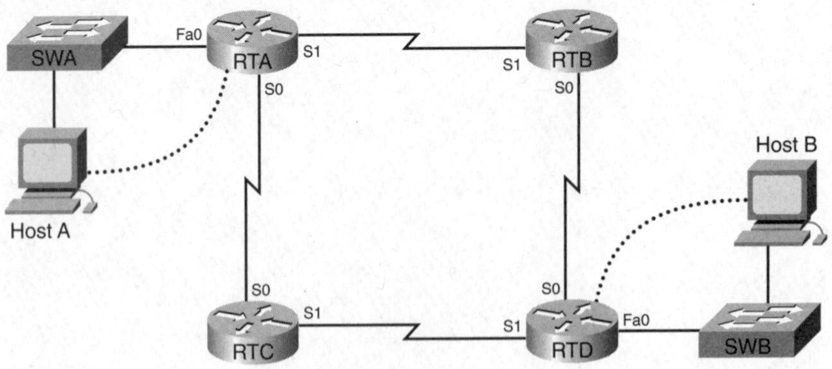

____

7. How would you gather information about other CDP-enabled devices in the network?

____

8. From RTB in Figure 4-1, what devices can you see in the output from CDP commands?

____

9. From RTC in Figure 4-1, what devices can you see in the output from CDP commands?

____

10. From RTD in Figure 4-1, what devices can you see in the output from CDP commands?

____

11. Complete the table that follows.

Command	Configuration Mode	Purpose
cdp run		
cdp enable		
clear cdp counters		
show cdp		
show cdp entry		
show cdp interface		
show cdp neighbors [**detail**]		

12. The **cdp run** command enables CDP globally on the router. By default, CDP is globally enabled. The **enable cdp** command enables CDP on a particular interface.

13. Fill in the appropriate commands in the configuration/output that follows:

```
RTC(config)#cdp run_ <-- Command that will start CDP
RTC(config)#interface Ethernet 0
RTC(config-if)#no cdp enable <-- Turn off CDP on this interface
RTC(config-if)#end
```

14. Why would you want to disable CDP on an interface or globally?

____

____

____

15. Fill in the appropriate commands in the configuration/output that follows:

```
RTC#______________________________________________________________
Global CDP information:
        Sending CDP packets every 60 seconds
        Sending a holdtime value of 180 seconds
        Sending CDPv2 advertisements is  enabled
RTC#____________________  <-- Command to display cdp statistics
CDP counters :
        Total packets output: 70, Input: 34
        Hdr syntax: 0, Chksum error: 0, Encaps failed: 0
        No memory: 0, Invalid packet: 0, Fragmented: 0
        CDP version 1 advertisements output: 0, Input: 0
        CDP version 2 advertisements output: 70, Input: 34
RTC# ____________________  <-- Command to reset traffic statistics
RTC# ____________________  <-- Command to display cdp statistics
CDP counters :
        Total packets output: 0, Input: 0
        Hdr syntax: 0, Chksum error: 0, Encaps failed: 0
        No memory: 0, Invalid packet: 0, Fragmented: 0
        CDP version 1 advertisements output: 0, Input: 0
        CDP version 2 advertisements output: 0, Input: 0
RTC# _____________________________________________________________
Capability Codes: R - Router, T - Trans Bridge, B - Source Route Bridge
                  S - Switch, H - Host, I - IGMP, r - Repeater

Device ID        Local Intrfce     Holdtme    Capability  Platform  Port ID
RTA               Ser 0              167          R          2500      Ser 0
RTB               Ser 1              129          R          2500      Ser 0
RTC# _____________________________________________________________
-------------------------
Device ID: RTA
Entry address(es):
  IP address: 172.17.0.2
Platform: cisco 2500,  Capabilities: Router
Interface: Serial0,  Port ID (outgoing port): Serial0
Holdtime : 130 sec

Version :
Cisco Internetwork Operating System Software
IOS (tm) 2500 Software (C2500-JS-L), Version 12.2(13b), RELEASE SOFTWARE (fc1)
Copyright (c) 1986-2003 by cisco Systems, Inc.
Compiled Thu 20-Feb-03 14:09 by pwade

advertisement version: 2
RTC# show cdp interface
Ethernet0 is up, line protocol is up
```

```
  Encapsulation ARPA
  Sending CDP packets every 60 seconds
  Holdtime is 180 seconds
Serial0 is up, line protocol is up
  Encapsulation HDLC
  Sending CDP packets every 60 seconds
  Holdtime is 180 seconds
Serial1 is administratively down, line protocol is down
  Encapsulation HDLC
  Sending CDP packets every 60 seconds
  Holdtime is 180 seconds
```

16. List and briefly describe the **debug** options displayed after entering the following command:

RTB#**debug cdp ?**

____

____

____

____

17. Fill in the table that follows.

Command	Description
clear cdp table	
show debugging	
debug cdp adjacency	
debug cdp events	
debug cdp ip	
cdp timers	
cdp holdtime	

Network Topology Discovery Exercise 1

You are the new network engineer at a small company with three locations. You have no documentation about the network, so your first job is to learn what Cisco devices are on the network and gather information about the platform, IOS, and IP addressing. You console into your local router, which is RTC, as shown in Figure 4-2, and begin to gather CDP information. Using the output from the **show cdp neighbors detail** command in the code that follows, determine the addressing scheme, device types, platforms, IOS versions, and network topology. Fill in the tables and draw the topology in the blank space provided following the output from RTC, RTB, and RTA.

Figure 4-2 Network Topology Discovery Exercise 1

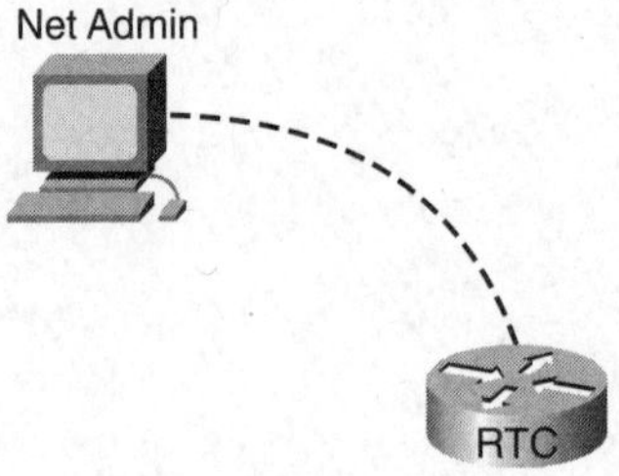


```
RTC>show cdp neighbors detail
-------------------------
Device ID: RTB
Entry address(es):
  IP address: 192.168.13.1
Platform: cisco 2500,  Capabilities: Router
Interface: Serial1,  Port ID (outgoing port): Serial1
Holdtime : 167 sec

Version :
Cisco Internetwork Operating System Software
IOS (tm) 2500 Software (C2500-JS-L), Version 12.2(13b), RELEASE SOFTWARE (fc1)
Copyright (c) 1986-2003 by cisco Systems, Inc.
Compiled Thu 20-Feb-03 14:09 by pwade

advertisement version: 2

-------------------------
Device ID: RTA
Entry address(es):
  IP address: 192.168.15.2
Platform: cisco 2500,  Capabilities: Router
Interface: Serial0,  Port ID (outgoing port): Serial1
Holdtime : 133 sec

Version :
Cisco Internetwork Operating System Software
IOS (tm) 2500 Software (C2500-JS-L), Version 12.2(13b), RELEASE SOFTWARE (fc1)
Copyright (c) 1986-2003 by cisco Systems, Inc.
Compiled Thu 20-Feb-03 14:09 by pwade

advertisement version: 2

-------------------------
Device ID: Switch_3
Entry address(es):
  IP address: 192.168.14.2
```

```
Platform: cisco WS-C2950-24,  Capabilities: Switch IGMP
Interface: FastEthernet0,  Port ID (outgoing port): FastEthernet0/12
Holdtime : 126 sec

Version :
Cisco Internetwork Operating System Software
IOS (tm) C2950 Software (C2950-I6Q4L2-M), Version 12.1(13)EA1, RELEASE SOFTWARE (fc1)
Copyright (c) 1986-2003 by cisco Systems, Inc.
Compiled Tue 04-Mar-03 02:14 by yenanh

advertisement version: 2
(output omitted)
```

```
RTB>show cdp neighbors detail
-------------------------
Device ID: RTC
Entry address(es):
  IP address: 192.168.13.2
Platform: cisco 1721,  Capabilities: Router
Interface: Serial1,  Port ID (outgoing port): Serial1
Holdtime : 145 sec

Version :
Cisco Internetwork Operating System Software
IOS (tm) C1700 Software (C1700-Y-M), Version 12.2(4)YB, EARLY DEPLOYMENT RELEASE
SOFTWARE (fc1)
Synched to technology version 12.2(6.8)T2
TAC Support: http://www.cisco.com/tac
Copyright (c) 1986-2002 by cisco Systems, Inc.
Compiled Fri 15-Mar-02 20:32 by ealyon

advertisement version: 2

-------------------------
Device ID: RTA
Entry address(es):
  IP address: 192.168.11.1
Platform: cisco 2500,  Capabilities: Router
Interface: Serial0,  Port ID (outgoing port): Serial0
Holdtime : 175 sec

Version :
Cisco Internetwork Operating System Software
IOS (tm) 2500 Software (C2500-JS-L), Version 12.2(13b), RELEASE SOFTWARE (fc1)
Copyright (c) 1986-2003 by cisco Systems, Inc.
Compiled Thu 20-Feb-03 14:09 by pwade
```

```
advertisement version: 2

-------------------------
Device ID: Switch_2
Entry address(es):
  IP address: 192.168.12.2
Platform: cisco WS-C2950-24,  Capabilities: Switch IGMP
Interface: Ethernet0,  Port ID (outgoing port): FastEthernet0/13
Holdtime : 154 sec

Version :
Cisco Internetwork Operating System Software
IOS (tm) C2950 Software (C2950-I6Q4L2-M), Version 12.1(13)EA1, RELEASE SOFTWARE (fc1)
Copyright (c) 1986-2003 by cisco Systems, Inc.
Compiled Tue 04-Mar-03 02:14 by yenanh

advertisement version: 2
(output omitted)
```

```
RTA>show cdp neighbors detail
-------------------------
Device ID: RTB
Entry address(es):
  IP address: 192.168.11.2
Platform: cisco 2500,  Capabilities: Router
Interface: Serial0,  Port ID (outgoing port): Serial0
Holdtime : 132 sec

Version :
Cisco Internetwork Operating System Software
IOS (tm) 2500 Software (C2500-JS-L), Version 12.2(13b), RELEASE SOFTWARE (fc1)
Copyright (c) 1986-2003 by cisco Systems, Inc.
Compiled Thu 20-Feb-03 14:09 by pwade

advertisement version: 2

-------------------------
Device ID: RTC
Entry address(es):
  IP address: 192.168.15.1
Platform: cisco 1721,  Capabilities: Router
Interface: Serial1,  Port ID (outgoing port): Serial0
Holdtime : 126 sec
```

```
Version :
Cisco Internetwork Operating System Software
IOS (tm) C1700 Software (C1700-Y-M), Version 12.2(4)YB, EARLY DEPLOYMENT RELEASE
SOFTWARE (fc1)
Synched to technology version 12.2(6.8)T2
TAC Support: http://www.cisco.com/tac
Copyright (c) 1986-2002 by cisco Systems, Inc.
Compiled Fri 15-Mar-02 20:32 by ealyon

advertisement version: 2

-------------------------
Device ID: Switch_1
Entry address(es):
  IP address: 192.168.16.2
Platform: cisco 1900,  Capabilities: Trans-Bridge Switch
Interface: Ethernet0,  Port ID (outgoing port): 6
Holdtime : 177 sec

Version :
V9.00

advertisement version: 2
(output omitted)
```

Note: I recommend that you use a pencil to fill out the following tables.

Device Name	Device Type	Platform	IOS Version

Device Name	Interface	IP Address

continues

Device Name	Interface	IP Address

Draw the network topology in the space provided.

Note: Practice on scratch paper first. Make sure that you label all devices, interfaces, and network addresses.

Network Topology Discovery Exercise 2

You are the new network engineer at a small company with three locations. You have no documentation about the network, so your first job is to learn what Cisco devices are on the network and gather information about the platform, IOS, and IP addressing. You console into your local router, which is CORE, as shown in Figure 4-3, and begin to gather CDP information. Using the output from the **show cdp neighbors detail** command in the code that follows, determine the addressing scheme, device types, platforms, IOS versions, and network topology. Fill in the tables and draw the topology in the blank space provided following the output from CORE, DIST_A, DIST_SW, DIST_B, AL_SWB, DIST_C, and AL_SWC.

Figure 4-3 Network Topology Discovery Exercise 2

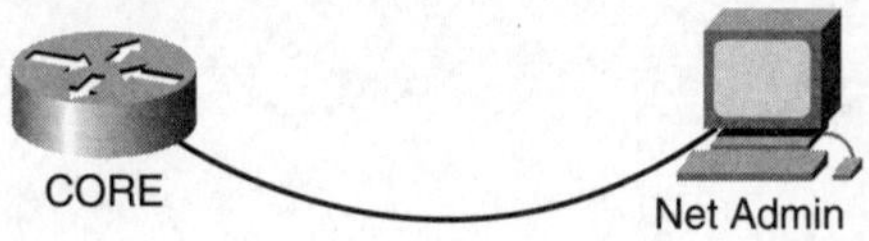


```
CORE#show cdp neighbors detail
-------------------------
Device ID: DIST_A
Entry address(es):
  IP address : 10.1.1.2
Platform: cisco C2600-I-M, Capabilities: Router
Interface: Serial0/0, Port ID (outgoing port): Serial0/0
Holdtime: 180

Version :
Cisco Internetwork Operating System Software
IOS (tm) C2600 Software (C2600-I-M), Version 12.2(28), RELEASE SOFTWARE (fc5)
Technical Support: http://www.cisco.com/techsupport
Copyright (c) 1986-2005 by cisco Systems, Inc.
Compiled Wed 27-Apr-04 19:01 by miwang

advertisement version: 2
Duplex: full
```

```
DIST_A#show cdp neighbors detail
-------------------------
Device ID: CORE
Entry address(es):
  IP address : 10.1.1.1
Platform: cisco C2600-I-M, Capabilities: Router
Interface: Serial0/0, Port ID (outgoing port): Serial0/0
Holdtime: 180

Version :
Cisco Internetwork Operating System Software
IOS (tm) C2600 Software (C2600-I-M), Version 12.2(28), RELEASE SOFTWARE (fc5)
Technical Support: http://www.cisco.com/techsupport
Copyright (c) 1986-2005 by cisco Systems, Inc.
Compiled Wed 27-Apr-04 19:01 by miwang
```

```
advertisement version: 2
Duplex: full
--------------------------

Device ID: DIST_SW
Entry address(es):
  IP address : 10.1.2.4
Platform: cisco WS-CSwitch-PT, Capabilities: Switch
Interface: FastEthernet0/0, Port ID (outgoing port): Vlan1
Holdtime: 180

Version :
Cisco Internetwork Operating System Software
IOS (tm) C2950 Software (C2950-I6Q4L2-M), Version 12.1(22)EA4, RELEASE SOFTWARE(fc1)
Copyright (c) 1986-2005 by cisco Systems, Inc.
Compiled Wed 18-May-05 22:31 by jharirba

advertisement version: 2
Duplex: full
```

```
DIST_SW#show cdp neighbors detail
--------------------------
Device ID: DIST_A
Entry address(es):
  IP address : 10.1.2.1
Platform: cisco C2600-I-M, Capabilities: Router
Interface: FastEthernet0/1, Port ID (outgoing port): FastEthernet0/0
Holdtime: 180

Version :
Cisco Internetwork Operating System Software
IOS (tm) C2600 Software (C2600-I-M), Version 12.2(28), RELEASE SOFTWARE (fc5)
Technical Support: http://www.cisco.com/techsupport
Copyright (c) 1986-2005 by cisco Systems, Inc.
Compiled Wed 27-Apr-04 19:01 by miwang

advertisement version: 2
Duplex: full
--------------------------

Device ID: DIST_B
Entry address(es):
  IP address : 10.1.2.2
Platform: cisco C2600-I-M, Capabilities: Router
Interface: FastEthernet0/2, Port ID (outgoing port): FastEthernet0/0
Holdtime: 180
```

```
Version :
Cisco Internetwork Operating System Software
IOS (tm) C2600 Software (C2600-I-M), Version 12.2(28), RELEASE SOFTWARE (fc5)
Technical Support: http://www.cisco.com/techsupport
Copyright (c) 1986-2005 by cisco Systems, Inc.
Compiled Wed 27-Apr-04 19:01 by miwang

advertisement version: 2
Duplex: full
---------------------------

Device ID: DIST_C
Entry address(es):
  IP address : 10.1.2.3
Platform: cisco C2600-I-M, Capabilities: Router
Interface: FastEthernet0/3, Port ID (outgoing port): FastEthernet0/0
Holdtime: 180

Version :
Cisco Internetwork Operating System Software
IOS (tm) C2600 Software (C2600-I-M), Version 12.2(28), RELEASE SOFTWARE (fc5)
Technical Support: http://www.cisco.com/techsupport
Copyright (c) 1986-2005 by cisco Systems, Inc.
Compiled Wed 27-Apr-04 19:01 by miwang

advertisement version: 2
Duplex: full
```

```
DIST_B#show cdp neighbors detail

Device ID: DIST_SW
Entry address(es):
  IP address : 10.1.2.4
Platform: cisco WS-CSwitch-PT, Capabilities: Switch
Interface: FastEthernet0/0, Port ID (outgoing port): Vlan1
Holdtime: 180

Version :
Cisco Internetwork Operating System Software
IOS (tm) C2950 Software (C2950-I6Q4L2-M), Version 12.1(22)EA4, RELEASE SOFTWARE(fc1)
Copyright (c) 1986-2005 by cisco Systems, Inc.
Compiled Wed 18-May-05 22:31 by jharirba
```

```
advertisement version: 2
Duplex: full
---------------------------

Device ID: AL_SWB
Entry address(es):
  IP address : 10.1.3.2
Platform: cisco WS-C2950T-24, Capabilities: Switch
Interface: FastEthernet0/1, Port ID (outgoing port): FastEthernet0/1
Holdtime: 180

Version :
Cisco Internetwork Operating System Software
IOS (tm) C2950 Software (C2950-I6Q4L2-M), Version 12.1(22)EA4, RELEASE SOFTWARE(fc1)
Copyright (c) 1986-2005 by cisco Systems, Inc.
Compiled Wed 18-May-05 22:31 by jharirba

advertisement version: 2
Duplex: full
```

```
AL_SWB#show cdp neighbors detail

Device ID: DIST_B
Entry address(es):
  IP address : 10.1.3.1
Platform: cisco C2600-I-M, Capabilities: Router
Interface: FastEthernet0/1, Port ID (outgoing port): FastEthernet0/1
Holdtime: 180

Version :
Cisco Internetwork Operating System Software
IOS (tm) C2600 Software (C2600-I-M), Version 12.2(28), RELEASE SOFTWARE (fc5)
Technical Support: http://www.cisco.com/techsupport
Copyright (c) 1986-2005 by cisco Systems, Inc.
Compiled Wed 27-Apr-04 19:01 by miwang

advertisement version: 2
Duplex: full
```

```
DIST_C#show cdp neighbors detail

Device ID: DIST_SW
Entry address(es):
  IP address : 10.1.2.4
Platform: cisco WS-CSwitch-PT, Capabilities: Switch
Interface: FastEthernet0/0, Port ID (outgoing port): Vlan1
Holdtime: 180
```

```
Version :
Cisco Internetwork Operating System Software
IOS (tm) C2950 Software (C2950-I6Q4L2-M), Version 12.1(22)EA4, RELEASE SOFTWARE(fc1)
Copyright (c) 1986-2005 by cisco Systems, Inc.
Compiled Wed 18-May-05 22:31 by jharirba

advertisement version: 2
Duplex: full
--------------------------

Device ID: AL_SWC
Entry address(es):
  IP address : 10.1.4.2
Platform: cisco WS-C2950-24, Capabilities: Switch
Interface: FastEthernet0/1, Port ID (outgoing port): FastEthernet0/1
Holdtime: 180

Version :
Cisco Internetwork Operating System Software
IOS (tm) C2950 Software (C2950-I6Q4L2-M), Version 12.1(22)EA4, RELEASE SOFTWARE(fc1)
Copyright (c) 1986-2005 by cisco Systems, Inc.
Compiled Wed 18-May-05 22:31 by jharirba

advertisement version: 2
Duplex: full
```

```
AL_SWC#show cdp neighbors detail

Device ID: DIST_C
Entry address(es):
  IP address : 10.1.4.1
Platform: cisco C2600-I-M, Capabilities: Router
Interface: FastEthernet0/1, Port ID (outgoing port): FastEthernet0/1
Holdtime: 180

Version :
Cisco Internetwork Operating System Software
IOS (tm) C2600 Software (C2600-I-M), Version 12.2(28), RELEASE SOFTWARE (fc5)
Technical Support: http://www.cisco.com/techsupport
Copyright (c) 1986-2005 by cisco Systems, Inc.
Compiled Wed 27-Apr-04 19:01 by miwang

advertisement version: 2
Duplex: full
```

Note: I recommend that you use a pencil to fill out the following tables.

Device Name	Device Type	Platform	IOS Version

Device Name	Interface	IP Address

Draw the network topology in the space provided.

Note: Practice on scratch paper first. Make sure that you label all devices, interfaces, and network addresses.

Getting Information and Troubleshooting Remote Devices

The Concept Questions exercise in this section reviews some of the most important tools at your disposal to gather information about and troubleshoot problems with remote devices. Ping is a quick end-to-end connectivity test, whereas tracing a route helps find where packets are failing on the way to the destination. Telnet allows you to access a remote device and view its configuration. After you are there, several powerful **show** commands help you quickly isolate any local problems.

Concept Questions

Answer the questions or fill in the blanks for the items that follow.

1. ______ provides a network terminal or remote login capability and verifies the application layer software between source and destination. Because it tests all seven layers of the OSI model, this is the most complete test mechanism available.
2. Cisco IOS software provides ____ vty lines numbered from __ to __.

3. Unlike **telnet**, **ping** only tests end-to-end connectivity up to and including the ________ layer of the OSI model. It uses the _____ protocol. __________ can test connectivity to each hop in the path from source to destination. It uses the ____ field in the IP header.

4. Fill in the empty boxes in Figure 4-4 with the following commands to indicate which layer of the OSI model that tool can test.

   - **show interfaces**
   - **ping**
   - **telnet**
   - **traceroute**
   - **show cdp neighbors**
   - **show ip route**

Figure 4-4 Testing by OSI Layers

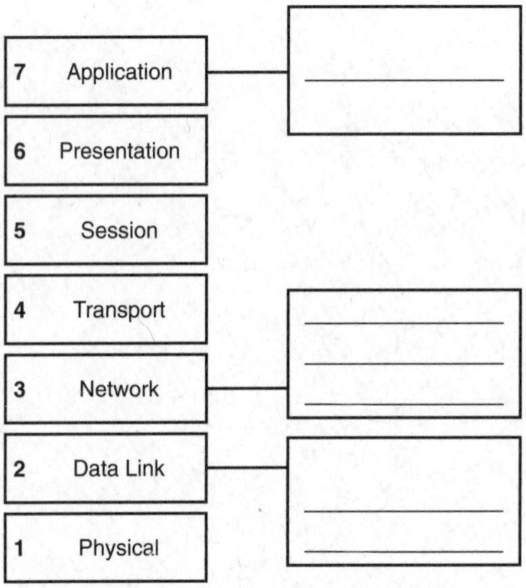

5. Review the following partial output from the **show run** command:

```
SAT#show run
Building Configuration...
!
hostname SAT
!
no ip domain-lookup
ip host DFW 192.168.1.1
!
(output omitted)
!
```

List four different commands that could be used to Telnet to DFW.

```
SAT#telnet dfw
SAT#telnet 192.168.1.1
SAT#DFW
SAT#192.168.1.1
```

6. In lab environments, you normally change the Telnet timeout value to "never" time out with the **exec-timeout 0 0** command. The user can terminate a Telnet session by typing either ____ or _____ at the user or privileged EXEC prompt.

7. What key combination suspends a Telnet session?

____

8. You have recently Telneted into both DFW and CRP. Your last Telnet session was with CRP, as shown in the following **show sessions** output:

```
SAT>show sessions
Conn    Host    Address         Idle    Conn Name
1       DFW     192.168.1.1     0       DFW
*2      CRP     192.168.11.2    0       CRP
```

If you want to resume the connection to DFW, what would you do?

____

9. How do you know that the last Telnet session in the preceding output was with CRP?

____

10. How can you quickly resume the session with CRP without typing a command?

____

11. IP addressing problems are common on IP networks. If the Physical layer and Data Link layers are operational, you can use the ________________ command to verify that all networks shown in the topology are being advertised and are listed in the local router's routing table.

12. Although Telnet is the most complete test for network connectivity, this is *not* its main purpose. What is the main purpose of Telnet?

____

13. Consider the following output from a **traceroute** command:

```
CRP#traceroute DFW
Type escape to abort.
Tracing the route to DFW (192.168.13.1)
  1 SAT (192.168.10.1) 8 msec 8 msec 4 msec
  2 AUS (192.168.11.2) 6 msec 8 msec 6 msec
  3 * * *
  4 * * *
  5 * * *
<user aborted>
```

What can you conclude from the output?

____

____

14. What would you do to find out more about this situation?

____

____

15. What key combination is used to abort the traceroute?

____

Lab Exercises

Command Reference

The commands for this chapter were thoroughly covered in the preceding Study Guide section. Refer to those exercises for the commands.

Curriculum Lab 4-1: Creating a Network Map Using CDP (4.1.4)

Figure 4-5 Topology for Lab 4-1

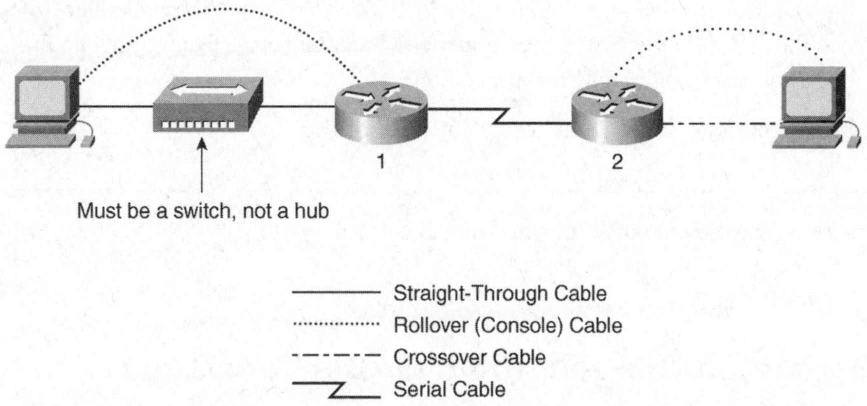

Table 4-1 Lab Equipment Configuration

Router Designation	Router Name	Interface Type	Serial 0 Clock	Serial 0 Address	Ethernet 0 Address
Router 1	GAD	DCE	56000	192.168.15.1	192.168.14.1
Router 2	BHM	DTE	Not set	192.168.15.2	192.168.16.1

The subnet mask for all interfaces on both routers is 255.255.255.0.

Objective:

The objective of this lab is to use CDP commands to get information about neighboring network devices.

Background/Preparation:

In this lab, the CDP commands are used. CDP discovers and shows information about directly connected Cisco devices (routers and switches).

Cable a network similar to the one shown in Figure 4-5. Be sure to use a switch and not a hub, because a hub cannot be discovered by CDP. You can use any router that meets the interface requirements displayed in the diagram (that is, 800, 1600, 1700, 2500, or 2600 routers, or a combination). Refer to the information in Appendix B, "Router Interface Summary," to correctly specify the interface identifiers to be used based on the equipment in your lab. The configuration output used in this lab is produced from 1721 Series routers. Any other router might produce slightly different output. The following tasks should be executed on each router unless you are specifically instructed otherwise.

Start a HyperTerminal session as you did in Lab 2-2, "Establishing a Console Session with HyperTerminal."

Refer to and implement the procedure documented in Appendix C, "Erasing and Reloading the Router," before continuing with this lab.

Task 1: Log in to Router 1 (GAD)

Why is it necessary to log on to Router 1 to see all the devices (routers and switches) in the network shown in Figure 4-5?

____

____

Task 2: Configure the Routers

Configure the routers according to the information in Table 4-1 so that CDP can collect information about them. Refer to Lab 3-4, "Configuring a Serial Interface," and Lab 3-6, "Configuring an Ethernet Interface," if you need help making changes to the configurations.

What should the clock rate be set to, and which interface is it set on?

____

Why is it necessary to use the **no shutdown** command on all interfaces?

____

Task 3: Gather Information About GAD's Interfaces

Enter the **show interface** command at either the user EXEC or the privileged EXEC router prompt.

How many interfaces are present? ______________________________

What type are they? ______________________________

Task 4: Display the CDP Updates Received on the Local Router

Step 1. Enter the **show cdp neighbors** command at the router prompt.

Step 2. Fill in Table 4-2.

Table 4-2 Entering CDP Neighbor Information

Device Port ID	Local Interface	Holdtime	Capability	Platform

Step 3. Upon completion of the previous tasks, log off (by typing **exit**) and turn the router off.

Curriculum Lab 4-2: Using CDP Commands (4.1.6)

Figure 4-6 Topology for Lab 4-2

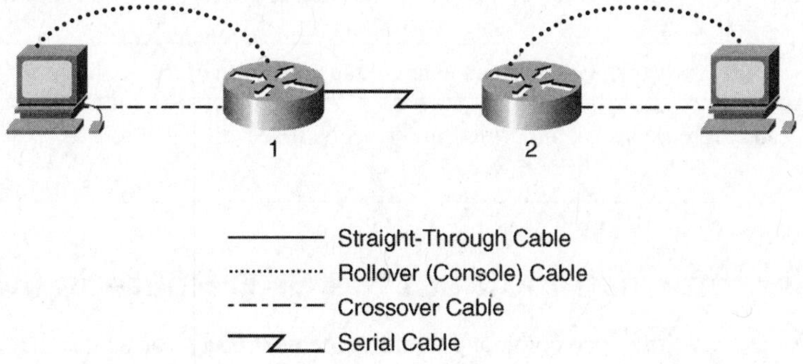

Table 4-3 Lab Equipment IP Address Information

Router Designation	Router Name	Interface Type	Serial 0 Clock	Serial 0 Address	Ethernet 0 Address
Router 1	GAD	DCE	56000	192.168.15.1	192.168.14.1
Router 2	BHM	DTE	Not set	192.168.15.2	192.168.16.1

The subnet mask for all interfaces on both routers is 255.255.255.0.

Objectives:

This lab contains the following objectives:

- Use CDP commands to obtain information about neighboring networks and devices
- Display information on how CDP is configured for its advertisement and discovery frame transmission
- Display CDP updates received on the local router

Background/Preparation:

In this lab, various CDP commands are used. CDP discovers and shows information about directly connected Cisco devices (routers and switches). CDP is a Cisco-proprietary protocol that runs at the Data Link layer (Layer 2) of the OSI model. This allows devices that might be running different network-layer (Layer 3) protocols, such as IP or Internetwork Packet Exchange (IPX), to learn about each other. CDP begins automatically upon a device's system startup. However, if Cisco IOS Release 10.3 or a newer version is used, CDP must be enabled on each of the device's interfaces by using the **cdp enable** command. Using the command **show cdp interface** gathers information that CDP uses for its advertisement and discovery frame transmission. Use the **show cdp neighbors** and **show cdp neighbors detail** commands to display the CDP updates received on the local router.

Cable a network similar to the one shown in Figure 4-6. You can use any router that meets the interface requirements displayed in the diagram (that is, 800, 1600, 1700, 2500 or 2600 routers, or a combination). Refer to the information in Appendix B to correctly specify the interface identifiers to be used based on the equipment in your lab. The configuration output used in this lab is produced from 1721 Series routers. Any other router might produce slightly different output. The following tasks should be executed on each router unless you are specifically instructed otherwise.

Start a HyperTerminal session as you did in Lab 2-2.

Refer to and implement the procedure documented in Appendix C before continuing with this lab.

Task 1: Configure the Routers

Configure the routers according to the information in Table 4-3 so that CDP can collect information about them. Refer to Lab 3-4 and Lab 3-6 if you need help making changes to the configurations.

Note: Do not use the **no shutdown** command on either of the router's interfaces at this time.

What should the clock rate be set to, and which interface is it set on?

____

Task 2: Gather Information About the GAD Router's Interfaces

Step 1. Enter the **show interface** command at either the user EXEC or the privileged EXEC router prompt. Document the following information about the router:

What is the name of the router? ______________________

Step 2. List the operational status of each interface in Table 4-4.

Table 4-4 Router Interface Operational Status

Interface	Interface Up or Down? (Carrier Detect Signal)	Line Protocol Up or Down? (Keepalives Being Received)

Task 3: Enable the Interfaces on GAD

To enable the interfaces on the GAD router, enter the following commands:

```
GAD(config)#interface serial 0
GAD(config-if)#no shutdown
GAD(config-if)#exit
GAD(config)#interface FastEthernet 0
GAD(config-if)#no shutdown
GAD(config-if)#exit
GAD(config)#exit
```

Task 4: Gather Information About the GAD Router Interfaces

Enter the **show interface** command at either the user EXEC or the privileged EXEC router prompt.

What is the name of the router? ______________________

List the operational status of each interface in Table 4-5.

Table 4-5 Router Interface Operational Status

Interface	Interface Up or Down? (Carrier Detect Signal)	Line Protocol Up or Down? (Keepalives Being Received)

Task 5: Display the Values of the CDP Timers, the Interface Status, and Encapsulation Used

Enter the **show cdp interface** command at the router prompt.

How often is the router sending CDP packets? ______________________

What is the holdtime value? ______________________

Global CDP settings can be seen by using the **show cdp** command by itself. What information is not displayed in the **show cdp** command?

____

Task 6: Display the CDP Updates Received on the Local Router

Enter the **show cdp neighbors** command at the router prompt.

Fill in the information in Table 4-6.

Table 4-6 CDP Neighbor Information

Device and Port ID	Local Interface	Hold Time	Capability	Platform

Task 7: Enable Serial 0 Interface on BHM

Enter the **no shutdown** command on the Serial 0 interface of Router 2. Return to Router 1 and repeat Task 4. Notice how the router now appears in the **show cdp neighbors** command display on GAD.

Task 8: Display Details About CDP Updates Received on the Local Router GAD

Enter the **show cdp neighbors detail** command from the router prompt.

Fill in the information in Table 4-7.

Table 4-7 CDP Neighbor Detail

Neighbor device ID	
Neighbor device capabilities	
IP address of interface attached to your router	
Port ID of your router that the neighbor is on	
Port ID of neighbor router that your router is on	
IOS version of neighbor router	

Task 9: Observe CDP Packets Being Sent and Received on Router GAD

Step 1. Enter the **debug cdp packets** command from privileged EXEC mode.

What is the output? (Wait for at least 2 minutes.)

Step 2. After observing the output, enter the **undebug all** command to stop debugging activity.

Task 10: Observe CDP Packet Traffic

Enter the following commands at the privileged EXEC mode prompt and record the results:

show cdp traffic

____

____

____

____

____

____

____

clear cdp counters

____

show cdp traffic

____

____

____

____

____

____

____

Curriculum Lab 4-3: Establishing and Verifying a Telnet Connection (4.2.2)

Figure 4-7 Topology for Lab 4-3

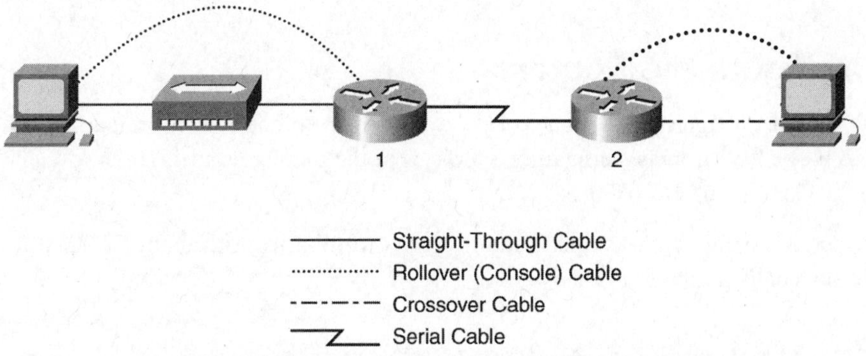

Table 4-8 Lab Equipment Configuration

Router Designation	Router Name	Ethernet 0 Address	Interface Type	Serial 0 Address
Router 1	GAD	192.168.14.1	DCE	192.168.15.1
Router 2	BHM	192.168.16.1	DTE	192.168.15.2

The routing protocol on both routers is Routing Information Protocol (RIP).

The enable secret password for both routers is **class**.

The enable/vty/console password for both routers is **cisco**.

The subnet mask for all interfaces on both routers is 255.255.255.0.

Objectives:

This lab contains the following objectives:

- Establish a Telnet connection to a remote router
- Verify that the Application layer between source and destination is working properly
- Retrieve information about remote routers using **show** commands
- Retrieve CDP information from routers not directly connected to you

Background/Preparation:

This lab focuses on the Telnet (remote terminal) utility to access routers remotely. Telnet connects from a local router to another remote router to simulate being at the console on the remote router. The local router acts as a Telnet client, and the remote router acts as a Telnet server. Telnet is a good testing and troubleshooting tool because it is an Application layer utility. A successful Telnet demonstrates that the entire TCP/IP protocol stack on both the client and server is functioning properly. You can Telnet from your workstation as a client in to any router with IP connectivity on your network. In addition, you can Telnet in to an Ethernet switch if an IP address has been assigned.

Cable a network similar to the one shown in Figure 4-7. You can use any router that meets the interface requirements displayed in the diagram (that is, 800, 1600, 1700, 2500, or 2600 routers, or a combination). Refer to the information in Appendix B to correctly specify the interface identifiers to be used based on the equipment in your lab. The configuration output used in this lab is produced from 1721 Series routers. Any other router might produce slightly different output. The following tasks should be executed on each router unless you are specifically instructed otherwise.

Start a HyperTerminal session as you did in Lab 2-2.

Refer to and implement the procedure documented in Appendix C before continuing with this lab.

Task 1: Configure the Routers

If you have trouble configuring hostnames or passwords, refer to Lab 3-2, "Configuring Router Passwords." If you have trouble configuring interfaces or the routing protocol, refer to Lab 3-4, Lab 3-6, and Lab 3-9, "Configuring Host Tables."

Verify the routers' configurations by performing a **show running-config** command on each router. If not correct, fix any configuration errors and verify.

Task 2: Log in to Router 1 and Verify the Connection to Router 2

Step 1. Log in to the GAD router in user mode.

Step 2. Verify the connection between the two routers by pinging the Serial 0 interface of the BHM router. If the ping is not successful, return to Task 1 and troubleshoot your configuration.

Task 3: Use help with the Telnet Command

Enter **telnet ?** at either the user EXEC or the privileged EXEC router prompt.

What did the router reply with?

____

Task 4: Telnet to a Remote Router

Enter **telnet** *router-name* (if IP host tables were configured) or **telnet** *ip-address* at the router prompt to connect to a remote router. Enter the password **cisco** to enter the remote router.

What prompt did the router display? ______________________________

Task 5: Look at the Interfaces on the Remote Router

Step 1. Enter **show interface** at the router prompt.

Step 2. List the interfaces, their IP addresses, and their subnet masks in Table 4-9.

Table 4-9 Remote Router Interface Information

Interface	IP Address	Subnet Mask

Task 6: Display the Protocols on the Remote Router

Step 1. Enter the **show protocols** command at the router prompt.

Step 2. Fill in Table 4-10 with the information that was generated by the remote-access router.

Table 4-10 Remote Router Interface Information Determined from show protocols

Interface	Is There a Carrier Signal?	Are the Keepalive Messages Being Received?

Task 7: Enter Privileged EXEC Mode

Enter **enable** at the command prompt. Enter the password **class**.

What prompt did the router display? ______________________________

What mode is this? ______________________________

Task 8: Look at the Running Configuration

Enter the **show running-config** command at the remote router prompt.

What file is being viewed on the remote router? Where is this file stored?

____

Task 9: Look at the Saved Configuration

Enter the **show startup-config** command at the router prompt.

What file is being viewed on the remote router? Where is this file stored?

____

____

What information is seen concerning the line vty connections?

____

Task 10: Look at the Neighbor Configuration

Step 1. Enter the **show cdp neighbors** command at the router prompt.

Step 2. List all device IDs that are connected to the remote router with a Telnet session.

____

Step 3. Upon completion of the previous tasks, log off (by typing **exit**) and turn the router off.

Curriculum Lab 4-4: Suspending and Disconnecting Telnet Sessions (4.2.3)

Figure 4-8 Topology for Lab 4-4

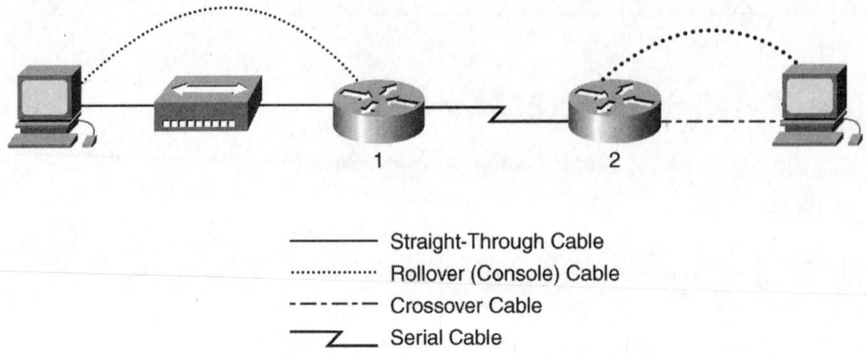

Table 4-11 Lab Equipment Configuration

Router Designation	Router Name	Ethernet 0 Address	Interface Type	Serial 0 Address
Router 1	GAD	192.168.14.1	DCE	192.168.15.1
Router 2	BHM	192.168.16.1	DTE	192.168.15.2

The routing protocol on both routers is RIP.

The enable secret password for both routers is **class**.

The enable/vty/console password for both routers is **cisco**.

The subnet mask for all interfaces on both routers is 255.255.255.0.

Objectives:

This lab contains the following objectives:

- Establish a Telnet session with a remote router
- Suspend and reestablish a Telnet session
- Display active Telnet sessions
- Disconnect a Telnet session

Background/Preparation:

This lab focuses on the ability to Telnet to a router, suspend that session, return to the local router console, and then reestablish the previous connection.

Cable a network similar to the one shown in Figure 4-8. You can use any router that meets the interface requirements displayed in the diagram (that is, 800, 1600, 1700, 2500, or 2600 routers, or a combination). Refer to the information in Appendix B to correctly specify the interface identifiers to be used based on the equipment in your lab. The configuration output used in this lab is produced from 1721 Series routers. Any other router might produce slightly different output. The following tasks should be executed on each router unless you are specifically instructed otherwise.

Start a HyperTerminal session as you did in Lab 2-2.

Refer to and implement the procedure documented in Appendix C before continuing with this lab.

Task 1: Configure the Routers

If you have trouble configuring hostnames or passwords, refer to Lab 3-2. If you have trouble configuring interfaces or the routing protocol, refer to Lab 3-4, Lab 3-6, and Lab 3-9.

Task 2: Log in to GAD and Verify the Connection to BHM

Step 1. Log in to the GAD router.

Step 2. Verify the connection between the two routers by pinging the serial 0 interface of the BHM router. If the ping is not successful, return to Task 1 and troubleshoot the configuration.

Task 3: Telnet to a Remote Router

Enter the **telnet BHM** command if IP host tables were configured. Otherwise, enter the IP address at the router prompt to connect to the remote router.

Enter the password **cisco** to enter the router.

What prompt did the router display? ____

Task 4: Look at the Interfaces on the Remote Router

Enter the **show interface** command at the router prompt.

Are both the Serial 0 and the FastEthernet 0 interfaces up? ______________________

Task 5: Suspend the Current Telnet Session

Press **Ctrl-Shift-6,x**. This suspends the remote session only and returns to the previous router. It does not disconnect from this router.

What prompt did the router display? ____

Task 6: Resume a Telnet session

Step 1. Press **Enter** at the router prompt. The router responds with the following:

```
[Resuming connection 1 to 192.168.15.2 ... ]
```

Step 2. Press **Enter**. This resumes the Telnet session that was previously suspended in Task 5.

What prompt did the router display? ________________________________

Task 7: Close a Telnet Session

Step 1. Enter the **exit** command while in a Telnet session. This terminates the session.

What prompt did the router display?________________________________

Note: To disconnect from a suspended Telnet session, type **disconnect** and press **Enter**.

Step 2. Upon completion of the previous tasks, log off (by typing **exit**) and turn the router off.

Curriculum Lab 4-5: Advanced Telnet Operations (4.2.4)

Figure 4-9 Topology for Lab 4-5

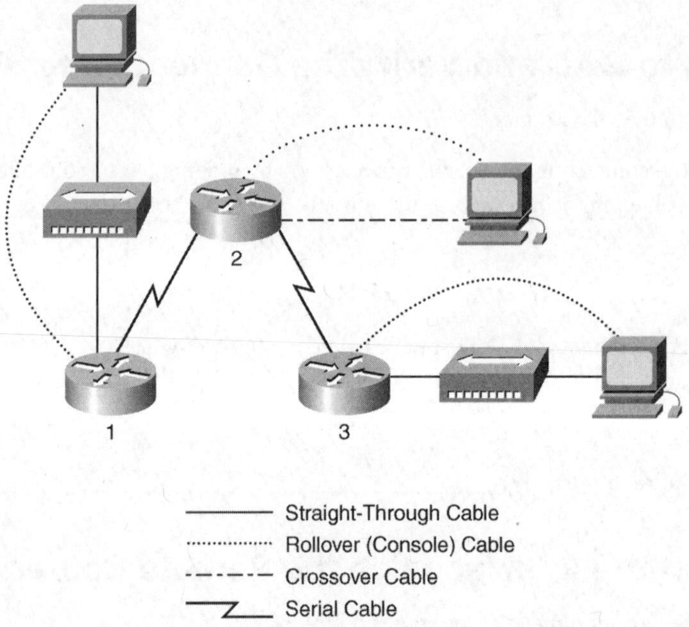

Table 4-12 Lab Equipment Configuration: Part I

Router Designation	Router Name	RIP Network Statements
Router 1	GAD	192.168.14.0
		192.168.15.0
Router 2	BHM	192.168.15.0
		192.168.13.0
		192.168.16.0
Router 3	PHX	192.168.13.0
		192.168.17.0

The routing protocol on both routers is RIP.

The enable secret password for both routers is **class**.

The enable/vty/console password for both routers is **cisco**.

Table 4-13 Lab Equipment Configuration: Part II

Router Designation	Router Name	FastEthernet 0 Address	Interface Type	Serial 0 Address	Interface Type	Serial 1 Address
Router 1	GAD	192.168.14.1	DCE	192.168.15.1	N/A	No address
Router 2	BHM	192.168.16.1	DTE	192.168.15.2	DCE	192.168.13.1
Router 3	PHX	192.168.17.1	N/A	No address	DTE	192.168.13.2

The subnet mask for all addresses on all routers is 255.255.255.0.

Objectives:

This lab contains the following objectives:

- Use the **telnet** command to remotely access other routers
- Verify that the Application layer between source and destination is working properly
- Suspend a Telnet session
- Engage in multiple Telnet sessions
- Return to the suspended session
- Disconnect from the Telnet session

Background/Preparation:

It is often desirable to have Telnet sessions to multiple routers simultaneously so that you can check and compare configuration information. This lab focuses on the ability the Telnet to multiple routers, suspend those sessions, and then switch between the active sessions. A list of active connections can also be displayed in the process.

Cable a network similar to the one shown in Figure 4-9. You can use any router that meets the interface requirements displayed in the diagram (that is, 800, 1600, 1700, 2500, or 2600 routers, or a combination). Refer to the information in Appendix B to correctly specify the interface identifiers to be used based on the equipment in your lab. The configuration output used in this lab is produced from 1721 Series routers. Any other router might produce slightly different output. The following tasks are intended to be executed on each router unless you are specifically instructed otherwise.

Start a HyperTerminal session as you did in Lab 2-2.

Refer to and implement the procedure documented in Appendix C before continuing with this lab.

Task 1: Configure the GAD, BHM, and PHX Routers Using the Tables

Step 1. Configure the three routers as indicated in Tables 4-12 and 4-13.

If you have trouble configuring hostnames or passwords, refer to Lab 3-2. If you have trouble configuring interfaces or the routing protocol, refer to Lab 3-4, Lab 3-6, and Lab 3-9.

Step 2. Verify the routers' configurations by performing a **show running-config** command on each router. If not correct, fix any configuration errors and verify.

Task 2: Log in to Router 1 and Verify the Connection to Routers 2 and 3

Step 1. Log in to the GAD router.

Step 2. Verify the connection between the two routers by pinging the serial 0 interface of the BHM and PHX routers. If the pings are not successful, return to Task 1 and troubleshoot the configuration.

Task 3: Telnet to a Remote Router

Step 1. Enter the **telnet BHM** command if IP host tables were configured. Otherwise, enter **telnet** *ip-address* at the router prompt to connect to the BHM router.

Step 2. Enter the password **cisco** to enter the router.

What prompt did the router display? ______________________

Task 4: Look at the Interfaces on the Remote Router

Enter the **show interface** command at the router prompt.

Are both the Serial 0 and the FastEthernet 0 interfaces up? ______________________

Task 5: Suspend the Current Telnet Session

Press **Ctrl-Shift-6,x**. This suspends the session only and returns to the previous router. It does not disconnect from this router.

What prompt did the router display? ______________________

Task 6: Establish Another Telnet Session

Step 1. Enter **telnet** *router-name* (if IP host tables were configured) or **telnet** *ip-address* at the router prompt to connect to the PHX router.

Step 2. Enter the password **cisco** to enter the router.

What prompt did the router display? ______________________

Task 7: Suspend the Current Telnet Session

Press **Ctrl-Shift-6,x**. This suspends the session only and returns to the previous router. It does not disconnect from this router.

What prompt did the router display? ______________________

Task 8: Use the show sessions Command to See the Connections

Enter the **show sessions** command at the router prompt. This reveals that two sessions are in use.

Task 9: Resume the Previously Suspended Telnet Session

Step 1. Type **resume** and the number of the session that is to be resumed, and press **Enter** at the router prompt. You can also just type the number of the session and press **Enter**. The router responds with the following:

```
[Resuming connection 1 to 192.168.X.X ... ]
```

Step 2. Press **Enter**. Pressing **Enter** also resumes a Telnet session that was previously suspended.

What prompt did the router display? ______________________

Task 10: Use the show sessions Command to See the Connections

Enter the **show sessions** command at the router prompt.

How many sessions are shown? ______________________

Two sessions were shown the last time you entered this command. What is the difference now?

____

Task 11: Close a Telnet Session

Enter the **exit** command while in a Telnet session. This terminates the Telnet session.

What prompt did the router display? ______________________________

Note: (Do not do this now.) To disconnect from a suspended Telnet session, type **disconnect** and press **Enter**.

Task 12: Use the show sessions Command to See the Connections

Enter the **show sessions** command at the router prompt.

How many sessions are shown?

____

Two sessions were shown on this router the last time. What is the difference?

____

Task 13: Resume the Previously Suspended Telnet Session

Step 1. Press **Enter**. The router responds with the following:

```
[Resuming connection 2 to 192.168.X.X ... ]
```

Step 2. Press **Enter**. This resumes a Telnet session that was previously suspended.

What prompt did the router display? ______________________________

Task 14: Close a Telnet Session

Enter the **exit** command while in a Telnet session. This terminates the Telnet session.

Task 15: Problems with Linked Telnet Sessions on Multiple Routers

When working with Telnet, one of the most common problems is remembering the focus of the session. *Focus* means "the device (router) that is the focus of the commands that you are issuing." Many times, people Telnet to a router and then Telnet from that router to another, and so on. Without hostnames, or if the routers have similar hostnames, confusion can occur. The following is an example of this:

Telnet to the PHX router. From the configuration prompt, type **no hostname**.

Task 16: Telnet to the BHM Router

From the configuration prompt, type **no hostname**.

Task 17: Telnet Back to the PHX Router

By looking at the prompt, it is not evident whether your Telnet worked.

Task 18: Telnet to the GAD Router

From the configuration prompt, type **no hostname**.

Task 19: Telnet to the BHM Router

Step 1. Type the **show sessions** command.

How many sessions are running? ______________________________

Why are that many sessions running?

____

Step 2. Type **exit** three times.

What router are you on? ______________________________

How many Telnet sessions are still open? ______________________________

Task 20: Exiting from All Sessions

Step 1. Keep typing **exit** until the following prompt appears:

```
Router con0 is now available.
```

Step 2. Press **Enter** to get started.

Step 3. Scroll back up the HyperTerminal listing.

How many session-closed messages were displayed? ______________________________

Is that the number listed in the "How many Telnet sessions are still open?" question from Task 19? ______________________________

Step 4. Upon completion of the previous tasks, log off (by typing **exit**) and turn the router off.

Curriculum Lab 4-6: Connectivity Tests—Ping (4.2.5a)

Figure 4-10 Topology for Lab 4-6

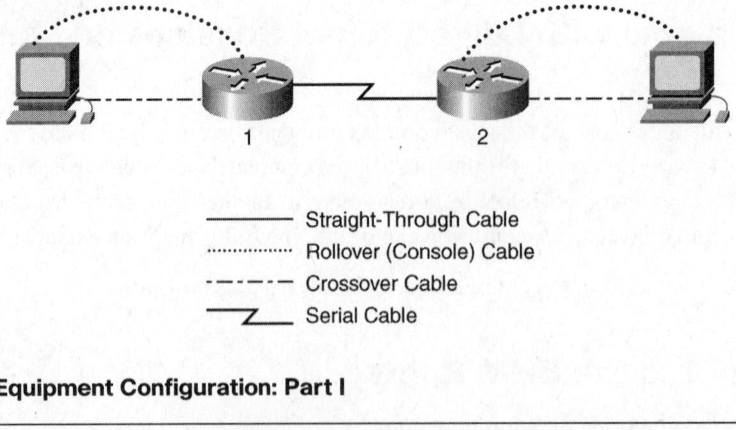

Table 4-14 Lab Equipment Configuration: Part I

Router Designation	Router Name	RIP Network Statements
Router 1	GAD	192.168.14.0, 192.168.15.0
Router 2	BHM	192.168.15.0, 192.168.16.0

The routing protocol on both routers is RIP.

The enable secret password for both routers is **class**.

The enable/vty/console password for both routers is **cisco**.

Table 4-15 Lab Equipment Configuration: Part II

Router Designation	Router Name	FastEthernet 0 Address	Interface Type Serial 0	Serial 0 Address
Router 1	GAD	192.168.14.1	DCE	192.168.15.1
Router 2	BHM	192.168.16.1	DTE	192.168.15.2

The subnet mask for all addresses on all routers is 255.255.255.0. The Serial 1 interface is inactive on both routers.

Objectives:

This lab contains the following objectives:

- Use the **ping** command to send Internet Control Message Protocol (ICMP) datagrams to the target host
- Verify that the Network layer between source and destination is working properly
- Retrieve information to evaluate the path-to-host reliability
- Determine delays over the path and know whether the host can be reached or is functioning
- Use the **extended ping** command to increase the number of packets

Background/Preparation:

The **ping** command is a good tool for troubleshooting Layers 1 through 3 of the OSI model and diagnosing basic network connectivity. With the **ping** command, a router sends an ICMP packet to the specified device (workstation, server, router, or switch) and then waits for a reply. The IP address or hostname can be pinged. To ping the hostname of a router, there must be a static host lookup table in the router or a Domain Name System (DNS) server for name resolution to IP addresses.

Cable a network similar to the one shown in Figure 4-10. You can use any router that meets the interface requirements displayed in the diagram (that is, 800, 1600, 1700, 2500, or 2600 routers, or a combination). Refer to the information in Appendix B to correctly specify the interface identifiers to be used based on the equipment in your lab. The configuration output used in this lab is produced from 1721 Series routers. Any other router might produce slightly different output. The following tasks should be executed on each router unless you are specifically instructed otherwise.

Start a HyperTerminal session as you did in Lab 2-2.

Refer to and implement the procedure documented in Appendix C before continuing with this lab.

Task 1: Configure the GAD and BHM Routers

If you have trouble configuring hostnames or passwords, refer to Lab 3-2. If you have trouble configuring interfaces or the routing protocol, refer to Lab 3-4, Lab 3-6, and Lab 3-9.

This lab requires that IP hostnames be configured.

Verify the routers' configurations by performing a **show running-config** command on each router. If not correct, fix any configuration errors and verify.

Task 2: Log in to GAD and Verify the Connection to BHM

Step 1. Log in to the GAD router.

Step 2. Verify the connection between the two routers by pinging the Serial 0 interface of the BHM router. If the ping is not successful, return to Task 1 and troubleshoot your configuration.

Task 3: Display Information About Host to Layer 3 Address Mappings

Step 1. Enter the **show host** command at the router prompt.

The router displays information about host to Layer 3 (IP) address mappings, how this information was acquired, and the age of the entry.

Step 2. List hostnames and the IP addresses for each one, and record the information in Table 4-16.

Table 4-16 Hostname/IP Address Information

Host Name	IP Address

Task 4: Use the ping Command

Enter **ping** *xxx.xxx.xxx.xxx*, where *xxx.xxx.xxx.xxx* is a listed IP address. Repeat with all IP addresses listed.

The router sends an ICMP packet to verify the hardware connection and Network layer address. The PC is acting as the console to the router; pinging from one router to another router is taking place.

Did all the IP addresses ping? ____________________

List four important pieces of information received from issuing the **ping** command.

____

Task 5: Examine the Results of the ping Command

Look at an example of the **ping** command generated by a router:

```
Router#ping 192.168.3.1
Type escape sequence to abort.
Sending 5, 100-byte ICMP Echoes to 192.168.3.1.1, timeout is 2 seconds: .!!!! Success
rate is 80 percent (4/5), round-trip min/avg/max = 68/68/168 ms
```

What does the exclamation point (!) indicate?

____

What does the period (.) indicate?

____

What does the **ping** command test for?

____

Task 6: Configure the Workstations

The configuration for the host connected to the GAD router is as follows:

```
IP address: 192.168.14.2
```

```
IP subnet mask: 255.255.255.0
Default gateway: 192.168.14.1
```

The configuration for the host connected to the BHM router is as follows:

```
IP address: 192.168.16.2
IP subnet mask: 255.255.255.0
Default gateway: 192.168.16.1
```

Task 7: Use the ping command from the Workstation

Step 1. In Windows, choose **Start** > **Programs** > **Accessories** > **Command Prompt**. This opens a command prompt window.

Step 2. To test that the TCP/IP stack and default gateway on the workstation are configured and working properly, use the MS-DOS window to ping the routers by issuing the following command:

```
C:\>ping 192.168.14.1
```

The **ping** should respond with successful results. If not, check the configurations on the host and directly connected router.

Task 8: Test Layer 3 Connectivity

Using the command prompt, enter **ping** and the IP address of all the routers' interfaces. This tests Layer 3 connectivity between the workstation and the routers.

Is the output from the workstation's **ping** command the same as the output from the **ping** command from a router?

____

Task 9: From the Host, Telnet to the Directly Connected Router

Step 1. Telnet to the connected router by typing **telnet** and the default gateway IP address of the router:

```
C:\>telnet 192.168.14.1
```

Step 2. The password prompt appears; enter **cisco**.

Task 10: Perform an Extended ping

Enter privileged EXEC mode by typing **enable** and then the password **class**. Type **ping** and press **Enter**. Fill out the rest of the prompts as you see them.

```
Protocol [ip]:
Target IP address: 192.168.16.1
Repeat count [5]: 50
Datagram size [100]:
Timeout in seconds [2]:
Extended commands [n]:
Sweep range of sizes [n]:
Type escape sequence to abort.
Sending 50, 100-byte ICMP Echos to 192.168.16.1, timeout is 2 seconds:
!!!!!!!!!!!!!!!!!!!!!!!!!!!!!!!!!!!!!!!!!!!!!!!!!!
```

```
Success rate is 100 percent (50/50), round-trip min/avg/max = 32/32/40 ms
GAD#
```

Notice how fast the ping response is. What was the average response time? ____________________

Task 11: Perform Another Extended ping

Step 1. Type **ping** and press **Enter**; then fill out the rest of the prompts as you see them.

Step 2. This time, during the ping, remove the crossover cable from BHM's Fast Ethernet port after ten pings have responded.

```
Protocol [ip]:
Target IP address: 192.168.16.1
Repeat count [5]: 50
Datagram size [100]: 1500
Timeout in seconds [2]:
Extended commands [n]:
Sweep range of sizes [n]:
Type escape sequence to abort.
Sending 50, 1500-byte ICMP Echos to 192.168.16.1, timeout is 2 seconds:
!!!!!!!!!!!!!!!U.U...........!!!!!!!!!!!!!!!!!!!!!
Success rate is 72 percent (36/50), round-trip min/avg/max = 432/434/464 ms
GAD#
```

What does the output from this extended ping say?

____

Step 3. Try doing this with a standard ping. Can the cable be removed before the ping is over? ______

What was the result of increasing the datagram size in the extended ping?

____

Task 12: Perform an Extended ping from the Host

Step 1. Exit the Telnet session and return to the host MS-DOS prompt. Type **ping** and press **Enter**.

Does the extended ping work the same way on the router as on the host? ________________

Type the following at the MS-DOS prompt:

```
C:\>ping 192.168.16.1-n 25
```

You should see 25 responses from the command.

Step 2. Experiment with other combinations of the extended `ping` commands on both the router and the host.

Step 3. Upon completion of the previous tasks, log off (by typing **exit**) and turn the router off.

Curriculum Lab 4-7: Connectivity Tests—Traceroute (4.2.5b)

Figure 4-11 Topology for Lab 4-7

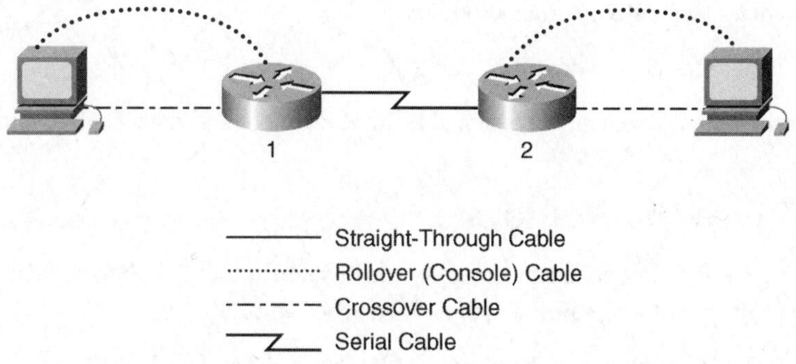

Table 4-17 Lab Equipment Configuration: Part I

Router Designation	Router Name	RIP Network Statements
Router 1	GAD	192.168.14.0, 192.168.15.0
Router 2	BHM	192.168.15.0, 192.168.16.0

The routing protocol on both routers is RIP.

The enable secret password for both routers is **class**.

The enable/vty/console password for both routers is **cisco**.

Table 4-18 Lab Equipment Configuration: Part II

Router Designation	Router Name	FastEthernet 0 Address	Interface Type Serial 0	Serial 0 Address
Router 1	GAD	192.168.14.1	DCE	192.168.15.1
Router 2	BHM	192.168.16.1	DTE	192.168.15.2

The subnet mask for all addresses on all routers is 255.255.255.0. The Serial 1 interface is inactive on both routers.

Objectives:

This lab contains the following objectives:

- Use the **traceroute** Cisco IOS software command from the source router to the destination router.
- Use the **tracert** MS-DOS command from the source workstation to the destination router. Verify that the Network layer between the source, destination, and each router along the way is working properly.
- Retrieve information to evaluate the end-to-end path reliability.
- Determine delays at each point over the path and know whether the host can be reached.

Background/Preparation:

The **traceroute** IOS command, abbreviated as **trace**, is an excellent utility for troubleshooting the path that a packet takes through an internetwork of routers. This command can help isolate problem links and routers along the way. The **traceroute** command uses ICMP packets and the error message generated by routers when the packet exceeds its Time-to-Live (TTL). The Windows version of this command is **tracert**.

Cable a network similar to the one shown in Figure 4-11. You can use any router that meets the interface requirements displayed in the diagram (that is, 800, 1600, 1700, 2500, or 2600 routers, or a combination). Refer to the information in Appendix B to correctly specify the interface identifiers to be used based on the equipment in your lab. The configuration output used in this lab is produced from 1721 Series routers. Any other router might produce slightly different output. The following tasks should be executed on each router unless you are specifically instructed otherwise.

Start a HyperTerminal session as you did in Lab 2-2.

Refer to and implement the procedure documented in Appendix C on all routers before continuing with this lab.

Task 1: Configure the Routers

If you have trouble configuring hostnames or passwords, refer to Lab 3-2. If you have trouble configuring interfaces or the routing protocol, refer to Lab 3-4, Lab 3-6, and Lab 3-9.

This lab requires that IP hostnames be configured.

Verify the routers' configurations by performing a **show running-config** command on each router. If not correct, fix any configuration errors and reverify.

Task 2: Configure the Workstations

The configuration for the host connected to the GAD router is as follows:

```
IP address: 192.168.14.2
IP subnet mask: 255.255.255.0
Default gateway: 192.168.14.1
```

The configuration for the host connected to the BHM router is as follows:

```
IP address: 192.168.16.2
IP subnet mask: 255.255.255.0
Default gateway: 192.168.16.1
```

Task 3: Use the ping Command from the Workstation

Step 1. From a Windows host, choose **Start** > **Programs** > **Accessories** > **Command Prompt**. This opens a command prompt window.

Step 2. To test that the TCP/IP stack and default gateway on the workstation are configured and working properly, use the MS-DOS window to ping the routers by issuing the following command:

```
C:\>ping 192.168.14.1
```

The ping should respond with successful results. If not, check the configurations on the host and directly connected router.

Task 4: Test Layer 3 Connectivity

Using the command prompt, enter **ping** and the IP address of all router interfaces. This tests Layer 3 connectivity between the workstation and the routers.

Is the output from the workstation's **ping** command the same as the output from the **ping** command from a router?

____

Task 5: Log in to the Router in User Mode

Log in to the GAD at the user EXEC mode prompt.

Task 6: Discover the traceroute Options

Type **traceroute** at the router prompt and press **Enter**.

With what did the router respond? ______________________________

Task 7: Use the Help Function with traceroute

Enter **traceroute ?** at the router prompt.

How did the router respond?

____
____
____
____
____
____
____

Task 8: Continue Discovering the traceroute Options

Enter privileged EXEC mode and type **traceroute ?**.

How did the router respond?

____
____
____
____
____
____
____
____

Was anything different between the two traceroute outputs?

____

If you noticed an added option of <cr>, that's good. This allows an extended ping at the privileged EXEC mode, which is unavailable at the user EXEC mode.

Task 9: Use the traceroute Command

Enter **traceroute ip** *xxx.xxx.xxx.xxx*, where *xxx.xxx.xxx.xxx* is the IP address of the target destination. Use one of the end routers and traceroute to the other end host. The **ip** keyword can be omitted if tracing to an IP address because it is the default.

```
GAD#traceroute 192.168.16.2
Type the escape sequence to abort.
```

```
Tracing the route to 192.168.16.2
  1 BHM (192.168.15.2) 16 msec 16 msec 16 msec
  2 192.168.16.2 16 msec 16 msec 12 msec
GAD#
```

If the output is not successful, check your router and host configurations.

Task 10: Continue Using traceroute

Log in to the other routers and repeat the **traceroute** command.

Task 11: Use the tracert Command from a Workstation

Step 1. From the console workstation, choose **Start** > **Programs** > **Accessories** > **Command Prompt**. An MS-DOS command prompt window opens.

Step 2. Enter **tracert** and the same IP address used in Task 5.

Step 3. The first hop is the default gateway or the near-side router interface on the LAN that the workstation is connected to. List the hostnames and IP addresses of the routers that the ICMP packet was routed through, as well as any other entries displayed, in Table 4-19.

Table 4-19 Hostname/IP Address Information

Hostname	IP Address

One more entry is found in the output of the **tracert** command when the trace is from the computer command prompt to the target host. Why?

____

Task 12: Trace to Cisco and Other Common Websites

From a Windows host that has Internet access, choose **Start** > **Programs** > **Accessories** > **Command Prompt**. An MS-DOS command prompt window opens, where you can enter the following:

```
C:\>tracert www.cisco.com
C:\>tracert www.yahoo.com
C:\>tracert www.aol.com
```

This procedure shows the IP address and the route of the destination.

What is the IP address of cisco.com?

____

How many hops did it take to get to cisco.com?

____

If a packet passes through a router, it is considered one hop, and the TTL of the packet is decremented by 1.

Task 13: Compare the IP Route traces to Cisco, Yahoo, and AOL

Where are the differences in the traces?

____

Why are they always the same in the beginning?

____

Upon completion of the previous tasks, log off (by typing **exit**) and turn the router off.

Curriculum Lab 4-8: Troubleshooting IP Address Issues (4.2.6)

Figure 4-12 Topology for Lab 4-8

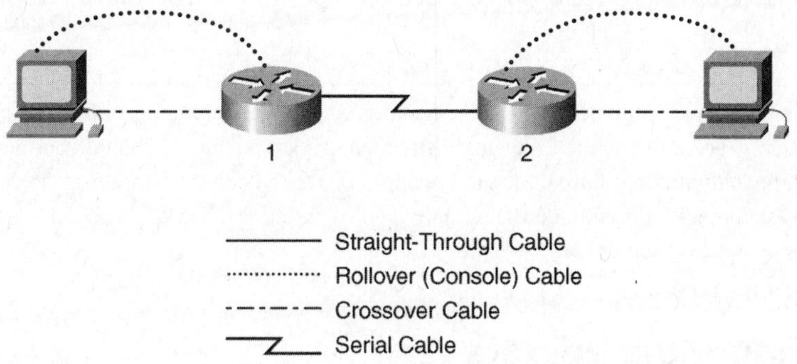

Table 4-20 Lab Equipment Configuration: Part I

Router Designation	Router Name	RIP Network Statements
Router 1	GAD	192.168.14.0, 192.168.15.0
Router 2	BHM	192.168.15.0, 192.168.16.0

The routing protocol on both routers is RIP.

The enable secret password for both routers is **class**.

The enable/vty/console password for both routers is **cisco**.

Table 4-21 Lab Equipment Configuration: Part II

Router Designation	Router Name	FastEthernet 0 Address	Interface Type Serial 0	Serial 0 Address
Router 1	GAD	192.168.14.1	DCE	192.168.16.1
Router 2	BHM	192.168.16.1	DTE	192.168.15.2

The subnet mask for all addresses on all routers is 255.255.255.0. The Serial 1 interface is inactive on both routers.

Objectives:

This lab contains the following objectives:

- Configure two routers and two workstations in a small WAN
- Troubleshoot problems introduced by incorrect configurations

Background/Preparation:

Cable a network similar to the one shown in Figure 4-12. You can use any router that meets the interface requirements displayed in the diagram (that is, 800, 1600, 1700, 2500, or 2600 routers, or a combination). Refer to the information in Appendix B to correctly specify the interface identifiers to be used based on the equipment in your lab. The configuration output used in this lab is produced from 1721 Series routers. Any other router might produce slightly different output. The following tasks should be executed on each router unless you are specifically instructed otherwise.

Start a HyperTerminal session as you did in Lab 2-2.

Refer to and implement the procedure documented in Appendix C on all routers before continuing with this lab.

Note: Work in teams of two. Team member 1 should configure the GAD router according to Table 4-21 and configure its attached workstation according to the following instructions. Team member 2 should configure the BHM router and its workstation. Both configurations have errors and result in IP-related communications problems. Team member 1 should then troubleshoot problems with the BHM router and workstations. Team member 2 can troubleshoot problems with the GAD router and workstations.

Task 1: Configure the Routers

If you have trouble configuring hostnames or passwords, refer to Lab 3-2. If you have trouble configuring interfaces or the routing protocol, refer to Lab 3-4, Lab 3-6, and Lab 3-9.

This lab requires that IP hostnames be configured.

Verify the routers' configurations by performing a **show running-config** command on each router. If not correct, fix any configuration errors and reverify.

Task 2: Configure the Workstations

The configuration for the host connected to the GAD router is as follows:

```
IP Address: 192.168.14.2
IP subnet mask: 255.255.255.0
Default gateway: 192.168.14.2
```

The configuration for the host connected to the BHM router is as follows:

```
IP Address: 192.168.16.2
IP subnet mask: 255.255.255.0
Default gateway: 192.168.16.1
```

Task 3: Use the ping Command from the Workstation

Step 1. From the Windows host, choose **Start** > **Programs** > **Accessories** > **Command Prompt**. This opens a command prompt window.

Step 2. To test that the TCP/IP stack and default gateway on the workstation are configured and working properly, use the MS-DOS window to ping the router by issuing the following command:

```
C:\>ping 192.168.14.1
```

The ping should respond with unsuccessful results, so check configurations on the host and routers.

Step 3. Two problems were introduced into the configurations. Correct the configurations to allow pinging of all the interfaces on the hosts and routers.

What was problem 1?

____

____

What was problem 2?

____

____

Step 4. Upon completion of the previous tasks, log off (by typing **exit**) and turn the router off.

Comprehensive Lab 4-9: CDP Commands

Figure 4-13 Using CDP Commands Topology

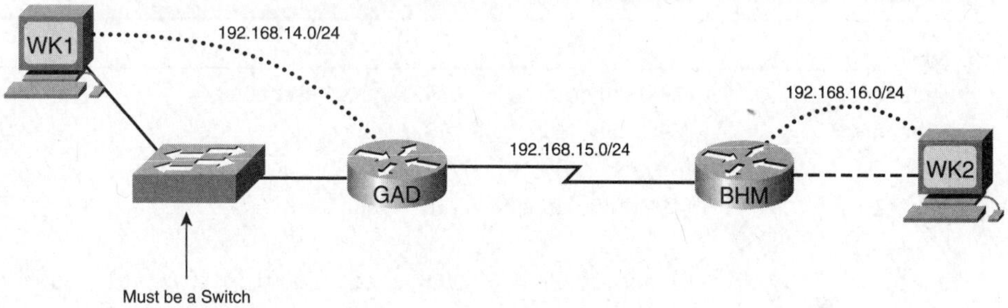

Objectives:

This lab contains the following objectives:

- Use CDP commands to obtain information about neighboring networks and devices
- Display information on how CDP is configured for its advertisement and discovery frame transmission
- Display CDP updates received on the local router

Task 1: Cabling, Basic Router Configuration, Workstation Configuration, and Verification

Step 1. Cable the lab according to the topology shown in Figure 4-13.

Step 2. Fill in the following table with appropriate configuration information for the interface type. For the LAN networks, assign the first address to the router interface and the second address to the workstation. For the WAN network, indicate which side you chose as data circuit–terminating equipment (DCE) or data terminal equipment (DTE). Assign the first address to GAD and the second address to BHM.

Device	Interface	DTE or DCE?	IP Address	Subnet Mask	Default Gateway
GAD					
BHM					
WK1					
WK2					

Step 3. Configure the routers, including any basic configurations required by your instructor.

Step 4. Verify that all configured interfaces are fully functional. Fill in the command that displays the following output:

```
GAD#________________________________________________
Interface          IP-Address     OK? Method Status                 Protocol
Ethernet0          192.168.14.1   YES manual up                     up

Ethernet1          unassigned     YES unset  administratively down down

Serial0            192.168.15.1   YES manual up                     up

Serial1            unassigned     YES unset  administratively down down
```

```
BHM#________________________________________________
Interface          IP-Address     OK? Method Status                 Protocol
Ethernet0          192.168.16.1   YES manual up                     up

Serial0            192.168.15.2   YES manual up                     up

Serial1            unassigned     YES unset  administratively down down
```

Step 5. Configure RIP routing on each router. Both routers belong to two networks. Only configure the router with its directly connected networks.

```
Router(config)#router rip
Router(config-router)#network network_address
Router(config-router)#network network_address
```

Step 6. Verify that routing tables are complete. Fill in the command that displays the following output.

```
GAD#show ip route
Codes: C - connected, S - static, I - IGRP, R - RIP, M - mobile, B - BGP
       D - EIGRP, EX - EIGRP external, O - OSPF, IA - OSPF inter area
       N1 - OSPF NSSA external type 1, N2 - OSPF NSSA external type 2
       E1 - OSPF external type 1, E2 - OSPF external type 2, E - EGP
       i - IS-IS, L1 - IS-IS level-1, L2 - IS-IS level-2, ia - IS-IS inter
area
       * - candidate default, U - per-user static route, o - ODR
       P - periodic downloaded static route

Gateway of last resort is not set

C    192.168.14.0/24 is directly connected, Ethernet0
```

```
C     192.168.15.0/24 is directly connected, Serial0
R     192.168.16.0/24 [120/1] via 192.168.15.2, 00:00:25, Serial0
```

```
BHM#show ip route
Codes: C - connected, S - static, I - IGRP, R - RIP, M - mobile, B - BGP
       D - EIGRP, EX - EIGRP external, O - OSPF, IA - OSPF inter area
       N1 - OSPF NSSA external type 1, N2 - OSPF NSSA external type 2
       E1 - OSPF external type 1, E2 - OSPF external type 2, E - EGP
       i - IS-IS, L1 - IS-IS level-1, L2 - IS-IS level-2, ia - IS-IS inter area
       * - candidate default, U - per-user static route, o - ODR
       P - periodic downloaded static route

Gateway of last resort is not set

R     192.168.14.0/24 [120/1] via 192.168.15.1, 00:00:11, Serial0
C     192.168.15.0/24 is directly connected, Serial0
C     192.168.16.0/24 is directly connected, Ethernet0
```

Verify that GAD can ping the LAN interface on BHM. Successful? ____________________

Verify that BHM can ping the LAN interface on GAD. Successful? ____________________

Step 7. Configure the workstations with the necessary IP address, subnet mask, and default gateway.

Verify the configuration on WK2. Fill in the commands that display the following output.

```
C:\>ipconfig

Windows IP Configuration



Ethernet adapter Local Area Connection:

        Connection-specific DNS Suffix  . :
        IP Address. . . . . . . . . . . . : 192.168.16.2
        Subnet Mask . . . . . . . . . . . : 255.255.255.0
        Default Gateway . . . . . . . . . : 192.168.16.1
```

Verify that WK2 can ping the default gateway. Successful? ____________________

```
C:\>ping 192.168.16.1

Pinging 192.168.16.1 with 32 bytes of data:

Reply from 192.168.16.1: bytes=32 time=2ms TTL=255
Reply from 192.168.16.1: bytes=32 time=2ms TTL=255
Reply from 192.168.16.1: bytes=32 time=2ms TTL=255
Reply from 192.168.16.1: bytes=32 time=2ms TTL=255

Ping statistics for 192.168.16.1:
    Packets: Sent = 4, Received = 4, Lost = 0 (0% loss),
Approximate round trip times in milli-seconds:
    Minimum = 2ms, Maximum = 2ms, Average = 2ms
```

Verify that WK2 can ping WK1. Successful? ____________________

```
C:\>ping 192.168.14.1

Pinging 192.168.14.1 with 32 bytes of data:

Reply from 192.168.14.1: bytes=32 time=25ms TTL=254
Reply from 192.168.14.1: bytes=32 time=20ms TTL=254
Reply from 192.168.14.1: bytes=32 time=20ms TTL=254
Reply from 192.168.14.1: bytes=32 time=20ms TTL=254

Ping statistics for 192.168.14.1:
    Packets: Sent = 4, Received = 4, Lost = 0 (0% loss),
Approximate round trip times in milli-seconds:
    Minimum = 20ms, Maximum = 25ms, Average = 21ms
```

Verify the configuration on WK1:

```
C:\>ipconfig

Windows IP Configuration


Ethernet adapter Local Area Connection:

        Connection-specific DNS Suffix  . :
        IP Address. . . . . . . . . . . . : 192.168.14.2
        Subnet Mask . . . . . . . . . . . : 255.255.255.0
        Default Gateway . . . . . . . . . : 192.168.14.1
```

Verify that WK1 can ping the default gateway. Successful? ______________________________

```
C:\>ping 192.168.14.1

Pinging 192.168.14.1 with 32 bytes of data:

Reply from 192.168.14.1: bytes=32 time=5ms TTL=255
Reply from 192.168.14.1: bytes=32 time=2ms TTL=255
Reply from 192.168.14.1: bytes=32 time=2ms TTL=255
Reply from 192.168.14.1: bytes=32 time=2ms TTL=255

Ping statistics for 192.168.14.1:
    Packets: Sent = 4, Received = 4, Lost = 0 (0% loss),
Approximate round trip times in milli-seconds:
    Minimum = 2ms, Maximum = 5ms, Average = 2ms
```

Verify that WK1 can ping WK2. Successful? ______________________________

```
C:\>ping 192.168.16.2

Pinging 192.168.16.2 with 32 bytes of data:

Reply from 192.168.16.2: bytes=32 time=27ms TTL=126
Reply from 192.168.16.2: bytes=32 time=18ms TTL=126
Reply from 192.168.16.2: bytes=32 time=18ms TTL=126
Reply from 192.168.16.2: bytes=32 time=21ms TTL=126
```

```
Ping statistics for 192.168.16.2:
    Packets: Sent = 4, Received = 4, Lost = 0 (0% loss),
Approximate round trip times in milli-seconds:
    Minimum = 18ms, Maximum = 27ms, Average = 21ms
```

Task 1 is now complete. You are ready to begin the lab objectives.

Task 2: Display the Values of the CDP Timers, the Interface Status, and the Encapsulation Used

Step 1. Enter the command that displays the value of CDP timers on one or all interfaces. What command did you use?

____

Step 2. Notice that the command you entered in Step 1 displays the interface status (for example, Ethernet0 is up, line protocol is up). What additional three pieces of information are displayed about the interface?

- ______________________________
- ______________________________
- ______________________________

These timer values are the defaults for CDP.

Step 3. Enter the command that displays global CDP settings. What command did you use?

____

What information is not shown in this command but is shown in the interface command?

____

Task 3: Display CDP Information About Other Devices

Step 1. What command displays brief information about directly connected Cisco devices?

____

Step 2. On GAD, shut down the Ethernet interface. What command did you use?

____

Step 3. Clear the CDP entries with the **clear cdp table** command.

Step 4. Enter the command that you listed in Step 1 to determine directly connected Cisco devices. What device or devices are listed?

____

What information is listed about the device or devices?

____

Step 5. Activate the Ethernet interface on GAD. What command did you use?

____

Step 6. Enter the command that you listed in Step 1 to determine directly connected Cisco devices. What device or devices are listed?

____

Step 7. What command displays detailed information about directly connected Cisco devices?

____

Step 8. Enter the command that you listed in Step 7 on GAD. List the additional information displayed about BHM.

____

____

Task 4: Monitoring and Observing CDP Traffic

Step 1. What command allows you to monitor CDP traffic on the local router as CDP packets are sent and received? (Hint: Use the help facility to determine the correct command.)

____

Step 2. On GAD, enter the command listed in Step 1 and watch the output for at least 2 minutes. Is GAD sending and receiving packets on both interfaces? ______________________

Step 3. Turn off the monitoring of CDP traffic. What command did you use?

____

Step 4. What command allows you to see the total number of CDP packets sent and received since the last reboot or clearing of counters?

____

Step 5. On GAD, enter the command listed in Step 4. How many CDP packets have been sent?

____

How many CDP packets have been received?

____

What version of CDP is GAD using?

____

Comprehensive Lab 4-10: Network Troubleshooting Commands

Figure 4-14 Using Troubleshooting Commands Topology

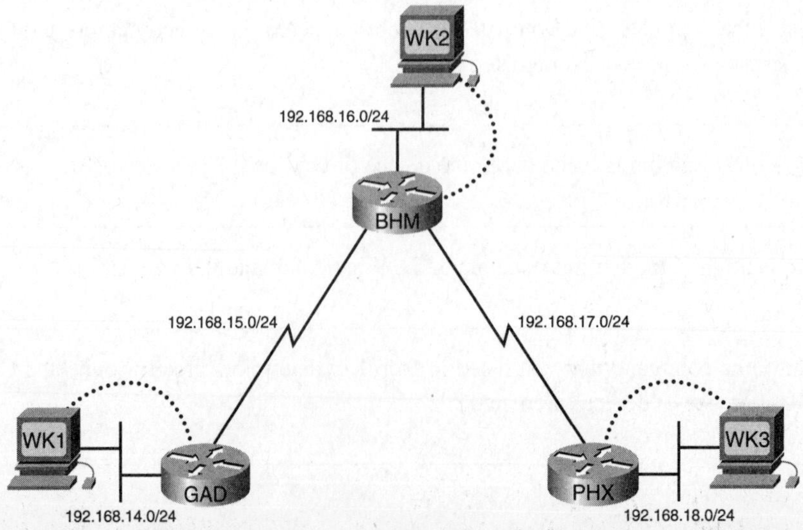

Objectives:

This lab contains the following objectives:

- Verify that the Network layer is operational using the **ping** command
- Extend the **ping** command from a workstation and a router by making use of available options
- Use **traceroute** and **tracert** commands to verify the path and to determine delays over the path from source to destination
- Establish, suspend, and reestablish Telnet sessions
- Display and disconnect an active Telnet session

Task 1: Cable and Configure the Topology

Step 1. Cable the lab according to the topology shown in Figure 4-14.

Step 2. Fill in the following table with the appropriate configuration information.

Device	Interface	DTE or DCE?	IP Address	Subnet Mask	Default Gateway

Step 3. Configure the routers with basic router configurations according to your instructor's specifications. Make sure that the **exec-timeout 0 0** command is entered under all line vty configurations.

Step 4. Configure routing using RIP as the routing protocol.

Step 5. Use the **show ip route** command to verify that all routers have five networks in the routing table.

Step 6. Configure each workstation with your assigned IP address, subnet mask, and default gateway.

Task 2: Verify Network Layer Connectivity

Step 1. From WK1, ping WK3. Successful? _______ If not, troubleshoot.

Step 2. From WK1, ping WK2. Successful? _______ If not, troubleshoot.

Step 3. From WK2, ping WK3. Successful? _______ If not, troubleshoot.

Why is it unnecessary to verify that WK3 can ping WK2 or WK1?

____

____

Step 4. From WK1, use **ping** options to continuously send ping packets to WK3 until stopped by you. (Hint: At the DOS prompt, type **ping** and then press **Enter** to see a list of options.)

What command did you use?

____

How did you stop the ping packets?

____

Step 5. From WK1, use **ping** options to specify that 100 packets should be sent to WK3.

What command did you use?

____

Step 6. From the GAD router, send 100 ping packets to the Ethernet interface attached to PHX. Use the Ethernet interface attached to GAD as the source IP address.

How would you complete the instruction for Step 6?

____

____

Why would you want to change the source IP address when pinging a destination IP address?

____

Task 3: Verify the Path from Source to Destination

Step 1. From GAD, discover the path that packets take to reach WK3. What command did you use?

____

Record the path and delays in the following space:

Step 2. From WK1, discover the path that packets take to reach WK3. What command did you use?

____

How many hops did it take? _______________________

Record the path and delays in the following space:

Task 4: Advanced Telnet Operations

Step 1. Before proceeding, make sure that all Telnet sessions, if any, are closed on all routers. What command, entered on each router, would verify that all Telnet sessions are closed?

____

Step 2. From GAD, Telnet to PHX and then suspend the Telnet session. What key combination suspends a Telnet session?

____

Step 3. From GAD, Telnet to PHX a second time and then suspend the Telnet session.

Step 4. From GAD, Telnet to PHX a third time and then suspend the Telnet session.

Step 5. From GAD, Telnet to PHX a fourth time and then suspend the Telnet session.

Step 6. From GAD, Telnet to PHX a fifth time and then suspend the Telnet session.

Step 7. From GAD, attempt to Telnet PHX a sixth time.

What message did you receive?

____

____

____

____

Why did you receive this message?

____

Step 8. From GAD, attempt to Telnet to BHM. Was your attempt successful? ____________

Why or why not?

____

Step 9. Make sure that you are at the GAD router prompt (suspend any Telnet session currently active, if necessary). Enter the command to display all Telnet sessions. What command did you use?

____

Step 10. You should have six sessions currently active. If not, you either did not configure the **exec-timeout 0 0** command as instructed in Task 1 or you did not connect and then suspend all the Telnet sessions correctly. Troubleshoot until you get command output that looks like this:

```
GAD#sh sessions
Conn Host                  Address            Byte  Idle Conn Name
   1 phx                   192.168.17.2          0     3 phx
   2 phx                   192.168.17.2          0     3
   3 phx                   192.168.17.2          0     3
   4 phx                   192.168.17.2          0     2
   5 phx                   192.168.17.2          0     2
*  6 bhm                   192.168.15.2          0     0 bhm
```

Step 11. If you press **Enter** at the GAD command prompt, what Telnet session will be resumed?

____

How can you tell which session will be resumed?

____

Step 12. If you press **Enter** in Step 11, you will need to suspend the Telnet session to go back to GAD. From the GAD router prompt, resume the third Telnet session with PHX. What command did you use?

____

Step 13. Permanently end this Telnet session with PHX by entering a command at the PHX prompt. What command did you use?

____

Step 14. From the GAD router prompt, end all Telnet sessions currently open. What command did you use to end Telnet sessions?

____

Step 15. Verify that all sessions are ended. What command did you use?

____

Task 5: Finalize Documentation and Restore Equipment Configurations

Step 1. Capture the configuration of all three routers. Clean up the scripts and keep them in your engineering journal.

Step 2. Erase and reload the routers.

Step 3. Remove the workstation configurations.

CHAPTER 5

Managing Cisco IOS Software

The Study Guide portion of this chapter uses a combination of fill-in-the-blank, open-ended questions, and unique custom exercises to test your knowledge of the theory of managing Cisco IOS software.

The Lab Exercises portion of this chapter includes all the online curriculum labs as well as a challenge lab to ensure that you have mastered the practical, hands-on skills needed for managing IOS.

Study Guide

Router Boot Sequence and Loading IOS Images

A Cisco router cannot operate without Cisco IOS software. Each Cisco router has a predetermined bootup sequence that locates and loads the Cisco IOS. The exercises in this section help you understand the stages and importance of this bootup procedure.

Vocabulary Exercise: Completion

Fill in the blanks for the items that follow.

1. When a router is first powered on, it completes a four-step initialization process:

1. Performing a ____

2. Loading a __________ program

3. Loading an _____

4. Loading a ______________ file

The last three of these steps require the router to copy the files into _____. Normally, most routers load an IOS image that is stored in _____ memory and an initial configuration stored in ________.

2. Routers use the following logic, in order, to attempt to load an IOS:

1. Load a limited-function IOS if the configuration register's last hex digit is set to ___ or ___.

2. Load an IOS based on the configuration of _________ commands in the startup-config file.

3. Load the first file in _______ as the IOS.

4. Use _____ broadcasts to find a _____ server and download an IOS from that server.

5. Load a limited-function IOS from _____.

In Step 1, the ___________________ is a __-bit number that Cisco routers store in a hidden area of ________. It can be set in a couple of ways and can be seen using the **show version** command. The most commonly used way to set its value is to use the **config-register** global configuration command. Routers use the 4 low-order bits of the configuration register as the ____ field, which tells the router what to do in the first of the preceding five decision steps. If the value of the field is set to ___, the router loads the ______________________, which is used for password recovery. If the value is set to ___, the router loads the _________ or ________, which can be used to copy a new IOS into flash. If the value is set to anything between ___ and ___, the router proceeds to Step 2.

In Step 2, the router looks in the ___________ file for any _________ commands and loads the IOS file listed. If multiple commands are configured, the router tries each of them sequentially. If no ____ _________ commands exist or all fail, the router proceeds to Step 3.

In Step 3, the router loads the first IOS listed in _____ memory.

In Step 4, the router broadcasts for a ____________, which is the last effort at finding and loading an IOS, but it is frankly seldom used outside a Cisco lab environment.

In Step 5, the router has given up trying to load a fully-functional IOS. So, the router loads one of the limited-function OSs. Depending on the platform, the router loads either the ________ OS or the ________ image.

Router Boot Sequence Exercise

Figure 5-1 displays an incomplete diagram of the default boot sequence of a router. Provide detail where information is missing.

Figure 5-1 Diagram of the Router Boot Sequence

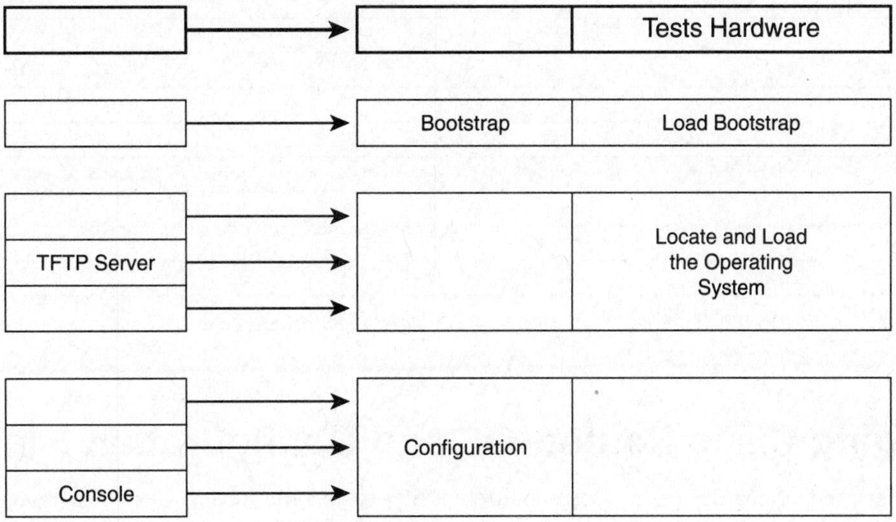

Boot System Commands Exercise

The default boot sequence for finding an IOS can be changed by configuring boot system commands. Record the commands to change the order the router uses to find an IOS to the following requirements:

- Boot image c1700-y-mz.122-11.T9.bin from TFTP at 10.0.0.2
- Boot image XXX-yyy-zzz from flash, which is not the first file listed in flash
- Boot image from ROM

Configuration Register Exercise

1. Fill in the following table with the correct configuration register values and describe what each means.

Value	Description

2. Record the command you would use to change the configuration register setting to 0x2102.

Journal Entry

Describe in short-essay format the router initialization process.

Managing Cisco Router IOS and Configuration Files

Cisco internetworking devices use several different files to operate, such as Cisco IOS images and configuration files. As a network engineer, you must be able to effectively manage these files to ensure that the proper versions are used and that necessary backups are performed and maintained. The exercises in this section can help you learn the Cisco IOS naming conventions and walk you through a file backup and a file restoration procedure.

IOS Naming Convention Exercise

The IOS image filename should never be changed because each part has a specific meaning according to the IOS naming convention. The image filename c2600-j1s3-mz.123-17a.bin can be broken into four parts, as shown in the following table. Briefly described what each part means.

Part of Name	Description
c2600	
jls3	
mz	
123-17a	

What does "mz" mean in an IOS filename?

Using the Cisco Feature Navigator at http://tools.cisco.com/ITDIT/CFN/jsp/index.jsp, answer the questions for each of the IOS image files that follow:

c1700-y-mz.122-11.T9.bin

The image only works with the _____ platform hardware. Which models within this platform support this IOS image?

____

What feature set does this IOS contain?

____

c2600-i-mz.121-5.bin

The image only works with the _____ platform hardware. Which models within this platform support this IOS image?

____

What feature set does this IOS contain?

____

c2600-j1s3-mz.123-17a.bin

The image only works with the _____ platform hardware. Which models within this platform support this IOS image?

____

What feature set does this IOS contain?

____

c2600-advsecurityk9-mz.123-13.bin

The image only works with the _____ platform hardware. Which models within this platform support this IOS image?

____

What feature set does this IOS contain?

____

c837-k9o3y6-mz.12.4-4.T

Which models support this IOS image?

____

What feature set does this IOS contain?

____

c2600-ik9o3s-mz.122-8.T10.bin

The image only works with the _____ platform hardware. Which models within this platform support this IOS image?

____

What feature set does this IOS contain?

____

____

Backing Up an IOS and Configuration File Exercise

Figure 5-2 Backing Up an IOS and Configuration File

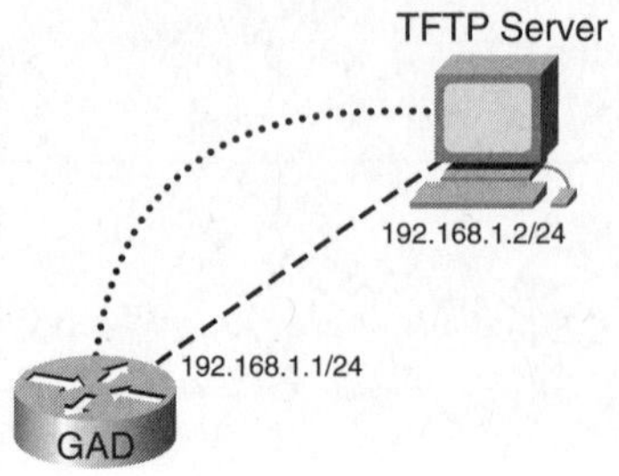

Refer to Figure 5-2. You have just installed and configured a new production router. Your final step is to back up the IOS and the configuration file to a TFTP server.

1. What kind of cable connection(s) do you need?

____

____

____

2. What kind of software do you need?

____

3. Explain the steps that you must take to get the PC ready to be a TFTP server.

____

____

4. Explain the step you must take to get the router ready to send files to the TFTP server.

____

5. How would you test that the PC and router can send and receive packets to and from each other?

____

____

6. Now that you know that the router and the PC can send packets, record the commands in the configuration that follows to send the configuration file to the TFTP server.

```
GAD#copy running-config tftp
Address or name of remote host []? ______________________________
Destination filename [GAD-confg]?
Write file GAD-config to __________? [confirm]:
Writing GAD-config  !!!  [OK - 880 bytes]
880 bytes copied in 0.869 secs (1013 bytes/sec)
```

7. Copy the IOS image to the TFTP server. What command do you use to discover the filename of the IOS stored in flash?

____

8. Record the commands in the configuration that follows to send the IOS to the TFTP server. Assume that the IOS filename is c1700-y-mz.122-11.T9.bin.

```
Router#______________________________________________
Source filename []? __________________________________
Address or name of remote host []? ____________________
```

```
Destination filename [c1700-y-mz.122-11.T9.bin]? ________________
!!!!!!!!!!!!!!!!!!!!!!!!!!!!!!!!!!!!!!!!!!!!!!!!!!!!!!!!!!!!!!!!!!!!!!!!!!!!!!!!!!!!!!!!!!
!!!!!!!!!!!!!!!!!!!!!!!!!!!!!!!!!!!!!!!!!!!!!!!!!!!!!!!!!!!!!!!!!!!!!!!!!!!!!!!!!!!!!!!!!!
!!!!!!!!!!!!!!!!!!!!!!!!!!!!!!!!!!!!!!!!!!!!!!!!!!!!!!!!!!!!!!!!!!!!!!!!!!!!!!!!!!!!!!!!!!
!!!!!!!!!!!!!!!!!!!!!!!
4288448 bytes bytes copied in 34.012 secs (126086 bytes/sec)
```

Using ROMMON and the tftpdnld Command Exercise

Refer to Figure 5-2. The IOS on your router is either corrupted or has been erased from flash, and your router is booting in ROMMON, or ROM Monitor, mode. To bring the router back to a production state, you need to restore the IOS.

1. You must use the **tftpdnld** command in ROMMON. In the following table, list the five environmental variables that must be set before you can use the **tftpdnld** command.

Environment Variable	Description
	The IP address of the router's first LAN interface.
	The subnet mask used on the router's first LAN interface.
	The IP address of the default gateway on the same LAN.
	The IP address of the TFTP server.
	The full name of the file to download from the TFTP server. The name can include the directory structure.

Note: You will not find these variables in the online version of the curriculum. Use the phrase "tftpdnld 1700" in your favorite search engine to find a link to the Cisco website, where ROMMON disaster recovery is discussed.

2. In the following list, record the environment variables along with the correct parameter for each. The first one is completed for you.

```
rommon 1>IP_ADDRESS=192.168.1.1
rommon 2>________________
rommon 3>________________
rommon 4>________________
rommon 5>________________
```

3. Enter the command that displays the environmental variables as configured.

```
rommon 6>________________
```

4. Record the command that begins the download process.

```
rommon 7>________________
<output omitted>
Invoke this command for disaster recovery only.
WARNING: all existing data in all partitions on flash will be lost!
Do you wish to continue? y/n: [n]: ________________
Receiving c1700-y-mz.122-11.T9.bin from 192.168.1.2
!!!!.!!!!!!!!!!!!!!!!!!!!.!!
File reception completed.
Copying file c2600-i-mz.121-5 to flash.
Erasing flash at 0x607c0000
program flash location 0x60440000
```

5. Record the command necessary to reboot the router. The command is *not* **reload**.

   `rommon 8>`______________________________

   The router should now reboot with the restored IOS.

Using ROMMON and XMODEM Exercise

Figure 5-3 Using ROMMON and XMODEM

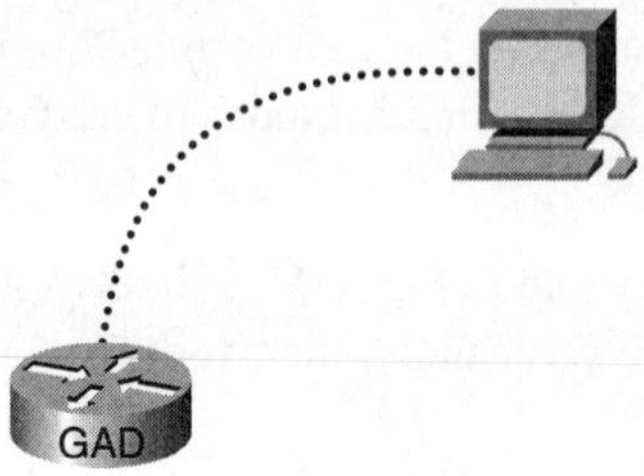

Your router IOS is either corrupted or has been erased from flash. You do *not* have access to an IOS through TFTP. To bring the router back to a production state, you must restore an IOS using XMODEM.

1. List and describe the three components you need to successfully use XMODEM.

   - ______________________________
   - ______________________________
     ____
   - ______________________________

2. A router's console port normally sends and receives at ____ bps. Record the command you would use to configure a faster speed.

```
rommon 1>______________________________
Configuration Summary
(Virtual Configuration Register: 0x1820)
enabled are:
break/abort has effect
console baud: 9600
boot: the ROM Monitor
do you wish to change the configuration? y/n [n]: ____________________
enable "diagnostic mode"? y/n [n]:[Enter]
enable "use net in IP bcast address"? y/n [n]: [Enter]
enable "load rom after netboot fails"? y/n [n]: [Enter]
enable "use all zero broadcast"? y/n [n]: [Enter]
disable "break/abort has effect"? y/n [n]: y
enable "ignore system config info"? y/n [n]: [Enter]
change console baud rate? y/n [n]: ____________________
enter rate: 0 = 9600, 1 = 4800, 2 = 1200, 3 = 2400
4 = 19200, 5 = 38400, 6 = 57600, 7 = 115200 [0]: 7
change the boot characteristics? y/n [n]: [Enter]
Configuration Summary
(Virtual Configuration Register: 0x1920)
enabled are:
```

```
console baud: 115200
boot: the ROM Monitor
do you wish to change the configuration? y/n [n]: n
```

3. Enter the command necessary to reboot the router so that the new console baud rate takes effect.

   `rommon 3 >`______________________________

4. What else must you do to ensure that you can interact with the router?

   ____

5. After the router reboots, you can configure it to be ready to receive the IOS image. Enter the command necessary to use XMODEM to receive the IOS file c1700-y-mz.122-11.T9.bin.

   `rommon 1.>`______________________________

```
Do not start the sending program yet...
Warning: All existing data in bootflash will be lost!
Invoke this application only for disaster recovery.
Do you wish to continue? y/n [n]: y
Ready to receive file c1700-y-mz.122-11.T9.bin...
```

6. What must be done now for the IOS to be sent to the router?

   ____

   ____

   ____

   After transfer is successful, make sure that you restore the router and the terminal to a 9600 baud rate.

Command Reference

In the table that follows, record the command, *including the correct router prompt,* that fits the description. Fill in any blanks with the appropriate missing information.

Command	Description
	Loads an IOS named *image-name*.
	Loads an IOS named *image-name* from a TFTP server located at 172.16.10.3.
	Loads the IOS from ROM.
	Saves the running configuration to NVRAM.
	The last line of the output from this command shows what the configuration register is set to.
	Displays a listing of the files stored in flash memory.
	Changes the configuration register setting to 2142.

Lab 5-1: Using the boot system Command (5.1.3)

Figure 5-4 Topology for Lab 5-1

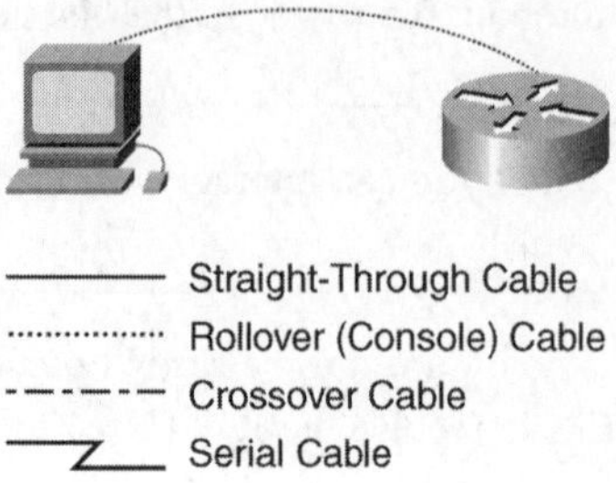

Table 5-1 Lab Equipment Configuration

Router Designation	Router Name	Enable Secret Password	Enable/vty/ Console Password
Router 1	GAD	class	cisco

Objectives

- Display information about the Cisco IOS Software image that is currently running.
- Determine where the IOS image is booting from.
- Check the amount of RAM, Flash memory, and nonvolatile RAM (NVRAM) memory the router has.
- Check the IOS image and Flash memory for space used and availability.
- Document the parts of the IOS image filename.
- Check and document the configuration register settings related to the boot method.
- Document a fallback boot sequence.

Background/Preparation

Cable a network similar to the one in Figure 5-4. You can use any router that meets the interface requirements in Figure 5-4 (that is, 800, 1600, 1700, 2500, and 2600 routers or a combination). Refer to the information in Appendix B, "Router Interface Summary," to correctly specify the interface identifiers based on the equipment in your lab. The 2600 Series routers produced the configuration output in this lab. Any other router might produce slightly different output.

Start a HyperTerminal session as you did in Lab 2-2, "Establishing a Console Session with HyperTerminal." Implement the procedure documented in Appendix C, "Erasing and Reloading the Router," before continuing with this lab.

Task 1: Log in to the Router

Connect to the router and log in.

Task 2: Enter Privileged EXEC Mode

Type **enable** at the command prompt.

Task 3: Save the Existing running-config to the startup-config

At the privileged EXEC command prompt, enter the following:

```
Router#copy running-config  startup-config Destination filename [startup-config]?  Enter
```

This task saves the current blank configuration.

Task 4: Configure the Router and View the Running Configuration File

Step 1. Configure the router with the information in Table 5-1.

Step 2. Enter **show running-config** at the router prompt. The router displays information on the running configuration file stored in RAM.

Do you see the configuration that you just entered? ______________________________

Task 5: Show Information About the Backup Configuration File

Enter **show startup-config** at the router prompt. The router displays information on the backup configuration file stored in NVRAM.

Do you see the configuration that you just entered? ______________________________

If not, why?

____

What command would make the running-config file and startup-config file identical?

____

Why is the startup-config file so important?

____

Is there any indication of the configuration register setting?

____

Task 6: Display the IOS Version and Other Important Information

Enter **show version** at the router prompt. The router returns information about the IOS image that is running in RAM.

What is the IOS version and rev level?

____

What is the name of the system image (IOS) file?

____

Where was the router IOS image booted from?

____

What type of processor and how much RAM does this router have?

____

What kind of router (platform type) is this?

____

The router backup configuration file is stored in NVRAM. How much NVRAM does this router have?

____

The router operating system (IOS) is stored in flash memory. How much flash memory does this router have?

____

What is the configuration register set to? What boot type does this setting specify?

____

Task 7: Create the Statements to Perform the Following Functions

Assuming that in Task 6, the configuration register was set to 0x2102, write the configuration mode commands to specify that the IOS image should be loaded from the following:

- ROM monitor: _______________
- Flash (without checking for **boot system** commands): _______________
- Flash (checks for **boot system** commands first): _______________
- ROM IOS: _______________

Note: ROM IOS is the default on older platforms.

Task 8: Show Information About the Flash Memory Device

Step 1. Enter **show flash** at the router prompt.

The router responds with information about the flash memory and what IOS image files are stored there.

Step 2. Document the following information:

How much flash memory is available and used?

____

What is the file that is stored in flash memory?

____

What is the size in bytes of the flash memory?

____

Task 9: Specify a Fallback Boot Sequence

Step 1. Write the **boot system** command to specify that the IOS image should be loaded from the following:

- Flash memory: _______________
- A Trivial File Transfer Protocol (TFTP) server: _______________
- ROM: _______________

Will this be a full IOS image? ___

To ensure that these commands are available for the router to use the next time you restart it, which task would need to be completed before reloading or power-cycling the router?

____

Step 2. When you finish the preceding tasks, log off (by typing **exit**) and turn off the router.

Lab 5-2: Troubleshooting Configuration Register Boot Problems (5.1.5)

Figure 5-5 Topology for Lab 5-2

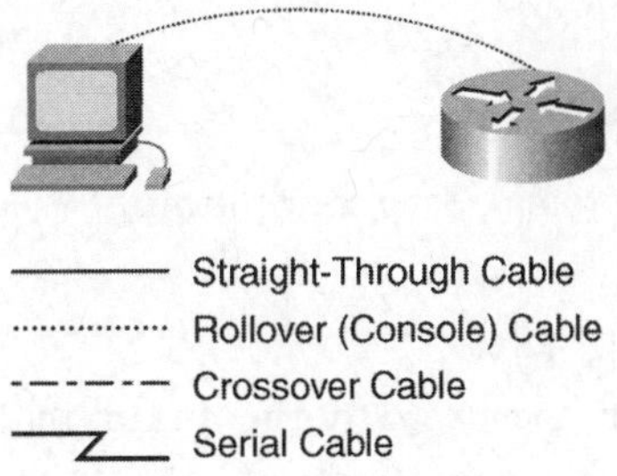

Table 5-2 Lab Equipment Configuration

Router Designation	Router Name	Enable Secret Password	Enable/vty/Console Password
Router 1	GAD	class	cisco

Objectives:

- Check and document the configuration register settings related to the boot method.
- Configure the router to boot using the configuration file in NVRAM, and reload the router.

Background/Preparation

Cable a network similar to the one in Figure 5-5. You can use any router that meets the interface requirements in Figure 5-5 (that is, 800, 1600, 1700, 2500, and 2600 routers or a combination). Refer to the information in Appendix B, "Router Interface Summary," to correctly specify the interface identifiers based on the equipment in your lab. The 1721 series routers produced the configuration output in this lab. Any other router might produce slightly different output.

Start a HyperTerminal session as you did in Lab 2-2.

Implement the procedure documented in Appendix C, "Erasing and Reloading the Router," before continuing with this lab.

Task 1: Log in to the Router

Connect to the router and log in.

Task 2: Configure the Router Name and Configuration Register Setting

Enter the following commands:

```
Router>enable
Router#configure terminal
Router(config)#hostname GAD
GAD(config)#config-register 0x2142
GAD(config)#exit
```

Task 3: Save the Existing running-config to the startup-config

At the privileged EXEC command prompt, enter the following:

```
GAD#copy running-config startup-config
Destination filename [startup-config]? Enter
```

Task 4: Restart the Router

At the privileged EXEC command prompt, enter the following:

```
GAD#reload
Proceed with reload? [confirm]  Enter
After the reload, the router responds with the following:
-- System Configuration Dialog --
Would you like to enter the initial configuration dialog? [yes/no]:  n
Type n and press  Enter.
```

Task 5: View the Running Configuration File

Enter **show running-config** at the privileged EXEC mode prompt. The router displays information on the running configuration file stored in RAM.

Do you see the configuration that you just entered? ______________________________

Task 6: Reload the Saved Configuration

At the privileged EXEC command prompt, enter the following:

```
Router#copy startup-config running-config
Destination filename [running-config]? Enter
```

Notice that the router name that was configured in Task 2 (GAD) is now displayed. Why did the Startup config file not load when you reloaded the router?

____

Task 7: Display the IOS Version and Other Important Information

Enter **show version** at the router prompt.

The router displays information about the IOS image that is running in RAM.

Notice that the end of the output shows a configuration register setting of 0x2142. This setting is the problem. The setting configures the router to ignore the Startup configuration file on bootup. The setting will be useful to boot up in the password recovery mode.

Task 8: Change the Configuration Register to Load the Startup Configuration File from NVRAM, Save, and Reload the Router

Enter global configuration mode and enter the following commands:

```
Router>enable
GAD#configure terminal
GAD(config)#config-register 0x2102
GAD(config)#exit
GAD#copy running-config  startup-config Destination filename [startup-config]?  Enter
```

```
GAD#reload
Proceed with reload? [confirm]Enter
```

Task 9. Verify the Configuration Register Setting and Log Out of the Router

After the router reboots, it should look to NVRAM for the Startup Configuration. Verify it by issuing the command **show version**:

```
GAD#show version
```

The results will be shown. You should be able to see the config-register 0x2102. When you finish these tasks, log off (by typing **exit**) and turn off the router.

Lab 5-3: Managing Configuration Files with TFTP (5.2.3)

Figure 5-6 Topology for Lab 5-3

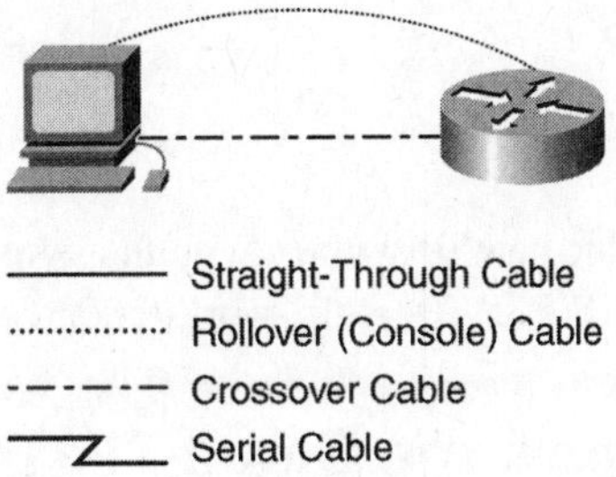

Table 5-3 Lab Equipment Configuration

Router Designation	Router Name	FastEthernet 0 Address	Subnet Mask
Router 1	GAD	192.168.14.1	255.255.255.0

The enable secret password for this router is **class**.

The enable, vty, and console passwords for this router are **cisco**.

Objectives:

- Back up a copy of a router's configuration file.
- Reload the backup configuration file from a TFTP server into RAM on a router.
- Save the new running-config to NVRAM.

Background/Preparation:

For documentation and recovery purposes, it is important to keep backup copies of router configuration files. You can store them in a central location such as a TFTP server for reference and retrieval if necessary.

Cable a network similar to the one in Figure 5-6. You can use any router that meets the interface requirements in Figure 5-6 (that is, 800, 1600, 1700, 2500, and 2600 routers or a combination). Refer to the information in Appendix B, "Router Interface Summary," to correctly specify the interface identifiers based on the equipment in your lab. The 1721 series routers produced the configuration output in this lab. Any other router might produce slightly different output.

Start a HyperTerminal session as you did in Lab 2-2.

Implement the procedure documented in Appendix C, "Erasing and Reloading the Router," before continuing with this lab.

Task 1: Configure the GAD Router

If you have trouble configuring the hostname, refer to Lab 3-2, "Configuring Router Passwords." If you have trouble configuring interfaces, refer to Lab 3-9, "Configuring Host Tables."

Verify the router's configuration by performing a **show running-config**. If it is not correct, fix any configuration errors and verify.

Task 2: Configure the Workstation

A workstation with the TFTP server software must be available for this lab. Verify that the software is available. If not, ask your instructor for assistance. The configuration for the TFTP server host connected to the GAD router is as follows:

- IP address: 192.168.14.2
- IP subnet mask: 255.255.255.0
- Default gateway: 192.168.14.1

Confirm that the host has accepted the new IP settings with the **winipcfg** command (Windows 9x) or the **ipconfig /all** command (Windows NT/200/XP) at the workstation command prompt.

Task 3: Start and Configure the Cisco TFTP Server

Start the TFTP server. If the computer is properly connected, there is no configuration for the Cisco TFTP server needed (see Figure 5-7). An alternative freeware TFTP server can also be used, such as tftpd32, which can be downloaded from http:// tftpd32.jounin.net/.

Figure 5-7 Cisco TFTP Server Setup

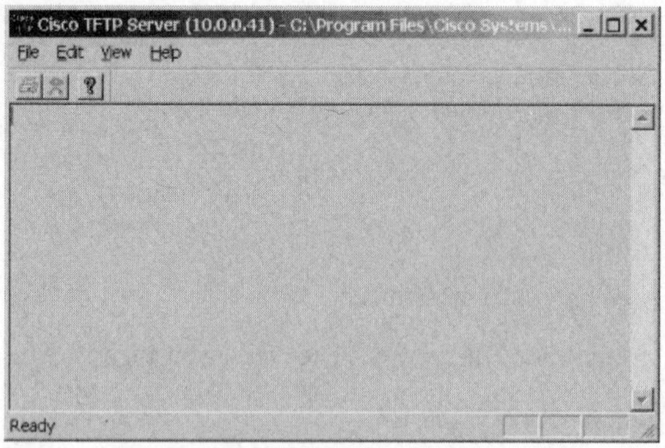

Task 4: Verify Connectivity by Pinging the TFTP Server

Step 1. Ping the TFTP server from the GAD router.

Step 2. If the ping fails, review the host and router configurations to resolve the problem.

Task 5: Copy the running-config to the TFTP Server

Step 1. Before copying the files, verify that the TFTP server is running.

Step 2. Record the IP address of the TFTP server. ______________________________

Step 3. Start the process by issuing the **copy running-config tftp** command from the privileged EXEC prompt, and then follow the prompts:

```
GAD#copy running-config tftp
Address or name of remote host []?  192.168.14.2
Destination filename [gad-confg]?  startup-config
!!
667 bytes copied in 0.036 secs (18528 bytes/sec)
```

Task 6: Verify the Transfer to the TFTP Server

Check the TFTP server log file by selecting **View > Log File.** The output should be similar to the following:

```
Mon Sep 16 14:10:08 2003: Receiving 'startup-config' file from 192.168.14.1 in binary mode
Mon Sep 16 14:11:14 2003: Successful.
```

Task 7: Copy the startup-config from the TFTP Server

Step 1. Now that you have backed up the startup-config, you need to test this image by restoring the file to the router. First, verify that the TFTP server is running, that it is sharing a network with the router, and that the router can reach it by pinging its IP address.

Step 2. Assume that the configuration on the GAD router has become corrupt. To simulate this, change the hostname of the router from GAD to "Router."

```
GAD(config)# hostname Router
```

What is the IP address of the TFTP server? ______________________________

Step 3. Complete the following to copy the startup-config file from the TFTP server to the router.

```
Router#copy tftp running-config
Address or name of remote host []?  192.168.14.2
Source filename []?  startup-config
Destination filename [running-config]?  [Enter]
Accessing tftp://192.168.14.2/startup-config...
Loading startup-config from 192.168.14.2 (via FastEthernet0): !
[OK - 667 bytes]
667 bytes copied in 9.584 secs (70 bytes/sec) GAD#
```

Task 8: Save the New running-config

Save the new running config to NVRAM using the following command:

```
GAD#copy running-config startup-config
Destination filename [startup-config]?[Enter]
Building configuration...
[OK]
```

Task 9: Test the Restored File

Issue the **show startup-config** command to verify the entire configuration. When you finish these tasks, log off (by typing **exit**) and turn off the router.

Lab 5-4: Managing IOS Images with TFTP (5.2.5)

Figure 5-8 Topology for Lab 5-4

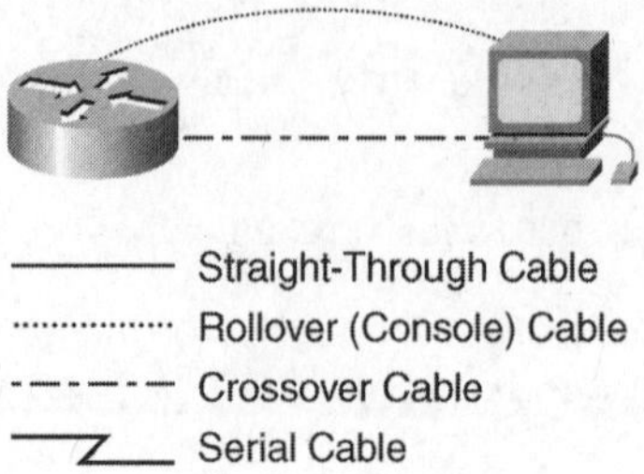

Table 5-4 Lab Equipment Configuration

Router Designation	Router Name	FastEthernet 0 Address	Subnet Mask
Router 1	GAD	192.168.14.1	255.255.255.0

Objectives:

- Back up a copy of a router's IOS from flash memory to a TFTP server.
- Reload the backup IOS image from a TFTP server into flash memory on a router.

Background/Preparation

For recovery purposes, it is important to keep backup copies of router IOS images. You can store them in a central location such as a TFTP server and retrieve them if necessary.

Cable a network similar to the one in Figure 5-8. You can use any router that meets the interface requirements in Figure 5-8 (that is, 800, 1600, 1700, 2500, and 2600 routers or a combination). Refer to the information in Appendix B, "Router Interface Summary," to correctly specify the interface identifiers based on the equipment in your lab. The 1721 Series routers produced the configuration output in this lab. Any other router might produce slightly different output.

Start a HyperTerminal session as you did in Lab 2-2.

Task 1: Configure the GAD Router

Step 1. If you have trouble configuring the hostname, refer to Lab 3-2. If you have trouble configuring interfaces, refer to Lab 3-9.

Step 2. Verify the router's configuration by performing a **show running-config** on the router. If it is not correct, fix any configuration errors and reverify.

Task 2: Configure the Workstation

A workstation with the TFTP server software must be available for this lab. Verify that the software is available. If not, ask your instructor for assistance. The configuration for the TFTP server host connected to the GAD router is as follows:

```
IP address: 192.168.14.2

IP subnet mask: 255.255.255.0

Default gateway: 192.168.14.1
```

Confirm that the host has accepted the new IP settings with the **ipconfig /all** command at the workstation command prompt.

Task 3: Collect Information to Document the Router

Issue the **show version** command.

What is the current value of the config register? ______________________________

How much flash memory does this router have? ______________________________

Is there at least 4 MB (4096 KB) of flash memory? ___ (This lab requires at least 4 MB of flash memory.)

What is the version number of boot ROM? ______________________________

Is the boot ROM version 5.2 or later? ___ (This lab requires 5.2 or later.)

Task 4: Collect More Information to Document the Router

Issue the **show flash** command.

Is a file already stored in flash memory? ______________________________

If so, what is the exact name of that file? ______________________________

How much flash memory is available (unused)? ______________________________

Task 5: Start and Configure the Cisco TFTP Server

Check with your instructor about the IP address of the Cisco TFTP server (see Figure 5-9). An alternative freeware TFTP server can also be used, such as tftpd32, which can be downloaded from http://tftpd32.jounin.net/.

Figure 5-9 Cisco TFTP Server

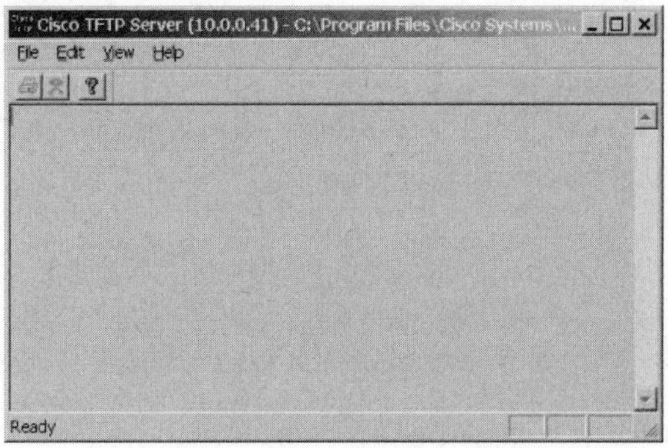

Task 6: Verify Connectivity by Pinging the TFTP Server

Ping the TFTP server from the GAD router.

If the ping fails, review the host and router configurations to resolve the problem.

Task 7: Prepare to Copy the IOS to the TFTP Server

Step 1. Before copying the files, verify that the TFTP server is running.

What is the IP address of the TFTP server?

____

Step 2. From the console session, enter **show flash**.

What is the name and length of the IOS image stored in Flash memory?

____

What attributes can you identify from codes in the IOS filename?

____

Task 8: Copy the IOS Image to the TFTP Server

From the console session in privileged EXEC mode, enter the **copy flash tftp** command. At the prompt, enter the IP address of the TFTP server.

```
GAD#copy flash tftp
Source filename [ ]? ________________________________
Address or name of remote host [ ]? ____________________
Destination filename [c1700-y-mz.122-11.T.bin]? _______________
```

After entering this command and answering the process requests, you should see the following output on the console. The process may take a few minutes, depending on the size of the image. Do *not* interrupt this process!

```
!!!!!!!!!!!!!!!!!!!!!!!!!!!!!!!!!!!!!!!!!!!!!!!!!!!!!!!!!!!!!!!!!!!!!!!!!!!!!!!!
!!!!!!!!!!!!!!!!!!!!!!!!!!!!!!!!!!!!!!!!!!!!!!!!!!!!!!!!!!!!!!!!!!!!!!!!!!!!!!!!
!!!!!!!!!!!!!!!!!!!!!!!!!!!!!!!!!!!!!!!!!!!!!!!!!!!!!!!!!!!!!!!!!!!!!!!!!!!!!!!!
!!!!!!!!!!!!!!!!!!!!!!!!!!!!!!!!!!!!!
4284648 bytes copied in 34.012 secs (125975 bytes/sec)
```

Task 9: Verify the Transfer to the TFTP Server

Step 1. Check the TFTP server log file by selecting **View > Log File.** The output should look something like the following:

```
Mon Sep 16 14:10:08 2003: Receiving 'c1700-y-mz.122-11.T.bin' in binary mode
Mon Sep 16 14:11:14 2003: Successful.
```

Step 2. Verify the Flash memory image size in the TFTP server directory. To locate it, choose **View > Options**. This command shows the TFTP server root directory. It should be similar to the following, unless the default directories were changed:

```
C:\Program Files\Cisco Systems\Cisco TFTP Server
```

Step 3. Locate this directory using Windows Explorer or My Computer and look at the detail listing of the file. The file length in the **show flash** command should be the same file size as the file stored on the TFTP server. If the file sizes are not identical, check with your instructor.

Note: If you aren't using the Cisco TFTP server, consult the supplied documentation for the default TFTP server root directory.

Task 10: Copy the IOS Image from the TFTP Server

Step 1. Now that the IOS image is backed up, you must test it and restore IOS to the router. Verify again that the TFTP server is running, that it is sharing a network with the router, and that the router can reach it by pinging the TFTP server IP address.

Step 2. Record the IP address of the TFTP server: ______________________________

Step 3. To start the actual copying, from the privileged EXEC prompt, type the following:

```
GAD#copy tftp flash
Address or name of remote host [ ]?192.168.14.2
Source filename []?c1700-y-mz.122-11.T.bin
Destination filename [c1700-y-mz.122-11.T.bin]?  Enter
%Warning:There is a file already existing with this name
Do you want to over write? [confirm]  Enter
Accessing tftp://192.168.14.2/c1700-y-mz.122-11.T.bin...
Erase flash: before copying? [confirm]  Enter
Erasing the flash filesystem will remove all files! Continue? [confirm]  Enter
Erasing device...
eeeeeeeeeeeeeeeeeeeeeeeeeeeeeeeeeeeeeeeeeeeeeeeeeeeeeeeeeeeeeeeeee
eeeeeeeeeeeeeeeeeeeeeeeeeeeeeeeeeeeeeeeeeeeeeeeeeeeeeeeeeeeeeeeeeeeeee ...erased
Erase of flash: complete
Loading c1700-y-mz.122-11.T.bin from 192.168.14.2 (via
FastEthernet0):!!!!!!!!!!
!!!!!!!!!!!!!!!!!!!!!!!!!!!!!!!!!!!!!!!!!!!!!!!!!!!!!!!!!!!!!!!!!!!!!!!!!!!!!!!!!
!!!!!!!!!!!!!!!!!!!!!!!!!!!!!!!!!!!!!!!!!!!!!!!!!!!!!!!!!!!!!!!!!!!!!!!!!!!!!!!!!
!!!!!!!!!!!!!!!!!!!!!!!!!!!!!!
[OK - 4284648 bytes]
Verifying checksum...  OK (0x9C8A)
4284648 bytes copied in 26.584 secs (555739 bytes/sec)
```

The router might prompt you to erase flash memory. Will the image fit in the available flash memory? ______________________________

If you erased the flash memory, what happened on the router console screen as it was doing so?

____

What is the size of the file being loaded?

____

What happened on the router console screen as the file was being downloaded?

____

Was the verification successful? ______________________________

Was the whole operation successful? ______________________________

Task 11: Test the Restored IOS Image

Step 1. To verify that the router image is correct, cycle the router power and observe the startup process to confirm that there were no Flash memory errors. If there are no errors, the router's IOS should start correctly.

Step 2. Further verify the IOS image in Flash memory by issuing the **show version** command, which shows output similar to the following:

```
System image file is "flash:c1700-y-mz.122-11.T.bin"
```

Step 3. When you finish Tasks 1 through 11, log off (by typing **exit**) and turn off the router.

Lab 5-5: Password Recovery Procedures (5.2.6a)

Figure 5-10 Topology for Lab 5-5

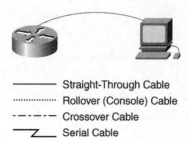

Straight-Through Cable
Rollover (Console) Cable
Crossover Cable
Serial Cable

Table 5-5 Lab Equipment Configuration

Router Designation	Router Name	Enable Secret Password	Enable/vty/Console Passwords
Router 1	GAD	class	cisco

Objective

- Gain access to a router with an unknown privileged EXEC mode (enable) password.

Background/Preparation

This lab demonstrates how you gain access to a router with an unknown privileged EXEC mode (enable) password. Anyone with this procedure and access to a console port on a router can change the password and take control of the router. That is why routers must also have physical security to prevent unauthorized access.

Cable a network similar to the one in Figure 5-10. You can use any router that meets the interface requirements in the diagram (that is, 800, 1600, 1700, 2500, and 2600 routers or a combination). Refer to the information in Appendix B, "Router Interface Summary," to correctly specify the interface identifiers to be used based on the equipment in your lab. The 1721 series routers produced the configuration output in this lab. Any other router might produce slightly different output.

Start a HyperTerminal session as you did in Lab 2-2.

Note: Configure the hostname and passwords on the router. Let an instructor, lab assistant, or other student configure a basic configuration, change the enable secret password, perform **copy running-config startup-config**, and reload the router.

Note: The version of HyperTerminal with Windows 95, 98, NT, and 2000 was developed for Microsoft by Hilgraeve. Some versions might not issue a "break" sequence as required for the Cisco router password-recovery technique. If you have this version, upgrade to HyperTerminal Private Edition (PE), which is free for personal and educational use. You can download the program at http://www.hilgraeve.com.

Task 1: Attempt to Log in to the Router

Make the necessary console connections and establish a HyperTerminal session with the router. Attempt to log in to the router using the privileged mode password **class**. Your output should look something like the following:

```
Router>enable
Password:
Password:
```

```
Password:
% Bad secrets
Router>
```

Task 2: Document the Current Configuration Register Setting

Step 1. At the user EXEC prompt, type **show ver**.

Step 2. Record the value displayed for the configuration register (for example, 0x2102): ___________

Task 3: Enter ROM Monitor Mode

Turn the router off, wait a few seconds, and turn it back on. When the router starts displaying "System Bootstrap, Version …" on the HyperTerminal screen, press the **Ctrl** key and the **Break** key together. The router will boot in ROM monitor mode. Depending on the router hardware, you get one of several prompts, such as **rommon 1 >** or simply >.

Task 4: Examine the ROM Monitor Mode Help

Type **?** at the prompt. The output should be similar to the following:

```
rommon 1 >?
alias                    set and display aliases command
boot                     boot up an external process
break                    set/show/clear the breakpoint
confreg                  configuration register utility
context                  display the context of a loaded image
dev                      list the device table
dir                      list files in file system
dis                      display instruction stream
help                     monitor builtin command help
history                  monitor command history
meminfo                  main memory information
repeat                   repeat a monitor command
reset                    system reset
set                      display the monitor variables
sysret                   print out info from last system return
tftpdnld                 tftp image download
xmodem                   x/ymodem image download
```

Task 5: Change the Configuration Register Setting to Boot Without Loading the Configuration File

From ROM monitor mode, type **confreg 0x2142** to change the configuration register.

```
rommon 2>confreg 0x2142
```

Task 6: Restart the Router

Step 1. From ROM monitor mode, type **reset** or power-cycle the router:

```
rommon 2>reset
```

Step 2. Because of the new configuration register setting, the router will not load the configuration file. When the system prompts, "Would you like to enter the initial configuration dialog? [yes]," enter **no** and press **Enter**.

Task 7: Enter Privileged EXEC Mode and Change the Password

Step 1. At the user EXEC mode prompt, type **enable** and press **Enter** to go to privileged EXEC mode without a password.

Step 2. Use the command **copy startup-config running-config** to restore the existing configuration. Because you are already in privileged EXEC mode, you do not need a password.

Step 3. Type **configure terminal** to enter global configuration mode.

Step 4. In global configuration mode, type **enable secret class** to change the secret password.

Step 5. While still in global configuration mode, type **config-register** *xxxxxxx*, where *xxxxxxx* is the original configuration register value recorded in Task 2, and press **Enter**.

Step 6. Press **Ctrl-Z** to return to privileged EXEC mode.

Step 7. Use the **copy running-config startup-config** command to save the new configuration.

Step 8. Before restarting the router, verify the new configuration setting. From the privileged EXEC prompt, enter the **show version** command and press **Enter**.

Step 9. Verify that the last line of output is the following:

```
Configuration register is 0x2142 (will be 0x2102 at next reload)
```

Step 10. Use the **reload** command to restart the router.

Task 8: Verify the New Password and Configuration

When the router reloads, the enable password will be **class**.

When you complete all eight tasks, log off (by typing **exit**) and turn the router off.

Lab 5-6: Managing IOS Images with ROMMON and Xmodem (5.2.6b)

Figure 5-11 Topology for Lab 5-6

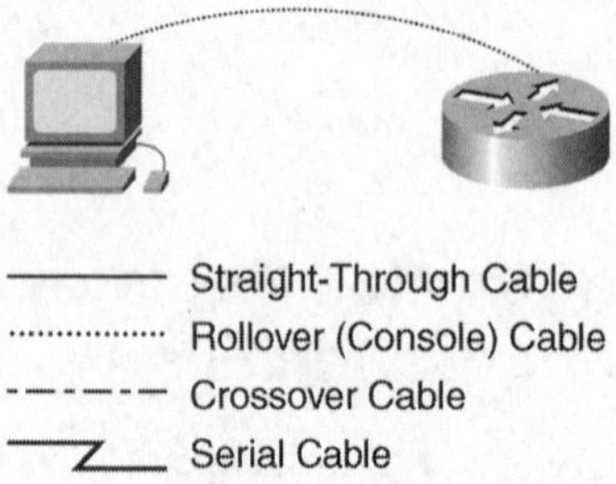

Objectives:

- Recover a Cisco router stuck in ROM monitor (ROMMON) mode due to a missing or corrupt IOS or boot flash memory image.
- Learn how to avoid having to use Xmodem to restore an IOS file.

Background/Preparation

You will need this process only in an emergency when a user deletes or erases the IOS and there is no possibility of uploading a new version of the IOS from a TFTP server. The first tasks show you how to avoid needing this procedure.

In case you cannot avoid the procedure, this lab explains how to use the **xmodem** command at the console to download IOS using ROMMON. You can use Xmodem on a group of routers and in disaster-recovery situations where the router has no valid IOS or boot flash memory image to boot from. (Hence, it boots only in ROMMON.) You can also use this procedure where there are no TFTP servers or network connections and a direct PC connection (or a modem connection) to the router's console is the only viable option. Because this procedure relies on the router's console speed and the PC's serial port, it can take a long time to download an image. Downloading a Cisco IOS Software Release 12.1(16) IP Plus image to a Cisco 1600 series router using a speed of 38,400bps takes approximately 25 minutes. This process is valid for the Cisco 827, 1600, 1700, 2600, 3600, and 3700 series routers.

Cable a network similar to the one in Figure 5-11. You can use any router that meets the interface requirements in Figure 5-11 (that is, 800, 1600, 1700, 2500, and 2600 routers or a combination). Refer to the information in Appendix B, "Router Interface Summary," to correctly specify the interface identifiers based on the equipment in your lab. The 1721 series routers produced the configuration output in this lab. Any other router might produce slightly different output.

Start a HyperTerminal session as you did in Lab 2-2.

Implement the procedure documented in Appendix C, "Erasing and Reloading the Router," before continuing with this lab.

Note: To complete this lab, a copy of the recommended Cisco IOS Software image (for example, **c1700-y-mz.122-11.T.bin**) must be available on your PC.

Task 1: Enter the ROM Monitor Mode

To simulate this, power-cycle the router and press **Ctrl-Break** to enter ROM monitor mode. Depending on the router hardware, one of several prompts, such as rommon 1 > or simply >, may appear.

Task 2: Find a Valid Image in Flash Memory

From the ROM Monitor prompt, issue the **dir flash:** command for each available device, and look for a valid IOS image.

```
rommon 3 >  dir  flash:
         File size             Checksum   File name
 3307884 bytes (0x804b4c)0x6ba0   c1700-ny-mz.121-6.bin
rommon 4 >
```

Task 3: Recover from the Listed Images if You See Any

Try to boot from any image that is listed in Task 1. If the image is valid, you will return to normal operation mode:

```
rommon 5 > boot flash:c1700-ny-mz.121-6.bin
program load complete, entry point: 0x80008000, size: 0x804a30
Self decompressing the image : ####################################
########...
```

Task 4: Record Information Using show version

Step 1. If none of the files are valid, you must download a new one using one of the following procedures. The first step is to record the **show version** information at initial setup. It will provide the information you need about the IOS image name.

```
Cisco Internetwork Operating System Software

IOS (tm) C1700 Software (C1700-Y-M), Version 12.2(11)T,  RELEASE SOFTWARE (fc1)
TAC Support: http://www.cisco.com/tac

Copyright  1986-2002 by cisco Systems, Inc.

Compiled Wed 31-Jul-02 09:08 by ccai

Image text-base: 0x80008124, data-base: 0x807E332C

ROM: System Bootstrap, Version 12.2(7r)XM1, RELEASE SOFTWARE (fc1)

Router uptime is 15 minutes

System returned to ROM by reload

System image file is "flash:c1700-y-mz.122-11.T.bin"

cisco 1721 (MPC860P) processor (revision 0x100) with 29492K/3276K bytes of
memory.

Processor board ID FOC06380F0T (479701011), with hardware revision 0000

MPC860P processor: part number 5, mask 2

Bridging software.

X.25 software, Version 3.0.0.

1 FastEthernet/IEEE 802.3 interface(s)

2 Serial(sync/async) network interface(s)

32K bytes of non-volatile configuration memory.

16384K bytes of processor board System flash (Read/Write)

 --More--

Configuration register is 0x2102
```

Step 2. Record the highlighted information in case you need to perform this procedure.

Task 5: Configure the Boot Register to Enter ROMMON Mode

Configure HyperTerminal for 8-N-1 at 9600 bps and connect your PC's serial port to the router's console port. When you are connected, you need to get to the ROMMON prompt (rommon 1>). Typically, if the router's IOS image and boot Flash memory image are both corrupt, the router only comes up in ROMMON mode. If you need to get to the ROMmon prompt, change the configuration register (typically 0x2102, as given by **show version**) to 0x0 as follows:

```
Router>ena

Router#configure terminal
```

Enter configuration commands, one per line. End with **Ctrl-Z**.

```
Router(config)#config-register 0x0

Router(config)#exit

Router#

*Mar  1 00:29:21.023: %SYS-5-CONFIG_I: Configured from console by console

Router#reload

System configuration has been modified. Save? [yes/no]:  n

Proceed with reload? [confirm][Enter]

*Mar  1 00:30:32.235: %SYS-5-RELOAD: Reload requested by console.

System Bootstrap, Version 12.2(7r)XM1, RELEASE SOFTWARE (fc1)
```

```
TAC Support: http://www.cisco.com/tac
Copyright  2001 by cisco Systems, Inc.
C1700 platform with 32768 Kbytes of main memory rommon 1 >
```

Task 6: View Available Commands from the ROMMON Prompt

Enter the following at the ROMMON prompt:

```
rommon 1 >?
alias                set and display aliases command
boot                 boot up an external process
break                set/show/clear the breakpoint
confreg              configuration register utility
context              display the context of a loaded image
dev                  list the device table
dir                  list files in file system
dis                  display instruction stream
help                 monitor builtin command help
history              monitor command history
meminfo              main memory information
repeat               repeat a monitor command
reset                system reset
set                  display the monitor variables
sync                 write monitor environment to NVRAM
sysret               print out info from last system return
tftpdnld             tftp image download
unalias              unset an alias
unset                unset a monitor variable
xmodem               x/ymodem image download
```

This lab uses **confreg** to reset the console speed and **xmodem** to transfer the file.

Task 7: Reset the Terminal Speed for a Faster Download

By specifying a data rate of 115,200bps, for example, you can increase the download rate, reducing download time. Follow these steps to reset the speed on the router:

```
rommon 2 >confreg
Configuration Summary
(Virtual Configuration Register: 0x1820)
enabled are:
break/abort has effect
console baud: 9600
boot: the ROM Monitor
do you wish to change the configuration? y/n  [n]:     y
enable  "diagnostic mode"? y/n  [n]:[Enter]
enable  "use net in IP bcast address"? y/n  [n]:  [Enter]
enable  "load rom after netboot fails"? y/n  [n]:  [Enter]
enable  "use all zero broadcast"? y/n  [n]:  [Enter]
disable "break/abort has effect"? y/n  [n]:     y
```

```
enable  "ignore system config info"? y/n  [n]:  [Enter]
change console baud rate? y/n  [n]:     y
enter rate: 0 = 9600,  1 = 4800,  2 = 1200,  3 = 2400
4 = 19200, 5 = 38400, 6 = 57600, 7 = 115200  [0]:     7
change the boot characteristics? y/n  [n]:  [Enter]
Configuration Summary
(Virtual Configuration Register: 0x1920)
enabled are:
console baud: 115200
boot: the ROM Monitor
do you wish to change the configuration? y/n  [n]:     y
```

You must reset or power cycle for new config to take effect

```
rommon 3 >reset
```

Note: You must change the HyperTerminal setting to reflect the new console speed of 115,200 instead of 9600. Otherwise, you will see garbled output until you change the settings.

```
System Bootstrap, Version 12.2(7r)XM1, RELEASE SOFTWARE (fc1) TAC Support:
http://www.cisco.com/tac
Copyright  2001 by cisco Systems, Inc.
C1700 platform with 32768 Kbytes of main memory
```

Task 8: Use the xmodem Command to Request a File from the Host

From the ROMMON prompt, issue the **xmodem** command. However, before issuing the **xmodem** command, *ensure that you have the new IOS image on your PC.*

```
rommon 2 > xmodem
usage: xmodem [-cyrx] <destination filename>
-c  CRC-16
-y  ymodem-batch protocol
-r  copy image to dram for launch
-x  do not launch on download completion
rommon 3 > xmodem c1700-y-mz.122-11.T.bin
Do not start the sending program yet...
   File size      Checksum             File name
   4284648 bytes (0x4160e8)   0x9c8a  c1700-y-mz.122-11.T.bin
WARNING: All existing data in bootflash will be lost!
Invoke this application only for disaster recovery.
Do you wish to continue? y/n  [n]:     y
Ready to receive file c1700-y-mz.122-11.T.bin ...
```

Task 9: Send the File from the HyperTerminal Program

Step 1. From the HyperTerminal program, send the IOS file using the tasks outlined in Figure 5-12.

Figure 5-12 Sending the IOS file using Hyper Terminal

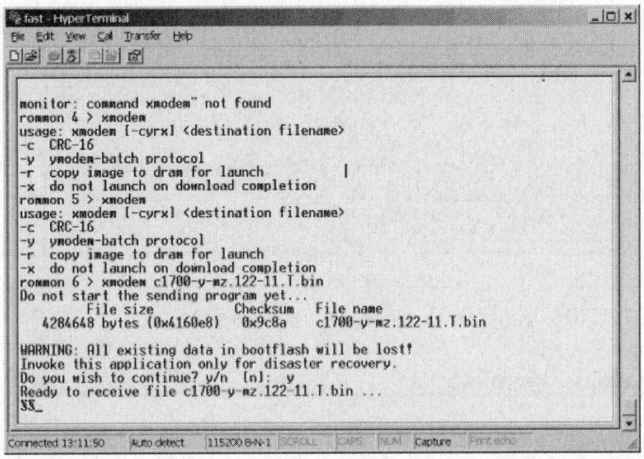

Step 2. Select **Transfer > Send File** and specify the location of the IOS file on the host hard drive, as shown in Figure 5-13.

Figure 5-13 Specifying the IOS File Location

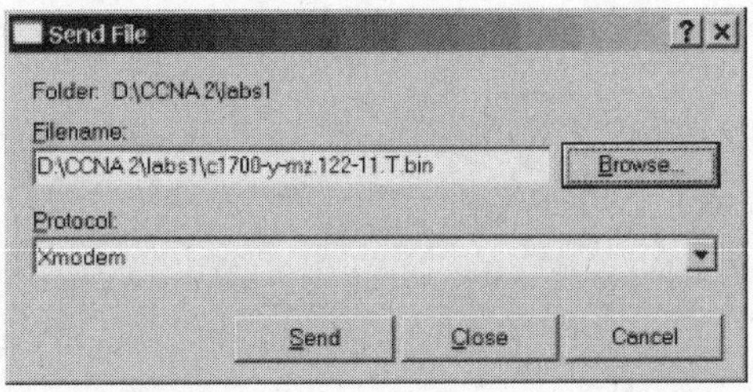

Step 3. Click **Send** to initiate the file transfer to the router (see Figure 5-14).

Figure 5-14 IOS File Transfer Initiated

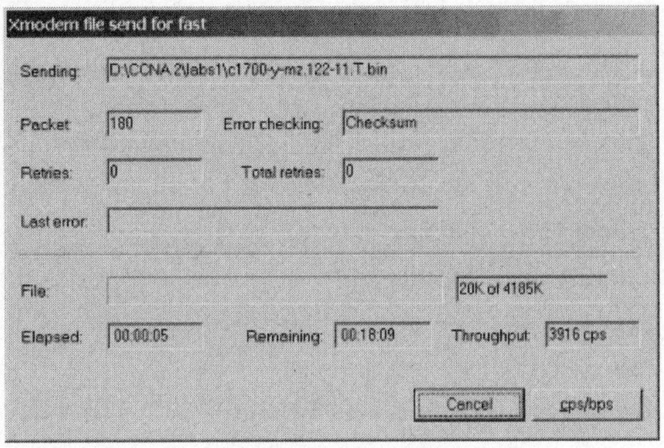

As the transfer progresses, it will look like Figure 5-15.

Figure 5-15 IOS File Transfer Progress

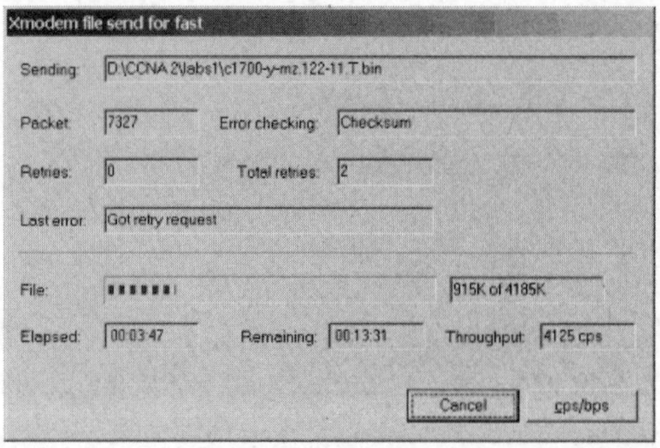

When finished, the transfer will look like Figure 5-16.

Figure 5-16 IOS File Transfer Complete

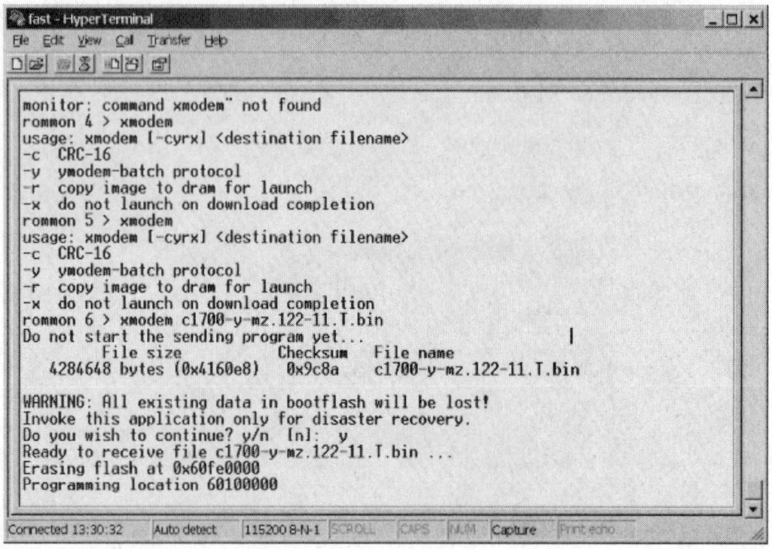

When the process is finished, the router reloads.

Task 10: Reset the Boot Register and the Console Speed

Step 1. From the configuration prompt, set the boot register back to 0x2102 or the original setting before the IOS transfer. Use the **config-register** command at the global configuration prompt:

```
Router(config)#config-register 0x2102
Router(config)#exit
Router#show flash
System flash directory:
File  Length   Name/status
  1   4284648  c1700-y-mz.122-11.T.bin
[4285452 bytes used, 12491764 available, 16777216 total]
16384K bytes of processor board System flash (Read/Write)
Reset the console speed in HyperTerminal to 9600.
Router(config)#line con 0
Router(config-line)#speed 9600
Router(config-line)#^Z
```

Step 2. HyperTerminal will stop responding. Reconnect to the router with HyperTerminal using 9600 bps, 8-N-1.c. Save the configuration to NVRAM on the router.

```
Router#copy running-config startup-config
```

Task 11: Review the New Settings

Reload the router and review the new settings using the **show version** command:

```
Router#show version
Cisco Internetwork Operating System Software
IOS (tm) C1700 Software (C1700-Y-M), Version 12.2(11)T,  RELEASE SOFTWARE (fc1)
TAC Support: http://www.cisco.com/tac
Copyright  1986-2002 by cisco Systems, Inc.
Compiled Wed 31-Jul-02 09:08 by ccai
Image text-base: 0x80008124, data-base: 0x807E332C
ROM: System Bootstrap, Version 12.2(7r)XM1, RELEASE SOFTWARE (fc1)
Router uptime is 12 minutes
System returned to ROM by power-on
System image file is "flash:c1700-y-mz.122-11.T.bin"
cisco 1721 (MPC860P) processor (revision 0x100) with 29492K/3276K bytes of memory
Processor board ID FOC06380F95 (3103823619), with hardware revision 0000
MPC860P processor: part number 5, mask 2
Bridging software.
X.25 software, Version 3.0.0.
1 FastEthernet/IEEE 802.3 interface(s)
2 Serial(sync/async) network interface(s)
32K bytes of non-volatile configuration memory.
16384K bytes of processor board System flash (Read/Write)
 --More--
Configuration register is 0x2102
```

Challenge Lab 5-7: Use TFTP to Load IOS and Configuration File

Figure 5-17 Using TFTP to Load an IOS and Configuration File

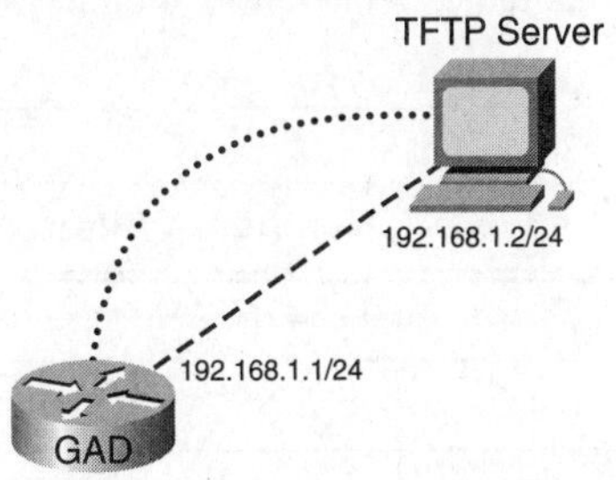

Objectives:

This lab contains the following objectives:

- Connect a router and workstation using a rollover cable
- Display and document information about the Cisco IOS image that is currently running

- Establish connectivity with a TFTP server on an attached workstation
- Check and document configuration register settings related to the boot method
- Change the boot sequence with boot system commands to load an IOS from the TFTP server
- Back up a copy of a router configuration file and IOS image to the TFTP server

Equipment:

You need a DB9–to–RJ-45 terminal adapter, a rollover cable, a crossover cable, a PC with HyperTerminal and TFTP server software, and a router. This lab can be done with any 1700, 2500, or 2600 Series router.

NetLab Compatibility Notes:

This lab cannot be effectively completed using NetLab.

Task 1: Cable the Lab and Gather Information

Step 1. Cable the lab according to the topology shown in Figure 5-17. A switch or hub is not needed, but can be used.

Step 2. Configure the router and workstation, including any basic configurations required by your instructor.

Step 3. Enter the correct command to list the information needed to fill in the table that follows and fill out column 2 in that table. What command did you enter?

____

IOS name	
Amount of RAM	
Type and number of interfaces	
Amount of NVRAM	
Amount of flash	
Configuration register setting	

Step 4. Enter the correct command to list the information needed to fill in the table that follows and fill out columns 2 and 3 in that table. What command did you enter?

____

Parameter	Number of Bytes	Number of Megabytes
Size of file stored flash bytes	12347672	11.78
Flash being used		
Flash available		
Total size of flash		

Step 5. You should have a backup IOS saved in your TFTP server's root folder. If not, ask your instructor how to proceed. What is the full name of the backup IOS stored in the TFTP server's root folder?

____

What is the file size in bytes?

____

Step 6. Make sure that your TFTP server is running on the attached workstation and then test connectivity. What command did you enter to test connectivity?

____

____

____

____

Successful? If not, troubleshoot.

Task 2: Change the Configuration Register Setting

Step 1. Your current configuration register setting should be 0x2102. What command would you enter to change the configuration register setting to 0x2102 if it was not the current setting?

____

____

Note: If the configuration was not 0x2102, set it to 0x2102 and reload the router.

Step 2. On most platforms, the 0x2102 setting usually means that the router looks for boot system commands in NVRAM. What are the fours steps a router follows to locate and load the IOS?

____

____

____

____

Task 3: Add Statements to Specify a Different Boot Sequence

Step 1. You will specify the TFTP server as the first place the router should look to locate and load the IOS. What command would specify that the IOS file on your TFTP server be loaded first?

____

Step 2. If the TFTP server fails, you want the router to look in flash. What command would specify that the IOS file in flash be loaded second?

____

____

Note: The image name does not have to specified unless the image is not the first file listed in the flash directory.

Step 3. If no IOS is available, you want the router to load the IOS in ROM. What command would specify that the IOS file in ROM be loaded last?

____

Task 4: Test Your Boot System Commands

Step 1. Because the router looks to NVRAM first for the boot system commands, back up your current configurations. What command did you enter?

____

Step 2. Again, make sure that your router can connect to the TFTP server on the workstation, and make sure that the TFTP server is running.

Step 3. Reload your router. The router should load the IOS stored in your TFTP root folder on the TFTP server. You can see evidence that the IOS is loading by watching either the TFTP or HyperTerminal window.

In HyperTerminal, you should see something similar to the following:

```
Loading c2600-ik9o3s-mz.122-8.T10.bin from 192.168.1.2 (via FastEthernet0/0):
!!!!!!!!!!!!!!!!!!!!!!!!!!!!!!!!!!!!!!!!!!!!!!!!!!!!!!!!!!!!!!!!!!!!!!!!!!!!!!
!!!!!!!!!!!!!!!!!!!!!!!!!!!!!!!!!!!!!!!!!!!!!!!!!!!!!!!!!!!!!!!!!!!!!!!!!!!!!!
!!!!!!!!!!!!!!!!!!!!!!!!!!!!!!!!!!!!!!!!!!!!!!!!!!!!!!!!!!!!!!!!!!!!!!!!!!!!!!
!!!!!!!!!!!!!!!!!!!!!!!!!!!!!!!!!!!!!
[OK - 14,341,200/16777216]
```

After the IOS is fully loaded, what does the router load next?

____

Step 4. Enter the command to display what IOS is currently running on the router.

____

Besides watching the progress of the upload in the router window or TFTP window, how do you know that the IOS for the TFTP server successfully loaded?

____

____

____

Task 5: Back Up the Configuration File to a TFTP Server

Enter the commands necessary to back up your current configuration to the TFTP server.

____

____

____

____

____

____

Was the backup successful? ____

How long did it take? ____

What is the name of the configuration file stored in your TFTP root folder? ____________________

What is the size of the configuration file? ____

Task 6: Back Up the IOS Stored in Flash to a TFTP Server

If you successfully uploaded the IOS from the TFTP server, the IOS in flash is probably a different version than the one currently running in RAM. You should have a backup of the IOS in Flash.

Step 1. Before you can back up the IOS, you need its filename. Enter the command necessary to view the IOS filename stored in flash.

____

Step 2. Enter the commands necessary to back up the IOS stored in Flash to the TFTP server.

____

____

____

____

____

____

____

____

____

Was the backup successful? ____

How long did it take? ____

Instructor Confirmation

Your instructor can now verify the following:

- The IOS loaded into RAM came from your TFTP server
- The TFTP server has a copy of your configuration file
- The TFTP server has a copy of your flash IOS

Instructor initials ___________

CHAPTER 6

Routing and Routing Protocols

The Study Guide portion of this chapter uses a combination of fill-in-the-blank, open-ended questions and unique custom exercises to test your knowledge of the theory of routing and routing protocols.

The Lab Exercises portion of this chapter includes all the online curriculum labs as well as a comprehensive lab and a challenge lab to ensure that you have mastered the practical, hands-on skills needed for routing and routing protocols.

Study Guide

Adding Connected and Static IP Routes

A router learns about directly connected networks for each local interface that is both configured with an IP address and in the "up and up" state. Routers also learn about routes that are manually configured by the network engineer or through dynamic processes. This section includes exercises to help you hone your skills in reading a Cisco IOS routing table. You also work through some static route configuration exercises and research the concept of administrative distance.

Dissecting a Routing Table Entry Exercise

Understanding entries in the routing table is a core skill you must learn to gather information about your network and troubleshoot connectivity problems. Refer to the following command output. Record the command that was entered to display this information.

```
RTB# show ip route
Codes: C - connected, S - static, R - RIP, M - mobile, B - BGP
       D - EIGRP, EX - EIGRP external, O - OSPF, IA - OSPF inter area
       N1 - OSPF NSSA external type 1, N2 - OSPF NSSA external type 2
       E1 - OSPF external type 1, E2 - OSPF external type 2
       i - IS-IS, su - IS-IS summary, L1 - IS-IS level-1, L2 - IS-IS level-2
       ia - IS-IS inter area, * - candidate default, U - per-user static route
       o - ODR, P - periodic downloaded static route

Gateway of last resort is 192.168.2.1 to network 0.0.0.0

C    192.168.4.0/24 is directly connected, Serial0/1
S    192.168.5.0/24 is directly connected, Serial0/1
R    192.168.1.0/24 [120/1] via 192.168.2.1, 00:00:17, Serial0/0
C    192.168.2.0/24 is directly connected, Serial0/0
C    192.168.3.0/24 is directly connected, FastEthernet0/0
S*   0.0.0.0/0 [1/0] via 192.168.2.1
```

Dissect the information by indicating what each of the following represents:

R

192.168.1.0

/24

[120

/1]

via 192.168.2.1

00:00:17

Serial0/0

Static Routing Configuration Exercise 1

Referring to Figure 6-1, neither static nor dynamic routing has yet been configured. However, all interfaces are in the "up and up" state.

Figure 6-1 Static Routing Configuration Exercise 1

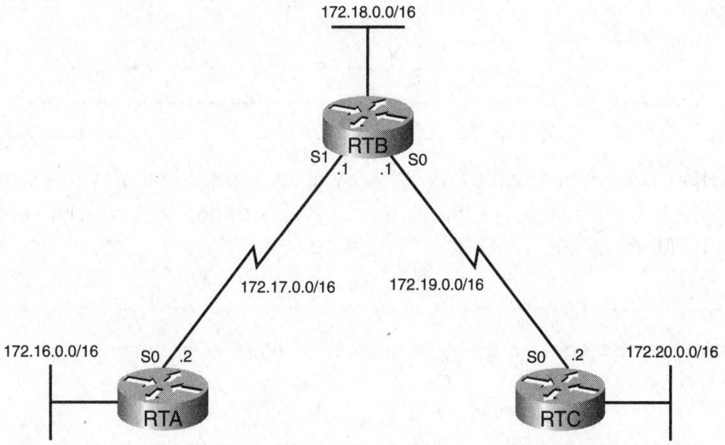

Use Figure 6-1 to answer the following questions:

1. List the details of the routes that are currently shown in each router's routing table.

   RTA:

   RTB:

RTC:

____

____

2. Assume that RTA will be the gateway router for RTB and RTC. What would you recommend configuring on RTB and RTC?

____

3. Record the command that you would enter on RTB using the *next-hop* IP address argument.

____

4. Record the command that you would enter on RTC using the *outbound-interface* argument.

____

5. Explain in detail the difference between the *next-hop* IP address argument and the *outbound-interface* argument?

____

____

____

____

____

____

6. RTA must establish connectivity with networks that are not listed in its routing table. How many networks does RTA still need to have statically configured?

____

7. Record the static route commands using the *next-hop* IP address argument to establish connectivity to these networks.

____

____

____

8. RTB has a default route pointing to RTA, which you configured in a previous step. Therefore, RTB has access to the LAN attached to RTA. However, RTB still does not have full connectivity. Which network is still not accessible by RTB?

____

9. Record the static route command using the *outbound-interface* argument to establish connectivity to this network.

____

10. Does RTC need further configuration? If so, what? If not, why not?

____

____

Static Routing Configuration Exercise 2

Note: You should complete Static Routing Configuration Exercise 1 before attempting this exercise.

Referring to Figure 6-2, neither static nor dynamic routing has been configured yet. However, all interfaces are in the "up and up" state. The ISDN link between RTA and RTC will be used only if one of the T1 links goes down.

Figure 6-2 Static Routing Configuration Exercise 2

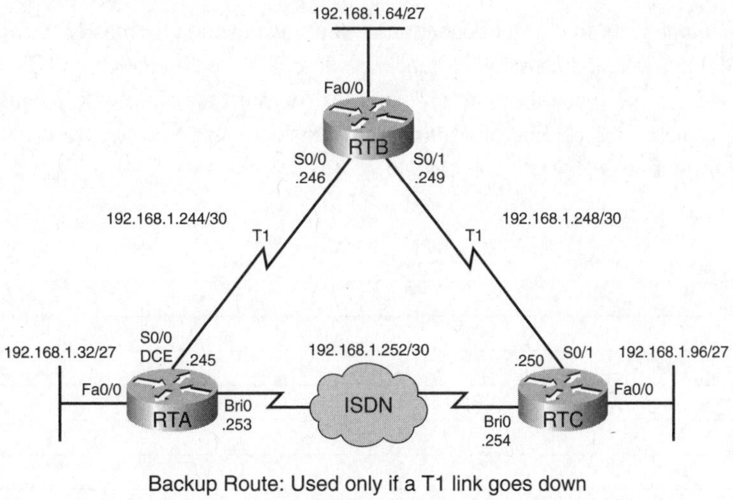

Use Figure 6-2 to answer the following questions:

1. Record the commands to configure static routes on RTA using the *outbound-interface* argument for all networks not directly connected. Skip the ISDN link for now.

____

____

____

2. Record the commands to configure static routes on RTB using the *next-hop* IP address argument for all networks not directly connected. Do not configure a route to the ISDN network.

____

____

3. Record the command to configure a default route on RTC using the *outbound-interface* argument and pointing to RTB.

____

4. Record the command to configure a backup static route using the *outbound-interface* argument on RTA pointing to the LAN on RTC. This route will use the ISDN network if the T1 link between RTA and RTB goes down.

____

5. Record the command to configure a backup default route using the *next-hop* IP address argument on RTC pointing to RTA. This route will use the ISDN network if the T1 link between RTB and RTC goes down.

____

Internet Research: What Is Administrative Distance?

Administrative distance is an important concept that you must eventually master. Search the Internet to see what you can find out about administrative distance, because it is used by the Cisco IOS. Define administrative distance, including its purpose and the values it can take. You must not simply "copy and paste" your answer, but rather express your understanding of administrative distance in your own words. Be sure to record the source of your information.

____
____
____
____
____
____
____
____

Concept Questions

1. What are the three ways that a router learns about routes to destination networks?

- ____
____
- ____
____
- ____
____
____

2. List at least three reasons why you would choose to use static routes instead of dynamic routes.

- ____
- ____
- ____
____
- ____
____
- ____
____

Routing Protocols Overview

In the previous section, you worked through exercises that focused on static routing. In this section, you turn your attention to dynamic routing through the use of routing protocols. The vocabulary exercises can help you with the terminology and concepts. Use the flow chart exercise as a visual snapshot of how routing protocols differ from one another. A couple of concept questions round out the section.

Vocabulary Exercise: Matching

Match the definition on the left with a term on the right.

Definitions

- **a.** Routing table
- **b.** Static route
- **c.** Connected subnets
- **d.** Stub network
- **e.** Default route
- **f.** Dynamic routing
- **g.** Routed protocol
- **h.** Routing protocol
- **i.** RIP
- **j.** Convergence
- **k.** Interior Gateway Protocol (IGP)
- **l.** EGP
- **m.** Autonomous system
- **n.** BGP
- **o.** Distance vector routing protocol
- **p.** Link-state routing protocol
- **q.** Balanced hybrid routing protocol
- **r.** Metric
- **s.** Link-state database
- **t.** OSPF
- **u.** Link-state advertisements (LSAs)
- **v.** SPF
- **w.** IGRP
- **x.** Load balancing

Terms

_____ Advertisements sent by OSPF

_____ Process by which all the routers collectively realize something has changed and update each other about the change

_____ After being configured, routers can learn routes automatically without assistance from the network engineer

_____ Blends the best of distance vector and link-state protocols

_____ Algorithm used by OSPF

_____ Protocols used between autonomous systems; also, the name of a specific routing protocol that is no longer used

_____ Listing of networks known by the router

_____ Cisco-proprietary routing protocol

_____ Route of last resort used if no other more specific route to the destination exists

_____ Networks attached to a router's interfaces

_____ Protocol that uses events to trigger updates to neighbors

_____ Using multiple routes to the same destination

_____ Used between routers to share information about networks

_____ Most widely used open-standard link-state routing protocol

_____ Defines packet structure, including the logical addressing used by routers to determine the destination network

_____ Route manually configured by an engineer

_____ Distance vector protocol that measures routes based on hop count

_____ Only EGP still in use today

_____ Protocol that sends periodic updates to neighbors

_____ Internetwork under the administrative control of a single organization

_____ Routing protocols used within an autonomous system

_____ Network with only one way out to other destination networks

_____ Measurement unit of a route

_____ Collection of all known networks within the internetwork; chooses the best route to install in the routing table

Vocabulary Exercise: Completion

Complete the paragraphs that follow by filling in appropriate words and phrases.

Routers add IP routes to their routing tables using three methods: ___________ routes, _________ routes (including default routes), and routes learned by using _____________ protocols. A ________ route is used when a router does not have a more specific route to the destination. A ___________ protocol defines the logical addressing of packets used by routers to find the destination network. A _________ protocol defines algorithms and processes that routers use to share information with neighbor routers. Regardless of the protocol used, the goal is to achieve ______________, which is an internetwork where all routers have a route to reach any destination.

Routing protocols can be classified into two main categories: ___________________________________, which are used within an __________________, and __________________________________, which are used between __________________. An __________________ is an internetwork under the administrative control of a single organization. IGPs for IP include ____________________________, and _________. The only current EGP in use is ___________________________.

IGPs can be further classified as follows, based on the type of algorithm they use:

- __________________ routing protocols, which use the Bellman-Ford algorithm
- __________________ routing protocols, which use the Dijkstra or SPF algorithm
- _______________ routing protocol, which uses the Cisco-proprietary Diffusing Update Algorithm (DUAL)

Distance vector routing protocols send _________ routing updates on a regular basis. For example, RIP sends out updates every ______ seconds. As long as RIP routers continue to hear the same routes with the same _________, the routing tables do not need to change. The _________, which is ___________ for RIP, measures the route so that RIP can determine the quality of the route. The best route is installed in the _________________. If two routes have the same metric to the same destination, RIP installs both routes and __________________ traffic sent to the destination.

___________________________ is the most popular link-state (LS) routing protocol. LS routing protocols send much more information in their routing updates than distance vector (DV) routing protocols. Therefore, LS protocols require more _________________________ power from the router. Initially, LS routers send information to every router in the internetwork. After this process, called ____________, every router has the same information about the internetwork as all the other routers. This information is stored in the __________________, which then finds the currently best routes to each subnet. The _________________, or _________________ (name of its inventor), algorithm calculates the best route to use from the LS database. The calculated best route is installed in the routing table.

Routing Protocols Flow Chart Exercise

Classify routing protocols by completing the flow chart in Figure 6-3. As a hint, a few of the phrases or acronyms you need include Interior Gateway Protocols, link-state, BGP, and IGRP.

Figure 6-3 Routing Protocols Flow Chart

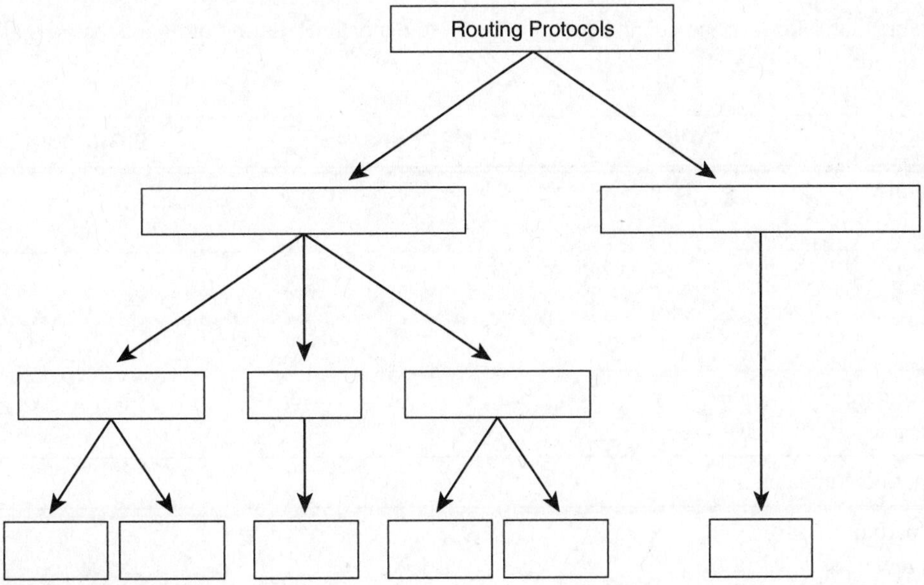

Concept Questions

1. Explain the meaning of the terms *routing protocol,* and *routed protocol* or *routable protocol.* Give an example of each.

____

____

____

____

____

____

2. List the main functions of a routing protocol.

____

- ____
- ____
- ____
- ____

Routing Protocols: Survey and Configuration

This last section focuses your attention on the main features of the more popular IGPs. The first exercise helps you compare and contrast features of RIP, OSPF, and EIGRP. You also work through some RIP configuration exercises that can, at the same time, help you with the concepts of routing.

Routing Protocol Characteristics Exercise

In the table that follows, compare and contrast the three major IGP routing protocols based on the feature listed.

Feature	RIPv1	OSPF	EIGRP
Algorithm			
Metric			
Open-standard or proprietary			
Sends periodic updates			
Full or partial routing updates			
Sends updates as broadcast or multicast			
Metric considered to be "infinite"			
Supports unequal-cost load balancing			

RIP Configuration Exercise 1

A concept often overlooked by the CCNA 2 student is what networks should be configured within a routing process. A good rule of thumb is to configure all the directly connected networks. Refer to Figure 6-4, which you used in the section "Static Routing Configuration Exercise 1" earlier in this chapter.

Figure 6-4 RIP Configuration Exercise 1

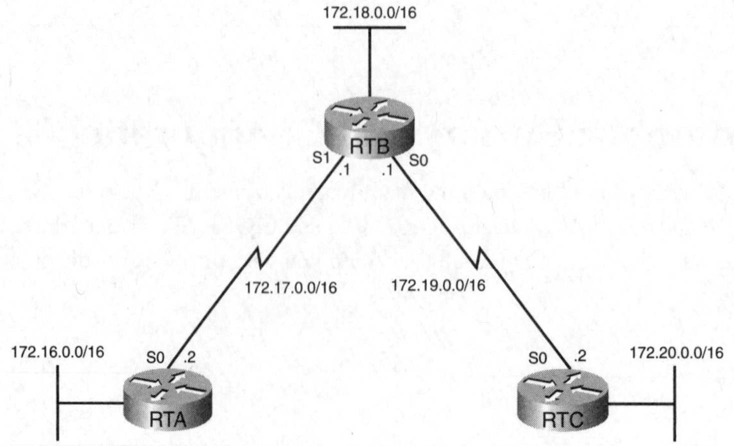

Record the commands, including router prompts, so that each router is using RIP and advertising all directly connected networks.

RTA:

RTB:

RTC:

RIP Configuration Exercise 2

Referring to Figure 6-5, record the commands, including router prompts, so that each router is using RIP and advertising all directly connected networks.

Figure 6-5 RIP Configuration Exercise 2

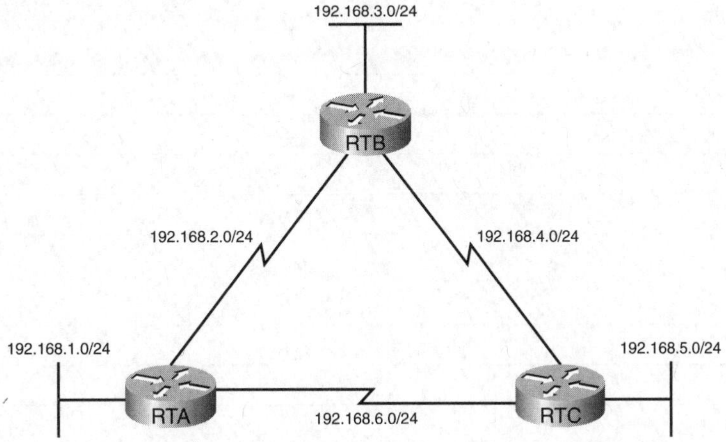

RTA:

RTB:

RTC:

Routing Configuration Challenge Exercise

The topology in Figure 6-6 requires a combination of static and dynamic routing. Record the commands, including router prompts, necessary to make sure that each router learns about the other routers' networks.

Figure 6-6 Routing Configuration Challenge Exercise

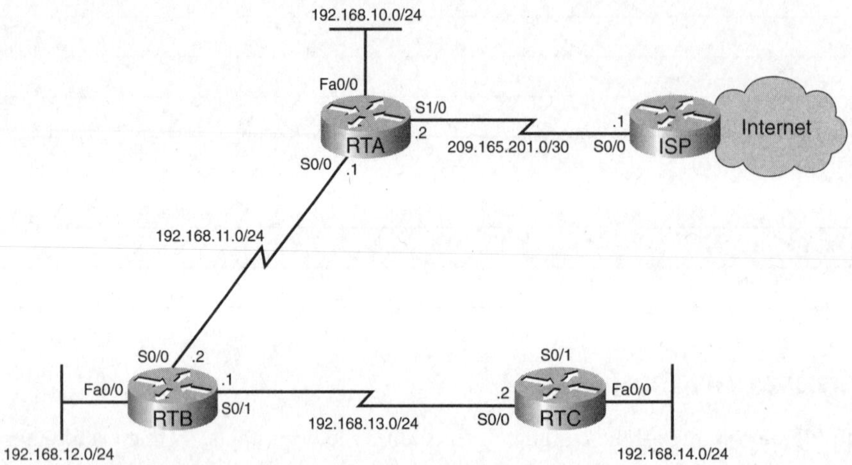

On RTA, do *not* configure the network between RTA and ISP as part of the RIP routing process. Make sure that each router has a gateway of last resort. You are not responsible for configuring ISP.

RTA:

____

____

____

____

____

RTB:

____

____

____

____

____

____

RTC:

____

____

____

____

____

Concept Questions

1. Although routers can be configured to do many things, describe the two main functions of every router, regardless of how simple or complex.

   ____

   - ____
   - ____

   ____

2. After you configure a network in the RIP routing process for a specific interface, what three actions does RIP begin to do related to that interface?

   ____

   ____

   ____

   ____

Lab Exercises

Command Reference

In the table that follows, record the command, *including the correct router prompt,* that fits the description. Fill in any blanks with the appropriate missing information.

Command	Description
	A static route to get to the 172.16.20.0/24 network can send packets to 172.16.10.2
	A static route to get to the 172.16.20.0/24 network can send packets out the s0/0 interface
	Sends all packets destined for networks not in my routing table to 172.16.10.2
	Sends all packets destined for networks not in my routing table out the s0/0 interface
	Displays the contents of the IP routing table
	Starts the routing process for RIP
	Adds the 10.0.0.0 network to the RIP routing process

Curriculum Lab 6-1: Configuring Static Routes (6.1.6)

Figure 6-7 Topology for Lab 6-1

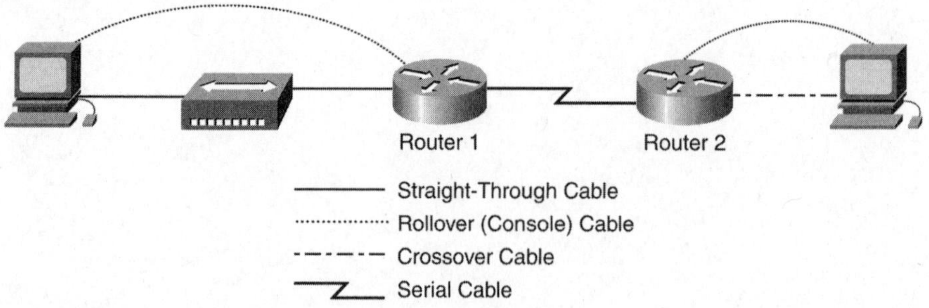

Part I of the lab equipment configuration is as follows:

Router Designation	Router Name	Routing Protocol	RIP Network Statement
Router 1	GAD	None	None
Router 2	BHM	None	None

The enable secret password for both routers is **class**.

The enable/vty/console password for both routers is **cisco**.

Part II of the lab equipment configuration is as follows:

Router Designation	Fast Ethernet 0 Address	Interface Type Serial 0	Serial 0 Address Table Entry	IP Host
Router 1	192.168.14.1	DCE	192.168.15.1	BHM
Router 2	192.168.16.1	DTE	192.168.15.2	GAD

No serial 1 address exists for either router.

The subnet mask for all addresses on both routers is 255.255.255.0.

The IP Host Table Entry column contents indicate the name(s) of the other router(s) in the IP host table.

Objective:

Configure static routes between routers to allow data transfer between networks without using dynamic routing protocols.

Background/preparation:

Cable a network similar to the one shown in Figure 6-7. You can use any router that meets the interface requirements in Figure 6-7 (that is, 800, 1600, 1700, 2500, or 2600 routers, or a combination). Refer to the information in Appendix B, "Router Interface Summary," to correctly specify the interface identifiers based on the equipment in your lab. The 1721 Series routers produced the configuration output in this lab. Any other router might produce slightly different output. You should execute the following steps on each router unless specifically instructed otherwise:

Step 1. Start a HyperTerminal session as you did in Lab 2-2, "Establishing a Console Session with HyperTerminal."

Step 2. Implement the procedure documented in Appendix C, "Erasing and Reloading the Router," before continuing with this lab.

Task 1: Configure Both Routers

Enter global configuration mode and configure the hostname as shown in the table for Part I of the lab equipment configuration. Then, configure the console, virtual terminal, and enable passwords. If you have trouble doing this, refer to Lab 3-2, "Configuring Router Passwords." Then, configure the interfaces and IP host tables. If you have trouble doing this, refer to Lab 3-2. Do not configure a routing protocol.

Task 2: Configure the Workstations with the Proper IP Address, Subnet Mask, and Default Gateway

Step 1. The configuration for the host connected to the GAD router is as follows:

- IP address: **192.168.14.2**
- IP subnet mask: **255.255.255.0**
- Default gateway: **192.168.14.1**

Step 2. The configuration for the host connected to the BHM router is as follows:

- IP address: **192.168.16.2**
- IP subnet mask: **255.255.255.0**
- Default gateway: **192.168.16.1**

Step 3. Check the connectivity between the workstations using the **ping** command. From the workstation attached to the GAD router, ping the workstation attached to the BHM router using the following code:

```
C:\>ping  192.168.16.2
Pinging 192.168.16.2 with 32 bytes of data: Request timed out.
Request timed out. Request timed out.
Request timed out.
Ping statistics for 192.168.16.2:
Packets: Sent = 4, Received = 0, Lost = 4 (100% loss), Approximate round trip
times in milli-seconds:
Minimum = 0ms, Maximum = 0ms, Average = 0ms
```

Was it successful? ______________________________

Why did the ping fail?

____

Task 3: Check the Interface Status

Check the interfaces on both routers with the command **show ip interface brief**. Are all the necessary interfaces up?

____

Task 4: Check the Routing Table Entries

Step 1. Using the command **show ip route**, view the IP routing table for the GAD router, as follows:

```
GAD>show ip route output eliminated

Gateway of last resort is not set

C     192.168.14.0/24 is directly connected, FastEthernet0
C     192.168.15.0/24 is directly connected, Serial0
```

Step 2. Using the command **show ip route**, view the IP routing table for the BHM router, as follows:

```
BHM>show ip route output eliminated

Gateway of last resort is not set

C     192.168.15.0/24 is directly connected, Serial0
C     192.168.16.0/24 is directly connected, FastEthernet0
```

Do all the routes you need appear in the routing tables of each router? ______________

Based on the output from the **show ip route** command on the GAD and BHM routers, can a host on network 192.168.16.0 connect to a host on network 192.168.14.0? ______________

If a route does not appear in the routing table of the router to which the host is connected, the host cannot reach the other host.

Task 5: Add Static Routes

How can you remedy this situation so that the hosts can ping each other? You add static routes to each router or run a routing protocol.

In global configuration mode, add a static route on Router 1 to network 192.168.16.0 using the following commands:

```
GAD(config)#ip  route  192.168.16.0  255.255.255.0  192.168.15.2
BHM(config)#ip  route  192.168.14.0  255.255.255.0  192.168.15.1
```

Why do you need a static route on both routers?

____

Task 6: Verify the New Routes

Step 1. Using the command **show ip route**, view the IP routing table for the GAD router, as follows:

```
GAD>show  ip  route output eliminated

Gateway of last resort is not set

C     192.168.14.0/24 is directly connected, FastEthernet0
C     192.168.15.0/24 is directly connected, Serial0
S     192.168.16.0/24 [1/0] via 192.168.15.2
```

Step 2. Using the command **show ip route**, view the IP routing table for the BHM router, as follows:

```
BHM>show ip route output eliminated
Gateway of last resort is not set
C     192.168.16.0/24 is directly connected, FastEthernet0
C     192.168.15.0/24 is directly connected, Serial0
S     192.168.14.0/24 [1/0] via 192.168.15.1
```

Do all the routes you need appear in the routing tables of each router?

____

Based on the output from the **show ip route** command on the GAD and BHM routers, can a host on network 192.168.16.0 connect to a host on network 192.168.14.0 now?

____

Task 7: Try to Ping Host to Host Again

Step 1. Check the connectivity between the workstations using the **ping** command. From the workstation attached to the GAD router, ping the workstation attached to the BHM router, as follows:

```
C:\>ping  192.168.16.2
Pinging 192.168.16.2 with 32 bytes of data:
Reply from 192.168.16.2: bytes=32 time=20ms TTL=254
Reply from 192.168.16.2: bytes=32 time=20ms TTL=254
Reply from 192.168.16.2: bytes=32 time=20ms TTL=254
Reply from 192.168.16.2: bytes=32 time=20ms TTL=254
Ping statistics for 192.168.16.2:
Packets: Sent = 4, Received = 4, Lost = 0 (0% loss), Approximate round trip
times in milli-seconds: Minimum = 20ms, Maximum = 20ms, Average = 20ms
```

Step 2. If the ping was not successful, check the routing table to make sure that the static routes are entered correctly. When you finish the preceding steps, log off (by typing **exit**) and turn the router off.

Comprehensive Lab 6-2: Static Routing with Migration to Dynamic Routing

Figure 6-8 Static Routing with Migration to Dynamic Routing

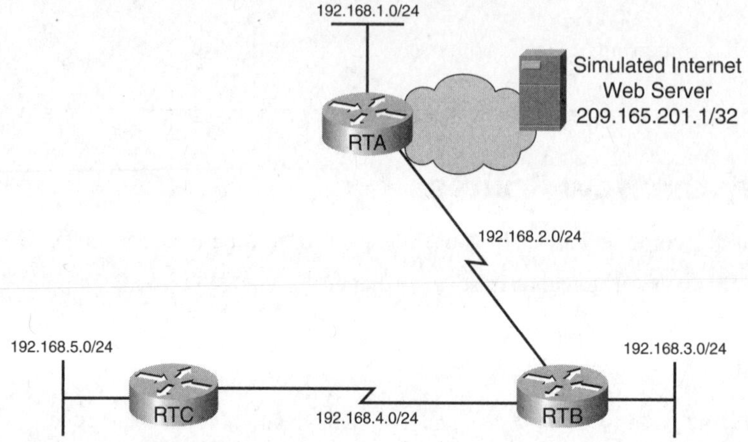

Objectives:

This lab contains the following objectives:

- Configure static routing
- Configure dynamic routing
- Verify full connectivity

Equipment:

This lab can be done with any combination of 1700, 2500, or 2600 Series routers.

NetLab Compatibility Notes:

This lab can be completed using NetLab.

Task 1: Cable the Lab

Step 1. Cable the lab as shown in the topology in Figure 6-8.

Step 2. Document the lab by filling in the following table with appropriate configuration information.

Router	Interface Type	IP Address	Subnet Mask	Clock Rate?
RTA				
	Lo0	209.165.201.1	255.255.255.255	No
RTB				
RTC				

Label the topology with the correct interface designation (for example, Fa0/0, S0/0, and so on).

Task 2: Basic Router Configurations

Step 1. Make sure that the routers have empty startup or running configurations. If necessary, what must be done to carry out this instruction?

____

____

Step 2. Configure RTA, RTB, and RTC with the following basic router configurations:

- Hostname
- Line configurations
- Global passwords
- Host tables
- Banner
- Other instructor-required global configurations

Step 3. Check your configurations. What command did you use?

____

Task 3: Interface Configurations

Step 1. Configure RTA, RTB, and RTC interfaces with IP addresses according to the table created in Task 1. For the Loopback 0 interface on RTA, use the following commands:

```
RTA(config)#interface loopback 0
RTA(config-if)#description Simulated Internet Web Server
RTA(config-if)#ip address 209.165.201.1 255.255.255.255
```

Note: Loopback interfaces are not physical interfaces but are created for a specific purpose. In this case, we are creating a loopback interface to test default routing. A loopback interface is always up if configured with an IP address and, therefore, can be pinged. You will use loopback interfaces for various reasons throughout your CCNA studies.

Step 2. Use the command **show ip interface brief** to verify interfaces on both routers are operational at the physical and data link layers.

Are RTA's interfaces fully operational? __________. If not, troubleshoot.

Are RTB's interfaces fully operational? __________. If not, troubleshoot.

Are RTC's interaces fully operational? __________. If not, troubleshoot.

Task 4: Static Routing Configurations

What command do you use to display the routing table?

____

Step 1. Configure RTA with static routes to every network not listed in its routing table. Use the next-hop IP address argument.

____

____

____

Step 2. Configure RTB with a static route to the LAN on RTC. Use the *outbound-interface* argument.

____

Step 3. Configure RTB with a default route pointing to RTA. Use the *outbound-interface* argument.

____

Step 4. Configure RTC with a default route pointing to RTB. Use the *next-hop-address* argument.

____

At this point, all routers should have full connectivity to every network shown in the topology. RTB and RTC should be able to ping the loopback interface on RTA.

Do you have full connectivity? __________. If not, troubleshoot.

Step 5. Verify that your routing tables look similar to the following:

```
RTA#show ip route
Codes: C - connected, S - static, R - RIP, M - mobile, B - BGP
       D - EIGRP, EX - EIGRP external, O - OSPF, IA - OSPF inter area
       N1 - OSPF NSSA external type 1, N2 - OSPF NSSA external type 2
       E1 - OSPF external type 1, E2 - OSPF external type 2
       i - IS-IS, su - IS-IS summary, L1 - IS-IS level-1, L2 - IS-IS level-2
       ia - IS-IS inter area, * - candidate default, U - per-user static route
       o - ODR, P - periodic downloaded static route

Gateway of last resort is not set

S    192.168.4.0/24 [1/0] via 192.168.2.2
     209.165.201.0/32 is subnetted, 1 subnets
C       209.165.201.1 is directly connected, Loopback0
S    192.168.5.0/24 [1/0] via 192.168.2.2
C    192.168.1.0/24 is directly connected, FastEthernet0/0
C    192.168.2.0/24 is directly connected, Serial0/0
S    192.168.3.0/24 [1/0] via 192.168.2.2
```

```
RTB#show ip route
Codes: C - connected, S - static, R - RIP, M - mobile, B - BGP
       D - EIGRP, EX - EIGRP external, O - OSPF, IA - OSPF inter area
       N1 - OSPF NSSA external type 1, N2 - OSPF NSSA external type 2
       E1 - OSPF external type 1, E2 - OSPF external type 2
       i - IS-IS, su - IS-IS summary, L1 - IS-IS level-1, L2 - IS-IS level-2
       ia - IS-IS inter area, * - candidate default, U - per-user static route
       o - ODR, P - periodic downloaded static route

Gateway of last resort is 192.168.2.1 to network 0.0.0.0

C    192.168.4.0/24 is directly connected, Serial0/1
S    192.168.5.0/24 is directly connected, Serial0/1
C    192.168.2.0/24 is directly connected, Serial0/0
C    192.168.3.0/24 is directly connected, FastEthernet0/0
S*   0.0.0.0/0 [1/0] via 192.168.2.1
```

```
RTC#show ip route
Codes: C - connected, S - static, R - RIP, M - mobile, B - BGP
       D - EIGRP, EX - EIGRP external, O - OSPF, IA - OSPF inter area
       N1 - OSPF NSSA external type 1, N2 - OSPF NSSA external type 2
       E1 - OSPF external type 1, E2 - OSPF external type 2
       i - IS-IS, su - IS-IS summary, L1 - IS-IS level-1, L2 - IS-IS level-2
```

```
        ia - IS-IS inter area, * - candidate default, U - per-user static route
        o - ODR, P - periodic downloaded static route

Gateway of last resort is 192.168.4.1 to network 0.0.0.0

C    192.168.4.0/24 is directly connected, Serial0/1
C    192.168.5.0/24 is directly connected, FastEthernet0/0
S*   0.0.0.0/0 [1/0] via 192.168.4.1
```

Task 5: Migrate to Dynamic Routing

Step 1. Now configure RIP as your routing protocol and remove the static routes. To maintain a converged network, add your RIP first and then remove the static routes. On RTA, enter the commands necessary to configure RIP as the routing protocol. *Do not configure* the loopback address 209.165.201.1 as part of RIP.

____

____

____

Step 2. On RTB, enter the commands necessary to configure RIP as the routing protocol.

____

____

____

____

Step 3. On RTC, enter the commands necessary to configure RIP as the routing protocol.

____

____

____

Step 4. Display the routing table on RTA. Notice that RTA is not using RIP routes to remote destinations. Why? Hint: Refer to your administrative distance research.

____

____

Step 5. Enter the commands necessary to remove all the static routes on RTA and the static route on RTB. However, leave the default routes configured on RTB and RTC.

____

____

____

Step 6. Verify that your routing tables look similar to the following output. If not, troubleshoot.

```
RTA#show ip route
Codes: C - connected, S - static, R - RIP, M - mobile, B - BGP
       D - EIGRP, EX - EIGRP external, O - OSPF, IA - OSPF inter area
       N1 - OSPF NSSA external type 1, N2 - OSPF NSSA external type 2
       E1 - OSPF external type 1, E2 - OSPF external type 2
       i - IS-IS, su - IS-IS summary, L1 - IS-IS level-1, L2 - IS-IS level-2
       ia - IS-IS inter area, * - candidate default, U - per-user static route
       o - ODR, P - periodic downloaded static route

Gateway of last resort is not set
```

```
R     192.168.4.0/24 [120/1] via 192.168.2.2, 00:00:03, Serial0/0
      209.165.201.0/32 is subnetted, 1 subnets
C        209.165.201.1 is directly connected, Loopback0
C     192.168.1.0/24 is directly connected, FastEthernet0/0
C     192.168.2.0/24 is directly connected, Serial0/0
R     192.168.3.0/24 [120/1] via 192.168.2.2, 00:00:03, Serial0/0
```

```
RTB#show ip route
Codes: C - connected, S - static, R - RIP, M - mobile, B - BGP
       D - EIGRP, EX - EIGRP external, O - OSPF, IA - OSPF inter area
       N1 - OSPF NSSA external type 1, N2 - OSPF NSSA external type 2
       E1 - OSPF external type 1, E2 - OSPF external type 2
       i - IS-IS, su - IS-IS summary, L1 - IS-IS level-1, L2 - IS-IS level-2
       ia - IS-IS inter area, * - candidate default, U - per-user static route
       o - ODR, P - periodic downloaded static route

Gateway of last resort is 192.168.2.1 to network 0.0.0.0

C     192.168.4.0/24 is directly connected, Serial0/1
R     192.168.5.0/24 [120/1] via 192.168.4.2, 00:00:16, Serial0/1
R     192.168.1.0/24 [120/1] via 192.168.2.1, 00:00:07, Serial0/0
C     192.168.2.0/24 is directly connected, Serial0/0
C     192.168.3.0/24 is directly connected, FastEthernet0/0
S*    0.0.0.0/0 [1/0] via 192.168.2.1
```

```
RTC#show ip route
Codes: C - connected, S - static, R - RIP, M - mobile, B - BGP
       D - EIGRP, EX - EIGRP external, O - OSPF, IA - OSPF inter area
       N1 - OSPF NSSA external type 1, N2 - OSPF NSSA external type 2
       E1 - OSPF external type 1, E2 - OSPF external type 2
       i - IS-IS, su - IS-IS summary, L1 - IS-IS level-1, L2 - IS-IS level-2
       ia - IS-IS inter area, * - candidate default, U - per-user static route
       o - ODR, P - periodic downloaded static route

Gateway of last resort is 192.168.4.1 to network 0.0.0.0

C     192.168.4.0/24 is directly connected, Serial0/1
C     192.168.5.0/24 is directly connected, FastEthernet0/0
R     192.168.1.0/24 [120/2] via 192.168.4.1, 00:00:27, Serial0/1
R     192.168.2.0/24 [120/1] via 192.168.4.1, 00:00:27, Serial0/1
R     192.168.3.0/24 [120/1] via 192.168.4.1, 00:00:27, Serial0/1
S*    0.0.0.0/0 [1/0] via 192.168.4.1
```

Challenge Lab 6-3: Static and Dynamic Routing Configuration

Figure 6-9 Static Routing and Dynamic Routing Configuration

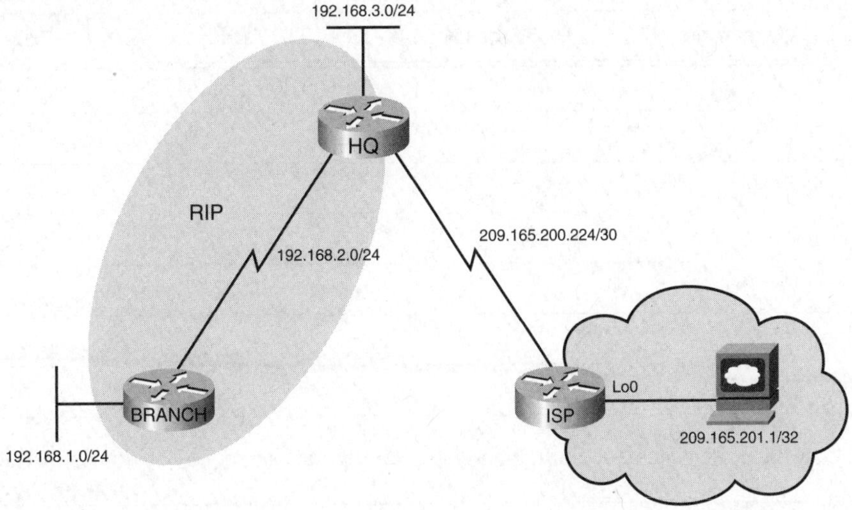

Objectives:

This lab contains the following objectives:

- Configure a combination of dynamic, static, and default routing
- Use the **ping** command to test end-to-end connectivity

Background/Preparation:

In this topology, two new concepts are introduced. First, the shaded area between the HQ and BRANCH routers is a common way to represent a routing domain. (You might also think of this shaded region as representing the autonomous system under the control of a single network administration.) In this case, RIP is the routing process used between HQ and BRANCH to advertise networks. Interfaces that are within the shaded region are part of the RIP process. In other words, the WAN link between HQ and ISP is *not* part of the RIP routing process. RIP is not configured on ISP. HQ uses a default route to send all "unroutable" packets to ISP. ISP uses a static route to reach HQ and BRANCH networks.

Second, this topology introduces the concept of using a loopback interface to simulate an attached device. Loopback interfaces are virtual interfaces on a router. This means that no physical interface exists. A loopback is a logical interface that can be assigned an IP address and subnet mask for testing and other purposes. If you completed Comprehensive Lab 6-2, "Static Routing with Migration to Dynamic Routing," you have already configured a loopback interface. In this lab, you add an ISP router configured with a loopback interface. This is a more realistic, "real-world" simulation of what occurs in a production network. The loopback on ISP simulates connectivity to any host on the Internet.

Equipment:

This lab can be done with any combination of 1700, 2500, or 2600 Series routers.

NetLab Compatibility Notes:

This lab can be completed using NetLab.

Note: Output shown in this lab is from NetLab 2600 routers.

Task 1: Cabling, Basic Router Configuration, and Verification

Step 1. Cable the lab according to the topology shown in Figure 6-9.

Step 2. Fill in the following table with the appropriate configuration information.

Device	Interface	DTE or DCE?	IP Address	Subnet Mask
ISP	Lo0	—	209.165.201.1	255.255.255.255
HQ				
BRANCH				

Step 3. Configure the routers, including any basic configurations required by your instructor.

Note: You should configure HQ and BRANCH with a host table entry for the simulated web server so that you can simply type in the name you assign instead of the IP address when testing connectivity to the simulated web server.

Do not configure routing yet. Refer to Comprehensive Lab 6-2, "Static Routing with Migration to Dynamic Routing," if you need help configuring a loopback interface.

Step 4. Verify that all configured interfaces are fully functional. What command did you use?

____

Task 2: Configure RIP Routing on HQ and BRANCH

Step 1. Configure HQ and BRANCH with RIP routing. Include the directly connected networks, but *do not* include the 209.168.200.224/30 network in the configuration for HQ.

Step 2. Verify that HQ can ping the LAN interface on BRANCH. Successful? ______ If not, troubleshoot.

Step 3. Verify that BRANCH can ping the LAN interface on HQ. Successful? ______ If not, troubleshoot.

Step 4. Verify that HQ can ping the WAN interface on ISP. Successful? ______ If not, troubleshoot.

Step 5. Verify that routing tables are complete. What command did you use?

____

Step 6. Verify that neither HQ nor BRANCH can ping the simulated web server, 209.165.201.1, configured on ISP by using the following code:

```
HQ#ping web

Type escape sequence to abort.
Sending 5, 100-byte ICMP Echos to 209.165.201.1, timeout is 2 seconds:
.....
Success rate is 0 percent (0/5)

BRANCH#ping web
```

```
Type escape sequence to abort.
Sending 5, 100-byte ICMP Echos to 209.165.201.1, timeout is 2 seconds:
.....
Success rate is 0 percent (0/5)
```

Why did these pings fail?

____

____

Task 3: Configure Static and Default Routing

Step 1. HQ and ISP use manually configured routes to provide full connectivity. HQ uses a default route to send data to ISP.

ISP uses a static route for all the networks within the client's autonomous system. On ISP, use network 192.168.0.0 and subnet mask 255.255.252.0 to configure a static route pointing to the next-hop IP address on HQ.

Note: The subnet mask 255.255.252.0 summarizes all three 192.168 networks attached to HQ and BRANCH. (You'll learn more about summarizing routes in your CCNA 3 studies.)

Record the command, including the router prompt, that you use to configure the static route on ISP.

____

Step 2. On HQ, configure a default route that can send "unroutable" packets to ISP. Use the *outbound-interface* argument instead of the *next-hop-address* argument when configuring the route. Record the command, including the router prompt, that you use to configure the static route on ISP.

____

What is the difference between using the *outbound-interface* argument and the *next-hop-address* argument?

____

____

____

____

____

Step 3. At this point, HQ should be able to ping the simulated web server at 209.165.201.1, and ISP should be able to ping the LAN interface attached to HQ. If not, troubleshoot.

BRANCH still cannot ping the simulated web server. Why not?

____

____

Step 4. You could enter a default route on BRANCH pointing to HQ. A better practice, however, is to have HQ advertise a default route to BRANCH. You can do this with the **default-information originate** command on HQ. This command configures RIP to "originate" the default route that you configured earlier and advertise it within the RIP routing process. The route is tagged as a default route and sent to BRANCH. If other RIP routers were attached to BRANCH, these routers would also receive the default information originated by HQ.

To configure HQ to advertise the default route, enter the following commands:

```
HQ(config)#router rip
HQ(config-router)#default-information originate
```

Step 5. Verify that all three routers have routing tables similar to the tables shown in the following code. Notice that both HQ and BRANCH have a "gateway of last resort" set.

Note: If BRANCH does not have a "gateway of last resort" set, you might have to reload both BRANCH and HQ. A small "bug" in the IOS sometimes prevents the **default-information originate** command from working properly. You might need to save your configurations to NVRAM and reload the routers.

```
BRANCH#show ip route
Codes: C - connected, S - static, R - RIP, M - mobile, B - BGP
       D - EIGRP, EX - EIGRP external, O - OSPF, IA - OSPF inter area
       N1 - OSPF NSSA external type 1, N2 - OSPF NSSA external type 2
       E1 - OSPF external type 1, E2 - OSPF external type 2
       i - IS-IS, su - IS-IS summary, L1 - IS-IS level-1, L2 - IS-IS level-2
       ia - IS-IS inter area, * - candidate default, U - per-user static route
       o - ODR, P - periodic downloaded static route

Gateway of last resort is 192.168.2.1 to network 0.0.0.0

C    192.168.1.0/24 is directly connected, FastEthernet0/0
C    192.168.2.0/24 is directly connected, Serial0/0
R    192.168.3.0/24 [120/1] via 192.168.2.1, 00:00:29, Serial0/0
R*   0.0.0.0/0 [120/1] via 192.168.2.1, 00:00:04, Serial0/0
```

```
HQ#show ip route
Codes: C - connected, S - static, R - RIP, M - mobile, B - BGP
       D - EIGRP, EX - EIGRP external, O - OSPF, IA - OSPF inter area
       N1 - OSPF NSSA external type 1, N2 - OSPF NSSA external type 2
       E1 - OSPF external type 1, E2 - OSPF external type 2
       i - IS-IS, su - IS-IS summary, L1 - IS-IS level-1, L2 - IS-IS level-2
       ia - IS-IS inter area, * - candidate default, U - per-user static route
       o - ODR, P - periodic downloaded static route

Gateway of last resort is 0.0.0.0 to network 0.0.0.0

     209.165.200.0/30 is subnetted, 1 subnets
C       209.165.200.224 is directly connected, Serial0/1
R    192.168.1.0/24 [120/1] via 192.168.2.2, 00:00:14, Serial0/0
C    192.168.2.0/24 is directly connected, Serial0/0
C    192.168.3.0/24 is directly connected, FastEthernet0/0
S*   0.0.0.0/0 is directly connected, Serial0/1
```

```
ISP#show ip route
Codes: C - connected, S - static, R - RIP, M - mobile, B - BGP
       D - EIGRP, EX - EIGRP external, O - OSPF, IA - OSPF inter area
       N1 - OSPF NSSA external type 1, N2 - OSPF NSSA external type 2
       E1 - OSPF external type 1, E2 - OSPF external type 2
       i - IS-IS, su - IS-IS summary, L1 - IS-IS level-1, L2 - IS-IS level-2
       ia - IS-IS inter area, * - candidate default, U - per-user static route
       o - ODR, P - periodic downloaded static route
```

```
Gateway of last resort is not set

     209.165.200.0/30 is subnetted, 1 subnets
C       209.165.200.224 is directly connected, Serial0/1
     209.165.201.0/32 is subnetted, 1 subnets
C       209.165.201.1 is directly connected, Loopback0
S    192.168.0.0/22 [1/0] via 209.165.200.226
```

Step 6. Verify that both BRANCH and HQ can now ping the simulated web server at 209.165.201.1. Successful? _______ If not, troubleshoot.

CHAPTER 7

Distance Vector Routing Protocols

The Study Guide portion of this chapter uses a combination of matching, fill-in-the-blank, and open-ended questions, and unique custom exercises to test your knowledge of the theory of distance vector routing protocols.

The Lab Exercises portion of this chapter includes all the online curriculum labs as well as a comprehensive lab and a challenge lab to ensure that you have mastered the practical, hands-on skills needed for TCP/IP for this chapter.

Study Guide

Avoiding Loops When Converging Using Distance Vector Routing Protocols

The simplicity of distance vector protocols introduces the possibility of routing loops. Routing loops occur when the routers forward packets so that the same single packet ends up back at the same routers repeatedly—wasting bandwidth and never delivering the packet. This first section reviews some vocabulary pertaining to loop avoidance. You also complete an exercise in which you are asked to apply your knowledge of how distance vector protocols avoid loops.

Vocabulary Exercise: Matching

Match the definition on the left with a term on the right.

Definitions

a. The process by which all the routers collectively realize something has changed and update each other about the change.

b. Until it expires, a router ignores new information about the downed route unless advertised by the neighbor that originally advertised the route.

c. Cisco's measurement of the trustworthiness of a routing information source.

d. A measurement of a route's quality; used by the routing protocol to pick the "best" route.

e. When at least one pair of subnets of the same classful network are separated by subnets of a different classful network.

f. Sends subnet mask information and supports variable-length subnet masks (VLSMs).

g. A metric assigned to routes that have failed; this metric is beyond the routing protocol's valid range of values.

h. A backup route that is installed in the routing table if the primary route becomes unavailable.

i. Occurs when routers forward packets so that the same single packet ends up back at the same routers repeatedly.

j. List of routes the router is currently using to forward traffic.

k. After this expires, the route is removed from the table.

l. An update with the metric set as infinite.

m. A rule for avoiding loops that states "For a given interface, any route whose outgoing interface is that same interface is not included in routing updates sent out that interface."

n. A distance vector routing protocol.

o. Sent immediately if a route fails.

p. Suspends split-horizon rules for a downed route.

q. Does not converge properly when discontiguous subnets have been used.

Terms

___ routing table

___ metric

___ routing loop

___ infinity

___ split horizon

___ route poisoning

___ poison reverse

___ triggered update

___ holddown timer

___ Routing Information Protocol (RIP)

___ classful routing protocol

___ classless routing protocols

___ discontiguous networks

___ flush timer

___ administrative distance

___ floating static route

___ convergence

Vocabulary Exercise: Completion

______________ occur when the routers forward packets so that the same single packet ends up back at the same routers repeatedly—wasting bandwidth and never delivering the packet. Several features of distance vector (DV) routing protocols prevent this from happening.

One way to avoid loops is to "spread the bad news" about a route failure through ______________, which refers to the practice of advertising a route with a special metric value called ________. Simply put, routers consider routes advertised with an _______ metric to have failed. For RIP, the value of this special metric is ________.

Another way DV routing protocols prevent loops is through the ___________ rule, which states "In routing updates sent out interface X, do not include routing information about routes that refer to interface X as the outgoing interface."

Finally, DV routing protocols use ______________, during which time a router does not believe any other routing information about the failed route, unless the information is learned from the neighbor that originally advertised the working route.

Routing Loop Avoidance Exercise

Refer to Figure 7-1 to answer the questions that follow.

Figure 7-1 Normal RIP Operations

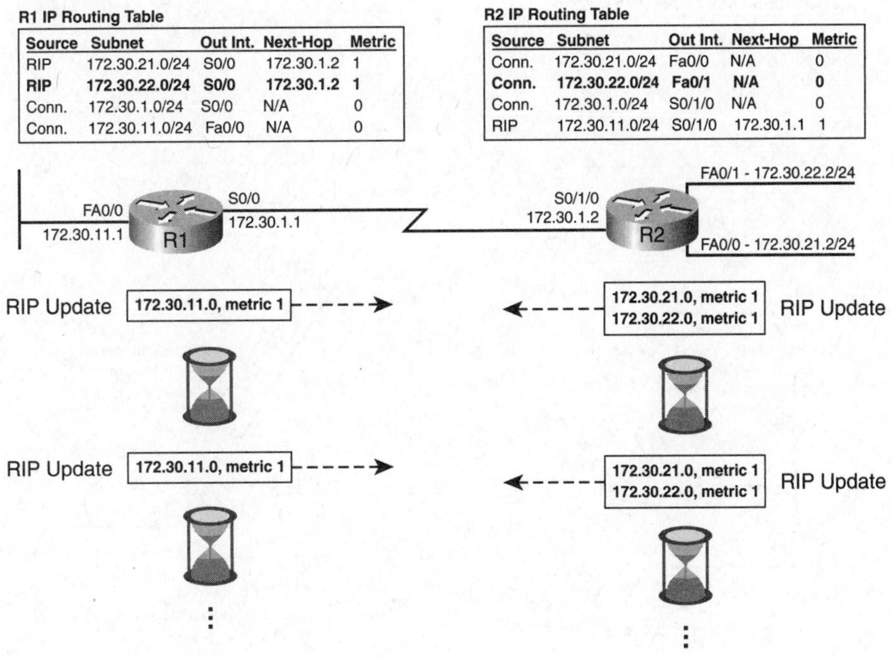

1. What is the meaning of "metric 1"?

____

2. How often does a RIP router send out updates?

____

3. What is the maximum value of RIP's metric?

____

4. RIP sends **full** updates. However, R1 includes only one network in its update. Why?

____

5. Explain what R2 does if the 172.30.22.0/24 network goes down.

____

6. What does R1 do when it hears about the failed network?

____

____

____

____

Refer to Figure 7-2 to answer the questions that follow.

Figure 7-2 RIP in a Redundant Network

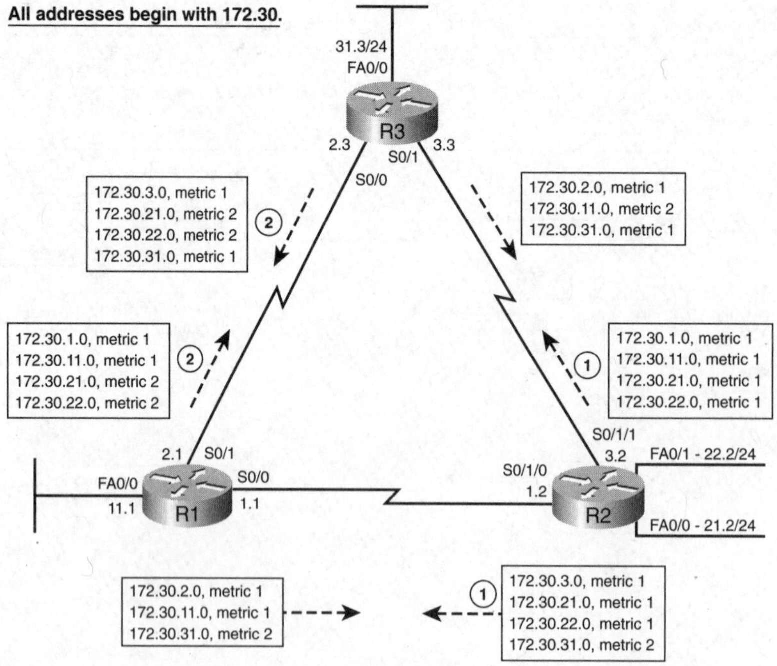

1. Notice how updates are not being sent out the Fast Ethernet interfaces. Normally, you would not want RIP updates sent out a LAN interface. In practice, how can you make this true?

____

2. Without the holddown timers in place, explain the details of what would happen if the 172.30.22.0/24 network goes down. Answering "a loop would occur" is not sufficient.

____
____
____
____
____

Routing Information Protocol

This section focuses specifically on RIP, covering its features and configuration and describing how to verify and troubleshoot a RIP installation. You first work through an exercise comparing and contrasting RIP v1 and v2. Then, you progress through a detailed RIP configuration exercise. Finally, you review some basic verification and troubleshooting tools.

RIP v1 and RIP v2 Comparison Exercise

Complete the following table that compares and contrasts RIP v1 and RIP v2.

Feature	v1	v2
What is the RFC?		
Uses hop count as the metric?		
What is the largest valid metric?		
What is the default update interval?		
Sends full periodic updates?		
Sends partial triggered updates when routes change?		
Uses route poisoning, poison reverse, split horizon, and holddown?		
Supports multiple equal-cost routes to same subnet?		
Sends updates as multicasts?		
Sends mask in updates, thereby supporting VLSM?		
Supports route tags?		
Supports authentication?		

Advanced RIP Concepts and Configuration Exercise

1. RIP v2 improved upon RIP v1 by adding information to the RIP routing update, including the following:

   - _____________, so that a router has confidence that the information it is receiving from a neighbor router is from a legitimate router

- Support for ______________________________ because RIP v2 sends the subnet mask information
- Reduction of broadcast traffic because RIP v2 ___________ updates

2. As a review, record the two commands, including the router prompt, necessary to enable RIP and configure it to advertise the 192.168.1.0 network.

____

____

3. You enter the following networks in the RIP routing process:

- 192.168.1.32
- 172.16.3.0
- 10.1.1.0

When you review the running configuration, you discover that the IOS does not list these subnets, but rather the classful networks. Record what you would see in the running configuration output.

____

____

____

____

4. Record the command, including the router prompt, that you would add to the RIP routing process to enable version 2.

____

5. In Figure 7-3, R1 is only sending RIP v1 updates and R3 is only sending RIP v2 updates. If you configure R2 with RIP v1, R3 cannot understand any of the updates from R2. If you configure R2 with RIP v2, R2 cannot understand any of the RIP updates. Record the commands, including the router prompt, that you enter on R2 to fix this problem. Changing the RIP version on R1 or R3 is not an option. Two possible solutions exist.

Figure 7-3 RIP v1 and RIP v2 Convergence

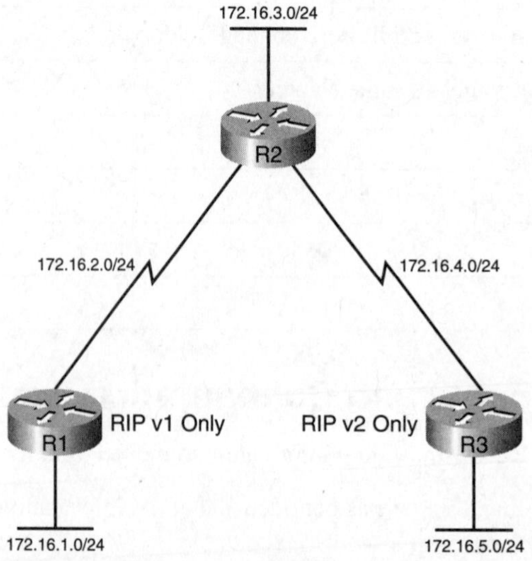

____
____
____
____
____
____
____
____
____
____
____
____

6. Because RIP v2 sends subnet mask information, it supports VLSM, which means that you can configure your network with ____________ subnets. A ____________ subnet occurs when at least one pair of subnets of the same classful network are separated by a subnet of a different classful network. To allow this situation in RIP v2, you must configure the ____________ command within the RIP routing process.

7. Although it is not normally recommended, you can change the timers that RIP uses for its routing updates and other timers. Record the command syntax, including the router prompt, to change the RIP timers.

____

8. In Figure 7-3, these routers should not send updates out their LAN interfaces. However, they will do so unless explicitly configured not to. Record the command, including the router prompt, necessary to stop RIP updates from being sent out these interfaces.

____

9. RIP is capable of load-balancing up to __ equal-cost routes (__ routes by default).

10. Record the command, including the router prompt, to change the default to the maximum.

____

11. Cisco routers use two types of load balancing. Explain the two load-balancing methods used by Cisco routers. Which method is the default, and how do you configure the other method?

____
____
____
____
____
____

12. In some cases, one router might need to use multiple routing protocols. Routers determine the best route in these cases by choosing the route with the lowest ____________________. Complete the following table.

Routing Information Source	AD
Connected interface	
Static route	
Enhanced Interior Gateway Routing Protocol (EIGRP) summary route	
External Border Gateway Protocol (BGP)	
Internal EIGRP	
IGRP	
Open Shortest Path First (OSPF)	
Intermediate System–to–Intermediate System (IS-IS)	
RIP	
External EIGRP	
Internal BGP	
Unknown	

13. You can also use administrative distance to configure a floating static route. Referring to Figure 7-4, record the commands, including the router prompt, to configure R-core with a default route using the T1 link, and then configure a floating default route that can use the dialup link if the T1 line goes down.

Figure 7-4 Configuring a Backup Route

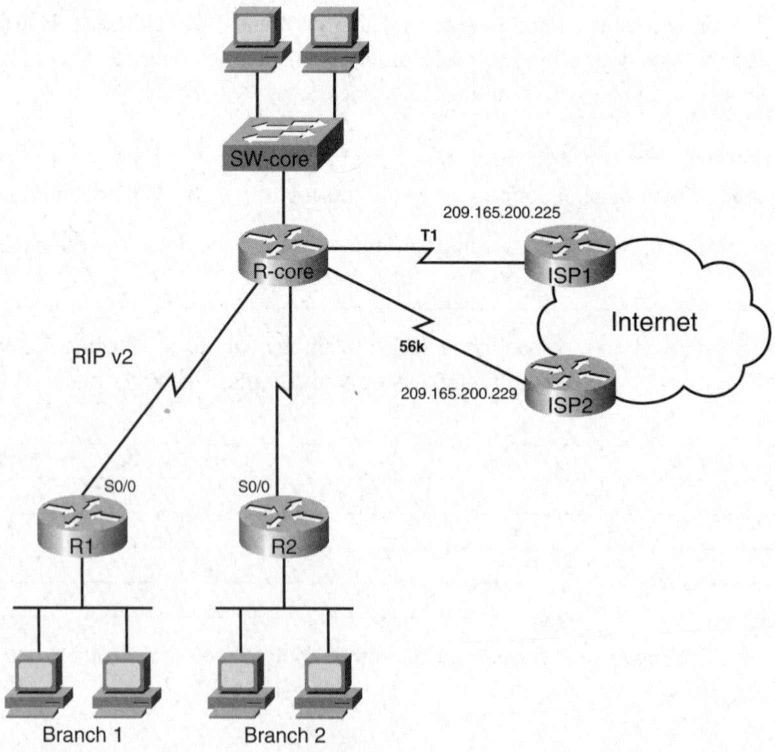

____

____

14. Instead of configuring every router in the organization with a default route pointing to R-core, you can configure R-core to redistribute the default route within the RIP routing process. Record the command, including the routing prompt.

____

____

____

15. RIP v1 is called a *classful routing protocol,* and RIP v2 is called a *classless routing protocol.* Classless routing protocols do the following:

- Send ____________ information in routing updates
- Support ______________________________ because of the inclusion of the mask in the routing updates
- Support designs that include ____________ networks

16. Besides RIP v1, the only other classful routing protocol is IGRP, which is no longer supported in newer Cisco IOSs. All other IP routing protocols are classless. List them.

____

17. Explain the purpose of the **ip classless** command, which is on by default in Cisco IOS Release 12.0 and higher. If necessary, search the Internet to find your answer. Regardless, list the source of your information.

____

____

____

____

____

18. Explain the difference between a classful and a classless network address.

____

____

____

____

Troubleshooting with show Commands

When you start using routing protocols to configure larger and more complex internetworks, you will find yourself using **show** commands to verify your configurations and troubleshoot problems. All too often, beginning students rely on the **show run** command as the one and only weapon in their troubleshooting arsenal. Rarely is **show run** the best choice for discovering the source of a problem. This exercise focuses your attention on three powerful **show** commands that can help you find almost any problem in your routing configuration.

1. After initially configuring an internetwork, the quickest way to verify connectivity to your neighbors is to make sure that all the required interfaces are active. What command generated the following output?

```
R2#____________________________________________
Interface            IP-Address      OK? Method Status     Protocol
FastEthernet0/0      172.16.3.1      YES NVRAM  up         up
Serial0/0            172.16.2.1      YES NVRAM  up         up
Serial0/1            172.16.4.1      YES NVRAM  up         up
```

2. After routing is configured, you want to verify that your internetwork is converged. What command generated the following output?

```
R1#____________________________________________
Codes: C - connected, S - static, R - RIP, M - mobile, B - BGP
       D - EIGRP, EX - EIGRP external, O - OSPF, IA - OSPF inter area
       N1 - OSPF NSSA external type 1, N2 - OSPF NSSA external type 2
       E1 - OSPF external type 1, E2 - OSPF external type 2
       i - IS-IS, su - IS-IS summary, L1 - IS-IS level-1, L2 - IS-IS level-2
       ia - IS-IS inter area, * - candidate default, U - per-user static route
       o - ODR, P - periodic downloaded static route

Gateway of last resort is 172.16.2.1 to network 0.0.0.0

     172.16.0.0/24 is subnetted, 5 subnets
R       172.16.4.0 [120/1] via 172.16.2.1, 00:00:14, Serial0/0
R       172.16.5.0 [120/2] via 172.16.2.1, 00:00:14, Serial0/0
C       172.16.1.0 is directly connected, FastEthernet0/0
C       172.16.2.0 is directly connected, Serial0/0
R       172.16.3.0 [120/1] via 172.16.2.1, 00:00:14, Serial0/0
R*   0.0.0.0/0 [120/1] via 172.16.2.1, 00:00:03, Serial0/0
```

3. For the following entry, what does the **2** mean in **[120/2]**?

R 172.16.5.0 [120/2] via 172.16.2.1, 00:00:14, Serial0/0

____

What does the **120** indicate?

____

What does **via 172.16.2.1** mean?

____

What does the **00:00:14** mean?

____

What does **Serial0/0** mean?

____

4. For the following entry, what does the **R** mean?

R* 0.0.0.0/0 [120/1] via 172.16.2.1, 00:00:03, Serial0/0

____

What does the asterisk (*) next to the **R** mean?

____

What does the **0.0.0.0/0** mean?

____

____

5. If your internetwork has not converged, the two previous commands are usually enough to quickly discover the source of the problem and fix it. However, sometimes what you thought would fix the problem doesn't work. Another **show** command can help. What command generated the following output?

```
R2#_______________________________________________
Routing Protocol is "rip"
  Sending updates every 30 seconds, next due in 25 seconds
  Invalid after 180 seconds, hold down 180, flushed after 240
  Outgoing update filter list for all interfaces is not set
  Incoming update filter list for all interfaces is not set
  Redistributing: rip
  Default version control: send version 1, receive any version
    Interface             Send  Recv  Triggered RIP  Key-chain
    FastEthernet0/0       1     1 2
    Serial0/0             1     1 2
    Serial0/1             1     1 2
  Automatic network summarization is in effect
  Maximum path: 2
  Routing for Networks:
    172.16.0.0
  Routing Information Sources:
    Gateway         Distance      Last Update
    172.16.4.2           120      00:00:02
    172.16.2.2           120      00:00:04
  Distance: (default is 120)
```

When will this router send out its next update? ______________________

What RIP version(s) is this router sending to its neighbors? ______________________

What RIP version(s) is this router allowed to receive from its neighbors? ______________________

How many equal-cost routes can this router use to forward traffic to a destination network? ________

What is the default number of equal-cost routes a Cisco router can use to forward traffic to a destination network? ______________________

What is the maximum number of equal-cost routes a Cisco router can use to forward traffic to a destination network? ______________________

What command, including router prompt, do you use to change this maximum number of equal-cost routes?

____

How many RIP neighbors does this router have? ______________________

Troubleshooting with debug Commands

Finally, if all else fails, you might want to use one of the many **debug** commands. Although these commands can severely impact the performance of production routers, you cannot harm anything in a lab environment. However, the output from these commands often generates faster than you can read it. Therefore, you should start a capture session within your terminal emulator. Then, after you are finished capturing the output, you can look at it at your leisure.

What command generated the output that follows?

```
R2#_______________________________________________________________
RIP: received v1 update from 172.16.2.2 on Serial0/0
     172.16.1.0 in 1 hops
RIP: received v1 update from 172.16.4.2 on Serial0/1
     172.16.5.0 in 1 hops
RIP: sending v1 update to 255.255.255.255 via Serial0/0 (172.16.2.1)
RIP: build update entries
   subnet 0.0.0.0 metric 1
   subnet 172.16.3.0 metric 1
   subnet 172.16.4.0 metric 1
   subnet 172.16.5.0 metric 2
RIP: sending v1 update to 255.255.255.255 via FastEthernet0/0 (172.16.3.1)
RIP: build update entries
   subnet 0.0.0.0 metric 1
   subnet 172.16.1.0 metric 2
   subnet 172.16.2.0 metric 1
   subnet 172.16.4.0 metric 1
   subnet 172.16.5.0 metric 2
RIP: sending v1 update to 255.255.255.255 via Serial0/1 (172.16.4.1)
RIP: build update entries
   subnet 0.0.0.0 metric 1
   subnet 172.16.1.0 metric 2
   subnet 172.16.2.0 metric 1
   subnet 172.16.3.0 metric 1
```

This output has been cleaned up so that you can better discuss what is going on. How many neighbors are sending updates to this router? _______________________________

How many updates is the router sending out? _______________________________

This command helps you identify where you can decrease RIP's use of bandwidth and improve security at the same time. Do you see where you are wasting bandwidth? How would you fix it?

____

____

____

____

Lab Exercises

Note about IGRP labs: According to the Cisco Networking Academy Program: "Beginning with Cisco IOS Release 12.3, Interior Gateway Routing Protocol (IGRP) will no longer be supported. As the number of IGRP networks decreases, IGRP coverage in future releases of Cisco Networking Academy Program courses will decrease as well. IGRP-related tasks will be reduced and eventually eliminated from Networking Academy program assessments and CCNA certification exams. These tasks include configuration commands, **debug** commands, and **show** commands. Next, the number of IGRP theory and concept assessment items will be reduced and eventually eliminated."

Completing the IGRP labs still has value for your later studies of EIGRP. (The 1721 router does not have IGRP, and these labs can be effectively done with EIGRP.) In particular, the section "Curriculum Lab 7-6: Default Routing with RIP and IGRP (7.3.6)" is important to your current understanding of default routing and should be completed even though it includes IGRP content. In addition, the section "Curriculum Lab 7-7: Unequal-Cost Load Balancing with IGRP (7.3.8)" is a fascinating journey into controlling traffic across multiple redundant links with different costs. These skills migrate well to EIGRP, which is the Cisco enhancement (thus the *E*) of its proprietary IGRP. Many of the IGRP configurations that you learn in these labs apply to EIGRP. However, you should realize that, at this point in your studies, you will not be assessed on IGRP concepts and configurations.

Command Reference

In the table that follows, record the command, *including the correct router prompt,* that fits the description. Fill in any blanks with the appropriate missing information.

Command	Description
	Instructs the IOS to forward packets destined for an unknown subnet to the best supernet router; on by default in IOS Release 12.0 and higher.
	Enables RIP as a routing protocol.
	Configures 172.16.0.0 as the network you want to advertise.
	Stops RIP updates from being sent out the Fa0/0 interface.
	Changes the default RIP times to 15, 45, 90, 135, and 180.
	Sets the number of equal-cost paths RIP uses to 6.
	Sends all static route information in RIP.
	Sends default route information in RIP.
	Enables RIP v2.
	This interface sends only RIP v1 updates.
	This interface sends only RIP v2 updates.
	This interface sends both RIP v1 and RIP v2 updates.

Command	Description
	This interface receives only RIP v1 updates.
	This interface receives only RIP v2 updates.
	This interface receives both RIP v1 and RIP v2 updates.
	Displays a summary of all interfaces, their states, and configured IP addresses.
	Displays the current routing table.
	Deletes the current routing table, forcing it to rebuild.
	Displays the current state of all active routing protocol processes.
	Displays all RIP activity in real time as it occurs.
	Turns off all debugging activity.

Lab 7-1: Configuring RIP (7.2.2)

Figure 7-5 Topology for Lab 7-1

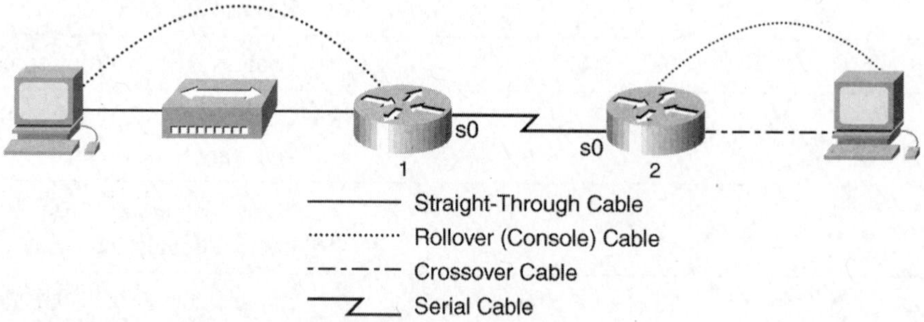

Table 7-1 Lab Equipment Configuration

Router Designation	Router Name	FastEthernet 0 Address	Interface Type	Serial 0 Address
Router 1	GAD	172.16.0.1	DCE	172.17.0.1
Router 2	BHM	172.18.0.1	DTE	172.17.0.2

The enable secret password for both routers is **class**.

The enable, vty, and console passwords for both routers are **cisco**. The subnet mask for both interfaces on both routers is 255.255.0.0.

Objectives:

- Set up an IP addressing scheme using Class B networks.
- Configure the dynamic Routing Information Protocol (RIP) on routers.

Background/Preparation

Cable a network similar to the one in Figure 7-5. You can use any router that meets the interface requirements in Figure 7-5 (that is, 800, 1600, 1700, 2500, and 2600 routers or a combination). Refer to the information in Appendix B, "Router Interface Summary," to correctly specify the interface identifiers based on the equipment in your lab. The 1721 series routers produced the configuration output in this lab. Any other router might produce slightly different output. You should execute the following tasks on each router unless specifically instructed otherwise.

Start a HyperTerminal session as you did in Lab 2-2, "Establishing a Console Session with HyperTerminal."

Implement the procedure documented in Appendix C, "Erasing and Reloading the Router," before continuing with this lab.

Task 1: Configure the Routers

On the routers, enter the global configuration mode and configure the router name as shown in Table 7-1. Then, configure the console, vty, and enable passwords.

If you have trouble doing this, refer to Lab 3-2, "Configuring Router Passwords." Next, configure the interfaces according to Table 7-1. If you have problems doing this, refer to Lab 3-9, "Configuring Host Tables."

Task 2: Check the Routing Table Entries

Step 1. Using the command **show ip route**, view the IP routing table for GAD.

```
GAD>show ip route output eliminated
Gateway of last resort is not set
C    172.16.0.0/16 is directly connected, FastEthernet0
C    172.17.0.0/16 is directly connected, Serial0
```

Step 2. Using the command **show ip route**, view the IP routing table for BHM.

```
BHM>show ip route output eliminated
Gateway of last resort is not set
C    172.17.0.0/24 is directly connected, Serial0
C    172.18.0.0/24 is directly connected, FastEthernet0
```

Task 3: Configure the Routing Protocol on the GAD Router

From the global configuration mode, enter the following:

```
GAD(config)#router rip
GAD(config-router)#network 172.16.0.0
GAD(config-router)#network 172.17.0.0
GAD(config-router)#exit
GAD(config)#exit
```

Task 4: Save the GAD Router Configuration

To save the GAD router configuration, enter the following command:

```
GAD#copy running-config startup-config
```

Task 5: Configure the Routing Protocol on the BHM Router

From global configuration mode, enter the following:

```
BHM(config)#router rip
BHM(config-router)#network 172.17.0.0
BHM(config-router)#network 172.18.0.0
BHM(config-router)#exit
BHM(config)#exit
```

Task 6. Save the BHM Router Configuration

To save the BHM router configuration, enter the following command:

```
BHM#copy running-config startup-config
```

Task 7: Configure the Hosts with the Proper IP Addresses, Subnet Masks, and Default Gateways

Task 8: Verify That the Internetwork Is Functioning by Pinging the FastEthernet Interface of the Other Router

Step 1. From the host attached to GAD, can you ping the BHM router's FastEthernet interface? _____

Step 2. From the host attached to BHM, can you ping the GAD router's FastEthernet interface? _____

Step 3. If the answer is no for either question, troubleshoot the router configurations to find the error. Then, do the pings again until the answer to both questions is yes.

Task 9: Show the Routing Tables for Each Router

From enable (privileged EXEC) mode, examine the routing table entries, using **show ip route** on each router.

What are the entries in the GAD routing table?

____

____

____

What are the entries in the BHM routing table?

____

____

____

When you finish this task, log off (by typing **exit**) and turn off the router.

Lab 7-2: Troubleshooting RIP (7.2.6)

Figure 7-6 Topology for Lab 7-2

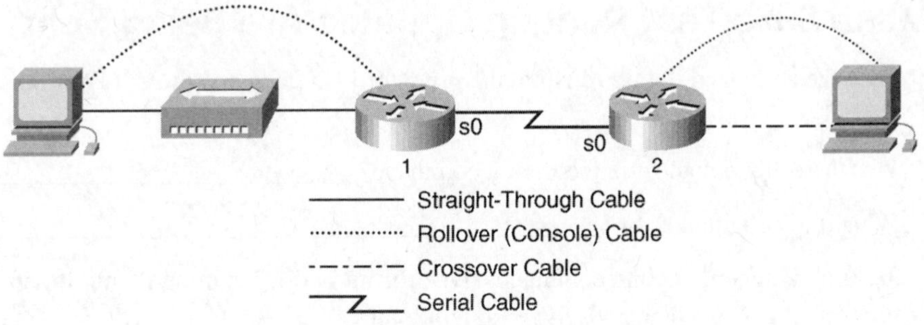

Table 7-2 Lab Equipment Configuration

Router Designation	Router Name	FastEthernet 0 Address	Interface Type	Serial 0 Address
Router 1	GAD	172.16.0.1	DCE	172.17.0.1
Router 2	BHM	172.18.0.1	DTE	172.17.0.2

The enable secret password for both routers is **class**.

The enable, vty, and console passwords for both routers are **cisco**. The subnet mask for both interfaces on both routers is 255.255.0.0.

Objectives:

- Set up an IP addressing scheme using Class B networks.
- Configure RIP on both routers.
- Observe routing activity using the **debug ip rip** command.
- Examine routes using the **show ip route** command.

Background/Preparation

Cable a network similar to the one in Figure 7-6. You can use any router that meets the interface requirements in Figure 7-6 (that is, 800, 1600, 1700, 2500, and 2600 routers or a combination). Refer to the information in Appendix B, "Router Interface Summary," to correctly specify the interface identifiers based on the equipment in your lab. The 1721 series routers produced the configuration output in this lab. Any other router might produce slightly different output. You should execute the following tasks on each router unless specifically instructed otherwise.

Start a HyperTerminal session as you did in Lab 2-2.

Implement the procedure documented in Appendix C, "Erasing and Reloading the Router," before continuing with this lab.

Task 1: Configure the Routers

On the routers, enter global configuration mode and configure the router name as shown in Table 7-2. Then, configure the console, vty, and enable passwords. If you have problems doing so, refer to Lab 3-2. Next, configure the interfaces according to Table 7-2. If you have problems doing so, refer to Lab 3-9. Finally, configure the RIP routing. Refer to Lab 7-1, "Configuring RIP," if you need help. Don't forget to save the configurations to the startup configuration file.

Task 2: Configure the Hosts with the Proper IP Addresses, Subnet Masks, and Default Gateways

Task 3: Make Sure That Routing Updates Are Being Sent

Step 1. Type the command **debug ip rip** at the privileged EXEC mode prompt. Wait for at least 45 seconds.

Was there any output from the **debug** command? ______________________________

What did the output show? ______________________________

Step 2. To turn off specific **debug** commands, type the **no** option, as in **no debug ip rip events.** To turn off all **debug** commands, type **undebug all.**

Task 4: Show the Routing Tables for Each Router

From enable (privileged EXEC) mode, examine the routing table entries, using **show ip route** on each router.

What are the entries in the GAD routing table?

____

____

____

What are the entries in the BHM routing table?

____

____

____

Task 5: Show the RIP Routing Table Entries for Each Router

Step 1. Enter **show ip route rip**.

Step 2. List the routes listed in the routing table:

____

____

What is the administrative distance? ______________________________

Task 6: Verify That the Internetwork Is Functioning by Pinging the FastEthernet Interface of the Other Router

Step 1. From the host attached to GAD, can you ping the BHM router's FastEthernet interface?______

Step 2. From the host attached to BHM, can you ping the GAD router's FastEthernet interface? _____

Step 3. If the answer is no for either question, troubleshoot the router configurations using **show ip route** to find the error. Also, check the workstation IP settings. Then, do the pings again until the answer to both questions is yes.

Step 4. When you finish these tasks, log off (by typing **exit**) and turn off the router.

Lab 7-3: Preventing Routing Updates Through an Interface (7.2.7)

Figure 7-7 Topology for Lab 7-3

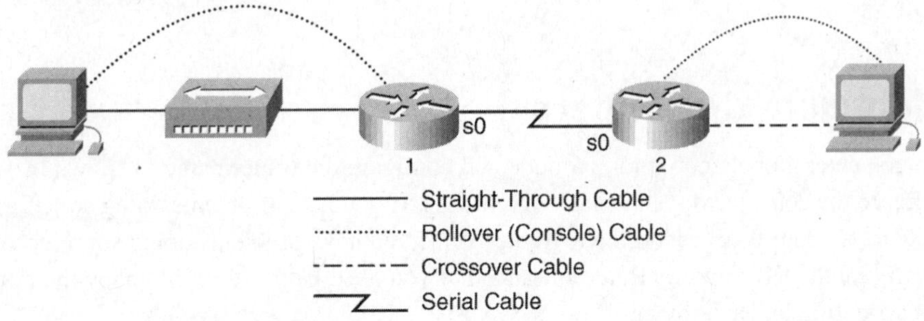

Table 7-3 Lab Equipment Configuration

Router Designation	Router Name	Routing Protocol	RIP Network Statements
Router 1	GAD	RIP	192.168.14.0
			192.168.15.0
Router 2	BHM	RIP	192.168.15.0
			192.168.16.0

The enable secret password for both routers is **class**.

The enable, vty, and console passwords for both routers are **cisco**.

Table 7-4 Lab Equipment IP Address and Interface Configuration

Router Designation	FastEthernet 0 Address	Interface Type Serial 0	Serial 0 Address	IP Host Table Entry
Router 1	192.168.14.1	DCE	192.168.15.1	BHM
Router 2	192.168.16.1	DTE	192.168.15.2	GAD

The subnet mask on all addresses for both routers is 255.255.255.0.

The IP Host Table Entry column contents indicate the name(s) of the other router(s) in the IP host table.

Objectives:

- Prevent routing updates through an interface to regulate advertised routes.
- Use the **passive-interface** command and add a default route.

Background/Preparation

This lab focuses on preventing routing updates through an interface to regulate advertised routes and observing the results. To make this work, you must use the **passive-interface** command and add a default route.

Cable a network similar to the one in Figure 7-7. You can use any router that meets the interface requirements in Figure 7-7 (that is, 800, 1600, 1700, 2500, and 2600 routers or a combination). Refer to the information in Appendix B, "Router Interface Summary," to correctly specify the interface identifiers based on the equipment in your lab. The 1721 series routers produced the configuration output in this lab. Any other router might produce slightly different output. You should execute the following tasks on each router unless specifically instructed otherwise.

Start a HyperTerminal session as you did in Lab 2-2.

Implement the procedure documented in Appendix C, "Erasing and Reloading the Router," before continuing with this lab.

Task 1: Configure the Routers

On the routers, enter global configuration mode and configure the router name as shown in Table 7-3. Then, configure the console, vty, and enable passwords. If you have problems doing so, refer to Lab 3.1.3. Next, configure the interfaces according to Table 7-4. If you have problems doing so, refer to Lab 3-9. Finally, configure the RIP routing. Refer to Lab 7-1 if you need help. Be sure to copy the **running-config** to the **startup-config** on each router.

Task 2: Configure the Hosts with the Proper IP Addresses, Subnet Masks, and Default Gateways

Test your configuration by pinging all interfaces from each host. If the pinging is not successful, troubleshoot your configuration.

Task 3: Check the Basic Routing Configuration

Step 1. Enter **show ip protocol** on each router.

In the configuration, is "Routing protocol is RIP" displayed? ____________________

Step 2. Enter the command **show ip route** on both routers. List how the route is connected (directly, RIP), the IP address, and the network or interface in Table 7-5.

Table 7-5 Lab Equipment IP Address and Interface Configuration

GAD	Route Connected	IP Address	Through Network/Interface

BHM	Route Connected	IP Address	Through Network/Interface

Task 4: Observe RIP Routing Updates

Step 1. From the GAD router, use the **debug ip rip** command to verify that the router is sending updates out the interface to the BHM router. Look for a section in the output that looks something like the following:

```
GAD#debug ip rip
RIP protocol debugging is on
```

```
GAD#
*Mar 1 03:12:17.555: RIP: sending v1 update to 255.255.255.255 via FastEthernet
0 (192.168.14.1)
*Mar 1 03:12:17.555: RIP: build update entries
*Mar 1 03:12:17.555:  network 192.168.15.0 metric 1
*Mar 1 03:12:17.555:  network 192.168.16.0 metric 2
*Mar 1 03:12:17.555: RIP: sending v1 update to 255.255.255.255 via Serial0
(192.168.15.1)
*Mar 1 03:12:17.555: RIP: build update entries
*Mar 1 03:12:17.555:  network 192.168.14.0 metric 1
*Mar 1 03:12:22.671: RIP: received v1 update from 192.168.15.2 on Serial0
*Mar 1 03:12:22.671:   192.168.16.0 in 1 hops
```

Other **debug** commands that function with RIP are as follows:

debug ip rip events

debug ip rip trigger

debug ip rip database

Step 2. To turn off specific **debug** commands, type the **no** option, as in **no debug ip rip events**. To turn off all **debug** commands, type **undebug all**.

Task 5: Stop Routing Updates from GAD to BHM

Step 1. On the console session for the GAD router, enter global configuration mode and then enter router mode with the command **router rip**. Enter the command **passive-interface serial 0** (refer to Appendix B for your model or router). This step prevents the GAD router from advertising its routes to the BHM router.

Step 2. To confirm this change, use the **debug ip rip events** command on the GAD router. Verify from the output that the router is not sending updates out the interface to the BHM router.

Step 3. Disable the debug output with the **no debug all** command.

Step 4. Also from the BHM router, issue **show ip route** to verify that you have removed the route to the GAD LAN. Attempt to ping from the computers in GAD to the computers in BHM.

What response do you get? ____

Step 5. Confirm that the BHM router is still sending updates to GAD. To do this, use the **debug ip rip events** command on the BHM router. Verify from the output that the router is sending updates out the interface to the GAD router.

How many routes are being sent? ____

Step 6. Disable the debug output with the **no debug all** command.

Task 6: Add a Default Route to BHM

Because BHM is not getting routing updates, it does not have a route to the outside world. You must provide it with a default route. A *default route* is the route by which the router sends data if the routing table does not have a specific route to use.

Step 1. From global configuration mode on the BHM router, enter the following:

```
BHM(config)#ip route 0.0.0.0 0.0.0.0 192.168.15.1
```

Step 2. Verify that the default route is in the BHM routing table by issuing the **show ip route** command. You should see output similar to the following:

```
BHM#show ip route
Codes: C - connected, S - static, I - IGRP, R - RIP, M - mobile, B - BGP
    D - EIGRP, EX - EIGRP external, O - OSPF, IA - OSPF inter area
    N1 - OSPF NSSA external type 1, N2 - OSPF NSSA external type 2
    E1 - OSPF external type 1, E2 - OSPF external type 2, E - EGP
    i - IS-IS, L1 - IS-IS level-1, * - candidate default
    U - per-user static route, o - ODR
Gateway of last resort is 192.168.15.1 to network 0.0.0.0
C   192.168.15.0/24 is directly connected, Serial0
C   192.168.16.0/24 is directly connected, FastEthernet0
S*  0.0.0.0/0 [1/0] via 192.168.15.1
BHM#
```

Step 3. Ensure that you can ping from the computers in GAD to the computers in BHM. If not, check the routing tables and interfaces.

Step 4. When you finish these tasks, log off (by typing **exit**) and turn off the router.

Lab 7-4: Load Balancing Across Multiple Paths (7.2.9)

Figure 7-8 Topology for Lab 7-4

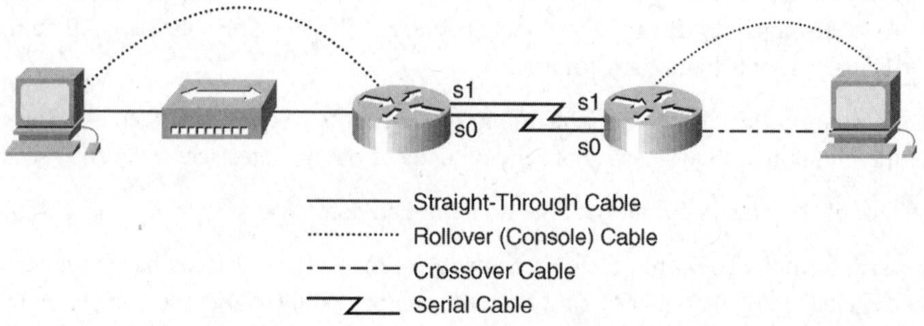

Table 7-6 Lab Equipment Configuration

Router Designation	Router Name	Routing Protocol	RIP Network Statements
Router 1	GAD	RIP	192.168.14.0
			192.168.15.0
			192.168.13.0
Router 2	BHM	RIP	192.168.15.0
			192.168.16.0
			192.168.13.0

The enable secret password for both routers is **class**.

The enable, vty, and console passwords for both routers are **cisco**.

Table 7-7 Lab Equipment IP Address and Interface Configuration

Router Designation	FastEthernet 0 Address	Interface Type Serial 0	Serial 0 Address	Interface Type Serial 1	Serial 1 Address	IP Host Table Entry
Router 1	192.168.14.1	DCE	192.168.15.1	DCE	192.168.13.1	BHM
Router 2	192.168.16.1	DTE	192.168.15.2	DTE	192.168.13.2	GAD

The subnet mask on all addresses for both routers is 255.255.255.0.

The IP Host Table Entry column contents indicate the name(s) of the other router(s) in the IP host table.

Objectives:

- Configure load balancing across multiple paths.
- Observe the load-balancing process.

Background/Preparation

Cable a network similar to the one in Figure 7-8. You can use any router that meets the interface requirements in Figure 7-8 (that is, 800, 1600, 1700, 2500, and 2600 routers or a combination). Refer to the information in Appendix B, "Router Interface Summary," to correctly specify the interface identifiers based on the equipment in your lab. The 1721 series routers produced the configuration output in this lab. Any other router might produce slightly different output. You should execute the following tasks on each router unless specifically instructed otherwise.

Start a HyperTerminal session as you did in Lab 2-2.

Implement the procedure documented in Appendix C, "Erasing and Reloading the Router," before continuing with this lab.

Task 1: Configure the Routers

On the routers, enter global configuration mode and configure the router name as shown in Table 7-6. Then, configure the console, vty, and enable passwords. If you have problems doing so, refer to Lab 3-2. Next, configure the interfaces and routing according to Table 7-7. If you have problems doing so, refer to Labs 3-9 and 7-1. Be sure to copy the **running-config** to the **startup-config** on each router so you won't lose the configuration if the router is power-cycled.

Task 2: Configure the Hosts with the Proper IP Addresses, Subnet Masks, and Default Gateways

Test your configuration by pinging all the interfaces from each host. If the pinging is not successful, troubleshoot your configuration.

Task 3: Check the Basic Routing Configuration

Step 1. Enter **show ip protocol** on each router.

In the configuration, is "Routing protocol is RIP" displayed?

Step 2. Enter the command **show ip route** on both routers. List how the route is connected (directly, RIP), the IP address, and through what network interface. You should list four routes for each. Record the information in Table 7-8.

Table 7-8 IP Route Information for GAD and BHM

GAD	Route Connected	IP Address	Through Network/Interface

BHM	Route Connected	IP Address	Through Network/Interface

Step 3. List the evidence of load balancing in the output from **show ip route**.

____

____

Task 4: Ensure That the Router Load-Balances on a Per-Packet Basis

Step 1. Configure the router to load-balance on a per-packet basis. Both serial interfaces must use process switching. *Process switching* forces the router to look in the routing table for the destination network of each routed packet. In contrast, fast switching (the default) stores the initial table lookup in a high-speed cache and uses the information to route packets to the same destination.

Step 2. Enable process switching on both serial interfaces.

```
GAD(config-if)#no ip route-cache
BHM(config-if)#no ip route-cache
```

Step 3. Verify that fast switching is disabled by using the **show ip interface** command.

Was fast switching disabled? ____

Task 5: Verify Per-Packet Load Balancing

Step 1. Because there are two routes to the destination network, half the packets are sent along one path and half travel over the other. The path selection alternates with each packet.

Observe this process by using the **debug ip packet** command on the GAD router.

Step 2. Send 30 ping packets across the network from the host attached to the BHM router to the host attached to the GAD router. This can be done with the **ping 192.168.16.2 -n 30** command on the host. As the pings are responded to, the router generates IP packet information. Stop the debug by using the command **undebug all** on the GAD router.

Step 3. Examine and record part of the debug output.

What is the evidence of load balancing in the output?

____

Task 6: Verify Per-Destination Load Balancing

Step 1. After verifying per-packet load balancing, configure the router to use per-destination load balancing. Both serial interfaces must use fast switching so that the they can use the route cache after the initial table lookup.

Use the command `GAD(config-if)#` **`ip route-cache`**.

Step 2. Use **show ip interface** to verify that fast switching is enabled.

Is fast switching enabled? ____

Step 3. The router consults the routing table only once per destination; therefore, packets that are part of a packet train to a specific host all follow the same path. Only when a second destination forces another table lookup or when the cached entry expires does the router use the alternate path.

Use the **debug ip packet** command and **ping** across the network. Note which serial interface the router sent the packet on.

Step 4. Examine and record part of the debug output. Which serial interface did the router send the packet on? ____

Step 5. When you finish this task, log off (by typing **exit**) and turn off the router.

Lab 7-5: Configuring IGRP (7.3.5)

Figure 7-9 Topology for Lab 7-5

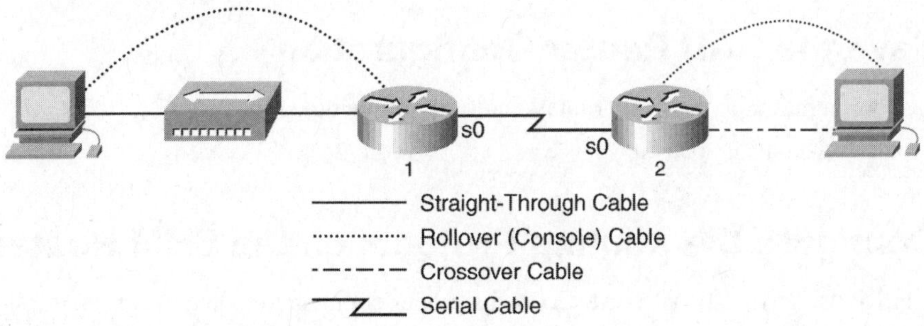

Table 7-9 Lab Equipment Configuration

Router Designation	Router Name	FastEthernet 0 Address	Interface Type	Serial 0 Address
Router 1	GAD	192.168.20.1	DCE	192.168.22.1
Router 2	BHM	192.168.25.1	DTE	192.168.22.2

The subnet mask for both interfaces on both routers is 255.255.255.0. The enable secret password for both routers is **class**.

The enable, vty, and console passwords for both routers are **cisco**.

Objectives:

- Set up an IP addressing scheme using Class C networks.
- Configure the Interior Gateway Routing Protocol (IGRP) on the routers.

Background/Preparation

Cable a network similar to the one in Figure 7-9. You can use any router that meets the interface requirements in Figure 7-9 (that is, 800, 1600, 1700, 2500, and 2600 routers or a combination). Refer to the information in Appendix B, "Router Interface Summary," to correctly specify the interface identifiers based on the equipment in your lab. The 1721 series routers produced the configuration output in this lab. Any other router might produce slightly different output. You should execute the following tasks on each router unless specifically instructed otherwise.

Start a HyperTerminal session as you did in Lab 2-2.

Implement the procedure documented in Appendix C, "Erasing and Reloading the Router," before continuing with this lab.

Task 1: Configure the Routers

On the routers, enter global configuration mode and configure the router name as shown in Table 7-9. Then, configure the console, vty, and enable passwords. If you have problems doing so, refer to Lab 3-2. Next, configure the interfaces according to Table 7-9. If you have problems doing so, refer to Lab 3-9.

Task 2: Configure the Routing Protocol on the GAD Router

Configure IGRP using autonomous system (AS) 101 on GAD. Go to the proper command mode and enter the following:

```
GAD(config)#router igrp 101
GAD(config-router)#network 192.168.22.0
GAD(config-router)#network 192.168.20.0
```

Task 3. Save the GAD Router Configuration

To save the configuration on the GAD router, enter the following command:

```
GAD#copy running-config startup-config
```

Task 4: Configure the Routing Protocol on the BHM Router

Configure IGRP using AS 101 on BHM. Go to the proper command mode and enter the following:

```
BHM(config)#router igrp 101
BHM(config-router)#network 192.168.25.0
BHM(config-router)#network 192.168.22.0
```

Task 5: Save the BHM Router Configuration

To save the configuration on the BHM router, enter the following command:

```
BHM#copy running-config startup-config
```

Task 6: Configure the Hosts with the Proper IP Addresses, Subnet Masks, and Default Gateways

Task 7: Verify That the Internetwork Is Functioning by Pinging the FastEthernet Interface of the Other Router

Step 1. From the host attached to GAD, can you ping the BHM host? ____________________

Step 2. From the host attached to BHM, can you ping the GAD host? ____________________

Step 3. If the answer is no for either question, troubleshoot the router configurations to find the error. Then, do the pings again until the answer to both questions is yes.

Task 8: Show the Routing Tables for Each Router

From enable (privileged EXEC) mode, examine the routing table entries using **show ip route** on each router.

What are the entries in the GAD routing table?

____

____

____

What are the entries in the BHM routing table?

____

____

____

Task 9: Verify the Routing Protocol

Type **show ip protocol** on both routers to verify IGRP is running and that it is the only protocol running.

Is IGRP the only protocol running on GAD? ____________________

Is IGRP the only protocol running on BHM? ____________________

Task 10: Verify the IGRP Statements in the Running Configuration of Both Routers

Step 1. Use the **show run | begin igrp** command on both routers.

Step 2. List the IGRP part of the configuration for GAD.

____

____

____

Task 11: Verify the IGRP Routing Updates Using the debug ip igrp events Command

Step 1. Type **debug ip igrp events** on the GAD router in privileged EXEC mode.

Do the routing updates appear? ____________________

Where are the updates being sent to? ____________________

Where are the updates being received from? ____________________

Step 2. Turn off debugging.

Task 12: Verify the IGRP Routing Updates Using the debug ip igrp transactions Command

Step 1. Type **debug ip igrp transactions** on the GAD router in privileged EXEC mode.

How is the output of the two **debug** commands **debug ip igrp events** and **debug ip igrp transactions** different?

____

____

Step 2. Turn off debugging.

Task 13: Analyze Specific Routes

Step 1. Type **show ip route 192.168.25.0** on the GAD router to see more detail on the route to the 192.168.25.0 network on BHM.

What is the total delay for this route?

____

What is the minimum bandwidth?

____

What is the reliability of this route?

____

What is the minimum maximum transmission unit (MTU) size for this route?

____

Step 2. Type **show ip route 192.168.25.0** on the BHM router.

What is the total delay for this route?

____

What is the minimum bandwidth?

____

What is the reliability of this route?

____

What is the minimum MTU size for this route?

____

Step 3. When you finish this task, log off (by typing **exit**) and turn off the router.

Lab 7-6: Default Routing with RIP and IGRP (7.3.6)

Figure 7-10 Topology for Lab 7-6

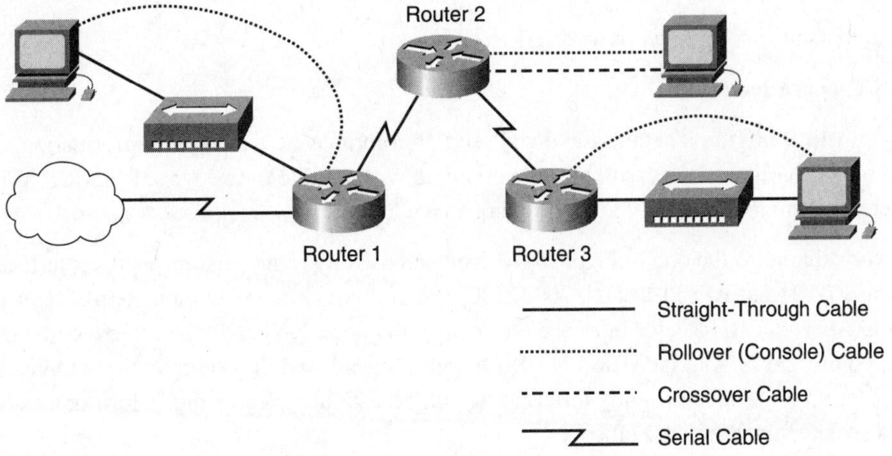

Table 7-10 Lab Equipment Configuration: Part I

Router Designation	Router Name	Routing Protocol	RIP Network Statements
Router 1	Centre	RIP	192.168.2.0
			192.168.3.0
Router 2	Boaz	RIP	192.168.1.0
			192.168.2.0
			192.168.4.0
Router 3	Mobile	RIP	192.168.1.0
			192.168.5.0

The enable secret password for all routers is **class**.

The enable, vty, and console passwords for all routers are **cisco**.

Table 7-11 Lab Equipment Configuration: Part II

Router Designation	FastEthernet 0 Address	Interface Type Serial 0	Serial 0 Address	Interface Type Serial 1	Serial 1 Address	IP Host Table Entry
Router 1	192.168.3.1	DTE	192.168.2.2	N/A	No address	Boaz Mobile
Router 2	192.168.4.1	DCE	192.168.1.1	DCE	192.168.2.1	Centre Mobile
Router 3	192.168.5.1	DTE	192.168.1.2	N/A	No address	Boaz Centre

The subnet mask on all addresses for all routers is 255.255.255.0.

The IP Host Table Entry column contents indicate the name(s) of the other router(s) in the IP host table.

Objectives:

- Configure a default route and use RIP to propagate this default information to other routers.
- Migrate the network from RIP to IGRP.
- Configure default routing to work with IGRP.

Background/Preparation

In this lab, you will configure a default route and use RIP to propagate this default information to other routers. When this configuration is working properly, you will migrate the network from RIP to IGRP and configure default routing to work with that protocol as well.

Cable a network similar to the one in Figure 7-10. You can use any router that meets the interface requirements in Figure 7-10 (that is, 800, 1600, 1700, 2500, and 2600 routers or a combination). Refer to the information in Appendix B, "Router Interface Summary," to correctly specify the interface identifiers based on the equipment in your lab. The 1721 Series routers produced the configuration output in this lab. Any other router might produce slightly different output. You should execute the following tasks on each router unless specifically instructed otherwise.

Start a HyperTerminal session as you did in Lab 2-2.

Implement the procedure documented in Appendix C, "Erasing and Reloading the Router," before continuing with this lab.

Task 1: Configure the Routers

On the routers, enter global configuration mode and configure the router name as shown in Table 7-10. Then, configure the console, vty, and enable passwords. If you have problems doing so, refer to Lab 3-2. Next, configure the interfaces and routing according to Tables 7-10 and 7-11. If you have problems doing so, refer to Labs 3-9 and 7-1. Be sure to copy the **running-config** to the **startup-config** on each router so you won't lose the configuration if the router is power-cycled.

Task 2: Configure the Hosts with the Proper IP Addresses, Subnet Masks, and Default Gateways

Test your configuration by pinging all the interfaces from each host. If the pinging is not successful, troubleshoot your configuration.

Task 3: Check the Basic Routing Configuration

Enter **show ip protocol** on each router.

In the configuration, does the Router RIP appear? ______________________________

Task 4: Verify Connectivity

To verify connectivity of the network you just set up, ping all the interfaces from each of the attached hosts. If you cannot ping all the interfaces, correct the configuration until you can.

Task 5: Configure Centre as the Connection to the Internet Service Provider (ISP)

Step 1. Configure Centre to simulate the existence of an outside network. You simulate the link between the company and its ISP by configuring a loopback interface with an IP address. Enter the following commands on the Centre router:

```
Centre(config)#interface loopback0
Centre(config-if)#ip address 172.16.1.1 255.255.255.255
```

Note: If you ping 172.16.1.1 from Centre's console, the loopback interface replies.

Step 2. From the Boaz console, attempt to ping 172.16.1.1. This ping should fail because the 172.16.0.0/16 network is not in the Boaz routing table.

If no default route exists, what does a router do with a packet destined for a network that is not in its table?

____

Task 6: Set Up a Default Route on the Centre Router

Step 1. You must create a default route on the Centre router pointed at the simulated ISP. Issue the following command on the Centre router in configuration mode:

```
Centre(config)#ip route 0.0.0.0 0.0.0.0 loopback0
```

This command statically configures the default route. The default route directs traffic destined for networks that are not in the routing table to the ISP WAN link (loopback 0).

Step 2. Unless you use Cisco IOS Software Release 12.1, RIP automatically propagates statically defined default routes. Depending on the IOS version, you might need to explicitly configure RIP to propagate this 0.0.0.0/0 route. Enter these commands on the Centre router in the proper command mode:

```
Centre(config)#router rip
Centre(config-router)#default-information originate
```

Task 7: Verify the Routing Tables

Step 1. Check the routing tables of Mobile and Boaz using the **show ip route** command. Verify that they both have received and installed a route to 0.0.0.0/0 in their tables.

On Boaz, what is the metric of this route? _______________________________

On Mobile, what is the metric of this route? _______________________________

Step 2. Mobile and Boaz still don't have routes to 172.16.0.0/16 in their tables. From Boaz, **ping 172.16.1.1**. This ping should be successful.

Why does the ping to 172.16.1.1 work, even though there is no route to 172.16.0.0/16 in the Boaz routing table?

____

Step 3. Ensure that Mobile can also ping 172.16.1.1. Troubleshoot if necessary.

Task 8: Migrate the Network from RIP to IGRP

Step 1. With default routing now working, you must migrate the network from RIP to IGRP for testing purposes. Issue the following command on all three routers:

```
Mobile(config)#no router rip
```

Note: With a normal migration, the IGRP routing protocol would be configured before removing the RIP routing protocol. IGRP routes would then replace the RIP routes in the routing table since they have a lower administrative distance and RIP could then be safely removed.

Step 2. With RIP removed from each router's configuration, configure IGRP on all three routers using AS 24, as shown:

```
Mobile(config)#router igrp 24
Mobile(config-router)#network 192.168.1.0
Mobile(config-router)#network 192.168.5.0
...
```

```
Boaz(config)#router igrp 24
Boaz(config-router)#network 192.168.1.0
Boaz(config-router)#network 192.168.2.0
Boaz(config-router)#network 192.168.4.0
...
```

```
Centre(config)#router igrp 24
Centre(config-router)#network 192.168.2.0
Centre(config-router)#network 192.168.3.0
```

Step 3. Use **ping** and **show ip route** to verify that IGRP is working properly. Don't worry about the 172.16.1.1 loopback address on Centre yet.

Task 9: Check Centre's Routing Table for the Static Default Route

Step 1. Check Centre's routing table. The static default route to 0.0.0.0/0 should still be there. To propagate this route with RIP, you issued the **default-information originate** command. (Depending on your IOS version, you might not have needed to do that.) The **default-information originate** command is not available in an IGRP configuration. Thus, you must use a different method to propagate default information in IGRP.

On Centre, issue the following commands:

```
Centre(config)#router igrp 24
Centre(config-router)#network 172.16.0.0
Centre(config-router)#exit
Centre(config)#ip default-network 172.16.0.0
```

These commands configure IGRP to update its neighbor routers about the network 172.16.0.0/16, which includes your simulated ISP link (loopback 0). Not only will IGRP advertise this network, but the **ip default-network** command also will flag this network as a candidate default route (denoted by an asterisk in the routing table). When a network is flagged as a default, that flag stays with the route as it passed from neighbor to neighbor by IGRP.

Step 2. Check the routing tables of Mobile and Boaz. If they don't yet have the 172.16.0.0/16 route with an asterisk, you might need to wait for another IGRP update (90 seconds). You can also issue the **clear ip route** * command on all three routers if you want to force them to immediately send new updates.

Step 3. When the 172.16.0.0/16 route appears as a candidate default in all three routing tables, proceed to the next task.

Task 10: Create a Second Loopback Interface on Centre to Test the Default Route

Step 1. Because the 172.16.0.0/16 network is known explicitly by Mobile and Boaz, you need to create a second loopback interface on Centre to test your default route. Issue the following commands on Centre:

```
Centre(config)#interface loopback1
Centre(config-if)#ip address 10.0.0.1 255.0.0.0
```

This loopback interface simulates another external network.

Step 2. Return to Mobile and check its routing table using the **show ip route** command.

Is there a route to the 10.0.0.0/8 network? ______________________________

Step 3. From Mobile, ping 10.0.0.1. This ping should be successful.

If there is no route to 10.0.0.0/8 and no route to 0.0.0.0/0, why does this ping succeed?

____

____

Lab 7-7: Unequal-Cost Load Balancing with IGRP (7.3.8)

Figure 7-11 Topology for Lab 7-7

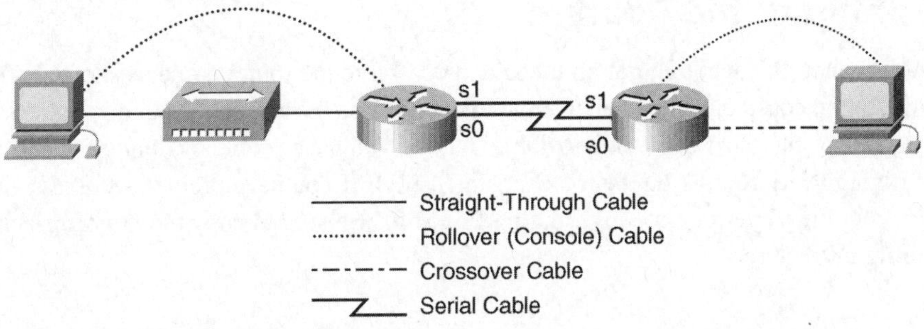

Table 7-12 Lab Equipment Configuration: Part I

Router Designation	Router Name	Routing Protocol	RIP Network Statements
Router 1	MAD	IGRP	192.168.41.0
			192.168.50.0
			192.168.52.0
Router 2	MIL	IGRP	192.168.50.0
			192.168.52.0
			192.168.33.0

The enable secret password for all routers is **class**.

The enable, vty, and console passwords for all routers are **cisco**.

Table 7-13 Lab Equipment Configuration: Part II

Router Designation	FastEthernet 0 Address	Interface Type Serial 0	Serial 0 Address	Interface Type Serial 1	Serial 1 Address	IP Host Table Entry
Router 1	192.168.41.1	DCE	192.168.50.1	DCE	192.168.52.1	MIL
Router 2	192.168.33.1	DTE	192.168.50.2	DTE	192.168.52.2	MAD

The subnet mask on all addresses for all routers is 255.255.255.0.

The IP Host Table Entry column contents indicate the name(s) of the other router(s) in the IP host table.

Objectives:

- Observe unequal-cost load balancing.
- Tune IGRP networks by using advanced **debug** commands.

Background/Preparation

Cable a network similar to the one in Figure 7-11. You can use any router that meets the interface requirements in Figure 7-11 (that is, 800, 1600, 1700, 2500, and 2600 routers or a combination). Refer to the information in Appendix B, "Router Interface Summary," to correctly specify the interface identifiers based on the equipment in your lab. The 1721 series routers produced the configuration output in this lab. Any other router might produce slightly different output. You should execute the following Tasks on each router unless specifically instructed otherwise.

Start a HyperTerminal session as you did in Lab 2-2.

Implement the procedure documented in Appendix C, "Erasing and Reloading the Router," before continuing with this lab.

Task 1: Configure the Routers

On the routers, enter global configuration mode and configure the router name as shown in Table 7-12. Then, configure the console, vty, and enable passwords. If you have problems doing so, refer to Lab 3-2. Next, configure the interfaces according to Table 7-13. If you have problems doing so, refer to Lab 3-9. Finally, configure IGRP routing on the routers using AS 34. If you have problems doing so, refer to Lab 7-5, "Configuring Interior Gateway Routing Protocol." Be sure to copy the **running-config** to the **startup-config** on each router.

Task 2: Configure Bandwidth on the MAD Router Interfaces

Step 1. To make unequal-cost load balancing work, you need to establish different metrics for the IGRP routes. You use the **bandwidth** command. Set the Serial 0 interface to a bandwidth of 56 kbps and the Serial 1 interface to a value of 384 kbps. You must also turn off the route cache for load balancing. Both serial interfaces must use process switching. Process switching forces the router to look in the routing table for the destination network of each routed packet. In contrast, fast switching (the default) stores the initial table lookup in a high-speed cache and uses the information to route packets to the same destination. Enter the following statements on the MAD router.

```
MAD(config)#interface serial 0/0
MAD(config-if)#bandwidth 56
MAD(config-if)#no ip route-cache
MAD(config-if)#interface serial 0/1
```

```
MAD(config-if)#bandwidth 384
MAD(config-if)#no ip route-cache
```

Because the IGRP metric includes bandwidth in its calculation, you must manually configure bandwidth on the serial interfaces to ensure accuracy. (For the purposes of this lab, the alternative paths to network 192.168.41.0 from the MAD router are not of unequal cost until you set the appropriate bandwidths.)

Step 2. Use the **show interface** command output to verify the correct bandwidth settings and the **show ip interface** command to ensure that fast switching is disabled.

Can you set the bandwidth of Ethernet interfaces manually? ______________________________

Task 3: Configure the Hosts with the Proper IP Addresses, Subnet Masks, and Default Gateways

Test your configuration by pinging all the interfaces from each host. If the pinging is not successful, troubleshoot your configuration.

Task 4: Use the variance Command to Configure Unequal-Cost Load Balancing

The variance value determines whether IGRP will accept unequal-cost routes. An IGRP router will only accept routes equal to the local best metric for the destination multiplied by the variance value. If an IGRP router's local best metric for a network is 10476 and the variance is 3, the router will accept unequal-cost routes with any metric up to 31428 (10,476 * 3), as long as the advertising router is closer to the destination. An IGRP router accepts only up to four paths to the same network.

Note: An alternate route is added to the route table only if the next-hop router in that path is closer to the destination (has a lower metric value) than the current route.

By default, IGRP's variance is set to 1, which means that only routes that are exactly 1 times the local best metric are installed. Thus, a variance of 1 disables unequal-cost load balancing.

Step 1. Configure the MAD router to enable unequal-cost load balancing using the following commands:

```
MAD(config)#router igrp 34
MAD(config-router)#variance 10
```

According to the help feature, what is the maximum variance value? ____________________

Step 2. Check the MAD routing table. It should have two routes to network 192.168.33.0 with unequal metrics.

What is the IGRP metric for the route to 192.168.33.0 through Serial 0? ________________

What is the IGRP metric for the route to 192.168.33.0 through Serial 1? ________________

Task 5: Check the Basic Routing Configuration

Step 1. Enter **show ip protocol** on each router.

Step 2. Enter the command **show ip route** on each router. List how the route is connected (directly, IGRP), the IP address, and the network. Each table should have four routes.

Table 7-14 IP Route Information for MAD and MIL

MAD	Route Connected	IP Address	Through Network/Interface

MIL	Route Connected	IP Address	Through Network/Interface

List the evidence of load balancing in the output from **show ip route**.

____

____

Task 6: Verify Per-Packet Load Balancing

Step 1. Because there are two routes to the destination network, half the packets are sent along one path and half travel over the other. The path selection alternates with each packet.

Observe this process by using the **debug ip packet** command on the MAD router.

Step 2. Send 30 ping packets across the network from the host attached to MIL router to the host attached to the MAD router. This can be done with the with the **ping 192.168.41.2 - n 30** command on the host. As the pings are responded to, the router outputs IP packet information. Stop the debug after the pings by using the command **undebug all**.

Step 3. Examine and record part of the debug output.

What is the evidence of load balancing in the output?

____

Task 7: Verify Per-Destination Load Balancing

Step 1. After verifying per-packet load balancing, configure the router to use per-destination load balancing. Both serial interfaces must use fast switching so that the routers can use the route cache after the initial table lookup.

Step 2. Use the command **ip route-cache** on both serial interfaces of the MAD router.

Step 3. Use the command **show ip interface** to verify that fast switching is enabled.

Is fast switching enabled? ____

The routers consult the routing table only once per destination; therefore, packets that are part of a packet train to a specific host all follow the same path. Only when a second destination forces another table lookup or when the cached entry expires does the router use the alternate path.

Step 4. Use the **debug ip packet** command and **ping** across the network. Note which serial interface the router sent the packet on.

Step 5. Examine and record part of the debug output.

On which serial interface did the router send the packet? ________________________________

Step 6. When you finish this task, log off (by typing **exit**) and turn off the router.

Comprehensive Lab 7-8: Advanced RIP Configuration and Troubleshooting

Figure 7-12 Advanced RIP Configuration and Troubleshooting

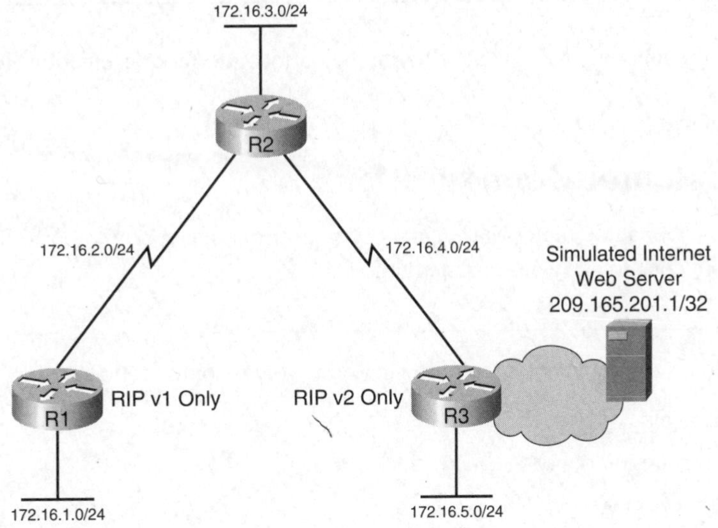

Objectives:

This lab contains the following objectives:

- Configure RIP v1 routing.
- Migrate to RIP v2 routing.
- Configure and distribute a default route.
- Optimize and verify RIP routing.

Equipment:

This lab can be done with any combination of 1700, 2500, and 2600 Series routers.

NetLab Compatibility Notes:

This lab can be completed using NetLab.

Task 1: Cable the Lab

Step 1. Cable the lab as shown in the topology in Figure 7-12.

Step 2. Document the lab by filling in the following table with appropriate configuration information.

Router	Interface Type	IP Address	Subnet Mask	Clock Rate? (Yes/No)
R1				
R2				
R3				

Step 3. Label the topology in Figure 7-12 with the correct interface designation (for example, Fa0/0, S0/0, and so on).

Task 2: Basic Router Configurations

Step 1. Make sure that the routers have empty startup or running configurations. If necessary, what must be done to carry out this instruction?

____

Step 2. Configure all routers with the following basic router configurations:

- Hostname
- Line configurations
- Global passwords
- Host tables
- Banner
- Other instructor-required global configurations

Step 3. Check your configurations. What command did you use?

____

Task 3: Interface Configurations

Step 1. Configure R1, R2, and R3 interfaces with IP addresses according to the table created in Task 1. At this point, *do not* configure the loopback interface.

Step 2. Use the **show ip interface brief** command to verify that interfaces on both routers are operational at the Physical and Data Link layers.

Are R1's interfaces fully operational? __________. If not, troubleshoot.

Are R2's interfaces fully operational? __________. If not, troubleshoot.

Are R3's interfaces fully operational? __________. If not, troubleshoot.

Task 4: Dynamic Routing Configurations

Step 1. Configure R1, R2, and R3 to use RIP routing and advertise the 172.16.0.0 network. *Do not* advertise the loopback on R3. *Do not* configure RIP v2 yet.

Step 2. Verify that all three routing tables have converged on the five routes in the internetwork:

```
R1#show ip route
Codes: C - connected, S - static, R - RIP, M - mobile, B - BGP
<some code output omitted>
       ia - IS-IS inter area, * - candidate default, U - per-user static route
       o - ODR, P - periodic downloaded static route

Gateway of last resort is not set

     172.16.0.0/24 is subnetted, 5 subnets
R       172.16.4.0 [120/1] via 172.16.2.1, 00:00:04, Serial0/0
R       172.16.5.0 [120/2] via 172.16.2.1, 00:00:04, Serial0/0
C       172.16.1.0 is directly connected, FastEthernet0/0
C       172.16.2.0 is directly connected, Serial0/0
R       172.16.3.0 [120/1] via 172.16.2.1, 00:00:04, Serial0/0
```

```
R2#show ip route
Codes: C - connected, S - static, R - RIP, M - mobile, B - BGP
<some code output omitted>
       ia - IS-IS inter area, * - candidate default, U - per-user static route
       o - ODR, P - periodic downloaded static route

Gateway of last resort is not set

     172.16.0.0/24 is subnetted, 5 subnets
C       172.16.4.0 is directly connected, Serial0/1
R       172.16.5.0 [120/1] via 172.16.4.2, 00:00:15, Serial0/1
R       172.16.1.0 [120/1] via 172.16.2.2, 00:00:15, Serial0/0
C       172.16.2.0 is directly connected, Serial0/0
C       172.16.3.0 is directly connected, FastEthernet0/0
```

```
R3#show ip route
Codes: C - connected, S - static, R - RIP, M - mobile, B - BGP
<some code output omitted>
       ia - IS-IS inter area, * - candidate default, U - per-user static route
       o - ODR, P - periodic downloaded static route

Gateway of last resort is not set

     172.16.0.0/24 is subnetted, 5 subnets
C       172.16.4.0 is directly connected, Serial0/1
C       172.16.5.0 is directly connected, FastEthernet0/0
R       172.16.1.0 [120/2] via 172.16.4.1, 00:00:00, Serial0/1
R       172.16.2.0 [120/1] via 172.16.4.1, 00:00:00, Serial0/1
R       172.16.3.0 [120/1] via 172.16.4.1, 00:00:00, Serial0/1
```

Task 5: Migration to RIP v2

Step 1. At this point, R1 and R2 remain RIP v1 routers. R3, however, is migrating to a RIP v2–only router. Configure R3 with RIP v2.

____

____

Step 2. On R3, turn on debugging for **ip rip events** and **ip rip database**. You must wait 3 minutes before RIP finally removes the routes from the routing table and another minute to see the flush timer take effect, removing the routes from memory. But it is interesting to watch how RIP v2 handles the RIP v1 updates and the removal of routes. The output that follows has been edited for brevity. You should turn on your terminal emulator's capture capability so that you can evaluate the debug output at your leisure.

```
R3(config-router)#end
!
!R3 displays current time when you exit configuration mode
!
03:22:07:%SYS-5-CONFIG_I: Configured from console by console
!
!Turn on debugging for ip rip events and ip rip database
!
R3#debug ip rip events
RIP event debugging is on
R3#debug ip rip database
RIP database events debugging is on
!
!From our debug ip rip events output, we see R3 is now sending RIP v2 updates
!
03:22:31: RIP: sending v2 update to 224.0.0.9 via FastEthernet0/0 (172.16.5.1)
03:22:31: RIP: Update contains 4 routes
03:22:31: RIP: Update queued
03:22:31: RIP: Update sent via FastEthernet0/0
03:22:33: RIP: sending v2 update to 224.0.0.9 via Serial0/1 (172.16.4.2)
03:22:33: RIP: Update contains 1 routes
03:22:33: RIP: Update queued
03:22:33: RIP: Update sent via Serial0/1
!
!The routing table still contains all the RIPv1 routes.
!Take note of the time since the last update
!
R3#show ip route
Codes: C - connected, S - static, R - RIP, M - mobile, B - BGP
       D - EIGRP, EX - EIGRP external, O - OSPF, IA - OSPF inter area
       N1 - OSPF NSSA external type 1, N2 - OSPF NSSA external type 2
       E1 - OSPF external type 1, E2 - OSPF external type 2
       i - IS-IS, su - IS-IS summary, L1 - IS-IS level-1, L2 - IS-IS level-2
       ia - IS-IS inter area, * - candidate default, U - per-user static route
       o - ODR, P - periodic downloaded static route

Gateway of last resort is not set

     172.16.0.0/24 is subnetted, 5 subnets
```

```
C       172.16.4.0 is directly connected, Serial0/1
C       172.16.5.0 is directly connected, FastEthernet0/0
R       172.16.1.0 [120/2] via 172.16.4.1, 00:00:37, Serial0/1
R       172.16.2.0 [120/1] via 172.16.4.1, 00:00:37, Serial0/1
R       172.16.3.0 [120/1] via 172.16.4.1, 00:00:37, Serial0/1
!
!Here we see from the debug ip events output that R3 is ignoring updates from
!R2
!
03:22:41.987: RIP: ignored v1 packet from 172.16.4.1 (illegal version)
!
!The show ip protocols displays our timers. The RIP v1 routes in the routing
!table should remain there for 3 minutes. After 4 minutes, they are removed
!from memory
!
R3#show ip protocols
Routing Protocol is "rip"
  Sending updates every 30 seconds, next due in 12 seconds
  Invalid after 180 seconds, hold down 180, flushed after 240
  Outgoing update filter list for all interfaces is not set
  Incoming update filter list for all interfaces is not set
  Redistributing: rip
  Default version control: send version 2, receive version 2
    Interface             Send  Recv  Triggered RIP  Key-chain
    FastEthernet0/0       2     2
    Serial0/1             2     2
  Automatic network summarization is in effect
  Maximum path: 4
  Routing for Networks:
    172.16.0.0
  Routing Information Sources:
    Gateway         Distance      Last Update
    172.16.4.1           120      00:00:45
  Distance: (default is 120)
!
!Notice in the above output that the last update was received 45 seconds ago
!That means routes from R2 will be removed in 2 minutes and 15 seconds if
!R3 does not receive a valid (v2) update
!
!Meanwhile R3 continues to send v2 and igore v1
!
03:22:58: RIP: sending v2 update to 224.0.0.9 via FastEthernet0/0 (172.16.5.1)
03:22:58: RIP: Update contains 4 routes
03:22:58: RIP: Update queued
03:22:58: RIP: Update sent via FastEthernet0/0
03:23:02: RIP: sending v2 update to 224.0.0.9 via Serial0/1 (172.16.4.2)
03:23:02: RIP: Update contains 1 routes
03:23:02: RIP: Update queued
03:23:02: RIP: Update sent via Serial0/1
03:23:09: RIP: ignored v1 packet from 172.16.4.1 (illegal version)
!
!Finally, after waiting 3 minutes our first debup ip rip database output shows
```

```
!that R3 has invalidated the old v1 routes and has removed them from the
!routing table
!
03:25:07: RIP-DB: invalidated route of 172.16.1.0/24 via 172.16.4.1
03:25:07: RIP-DB: Remove 172.16.1.0/24, (metric 4294967295) via 172.16.4.1,
Serial0/1
03:25:07: RIP-DB: invalidated route of 172.16.2.0/24 via 172.16.4.1
03:25:07: RIP-DB: Remove 172.16.2.0/24, (metric 4294967295) via 172.16.4.1,
Serial0/1
03:25:07: RIP-DB: invalidated route of 172.16.3.0/24 via 172.16.4.1
03:25:07: RIP-DB: Remove 172.16.3.0/24, (metric 4294967295) via 172.16.4.1,
Serial0/1
!
!The routing table now only contains connected routes
!
R3#show ip route
Codes: C - connected, S - static, R - RIP, M - mobile, B - BGP
       D - EIGRP, EX - EIGRP external, O - OSPF, IA - OSPF inter area
       N1 - OSPF NSSA external type 1, N2 - OSPF NSSA external type 2
       E1 - OSPF external type 1, E2 - OSPF external type 2
       i - IS-IS, su - IS-IS summary, L1 - IS-IS level-1, L2 - IS-IS level-2
       ia - IS-IS inter area, * - candidate default, U - per-user static route
       o - ODR, P - periodic downloaded static route

Gateway of last resort is not set

     172.16.0.0/24 is subnetted, 2 subnets
C       172.16.4.0 is directly connected, Serial0/1
C       172.16.5.0 is directly connected, FastEthernet0/0
!
!After one more minute, the routes are flushed completely from memory
!
03:26:07: RIP-DB: garbage collect 172.16.1.0/24
03:26:07: RIP-DB: garbage collect 172.16.2.0/24
03:26:07: RIP-DB: garbage collect 172.16.3.0/24
!
!Turn off debugging
!
R3#undebug all
All possible debugging has been turned off
```

Step 3. The importance of going through the process in Step 2 as a learning tool cannot be overstated. At this point, repeat Steps 1 and 2. Pay close attention to everything that is happening. Try to see the big picture of what is going on. What is happening on R1 and R2? How can you get R3 to accept updates from R2? Do you need to do anything on R1? If you are not sure what is happening, find out. Ask your instructor. Review your notes.

Step 4. Most of the time, you don't want to wait for your routing protocol to remove routes from the routing table. What command can you use to force the router to delete its current routing table?

____

Step 5. Display the routing tables for R1 and R2. What do you notice?

____

Step 6. Can R1 ping the Fast Ethernet interface on R3? Why not? Try tracing the ping if you're not sure.

____

____

Step 7. Configure R3 to send and receive both RIP v1 and RIP v2 updates to R2. This causes R3 to send out two different updates to R2, as shown in the **debug ip rip events** output that follows. Notice that R3 now accepts v1 updates from R3 but sends only v2 out the Fast Ethernet interface.

____

____

____

```
R3#debug ip rip events
RIP event debugging is on

00:04:25: RIP: sending v2 update to 224.0.0.9 via FastEthernet0/0 (172.16.5.1)
00:04:25: RIP: Update contains 4 routes
00:04:25: RIP: Update queued
00:04:25: RIP: Update sent via FastEthernet0/0

00:04:41: RIP: received v1 update from 172.16.4.1 on Serial0/1
00:04:41: RIP: Update contains 3 routes

00:04:47: RIP: sending v1 update to 255.255.255.255 via Serial0/1 (172.16.4.2)
00:04:47: RIP: Update contains 1 routes
00:04:47: RIP: Update queued
00:04:47: RIP: Update sent via Serial0/1

00:04:47: RIP: sending v2 update to 224.0.0.9 via Serial0/1 (172.16.4.2)
00:04:47: RIP: Update contains 1 routes
00:04:47: RIP: Update queued
00:04:47: RIP: Update sent via Serial0/1
```

Your internetwork should now be converged again. R1 should be able to ping the Fast Ethernet interface on R3, and R3 should have a complete routing table:

```
R1#ping 172.16.5.1

Type escape sequence to abort.
Sending 5, 100-byte ICMP Echos to 172.16.5.1, timeout is 2 seconds:
!!!!!
Success rate is 100 percent (5/5), round-trip min/avg/max = 56/56/60 ms
------------------------------------------------------------
R3#show ip route
Codes: C - connected, S - static, R - RIP, M - mobile, B - BGP
       D - EIGRP, EX - EIGRP external, O - OSPF, IA - OSPF inter area
       N1 - OSPF NSSA external type 1, N2 - OSPF NSSA external type 2
       E1 - OSPF external type 1, E2 - OSPF external type 2
       i - IS-IS, su - IS-IS summary, L1 - IS-IS level-1, L2 - IS-IS level-2
       ia - IS-IS inter area, * - candidate default, U - per-user static route
       o - ODR, P - periodic downloaded static route
```

```
Gateway of last resort is not set

         172.16.0.0/24 is subnetted, 5 subnets
C           172.16.4.0 is directly connected, Serial0/1
C           172.16.5.0 is directly connected, FastEthernet0/0
R           172.16.1.0 [120/2] via 172.16.4.1, 00:00:17, Serial0/1
R           172.16.2.0 [120/1] via 172.16.4.1, 00:00:17, Serial0/1
R           172.16.3.0 [120/1] via 172.16.4.1, 00:00:17, Serial0/1
```

Task 6: Configure and Redistribute a Default Route

Step 1. Configure the loopback interface on R3. You will use this IP address to simulate Internet connectivity.

____

____

____

Step 2. Configure R2 with a static default route using the outbound interface that points to R3.

____

Step 3. R2 can now ping the simulated web server at 209.165.201.1, but R3 cannot:

```
R2#ping web

Type escape sequence to abort.
Sending 5, 100-byte ICMP Echos to 209.165.201.1, timeout is 2 seconds:
!!!!!
Success rate is 100 percent (5/5), round-trip min/avg/max = 28/29/32 ms

R1#ping web

Type escape sequence to abort.
Sending 5, 100-byte ICMP Echos to 209.165.201.1, timeout is 2 seconds:
.....
Success rate is 0 percent (0/5)
```

As a side note, what command enables you to simply type **ping web** instead of **ping 209.165.201.1**?

____

Step 4. Redistribute the default route within RIP. You can use one of two commands. Which command did you use, and what is the difference between the two commands?

____

____

____

____

____

____

Step 5. Verify that R1 can ping the simulated web server:

```
R1#ping web

Type escape sequence to abort.
Sending 5, 100-byte ICMP Echos to 209.165.201.1, timeout is 2 seconds:
!!!!!
Success rate is 100 percent (5/5), round-trip min/avg/max = 56/56/60 ms
```

Task 7: Optimize and Verify RIP Routing

Step 1. The final task before capturing verification output and configurations is to optimize RIP. You might have already asked, "Why am I sending out RIP updates on the LAN interfaces?" This is a good question! If you do not have a good reason, it is best to stop these updates. Configure all three routers to stop sending updates out their LAN interfaces.

____

____

____

____

____

____

Step 2. You can verify the previous configurations by looking at the routing process. What command generated the output that follows?

```
R1#show ip protocols
Routing Protocol is "rip"
  Sending updates every 30 seconds, next due in 22 seconds
  Invalid after 180 seconds, hold down 180, flushed after 240
  Outgoing update filter list for all interfaces is not set
  Incoming update filter list for all interfaces is not set
  Redistributing: rip
  Default version control: send version 1, receive any version
    Interface             Send  Recv  Triggered RIP  Key-chain
    Serial0/0             1     1 2
  Automatic network summarization is in effect
  Maximum path: 4
  Routing for Networks:
    172.16.0.0
  Passive Interface(s):
    FastEthernet0/0
  Routing Information Sources:
    Gateway          Distance      Last Update
    172.16.2.1            120      00:00:23
  Distance: (default is 120)
```

Step 3. Verify that all your routing tables look like the following:

```
R1#show ip route
Codes: C - connected, S - static, R - RIP, M - mobile, B - BGP
```

```
       D - EIGRP, EX - EIGRP external, O - OSPF, IA - OSPF inter area
       N1 - OSPF NSSA external type 1, N2 - OSPF NSSA external type 2
       E1 - OSPF external type 1, E2 - OSPF external type 2
       i - IS-IS, su - IS-IS summary, L1 - IS-IS level-1, L2 - IS-IS level-2
       ia - IS-IS inter area, * - candidate default, U - per-user static route
       o - ODR, P - periodic downloaded static route

Gateway of last resort is 172.16.2.1 to network 0.0.0.0

     172.16.0.0/24 is subnetted, 5 subnets
R       172.16.4.0 [120/1] via 172.16.2.1, 00:00:09, Serial0/0
R       172.16.5.0 [120/2] via 172.16.2.1, 00:00:09, Serial0/0
C       172.16.1.0 is directly connected, FastEthernet0/0
C       172.16.2.0 is directly connected, Serial0/0
R       172.16.3.0 [120/1] via 172.16.2.1, 00:00:09, Serial0/0
R*   0.0.0.0/0 [120/1] via 172.16.2.1, 00:00:09, Serial0/0
```

```
R2#show ip route
Codes: C - connected, S - static, R - RIP, M - mobile, B - BGP
       D - EIGRP, EX - EIGRP external, O - OSPF, IA - OSPF inter area
       N1 - OSPF NSSA external type 1, N2 - OSPF NSSA external type 2
       E1 - OSPF external type 1, E2 - OSPF external type 2
       i - IS-IS, su - IS-IS summary, L1 - IS-IS level-1, L2 - IS-IS level-2
       ia - IS-IS inter area, * - candidate default, U - per-user static route
       o - ODR, P - periodic downloaded static route

Gateway of last resort is 0.0.0.0 to network 0.0.0.0

     172.16.0.0/24 is subnetted, 5 subnets
C       172.16.4.0 is directly connected, Serial0/1
R       172.16.5.0 [120/1] via 172.16.4.2, 00:00:24, Serial0/1
R       172.16.1.0 [120/1] via 172.16.2.2, 00:00:01, Serial0/0
C       172.16.2.0 is directly connected, Serial0/0
C       172.16.3.0 is directly connected, FastEthernet0/0
S*   0.0.0.0/0 is directly connected, Serial0/1
```

```
R3#show ip route
Codes: C - connected, S - static, R - RIP, M - mobile, B - BGP
       D - EIGRP, EX - EIGRP external, O - OSPF, IA - OSPF inter area
       N1 - OSPF NSSA external type 1, N2 - OSPF NSSA external type 2
       E1 - OSPF external type 1, E2 - OSPF external type 2
```

```
       i - IS-IS, su - IS-IS summary, L1 - IS-IS level-1, L2 - IS-IS level-2
       ia - IS-IS inter area, * - candidate default, U - per-user static route
       o - ODR, P - periodic downloaded static route

Gateway of last resort is 172.16.4.1 to network 0.0.0.0

     172.16.0.0/24 is subnetted, 5 subnets
C       172.16.4.0 is directly connected, Serial0/1
C       172.16.5.0 is directly connected, FastEthernet0/0
R       172.16.1.0 [120/2] via 172.16.4.1, 00:00:01, Serial0/1
R       172.16.2.0 [120/1] via 172.16.4.1, 00:00:01, Serial0/1
R       172.16.3.0 [120/1] via 172.16.4.1, 00:00:01, Serial0/1
     209.165.201.0/32 is subnetted, 1 subnets
C       209.165.201.1 is directly connected, Loopback0
R*   0.0.0.0/0 [120/1] via 172.16.4.1, 00:00:01, Serial0/1
```

Step 4. For each router, capture the following commands. Clean up the output and save for future reference.

- **show run**
- **show ip interface brief**
- **show ip route**
- **show ip protocols**

Challenge Lab 7-9: RIP and Default Routing to ISP

Figure 7-13 RIP and Default Routing to ISP

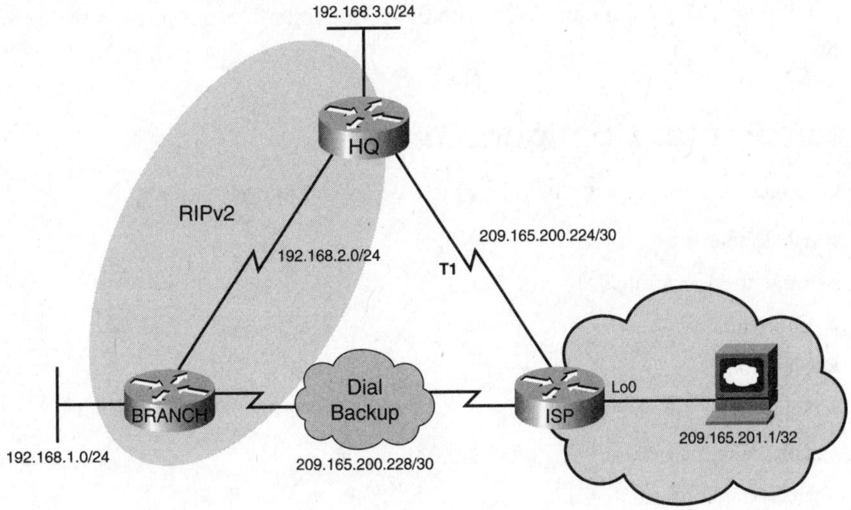

Objectives:

This lab contains the following objectives:

- Configure RIP v2 routing.
- Configure and distribute a default route.
- Configure a backup default route.

Equipment:

This lab can be done with any combination of 1700, 2500, and 2600 Series routers.

NetLab Compatibility Notes:

This lab can be completed using NetLab.

Task 1: Cable the Lab

Step 1. Cable the lab as shown in the topology in Figure 7-13.

Step 2. Document the lab by filling in the following table with the appropriate configuration information.

Router	Interface Type	IP Address	Subnet Mask	Clock Rate? (Yes/No)
BRANCH				
HQ				
ISP				
	Lo0	209.165.201.1	255.255.255.255	N/A

Step 3. Label the topology in Figure 7-13 with the correct interface designation (for example, Fa0/0, S0/0, and so on).

Task 2: Basic Router Configurations

Step 1. Configure all routers with the following basic router configurations:

- Hostname
- Line configurations
- Global passwords
- Host tables
- Banner
- Other instructor-required global configurations

Step 2. Verify your configurations.

Task 3: Interface Configurations

Step 1. Configure the interfaces with IP addresses according to the table you created in Task 1.

Step 2. Verify that interfaces for all routers are operational at the Physical and Data Link layers.

Task 4: Dynamic Routing Configuration for BRANCH and HQ

Step 1. Configure BRANCH and HQ to use RIP v2 routing. Neither router should advertise the link to ISP.

Step 2. Stop BRANCH and HQ from sending RIP updates out their LAN interfaces. Afterward, your RIP routing process should look like the following:

```
HQ#show ip protocols
Routing Protocol is "rip"
  Sending updates every 30 seconds, next due in 5 seconds
  Invalid after 180 seconds, hold down 180, flushed after 240
  Outgoing update filter list for all interfaces is not set
  Incoming update filter list for all interfaces is not set
  Redistributing: rip
  Default version control: send version 2, receive version 2
    Interface             Send  Recv  Triggered RIP  Key-chain
    Serial0/0             2     2
  Automatic network summarization is in effect
  Maximum path: 4
  Routing for Networks:
    192.168.2.0
    192.168.3.0
  Passive Interface(s):
    FastEthernet0/0
  Routing Information Sources:
    Gateway         Distance      Last Update
    192.168.2.1          120      00:00:27
  Distance: (default is 120)
```

Step 3. Verify that BRANCH and HQ routing tables look like the following:

```
BRANCH#show ip route
Codes: C - connected, S - static, R - RIP, M - mobile, B - BGP
       D - EIGRP, EX - EIGRP external, O - OSPF, IA - OSPF inter area
       N1 - OSPF NSSA external type 1, N2 - OSPF NSSA external type 2
       E1 - OSPF external type 1, E2 - OSPF external type 2
       i - IS-IS, su - IS-IS summary, L1 - IS-IS level-1, L2 - IS-IS level-2
       ia - IS-IS inter area, * - candidate default, U - per-user static route
       o - ODR, P - periodic downloaded static route

Gateway of last resort is not set

     209.165.200.0/30 is subnetted, 1 subnets
C       209.165.200.228 is directly connected, Serial0/1
C    192.168.1.0/24 is directly connected, FastEthernet0/0
C    192.168.2.0/24 is directly connected, Serial0/0
R    192.168.3.0/24 [120/1] via 192.168.2.2, 00:00:10, Serial0/0
```

```
HQ#show ip route
Codes: C - connected, S - static, R - RIP, M - mobile, B - BGP
       D - EIGRP, EX - EIGRP external, O - OSPF, IA - OSPF inter area
```

```
       N1 - OSPF NSSA external type 1, N2 - OSPF NSSA external type 2
       E1 - OSPF external type 1, E2 - OSPF external type 2
       i - IS-IS, su - IS-IS summary, L1 - IS-IS level-1, L2 - IS-IS level-2
       ia - IS-IS inter area, * - candidate default, U - per-user static route
       o - ODR, P - periodic downloaded static route

Gateway of last resort is not set

     209.165.200.0/30 is subnetted, 1 subnets
C       209.165.200.224 is directly connected, Serial0/1
R    192.168.1.0/24 [120/1] via 192.168.2.1, 00:00:13, Serial0/0
C    192.168.2.0/24 is directly connected, Serial0/0
C    192.168.3.0/24 is directly connected, FastEthernet0/0
```

Task 5: Configure Static Routing on ISP

Step 1. Configure static routes to the 192.168.1.0/24, 192.168.2.0/24, and 192.168.3.0/24 networks. Use the next-hop IP address at HQ.

____

____

____

Step 2. If the primary T1 link goes down, ISP will use the secondary Dial Backup link. Configure three floating static routes to the 192.168.1.0/24, 192.168.2.0/24, and 192.168.3.0/24 networks that point to the next-hop IP address at BRANCH.

____

____

____

Step 3. Verify that ISP's routing table looks like the one that follows. Notice that the floating static routes are *not* in the routing table.

```
ISP#show ip route
Codes: C - connected, S - static, R - RIP, M - mobile, B - BGP
       D - EIGRP, EX - EIGRP external, O - OSPF, IA - OSPF inter area
       N1 - OSPF NSSA external type 1, N2 - OSPF NSSA external type 2
       E1 - OSPF external type 1, E2 - OSPF external type 2
       i - IS-IS, su - IS-IS summary, L1 - IS-IS level-1, L2 - IS-IS level-2
       ia - IS-IS inter area, * - candidate default, U - per-user static route
       o - ODR, P - periodic downloaded static route

Gateway of last resort is not set

     209.165.200.0/30 is subnetted, 2 subnets
C       209.165.200.228 is directly connected, Serial0/0
C       209.165.200.224 is directly connected, Serial0/1
     209.165.201.0/32 is subnetted, 1 subnets
C       209.165.201.1 is directly connected, Loopback0
S    192.168.1.0/24 [1/0] via 209.165.200.226
S    192.168.2.0/24 [1/0] via 209.165.200.226
S    192.168.3.0/24 [1/0] via 209.165.200.226
```

Task 6: Configure Primary Default Routing on HQ

Step 1. Configure HQ with a default route using the outbound interface to point to ISP.

____

Step 2. Redistribute the default route within RIP.

____

Step 3. Verify that HQ and BRANCH both have routing tables that look like the following:

```
HQ#show ip route
Codes: C - connected, S - static, R - RIP, M - mobile, B - BGP
       D - EIGRP, EX - EIGRP external, O - OSPF, IA - OSPF inter area
       N1 - OSPF NSSA external type 1, N2 - OSPF NSSA external type 2
       E1 - OSPF external type 1, E2 - OSPF external type 2
       i - IS-IS, su - IS-IS summary, L1 - IS-IS level-1, L2 - IS-IS level-2
       ia - IS-IS inter area, * - candidate default, U - per-user static route
       o - ODR, P - periodic downloaded static route

Gateway of last resort is 0.0.0.0 to network 0.0.0.0

     209.165.200.0/30 is subnetted, 1 subnets
C       209.165.200.224 is directly connected, Serial0/1
R    192.168.1.0/24 [120/1] via 192.168.2.1, 00:00:13, Serial0/0
C    192.168.2.0/24 is directly connected, Serial0/0
C    192.168.3.0/24 is directly connected, FastEthernet0/0
S*   0.0.0.0/0 is directly connected, Serial0/1
```

```
BRANCH#show ip route
Codes: C - connected, S - static, R - RIP, M - mobile, B - BGP
       D - EIGRP, EX - EIGRP external, O - OSPF, IA - OSPF inter area
       N1 - OSPF NSSA external type 1, N2 - OSPF NSSA external type 2
       E1 - OSPF external type 1, E2 - OSPF external type 2
       i - IS-IS, su - IS-IS summary, L1 - IS-IS level-1, L2 - IS-IS level-2
       ia - IS-IS inter area, * - candidate default, U - per-user static route
       o - ODR, P - periodic downloaded static route

Gateway of last resort is 192.168.2.2 to network 0.0.0.0

     209.165.200.0/30 is subnetted, 1 subnets
C       209.165.200.228 is directly connected, Serial0/1
C    192.168.1.0/24 is directly connected, FastEthernet0/0
C    192.168.2.0/24 is directly connected, Serial0/0
R    192.168.3.0/24 [120/1] via 192.168.2.2, 00:00:10, Serial0/0
R*   0.0.0.0/0 [120/1] via 192.168.2.2, 00:00:10, Serial0/0
```

Step 4. Both routers should now be able to ping the simulated web server on ISP. If not, troubleshoot.

Task 7: Configure BRANCH with a Floating Static Default Route

Step 1. The last configuration is to set up BRANCH as a secondary gateway to the Internet. To do this, configure a floating static default route using the outbound interface that points to ISP over the simulated Dial Backup link. (Hint: You must use an administrative distance value that is higher than RIP's AD value.)

Step 2. Your routing table for BRANCH will *not* show this route, which is the correct configuration. You test the backup route in the next task.

```
BRANCH#show ip route
Codes: C - connected, S - static, R - RIP, M - mobile, B - BGP
       D - EIGRP, EX - EIGRP external, O - OSPF, IA - OSPF inter area
       N1 - OSPF NSSA external type 1, N2 - OSPF NSSA external type 2
       E1 - OSPF external type 1, E2 - OSPF external type 2
       i - IS-IS, su - IS-IS summary, L1 - IS-IS level-1, L2 - IS-IS level-2
       ia - IS-IS inter area, * - candidate default, U - per-user static route
       o - ODR, P - periodic downloaded static route

Gateway of last resort is 192.168.2.2 to network 0.0.0.0

     209.165.200.0/30 is subnetted, 1 subnets
C       209.165.200.228 is directly connected, Serial0/1
C    192.168.1.0/24 is directly connected, FastEthernet0/0
C    192.168.2.0/24 is directly connected, Serial0/0
R    192.168.3.0/24 [120/1] via 192.168.2.2, 00:00:10, Serial0/0
R*   0.0.0.0/0 [120/1] via 192.168.2.2, 00:00:10, Serial0/0
```

Task 8: Test the Backup Route

Step 1. Test your backup route by sending a large number of pings to the simulated web server from the BRANCH router. While the BRANCH router is sending the pings, shut down the interface between HQ and BRANCH, either by entering the **no shutdown** command on HQ or by unplugging the interface. You should see a few pings fail while BRANCH reconverges on the downed route and begins using the backup route.

Note: You must use an extended ping on BRANCH to change the number of ping packets sent. This is a great time for you to explore this command. To access extended ping, simply type **ping** at the router prompt and press **Enter**. Follow the prompts, accepting the defaults, except change the repeat count to a high number. A 500 count should be high enough.

```
BRANCH#ping
Protocol [ip]:
Target IP address: 209.165.201.1
Repeat count [5]: 500
<output omitted>
.
.
Type escape sequence to abort.
Sending 500, 100-byte ICMP Echos to 209.165.201.1, timeout is 2 seconds:
!!!!!!!!!!!!!!!!!!!!!!!!!!!!!!!!!!!!!!!!!!!!!!!!!!!!!!!!!!!!!!!!!!!!!!
!!!!!!!!!!!!!!!!!!!!!!!!!!!!!!!!!.
*Mar  1 01:25:32.439: %LINK-3-UPDOWN: Interface Serial0/0, changed state to
down
*Mar  1 01:25:33.439: %LINEPROTO-5-UPDOWN: Line protocol on Interface
Serial0/0,
 changed state to down.!!!!!!!!!!!!!!!!!!!!!!!!!!!!!!!!!!!!
```

```
!!!!!!!!!!!!!!!!!!!!!!!!!!!!!!!!!!!!!!!!!!!!!!!!!!!!!!!!!!!!!!!!!!!!!!
!!!!!!!!!!!!!!!!!!!!!!!!!!!!!!!!!!!!!!!!!!!!!!!!!!!!!!!!!!!!!!!!!!!!!!
!!!!!!!!!!!!!!!!!!!!!!!!!!!!!!!!!!!!!!!!!!!!!!!!!!!!!!!!!!!!!!!!!!!!!!
!!!!!!!!!!!!!!!!!!!!!!!!!!!!!!!!!!!!!!!!!!!!!!!!!!!!!!!!!!!!!!!!!!!!!!
!!!!!!!!!!!!!!!!!!!!!!!!!!!!!!!!!!!!!!!!!!!!!!!!!!!!!!!!!!!!!!!!!!!!!!
!!!!!!!!!!
Success rate is 99 percent (498/500), round-trip min/avg/max = 28/32/68 ms
```

Step 2. From the output in Step 1, notice that BRANCH lost only two pings and quickly began using the backup route. BRANCH's routing table now has the floating static default route installed:

```
BRANCH#show ip route
Codes: C - connected, S - static, R - RIP, M - mobile, B - BGP
       D - EIGRP, EX - EIGRP external, O - OSPF, IA - OSPF inter area
       N1 - OSPF NSSA external type 1, N2 - OSPF NSSA external type 2
       E1 - OSPF external type 1, E2 - OSPF external type 2
       i - IS-IS, su - IS-IS summary, L1 - IS-IS level-1, L2 - IS-IS level-2
       ia - IS-IS inter area, * - candidate default, U - per-user static route
       o - ODR, P - periodic downloaded static route

Gateway of last resort is 0.0.0.0 to network 0.0.0.0

     209.165.200.0/30 is subnetted, 1 subnets
C       209.165.200.228 is directly connected, Serial0/1
C    192.168.1.0/24 is directly connected, FastEthernet0/0
S*   0.0.0.0/0 is directly connected, Serial0/1
```

Because of the way you configured ISP, both HQ and BRANCH should be able to ping each other's LAN interfaces.

Note: The way you configured ISP is technically incorrect. You would, at the very least, be using a Network Address Translation (NAT) configuration on both BRANCH and HQ, which allows a more realistic configuration. But NAT is beyond the scope of your CCNA 2 studies. When you study CCNA 4, you can revisit this lab and implement a more appropriate solution.

Step 3. Reestablish connectivity between HQ and BRANCH, after which BRANCH should have the following routing table:

```
BRANCH#show ip route
Codes: C - connected, S - static, R - RIP, M - mobile, B - BGP
       D - EIGRP, EX - EIGRP external, O - OSPF, IA - OSPF inter area
       N1 - OSPF NSSA external type 1, N2 - OSPF NSSA external type 2
       E1 - OSPF external type 1, E2 - OSPF external type 2
       i - IS-IS, su - IS-IS summary, L1 - IS-IS level-1, L2 - IS-IS level-2
       ia - IS-IS inter area, * - candidate default, U - per-user static route
       o - ODR, P - periodic downloaded static route

Gateway of last resort is 192.168.2.2 to network 0.0.0.0

     209.165.200.0/30 is subnetted, 1 subnets
C       209.165.200.228 is directly connected, Serial0/1
C    192.168.1.0/24 is directly connected, FastEthernet0/0
C    192.168.2.0/24 is directly connected, Serial0/0
R    192.168.3.0/24 [120/1] via 192.168.2.2, 00:00:07, Serial0/0
R*   0.0.0.0/0 [120/1] via 192.168.2.2, 00:00:07, Serial0/0
```

Task 9: Capture and Document Your Configurations

For each router, capture the following commands. Clean up the output and save for future reference.

- **show run**
- **show ip interface brief**
- **show ip route**
- **show ip protocols**

CHAPTER 8

TCP/IP Suite Error and Control Messages

The Study Guide portion of this chapter uses a combination of fill-in-the-blank and open-ended questions, and unique custom exercises to test your knowledge of the theory of ICMP.

There are no Lab Exercises for this chapter.

Study Guide

TCP/IP Error Messages: ICMP

IP is limited because it is a best-effort delivery system. This means that IP, by itself, cannot ensure reliable delivery of data. Delivery can fail for any number of reasons, such as hardware problems, configuration errors, and disconnected devices. To inform source hosts that an error in delivery has occurred, IP relies on ICMP. Many of the ICMP messages are no longer relevant in today's networks. However, a few are still important to your studies. This chapter contains a few exercises to help you understand the most import ICMP messages: ping, destination unreachable, and time exceeded.

Vocabulary Exercise: Completion

Complete the paragraphs that follow by filling in appropriate words and phrases.

By design, the Internet Protocol (IP) is ___________ because it does not recover packets that the IP forwarding process cannot deliver. When an application needs reliability, it depends on ______. Although IP provides no error recovery, devices that discard IP packets can send a message to the source reporting the lost packet. This error message belongs to a group of messages that are part of the ___________________________________ (ICMP).

ICMP defines a set of messages that can be used to control and inform hosts about anything having to do with the operation of the TCP/IP Internet layer. ICMP is one of the three Internet-layer protocols. The other two are ____ and ____________________________.

The ICMP message you have used to verify connectivity is sent with the ____ command. The initial message is called an ICMP ____________. The response is called an ICMP __________. In the Windows XP OS, four pings are sent to the destination by default. As responses are received, the output on the screen includes the IP address of the destination, the size of the packet, the round-trip time (RTT), and a TTL value. The TTL, or __________, field in an IP packet can be used to check the length of a route as measured by hops.

The ICMP __________ message can be sent by routers and hosts, indicating that a packet cannot be delivered. The host or router sends the message to the _______ IP address listed in the discarded packet.

Routing begins with a host sending a packet, either directly to another host on the same subnet or by sending the packet to its default ______________. Before a host can send a packet on an IP network, it must be configured with an __________, __________, and __________. To send a packet to a destination, the source host must have an IP address for the destination.

Routers and hosts define a limit on the size of IP packets they can both receive and forward on each interface. This configurable limit, typically _____ bytes, is called the _______________________ (MTU) of the interface. If a router needs to forward a packet out an interface, and the packet is larger than the MTU, the router fragments the packet. If a packet needs to be fragmented but has the "do not fragment" (DF) bit set, a router sends the Type __ destination unreachable message. This can happen with encrypted Virtual Private Network (VPN) packets.

The Time Exceeded message type ___ is sent when a router receives a packet and has to decrement the ____ field to ___. The packet is __________.

IP Packet Header Exercise

The IP header contains important information used by the routing and filtering processes to forward or discard packets. A few of the fields the header includes are the address fields, quality of service (QoS) fields, and fields to track fragmented packets. Figure 8-1 shows the fields of an IP packet header without the field names. Fill in the field names. Then briefly describe each field, box in your description, and draw an arrow pointing from the description to the field it describes. The first field, the VERS field, is already done for you as an example. You might need to do research to complete this activity.

Figure 8-1 IP Packet Header

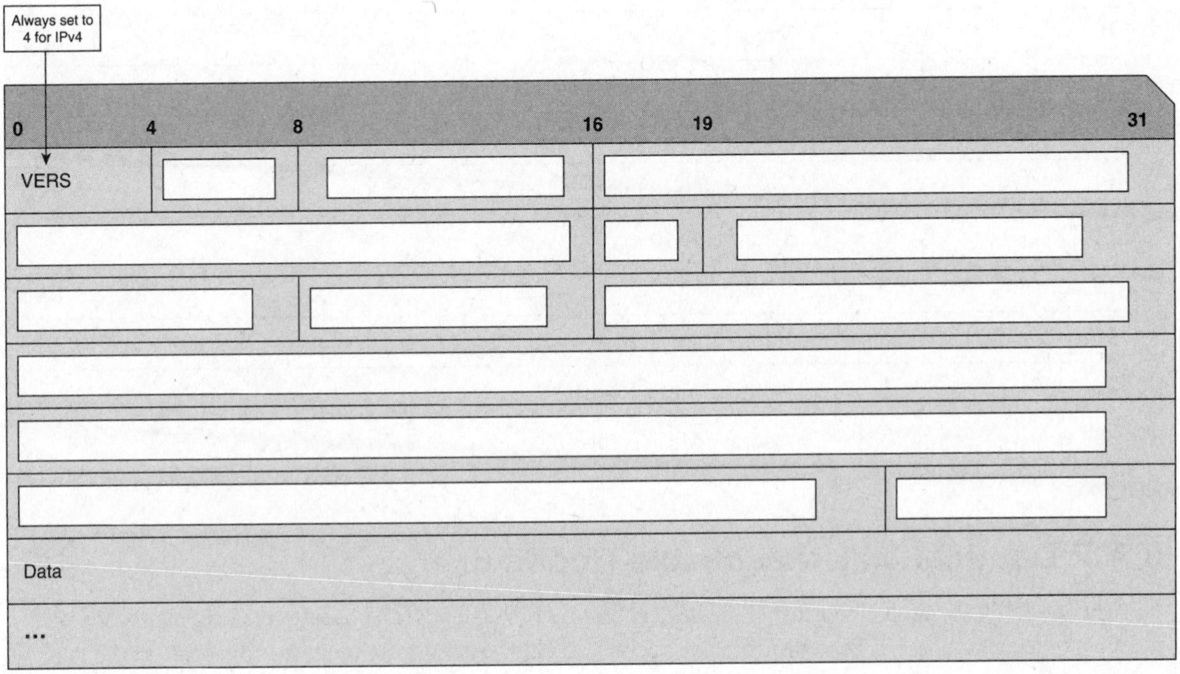

ICMP Message Type Exercise

ICMP messages are encapsulated within an IP packet. Common fields to all ICMP messages include a Type and Code field. Most messages also include a checksum. If the message is an error message, the first 576 bytes of the original packet's data should be included in the ICMP message. Many of the original ICMP message types are no longer used in most network implementations because the services they provided have been replaced by other processes. For example, the Timestamp Request and Timestamp Reply message types 13 and 14, respectively, have been largely replaced by the Network Time Protocol (NTP).

However, you should be familiar with the ICMP types that are still commonly used. Fill in the following table with the missing type numbers and descriptions.

Type Value	Description
4	Source Quench
5	Redirect/Change Request
9	Router Advertisement
10	Router Selection
12	Parameter Problem
13	Timestamp Request
14	Timestamp Reply
15	Information Request
16	Information Reply
17	Address Mask Request
18	Address Mask Reply

ICMP Destination Unreachable Codes Exercise

The ICMP Destination Unreachable message is sent by routers and hosts back to the originating source host of a packet that has been discarded. A packet can be discarded for a number of reasons. In the table that follows, record the reason for the corresponding ICMP destination unreachable code.

Code Value	Description
0	
1	
2	
3	
4	
5	
6	
7	
8	
9	
10	
11	
12	

Concept Questions

1. Explain the difference between reliable and unreliable protocols.

2. What does a process using IP do about a packet that is undeliverable?

3. How are packets guaranteed delivery?

4. What is the purpose of a default gateway?

Lab Exercises

There are no labs for this chapter.

CHAPTER 9

Basic Router Troubleshooting

The Study Guide portion of this chapter uses a combination of fill-in-the-blank, open-ended questions and unique custom exercises to test your knowledge of the theory of basic router troubleshooting.

The Lab Exercises portion of this chapter includes all the online curriculum labs as well as a challenge lab to ensure that you have mastered the practical, hands-on skills needed for basic router troubleshooting.

Study Guide

Examining the Routing Table

When you're a network engineer, an important part of your job is to interpret the output displayed by various commands that provide information about the routing process. One of the most important **show** commands in the Cisco IOS software is the **show ip route** command. You have already used this command in previous chapters. This section concentrates on all the details of what this command displays as well as how the router determines what routes to install in the routing table.

Vocabulary Exercises: Completion

Complete the paragraphs that follow by filling in appropriate words and phrases.

_______________ (also called forwarding) is the process by which a router receives a packet on one interface, looks for a matching destination network, and then forwards the packet based on the match out the appropriate interface. _______________ are the messages and rules used by routers to learn all possible routes, choose the best routes, and then add these routes to the routing table.

To fully appreciate routing, you need a solid understanding of the contents of a router's IP _______________, as stored in a router's ___________ and displayed using the **show ip route** command.

This table lists all the routes the router has learned through connected networks, _____________ routing, and _____________ routing. If a router does not have a route for a destination, it _____________ the packet. Therefore, the router should have a gateway of last resort, or _____________ route, which it can use if no other more specific route is available. Besides using the **default-information originate** command discussed in Chapter 7, "Distance Vector Routing Protocols," a router could be configured to advertise a default route with the **ip default-network** command.

A router can learn a route to the same destination from two or more different routing sources. For example, the router could receive a Routing Information Protocol (RIP) update advertising 192.168.1.0/24 and also be configured with a static route to the same 192.168.1.0/24. In such cases, the router chooses the route based on ____________________________. In the 192.168.1.0/24 scenario, the _____________ route is believed over the _____________ route because ________________ routes have a lower ________________________________.

If two or more routes to the same destination are learned from the same routing source, the router chooses the route with the ___________________ metric value for that routing source. For RIP, the metric is _____________. For Interior Gateway Routing Protocol (IGRP) and Enhanced Interior Gateway Routing Protocol (EIGRP), the metric is a composite of _____________ and _____________. For Open Shortest Path First (OSPF), the metric is _____________, which is a measure of _____________ in the Cisco IOS software.

You might need to determine when the last update was received from a routing process that uses periodic updates. RIP sends updates every ___________ seconds, and IGRP sends updates every ________ seconds. Two commands in particular can display when the last update was received: **show ip route** and **show ip protocols**. In addition, the **show ip rip** database command can also display the last time an update was received by a RIP neighbor. In the following output, notice that all three commands show how many seconds since the last update. Fill in the missing commands.

R2#____

```
0.0.0.0/0    auto-summary
0.0.0.0/0    redistributed
   [1] via 0.0.0.0,
192.168.1.0/24    auto-summary
192.168.1.0/24
   [1] via 192.168.2.1, 00:00:06, Serial0/0
192.168.2.0/24    auto-summary
192.168.2.0/24    directly connected, Serial0/0
192.168.3.0/24    auto-summary
192.168.3.0/24    directly connected, FastEthernet0/0
192.168.4.0/24    auto-summary
192.168.4.0/24    directly connected, Serial0/1
```

R2#____

```
Routing Protocol is "rip"
  Sending updates every 30 seconds, next due in 11 seconds
  Invalid after 180 seconds, hold down 180, flushed after 240
  Outgoing update filter list for all interfaces is not set
  Incoming update filter list for all interfaces is not set
  Redistributing: rip
  Default version control: send version 1, receive any version
    Interface            Send  Recv  Triggered RIP  Key-chain
    FastEthernet0/0      1     1 2
    Serial0/0            1     1 2
    Serial0/1            1     1 2
  Automatic network summarization is in effect
  Maximum path: 4
  Routing for Networks:
    192.168.2.0
    192.168.3.0
    192.168.4.0
  Routing Information Sources:
    Gateway         Distance      Last Update
    192.168.2.1          120      00:00:06
  Distance: (default is 120)
```

R2#____

```
! legend omitted for brevity
Gateway of last resort is 0.0.0.0 to network 0.0.0.0

C*   192.168.4.0/24 is directly connected, Serial0/1
R    192.168.1.0/24 [120/1] via 192.168.2.1, 00:00:06, Serial0/0
C    192.168.2.0/24 is directly connected, Serial0/0
C    192.168.3.0/24 is directly connected, FastEthernet0/0
S*   0.0.0.0/0 is directly connected, Serial0/1
```

Interpreting a Routing Table Entry Exercise

Understanding entries in the routing table is a core skill you must learn to gather information about your network and to troubleshoot connectivity problems. Look at the following output:

```
RTB# show ip route
Codes: C - connected, S - static, R - RIP, M - mobile, B - BGP
       D - EIGRP, EX - EIGRP external, O - OSPF, IA - OSPF inter area
       N1 - OSPF NSSA external type 1, N2 - OSPF NSSA external type 2
       E1 - OSPF external type 1, E2 - OSPF external type 2
       i - IS-IS, su - IS-IS summary, L1 - IS-IS level-1, L2 - IS-IS level-2
       ia - IS-IS inter area, * - candidate default, U - per-user static route
       o - ODR, P - periodic downloaded static route

Gateway of last resort is 192.168.2.1 to network 0.0.0.0

C    192.168.4.0/24 is directly connected, Serial0/1
S    192.168.5.0/24 is directly connected, Serial0/1
R    192.168.1.0/24 [120/1] via 192.168.2.1, 00:00:17, Serial0/0
C    192.168.2.0/24 is directly connected, Serial0/0
C    192.168.3.0/24 is directly connected, FastEthernet0/0
S*   0.0.0.0/0 [1/0] via 192.168.2.1
```

Referring to the highlighted entry, dissect the information by indicating what each of the following represents in Table 9-1.

Table 9-1 Routing Table Entry Interpretation

Entries	Description
R	
192.168.1.0	
/24	
[120	
/1]	
via 192.168.2.1	
00:00:17	
Serial0/0	

The show ip route Options Exercise

You can filter the output of the **show ip route** command so that it displays only the routes you want to see. On a live router, enter the **show ip route** command, then a space, and then a question mark (**?**) to access the additional parameters for the command. List all the available options in the space that follows.

Layer 2 and Layer 3 Address Exercise

Refer to Figure 9-1, which shows the Layer 2 (L2) and Layer 3 (L3) addresses. For Frame Relay, the L2 address is the data-link connection identifier (DLCI). For the PPP WAN protocol, the L2 address field has no meaning because it uses a direct link between two devices. Therefore, the address field is always filled with 8 1 bits (11111111, 0xFF, 255).

Figure 9-1 Topology of Layer 2 and Layer 3 Addresses

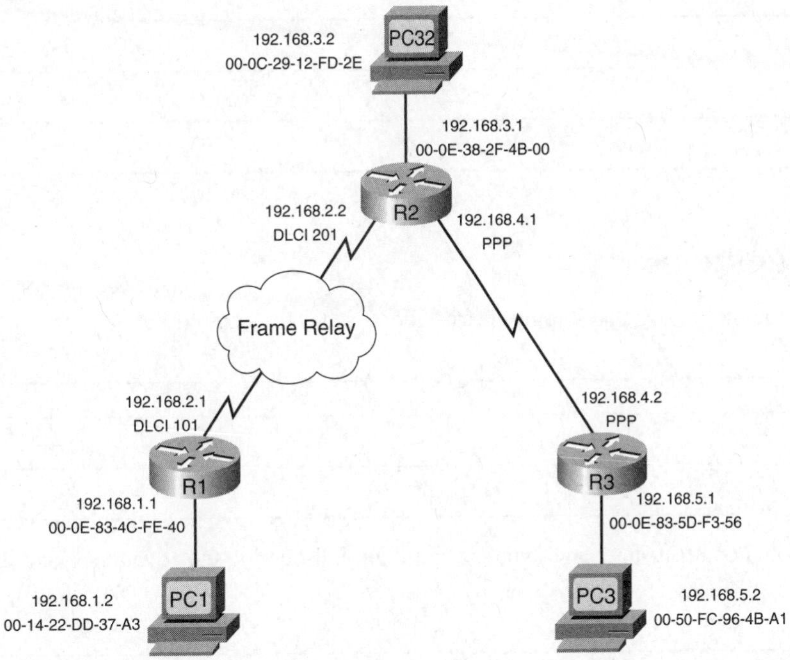

Fill in Table 9-2 with the correct L2 and L3 addresses at each stage as a packet travels from PC1 to PC3.

Table 9-2 Layer 2 and Layer 3 Addresses

Stage	Destination (L2)	Source (L2)	Source (L3)	Destination (L3)
PC1 to R1				
R1 to R2				
R2 to R3				
R3 to PC3				

Complete the Administrative Distance Table Exercise

You should memorize the administrative distance values for all the interior gateway protocols. The Border Gateway Protocol (BGP) and Intermediate System–to–Intermediate System (IS-IS) Protocol are not discussed until the CCNP level. Complete the following table with the correct default value for administrative distance (AD).

Protocol or Source of Routing Information	Default AD
Connected interface	
Static route	
EIGRP summary route	
External BGP	
Internal EIGRP	
IGRP	
OSPF	
IS-IS	
RIP	
External EIGRP	
Internal BGP	
Unknown	

Concept Questions

1. Describe the three ways that a router learns about routes to networks.

   - ____________________
   - ____________________
   - ____________________

2. Compare and contrast static and dynamic routing by discussing the advantages and disadvantages of each.

   ____

3. Explain the purpose of administrative distance.

   ____

Network Testing Methods and Tips

If you have not yet experienced problems with your networked labs, you have not done enough labs! Even in the simple lab scenarios in the CCNA curriculum, you should have already experienced errors in your configurations—either software or hardware, or both. The best way to develop a method for troubleshooting errors is to decide on a standard, structured procedure that you can use each time you test your network. This section focuses on one method—using the layers of the OSI model—and some of the tools that are at your disposal to troubleshoot most errors in your network configurations. The section "Router and Routing Troubleshooting Tips" focuses specifically on the **show** and **debug** commands used for troubleshooting.

Using the OSI Model to Troubleshoot

Many times a problem can be traced to the Physical layer. Therefore, a structured approach to troubleshooting that uses the conceptual framework of the OSI model can start at Layer 1. From Layer 1, the process continues up the layers until the problem is solved.

1. List common Layer 1 errors:
   - ______________________________
   - ______________________________
   - ______________________________
   - ______________________________
   - ______________________________
   - ______________________________
   - ______________________________
2. List common Layer 2 errors:
   - ______________________________
   - ______________________________
   - ______________________________
   - ______________________________
   - ______________________________
3. List common Layer 3 errors:
   - ______________________________
   - ______________________________
   - ______________________________
   - ______________________________
   - ______________________________
   - ______________________________
   - ______________________________
   - ______________________________

Match the Tool to the Layer Exercise

In Figure 9-2, in the Typical Tools column, record at which layer the following troubleshooting tools would be used: ping, Telnet, CDP, check cables, traceroute.

Figure 9-2 Troubleshooting Tools

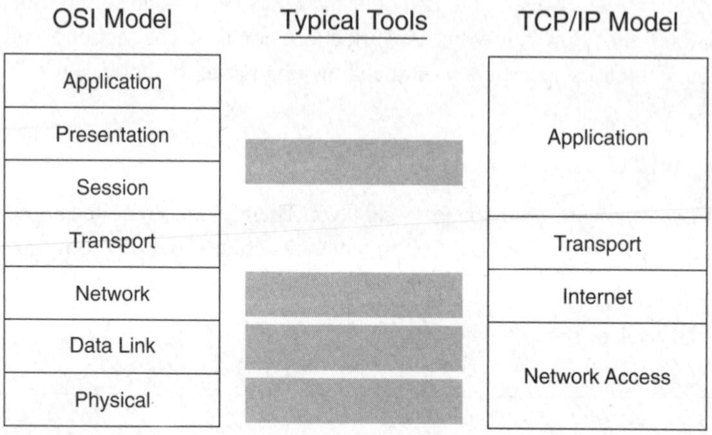

Concept Questions

1. What is a structured approach to troubleshooting, and why is it important to use a structured approach to solve problems?

____

____

____

____

____

2. Explain the extended **ping** command, including how to use it and the benefits of using it.

____

____

____

____

Router and Routing Troubleshooting Tips

A prerequisite to testing and troubleshooting your network is a firm understanding of the topology and addressing scheme in use. You must know what you are testing before you can successfully test it. You also must know what is missing or what errors to look for to troubleshoot misconfigurations. Too often, students jump in and send a ping packet across a newly configured network to test Layer 3 connectivity. Internet Control Message Protocol (ICMP) echo requests and replies test only direct connectivity between two hosts. The **ping** command can verify only a small portion of your network. To verify your configurations, you should start with a series of **show** commands on each router. If you know that each router has all the necessary interfaces active and that each routing table is complete, you can quickly isolate connectivity problems to the hosts that cannot access the network. This section focuses on some of the most important commands you can use to discover and troubleshoot network misconfigurations and errors: **show**, **traceroute**, and **debug**.

For all the exercises in this section, use Figure 9-3.

Figure 9-3 Router and Routing Troubleshooting

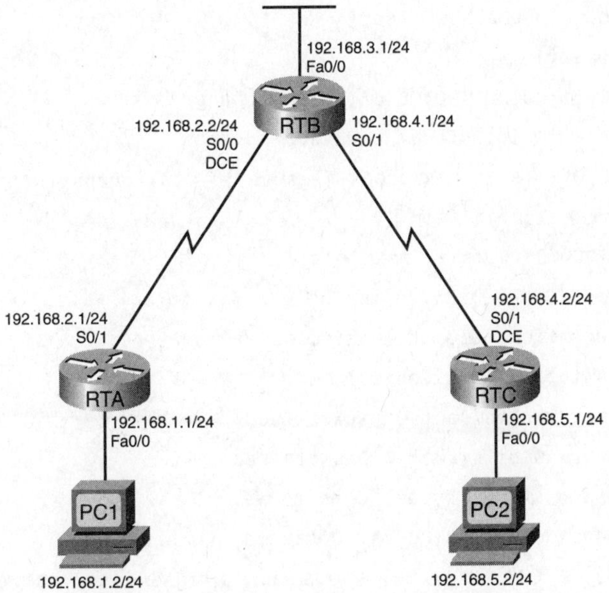

The show Command Exercise

You have already worked through an exercise for the **show ip route** command, which displays the current routing table. Your ability to interpret the output from this command is one of your most relied-upon skills. For example, the routing table for RTB is shown as follows. For the topology shown in Figure 9-3, what is missing, and what would you do to begin the process of fixing the problem?

```
RTB#show ip route
!Codes omitted for brevity

Gateway of last resort is not set

C     192.168.4.0/24 is directly connected, Serial0/1
R     192.168.5.0/24 [120/1] via 192.168.4.2, 00:00:10, Serial0/1
C     192.168.2.0/24 is directly connected, Serial0/0
C     192.168.3.0/24 is directly connected, FastEthernet0/0
```

____

____

____

____

The **show interface serial 0/1** command was entered to display the following output. The first line of the output indicates "up and up." What does this mean?

____

```
RTA#show interface serial 0/1
Serial0/1 is up, line protocol is up
  Hardware is PowerQUICC Serial
  Description: Link to RTC
```

```
Internet address is 192.168.2.1/24
MTU 1500 bytes, BW 1544 Kbit, DLY 20000 usec,
   reliability 255/255, txload 1/255, rxload 1/255
Encapsulation HDLC, loopback not set
Keepalive set (10 sec)
Last input 00:00:05, output 00:00:02, output hang never
Last clearing of "show interface" counters never
Input queue: 0/75/0/0 (size/max/drops/flushes); Total output drops: 0
Queueing strategy: weighted fair
Output queue: 0/1000/64/0 (size/max total/threshold/drops)
   Conversations  0/3/256 (active/max active/max total)
   Reserved Conversations 0/0 (allocated/max allocated)
   Available Bandwidth 1158 kilobits/sec
5 minute input rate 0 bits/sec, 0 packets/sec
5 minute output rate 0 bits/sec, 0 packets/sec
   364 packets input, 27762 bytes, 0 no buffer
   Received 359 broadcasts, 0 runts, 0 giants, 0 throttles
   0 input errors, 0 CRC, 0 frame, 0 overrun, 0 ignored, 0 abort
   375 packets output, 26482 bytes, 0 underruns
   0 output errors, 0 collisions, 8 interface resets
   0 output buffer failures, 0 output buffers swapped out
   2 carrier transitions
   DCD=up  DSR=up  DTR=up  RTS=up  CTS=up
```

In the preceding output, if Layer 2 issues existed, what statistics would indicate this as a problem?

- ______________________________
- ______________________________
- ______________________________
- ______________________________

The output from the preceding command has more meaning if you know how long the interface has been collecting statistics. The time is usually based on how long it has been since the last router reboot. What command displays how long a router has been up?

____

You can also reset the statistics to 0 values. What command, including the router prompt, resets the interface statistics?

____

____

____

____

From the preceding command output, what statistics indicate Layer 2 issues?

- ______________________________
- ______________________________
- ______________________________
- ______________________________
- ______________________________

The preceding command displays a detailed picture of the status of the interface. However, to see an abbreviated listing of all interfaces and their statuses, use the **show ip interface brief** command to display the following output:

```
RTB#show ip interface brief
Interface              IP-Address      OK? Method Status                Protocol
FastEthernet0/0        192.168.3.1     YES manual up                    up

Serial0/0              192.168.2.2     YES manual up                    up

FastEthernet0/1        unassigned      YES unset  administratively down down

Serial0/1              192.168.4.1     YES manual up                    up
```

In lab environments, you often connect routers back to back using the serial interfaces, as shown in Figure 9-3. A common mistake students make is configuring the clock rate on the wrong side of the DCE/DTE link. You can always leave your console session and check the cable connections. However, you can also use the **show controllers** command to quickly display what side of the DCE/DTE cable is currently attached to the interface. In the following output, the serial 0/1 interface is the DTE side and has detected a clocking from the other side, RTB. Therefore, you can assume that RTB is configured with a clock rate.

```
RTA#show controllers serial 0/1
Interface Serial0/1
Hardware is PowerQUICC MPC860
DTE V.35 TX and RX clocks detected.
!output omitted for brevity
```

On the RTB side of the link, the same command shows that RTB is indeed the DCE side and is configured with a clock rate of 64000.

```
RTB#show controllers serial 0/0
Interface Serial0/0
Hardware is PowerQUICC MPC860
DCE V.35, clock rate 64000
!output omitted for brevity
```

If the routing table is incomplete but all your interfaces are in the "up and up" state, you probably have a routing configuration problem. The **show ip protocols** command can display details about the current dynamic routing configuration on the local router.

```
RTB#show ip protocols
Routing Protocol is "rip"
  Sending updates every 30 seconds, next due in 22 seconds
  Invalid after 180 seconds, hold down 180, flushed after 240
```

```
Outgoing update filter list for all interfaces is not set
Incoming update filter list for all interfaces is not set
Redistributing: rip
Default version control: send version 1, receive any version
  Interface             Send  Recv  Triggered RIP  Key-chain
  FastEthernet0/0       1     1 2
  Serial0/0             1     1 2
  Serial0/1             1     1 2
Automatic network summarization is in effect
Maximum path: 4
Routing for Networks:
  192.168.2.0
  192.168.3.0
  192.168.4.0
Routing Information Sources:
  Gateway         Distance      Last Update
  192.168.3.2          120      02:58:32
  192.168.2.1          120      00:00:02
  192.168.4.2          120      00:00:20
Distance: (default is 120)
```

In Chapter 4, "Learning About Other Devices," you read about the Cisco Discovery Protocol and learned how valuable a tool it can be to discover information about directly connected neighbors. As a review, record the commands that display the following output.

```
RTB#show cdp neighbors
Capability Codes: R - Router, T - Trans Bridge, B - Source Route Bridge
                  S - Switch, H - Host, I - IGMP, r - Repeater

Device ID        Local Intrfce     Holdtme    Capability  Platform  Port ID
RTC              Ser 0/1            164           R         2621XM    Ser 0/1
RTA              Ser 0/0            128           R         2611XM    Ser 0/1

RTB#show cdp neighbors detail
-------------------------
Device ID: RTC
Entry address(es):
  IP address: 192.168.4.2
Platform: cisco 2621XM,  Capabilities: Router
Interface: Serial0/1,  Port ID (outgoing port): Serial0/1
Holdtime : 157 sec

Version :
Cisco Internetwork Operating System Software
IOS (tm) C2600 Software (C2600-J1S3-M), Version 12.3(17a), RELEASE SOFTWARE (fc2)
Technical Support: http://www.cisco.com/techsupport
Copyright (c) 1986-2005 by cisco Systems, Inc.
Compiled Mon 12-Dec-05 14:12 by evmiller
```

```
advertisement version: 2

-------------------------
Device ID: RTA
Entry address(es):
  IP address: 192.168.2.1
Platform: cisco 2611XM,  Capabilities: Router
Interface: Serial0/0,  Port ID (outgoing port): Serial0/1
Holdtime : 120 sec

Version :
Cisco Internetwork Operating System Software
IOS (tm) C2600 Software (C2600-J1S3-M), Version 12.3(17a), RELEASE SOFTWARE (fc2)
Technical Support: http://www.cisco.com/techsupport
Copyright (c) 1986-2005 by cisco Systems, Inc.
Compiled Mon 12-Dec-05 14:12 by evmiller

advertisement version: 2

RTB#________________________________________
Global CDP information:
        Sending CDP packets every 60 seconds
        Sending a holdtime value of 180 seconds
        Sending CDPv2 advertisements is  enabled

RTB#________________________________________
FastEthernet0/0 is up, line protocol is up
  Encapsulation ARPA
  Sending CDP packets every 60 seconds
  Holdtime is 180 seconds
Serial0/0 is up, line protocol is up
  Encapsulation HDLC
  Sending CDP packets every 60 seconds
  Holdtime is 180 seconds
FastEthernet0/1 is administratively down, line protocol is down
  Encapsulation ARPA
  Sending CDP packets every 60 seconds
  Holdtime is 180 seconds
Serial0/1 is up, line protocol is up
  Encapsulation HDLC
  Sending CDP packets every 60 seconds
  Holdtime is 180 seconds
```

The debug Command Exercise

Occasionally, the **show** commands you have studied so far do not point to a particular problem. In such situations, you can choose to use a **debug** command. The **debug** commands display information about processes that are currently happening. For example, you can watch RIP operations with the **debug ip rip** command. The debug output displays detailed information about the updates sent and received, as shown in the following output:

```
RTA#debug ip rip
RIP protocol debugging is on
*Mar  1 03:47:25.933: RIP: sending v1 update to 255.255.255.255 via Serial0/1
(192.168.2.1)
*Mar  1 03:47:25.933: RIP: build update entries
*Mar  1 03:47:25.933:   network 192.168.1.0 metric 1
*Mar  1 03:47:33.381: RIP: sending v1 update to 255.255.255.255 via FastEthernet
0/0 (192.168.1.1)
*Mar  1 03:47:33.381: RIP: build update entries
*Mar  1 03:47:33.381:   network 192.168.2.0 metric 1
*Mar  1 03:47:33.381:   network 192.168.3.0 metric 2
*Mar  1 03:47:33.381:   network 192.168.4.0 metric 2
*Mar  1 03:47:33.381:   network 192.168.5.0 metric 3
*Mar  1 03:47:42.640: RIP: received v1 update from 192.168.2.2 on Serial0/1
*Mar  1 03:47:42.640:      192.168.3.0 in 1 hops
*Mar  1 03:47:42.644:      192.168.4.0 in 1 hops
*Mar  1 03:47:42.644:      192.168.5.0 in 2 hops
```

To turn off debugging, use the **no** form of the command. What command turns off all possible debugging?

```
RTA#______________________________________________________________
All possible debugging has been turned off
```

The available **debug** commands are numerous. Use the help facility to find a **debug** command to fit your specific situation.

Finally, if you telnet into a remote router and want "debug out" displayed on the console, you must use the **terminal monitor** command:

```
RTA#rtb
Trying RTB (192.168.2.2)... Open
RTB>en
RTB#terminal monitor
```

Concept Questions

Explain in detail how the **trace** commands (**traceroute** on a router or **tracert** on a PC) work.

Lab Exercises

Command Reference

In the table that follows, record the command, *including the correct router prompt,* that fits the description. Fill in any blanks with the appropriate missing information.

Command	Description
	Displays the entire routing table
	Displays all the RIP routes in the routing table
	Displays information about route 192.168.1.0
	Displays a summary of the status of all interfaces on the router
	Displays detailed information about the serial 0/0 interface
	Resets the statistics on all interfaces to 0
	Displays the type of cable plugged into the serial interface (DTE or DCE) and the clock rate, if it was set
	Displays detailed information about the IP routing protocols currently configured
	Command used to enter extended ping mode
	Discovers details about the path used to reach destination 192.168.5.1
	Turns on all possible debugging
	Turns off all possible debugging
	Lists what **debug** commands are on
	Debug output can now be seen through a Telnet session (the default is to only send output on a console screen)

Lab 9-1: Using show ip route to Examine Routing Tables (9.1.1)

Figure 9-4 **Topology for Lab 9-1**

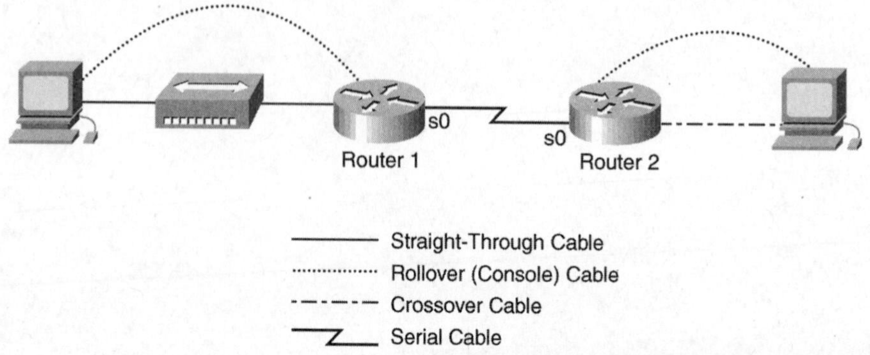

Table 9-3 Lab Equipment Configuration

Router Designation	Router Name	FastEthernet 0 Address	Interface Type Serial 0	Serial 0 Address
Router 1	BHM	172.16.0.1	DCE	172.17.0.1
Router 2	GAD	172.18.0.1	DTE	172.17.0.2

The enable secret password for both routers is **class**.

The enable, vty, and console passwords for both routers are **cisco**. The subnet mask for both interfaces on both routers is 255.255.0.0.

Objectives

- Set up an IP addressing scheme using Class B networks.
- Configure the Routing Information Protocol (RIP) and Interior Gateway Routing Protocol (IGRP) on the routers.
- Examine the impact on the routing table of multiple routing protocols using the **show ip route** command.

Background/Preparation

Cable a network similar to the one in Figure 9-1. You can use any router that meets the interface requirements in Figure 9-3 (that is, 800, 1600, 1700, 2500, and 2600 routers or a combination). Refer to the information in Appendix B, "Router Interface Summary," to correctly specify the interface identifiers based on the equipment in your lab. The 1721 Series routers produced the configuration output in this lab. Any other router might produce slightly different output. You should execute the following tasks on each router unless specifically instructed otherwise.

Start a HyperTerminal session as you did in Lab 2-2.

Implement the procedure documented in Appendix C, "Erasing and Reloading the Router," before continuing with this lab.

Task 1: Configure the Routers

On the routers, enter global configuration mode and configure the router name as shown in Table 9-3. Then, configure the console, vty, and enable passwords. If you have problems doing so, refer to Lab 3-2. Next, configure the interfaces according to Table 9-3. If you have problems doing so, refer to Lab 3-9. Finally, configure the RIP routing. Refer to Lab 7-1 if you need help. Don't forget to save the configurations to the startup configuration file.

Task 2: Configure the Hosts with the Proper IP Addresses, Subnet Masks, and Default Gateways

Task 3: Verify That the Internetwork Is Functioning by Pinging the FastEthernet Interface of the Other Router

Step 1. From the host attached to GAD, can you ping the BHM router's FastEthernet interface? _____

Step 2. From the host attached to BHM, can you ping the GAD router's FastEthernet interface? _____

Step 3. If the answer is no for either question, troubleshoot the router configurations to find the error. Then do the pings again until the answer to both questions is yes.

Task 4: Make Sure That Routing Updates Are Being Sent

Step 1. On the GAD router, type the command **debug ip rip** at the privileged EXEC mode prompt. Wait for at least 45 seconds.

Was there any output from the **debug** command? ______________________________

What did the output display? ______________________________

Step 2. Stop the debug with **no debug ip rip**.

Task 5: Show the Routing Tables for Each Router

Examine the routing table entries using **show ip route** on each router.

What are the entries in the GAD routing table?

____

____

____

What are the entries in the BHM routing table?

____

____

____

Task 6: Enable IGRP Routing on Both Routers

Step 1. Leave RIP enabled, but enter **router igrp 25** on both routers at the configuration prompt. Enter the appropriate **network** statements for each router.

```
GAD(config)#router igrp 25
GAD(config-router)#network 172.16.0.0
GAD(config-router)#network 172.17.0.0
BHM(config)#router igrp 25
BHM(config-router)#network 172.18.0.0
BHM(config-router)#network 172.17.0.0
```

Step 2. On the same router used in Task 4, enter **debug ip rip and debug ip igrp events**. Then, wait at least 2 minutes.

What types of routing updates are being sent? ______________________________

Why are both protocols sending updates? ______________________________

Task 7: Show the Routing Tables for Each Router Again

Examine the routing table entries using **show ip route** on each router.

What are the entries in the GAD routing table?

____

____

____

What are the entries in the BHM routing table?

____

____

____

Why are the RIP routes not in the tables?

____

What should you do for this network to be more efficient?

____

Task 8: Add a Second Serial Cable Between Routers

Step 1. Add a second serial cable between Interface S1 on GAD and Serial S1 on BHM. GAD is the DCE.

Step 2. Configure the GAD router with the following additional statements:

```
GAD(config)#interface Serial1
GAD(config-if)#ip address 172.22.0.2 255.255.0.0
GAD(config-if)#clockrate 56000
GAD(config-if)#no shutdown
```

Step 3. Configure the BHM router with the following additional statements:

```
BHM(config)#interface Serial1
BHM(config-if)#ip address 172.22.0.1 255.255.0.0
BHM(config-if)#no shutdown
```

Step 4. On the BHM router, remove the IGRP network statement **network 172.18.0.0** so your **router IGRP 25** contains only the **network 172.17.0.0** statement.

Task 9: Clear the Routing Tables on Both Routers

Type the command **clear ip route *** at the privileged EXEC prompt on both routers. Wait at least 90 seconds and then type the command **show ip route** on both routers.

What types of routes appear on GAD?

____

What types of routes appear on BHM?

____

Why is this?

____

____

____

Task 10: Use show ip route to See Different Routes by Type

Step 1. Enter **show ip route** while connected to the GAD router.

What networks appear?

____

____

____

What interface(s) is/are directly connected?

____

Step 2. Enter **show ip route rip**.

List the routes in the routing table:

____

What is the administrative distance? _______________________

Step 3. Enter **show ip route** while connected to the BHM router.

What networks appear?

____

____

____

What interface(s) is/are directly connected?

____

Step 4. Enter **show ip route rip**.

List the routes in the routing table. _______________________

If you saw none, that is correct. Why?

____

Step 5. Enter **show ip route igrp**.

List the routes in the routing table:

____

What is the administrative distance? _______________________

Step 6. When you finish these tasks, log off (by typing **exit**) and turn off the router.

Lab 9-2: Gateway of Last Resort (9.1.2)

Figure 9-5 Topology for Lab 9-2

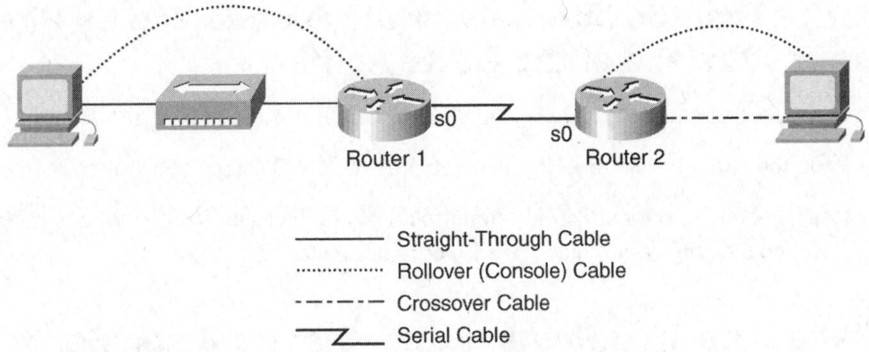

Table 9-4 Lab Equipment Configuration

Router Designation	Router Name	FastEthernet 0 Address	Interface Type Serial 0	Serial 0 Address
Router 1	GAD	172.16.0.1	DCE	172.17.0.1
Router 2	BHM	172.18.0.1	DTE	172.17.0.2

The enable secret password for both routers is **class**.

The enable, vty, and console passwords for both routers are **cisco**. The subnet mask for both interfaces on both routers is 255.255.0.0.

Objectives

- Configure RIP routing and add default routes (gateways) to the routers.
- Remove RIP and the default routes.
- Configure IGRP routing and add default routes (gateways) to the routers.

Background/Preparation

This lab shows the purpose of the gateway of last resort, also known as the default gateway. Cable a network similar to the one in Figure 9-5. You can use any router that meets the interface requirements in Figure 9-5 (that is, 800, 1600, 1700, 2500, and 2600 routers or a combination). Refer to the information in Appendix B, "Router Interface Summary," to correctly specify the interface identifiers based on the equipment in your lab. The 1721 Series routers produced the configuration output in this lab. Any other router might produce slightly different output. You should execute the following tasks on each router unless specifically instructed otherwise.

Start a HyperTerminal session as you did in Lab 2-2.

Implement the procedure documented in Appendix C, "Erasing and Reloading the Router," before continuing with this lab.

Task 1: Configure the Routers

On the routers, enter global configuration mode and configure the router name as shown in Table 9-4. Then, configure the console, vty, and enable passwords. If you have trouble doing so, refer to Lab 3-2. Next, configure the interfaces according to Table 9-4. If you have trouble doing so, refer to Lab 3-9. Finally, configure the RIP routing, which is covered in Lab 7-1 in case you need help. Don't forget to save the configurations to the startup configuration file.

Task 2: Configure the Hosts with the Proper IP Addresses, Subnet Masks, and Default Gateways

Task 3: Verify That the Internetwork Is Functioning by Pinging the FastEthernet Interface of the Other Router

Step 1. From the host attached to GAD, can you ping the BHM router's FastEthernet interface? _____

Step 2. From the host attached to BHM, can you ping the GAD router's FastEthernet interface? _____

Step 3. If the answer is no for either question, troubleshoot the router configurations to find the error. Then, do the pings again until the answer to both questions is yes.

Task 4: Make Sure That Routing Updates Are Being Sent

Step 1. Enter the command **debug ip rip** at the privileged EXEC mode prompt. Wait for at least 45 seconds.

Was there any output from the **debug** command? ______________________________

What did the output display?

____

Step 2. Enter **undebug all** to turn off debugging.

Task 5: Show the Routing Tables for Each Router

Examine the routing table entries using **show ip route** on each router.

What are the entries in the GAD routing table?

____

____

____

What are the entries in the BHM routing table?

____

____

____

Task 6: Add the Default Route to the BHM Router

Step 1. Enter the command **ip route 0.0.0.0 0.0.0.0 172.17.0.1** at the configuration mode prompt.

Step 2. Enter **show ip route** in privileged EXEC mode.

What is the gateway of last resort?

____

What does the gateway of last resort mean?

____

____

Task 7: Add the Default Route to the GAD Router

Step 1. Enter the command **ip route 0.0.0.0 0.0.0.0 172.17.0.2** at the configuration prompt.

Step 2. Enter **show ip route** in privileged EXEC mode.

What is the gateway of last resort?

____

Are there any other new entries in the routing table? _______________________

Task 8: Remove RIP Routing from Both Routers

To remove RIP routing, type the **no router rip** command at the configuration mode prompt. Then, ping the FastEthernet 0 interface on the GAD router from the BHM router.

What were the results of the ping?

____

Why was the ping successful?

____

Task 9: Remove the Default Route from Only the GAD Router

Step 1. Remove the gateway of last resort on the GAD router by typing **no ip route 0.0.0.0 0.0.0.0 172.17.0.2** at the configuration mode prompt on the GAD router.

Step 2. Enter **show ip route** in privileged EXEC mode.

What is the gateway of last resort?

____

Why is the gateway gone?

____

Step 3. Ping the FastEthernet 0 interface on the GAD router from the BHM router.

What were the results of the ping?

____

Why was the ping successful?

____

Step 4. Ping the FastEthernet 0 interface on the BHM router from the GAD router.

What were the results of the ping?

____

Why was the ping unsuccessful?

____

Step 5. Remove the gateway of last resort from the BHM router.

Task 10: Remove RIP Routing from the Routers and Use IGRP Instead

Step 1. Remove RIP routing by using the **no** form of the **rip routing** command. Then, set up IGRP routing using 30 as the autonomous system (AS) number. Remember to wait for the routes to propagate to the other router.

Step 2. Check the new routing protocol by typing **show ip route** at the privileged EXEC mode prompt. There should be two connected routes and two IGRP routes in **show ip route** output.

Task 11: Enter a Default Network Entry on the BHM Router

Step 1. Enter the command **ip default-network 172.17.0.0** at the configuration mode prompt.

Step 2. Enter the **show ip route** command in privileged EXEC mode.

Is a default route listed? ____

Step 3. When you finish these tasks, log off (by typing **exit**) and turn off the router.

Lab 9-3: Last Route Update (9.1.8)

Figure 9-6 Topology for Lab 9-3

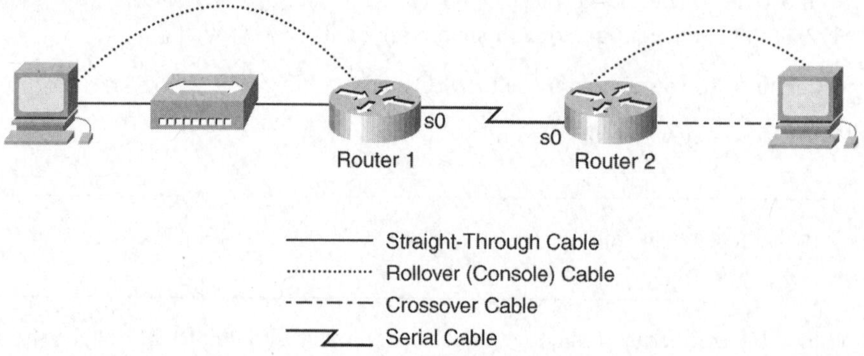

Table 9-5 Lab Equipment Configuration

Router Designation	Router Name	FastEthernet 0 Address	Interface Type Serial 0	Serial 0 Address
Router 1	GAD	172.16.0.1	DCE	172.17.0.1
Router 2	BHM	172.18.0.1	DTE	172.17.0.2

The enable secret password for both routers are **class**.

The enable, vty, and console passwords for both routers are **cisco**. The subnet mask for both interfaces on both routers is 255.255.0.0.

Objective

- Gather information about routing updates and routing protocols.

Background/Preparation

Cable a network similar to the one in Figure 9-6. You can use any router that meets the interface requirements in Figure 9-6 (that is, 800, 1600, 1700, 2500, and 2600 routers or a combination). Refer to the information in Appendix B, "Router Interface Summary," to correctly specify the interface identifiers based on the equipment in your lab. The 1721 Series routers produced the configuration output in this lab. Any other router might produce slightly different output. You should execute the following tasks on each router unless specifically instructed otherwise.

Start a HyperTerminal session as you did in Lab 2-2.

Implement the procedure documented in Appendix C, "Erasing and Reloading the Router," before continuing with this lab.

Task 1: Configure the Routers

On the routers, enter global configuration mode and configure the router name as shown in Table 9-5. Then, configure the console, vty, and enable passwords. If you have trouble doing so, refer to Lab 3-2. Next, configure the interfaces according to Table 9-5. If you have trouble doing so, refer to Lab 3-9. Finally, configure the RIP routing, which is covered in Lab 7-1 in case you need help. Don't forget to save the configurations to the startup configuration file.

Task 2: Configure the Hosts with the Proper IP Addresses, Subnet Masks, and Default Gateways

Task 3: Verify That the Internetwork Is Functioning by Pinging the FastEthernet Interface of the Other Router

Step 1. From the host attached to GAD, can you ping the BHM router's FastEthernet interface? _____

Step 2. From the host attached to BHM, can you ping the GAD router's FastEthernet interface? _____

Step 3. If the answer is no for either question, troubleshoot the router configurations to find the error. Then, do the pings again until the answer to both questions is yes.

Task 4: Make Sure That Routing Updates Are Being Sent

Step 1. Enter the command **debug ip rip** at the privileged EXEC mode prompt. Wait for at least 45 seconds.

Was there any output from the **debug** command? ____________________

Step 2. Enter **undebug all** to turn off debugging.

Task 5: Show the Routing Tables for Each Router

Examine the routing table entries using **show ip route** on each router.

Task 6: Check the Routing Table for a Specific Route

Step 1. From the privileged EXEC mode prompt on BHM, enter **show ip route 172.16.0.0**.

When was the last update? ____________________

When did BHM receive the last RIP update? ____________________

Step 2. Wait 5 seconds and enter **show ip route 172.16.0.0** a second time.

What has changed from the first time? ____________________

Step 3. Wait 5 seconds and enter **show ip route 172.16.0.0** a third time.

What has changed from the second time? ____________________

What is the default update time for RIP? ____________________

Task 7: Check the IP RIP Database on the BHM Router

Note: The router must use Cisco IOS Software Release 12.0 or later.

Step 1. Enter **show ip rip database** from the privileged EXEC mode prompt.

When was the last update? ______________________________

Step 2. Wait 5 seconds and enter **show ip rip database**.

What has changed from the first time? ______________________________

Step 3. Wait 5 seconds and enter **show ip rip database**.

What has changed from the second time? ______________________________

Task 8: Configure IGRP Using AS Number 101 on All Routers

Make sure that when you configure IGRP using AS number 101 on all routers you leave RIP on all routers.

Task 9: From BHM, Enter show ip route

Step 1. List the routes displayed in the routing table.

____

____

____

When did BHM receive the last IGRP update? ______________________________

Step 2. Wait 5 seconds and enter **show ip route**.

What has changed from the first time? ______________________________

Step 3. Wait 5 seconds and enter **show ip route**.

What has changed from the second time? ______________________________

What is the default update time for IGRP? ______________________________

Task 10: Check the Routing Protocol on Router BHM

Step 1. From privileged EXEC mode on BHM, enter **show ip protocols**.

What protocols appear? ______________________________

In how many seconds is the next update due for each protocol? ______________________________

Step 2. When you finish these tasks, log off (by typing **exit**) and turn off the router.

Lab 9-4: Troubleshooting Using ping and telnet (9.2.6)

Figure 9-7 Topology for Lab 9-4

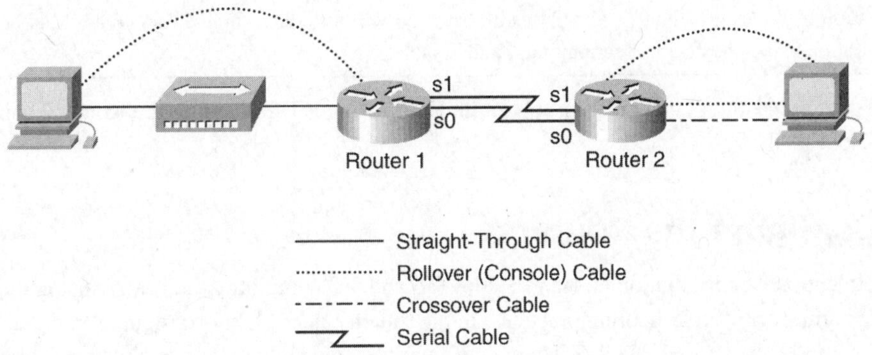

Table 9-6 Lab Equipment Configuration: Part I

Router Designation	Router Name	Routing Protocol	RIP Network Statements
Router 1	GAD	RIP	192.168.14.0
			192.168.15.0
Router 2	BHM	RIP	192.168.16.0
			192.168.13.0

The enable secret password for both routers is **class**.

The enable, vty, and console passwords for both routers are **cisco**.

Table 9-7 Lab Equipment Configuration: Part II

Router Designation	FastEthernet 0 Address	Interface Type Serial 0	Serial 0 Address	Interface Type Serial 1	Serial 1 Address	IP Host Table Entry
Router 1	192.168.14.1	DCE	192.168.15.1	DCE	192.168.13.1	BHM
Router 2	192.168.16.1	DTE	192.168.15.2	DTE	192.168.13.2	GAD

The subnet mask for all addresses on both routers is 255.255.255.0.

The IP Host Table Entry column contents indicate the name(s) of the other router(s) in the IP host table.

Objectives

- Use your knowledge of the Open System Interconnection (OSI) model Layers 1, 2, and 3 to diagnose network configuration errors.
- Use the ping and Telnet utilities in testing.

Background/Preparation

Cable a network similar to the one in Figure 9-7. You can use any router that meets the interface requirements in Figure 9-7 (that is, 800, 1600, 1700, 2500, and 2600 routers or a combination). Refer to the information in Appendix B, "Router Interface Summary," to correctly specify the interface identifiers based on the equipment in your lab. The 1721 Series routers produced the configuration output in this lab. Any other router might produce slightly different output. You should execute the following tasks on each router unless specifically instructed otherwise.

Start a HyperTerminal session as you did in Lab 2-2, "Establishing a Console Session with HyperTerminal."

Note: Work in teams of two. Team Member 1 should cable and configure the routers and workstations according to the information in Tables 9-6 and 9-7. Using this information will introduce some errors. Team Member 2 should test the configuration using physical inspection, ping, and Telnet.

Implement the procedure documented in Appendix C, "Erasing and Reloading the Router," before continuing with this lab.

Task 1: Configure the Routers

There are intentional configuration errors in Tables 9-6 and 9-7. Configure the routers using these parameters to introduce errors for troubleshooting practice. On the routers, enter global configuration mode and configure the router name as shown in Table 9-6. Then, configure the console, vty, and enable passwords. If you have problems doing so, refer to Lab 3-2, "Configuring Router Passwords." Next, configure the interfaces and routing according to the chart. If you have problems doing so, refer to Lab 3-9, "Configuring Host Tables," and Lab 7-1, "Configuring RIP." Make sure to copy the **running-config** to the **startup-config** on each router so you won't lose the configuration if the router is power-recycled.

Task 2: Configure the Hosts with the Proper IP Addresses, Subnet Masks, and Default Gateways

Test the configuration by pinging all the interfaces from each host. If the pinging is not successful, go on to Task 3.

If the pinging is successful, advise the instructor that the configuration is operational. The instructor will introduce fault(s) into the configuration for you to diagnose and repair.

Task 3: Check the Connections

Step 1. Review the physical connections on the standard lab setup.

Step 2. Check all physical devices, cables, and connections.

Task 4: Troubleshoot

Troubleshoot the network problems using the commands **ping** and **telnet** to discover problems.

Task 5: List the Findings

Step 1. Write down the problems as you encounter them.

Step 2. Write down what you did to correct the problems.

Step 3. Use Table 9-8 to record the information.

Step 4. Have the instructor verify that you corrected all the problems.

Table 9-8 Troubleshooting Documentation Table

Problem Number	Problem Discovered	Solution	Instructor Verification

Task 6: Perform the Lab Again with Team Members 1 and 2 Switching Roles

When you finish the preceding tasks, log off (by typing **exit**) and turn off the router.

Lab 9-5: Troubleshooting Using traceroute (9.3.4)

Figure 9-8 Topology for Lab 9-5

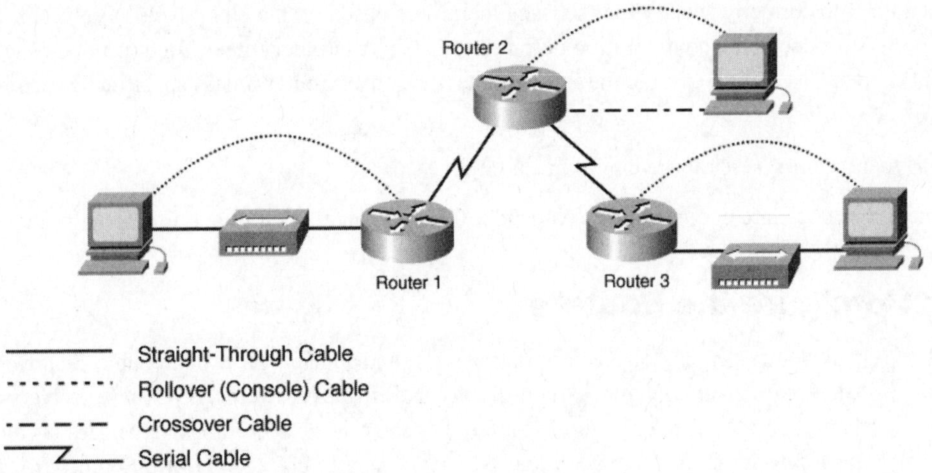

Table 9-9 Lab Equipment Configuration: Part I

Router Designation	Router Name	Routing Protocol	RIP Network Statements
Router 1	GAD	RIP	192.168.14.0
			192.168.15.0
Router 2	BHM	RIP	192.168.15.0
			192.168.13.0
			192.168.16.0
Router 3	PHX	RIP	192.168.13.0
			192.168.17.0

The enable secret password for all routers is **class**.

The enable, vty, and console passwords for all routers are **cisco**.

Table 9-10 Lab Equipment Configuration: Part II

Router Designation	FastEthernet 0 Address	Interface Type Serial 0	Serial 0 Address	Interface Type Serial 1	Serial 1 Address	IP Host Table Entries
Router 1	192.168.14.1	DCE	192.168.15.1	N/A	No address	BHM PHX
Router 2	192.168.16.1	DTE	192.168.15.2	DCE	192.168.13.1	GAD PHX
Router 3	192.168.17.1	N/A	No address	DTE	192.168.13.2	GAD BHM

The subnet mask for all addresses on both routers is 255.255.255.0.

Objectives

- Use the **traceroute** Cisco IOS Software command from source router to destination router.
- Use the **tracert** MS-DOS command from source workstation to destination router.
- Verify that the network layer between source, destination, and each router along the way is working properly.
- Retrieve information to evaluate the end-to-end path reliability.

Background/Preparation

Cable a network similar to the one in Figure 9-8. You can use any router that meets the interface requirements in Figure 9-8 (that is, 800, 1600, 1700, 2500, and 2600 routers or a combination). Refer to the information in Appendix B to correctly specify the interface identifiers based on the equipment in your lab. The 1721 Series routers produced the configuration output in this lab. Any other router might produce slightly different output. You should execute the following tasks on each router unless specifically instructed otherwise.

Start a HyperTerminal session as you did in Lab 2-2.

Implement the procedure documented in Appendix C on all routers before continuing with this lab.

Task 1: Configure the Routers

Step 1. On the routers, enter global configuration mode and configure the router name as shown in Tables 9-9 and 9-10. Then, configure the console, vty, and enable passwords. If you have problems doing so, refer to Lab 3-2. Next, configure the interfaces and routing according to the chart. If you have problems doing so, refer to Labs 3-9 and 7-1. Make sure to copy the **running-config** to the **startup-config** on each router so you won't lose the configuration if the router is power-recycled.

This lab requires that the routers have IP hostnames configured.

Step 2. Verify the routers' configurations by performing a **show running-config** on each router. If they are not correct, fix any configuration errors and reverify.

Task 2: Configure the Workstations with the Appropriate IP Address Subnet Masks and Default Gateways

Task 3: Ping from the Workstations

Step 1. From a Windows host, choose **Start > Programs > Accessories > MS-DOS**. This task opens a command-prompt window. (If this not the correct location, see the instructor for the proper location on this computer.)

Step 2. To test that the TCP/IP stack and default gateway on the workstation are configured and working properly, use the MS-DOS window to ping the routers by issuing the following command:

```
C:\>ping 192.168.14.1
```

Step 3. The ping should respond with successful results. If not, check the configurations on the host and directly connected router.

Task 4: Test Layer 3 Connectivity

Using the command prompt, enter **ping** and the IP addresses of all routers' interfaces. This task tests Layer 3 connectivity between the workstation and the routers.

Is the output from the workstation's **ping** command the same as the output from the **ping** command from a router?

____

____

Task 5: Log in to the Router in User Mode

Log in to the GAD router and enter privileged EXEC mode.

Task 6: Discover the trace Options

Enter **traceroute** at the router prompt.

What did the router respond with?

____

____

Task 7: Use the traceroute Command

Step 1. Enter **traceroute ip** *xxx.xxx.xxx.xxx* where *xxx.xxx.xxx.xxx* is the IP address of the target destination. *Note:* Use one of the end routers and **traceroute ip** to the other end host. The router responds with the following:

```
GAD#traceroute ip 192.168.16.2
Type escape sequence to abort. Tracing the route to 192.168.16.2

 1 BHM (192.168.15.2) 16 msec 16 msec 16 msec
 2 192.168.16.2 16 msec 16 msec 12 msec
GAD#
```

Step 2. If the output is not successful, check the router and host configurations.

Note: If the **ip** keyword is omitted, traceroute defaults to IP.

Task 8: Continue Using traceroute

Repeat Tasks 5 through 7 with all other routers on the network.

Task 9: Use the tracert Command from a Workstation

Step 1. From the console workstation, choose **Start > Programs > Command Prompt**. An MS-DOS command-prompt window opens.

Step 2. Enter **tracert** and the same IP address you used in Task 5.

Step 3. The first hop is the default gateway or the near-side router interface on the LAN that the workstation is connected to. List the hostname and IP address of the router that the ICMP packet was routed through in Table 9-11.

Table 9-11 Recording Hostnames and IP Addresses of Routed ICMP Packets

Hostname	IP Address

There is one more entry in the output of the **tracert** command when the trace is from the computer command prompt to the target host. Why?

____

Step 4. When you finish the preceding tasks, log off (by typing **exit**) and turn off the router.

Lab 9-6: Troubleshooting Routing Issues with show ip route and show ip protocols (9.3.5)

Figure 9-9 Topology for Lab 9-6

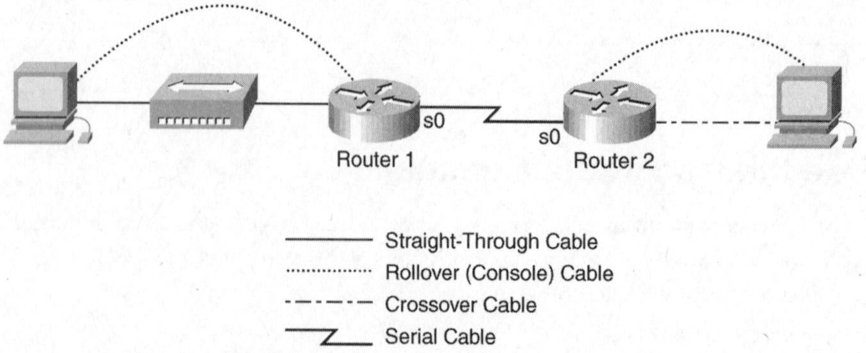

Table 9-12 Lab Equipment Configuration

Router Designation	Router Name	FastEthernet 0 Address	Interface Type Serial 0	Serial 0 Address
Router 1	GAD	192.168.1.1	DCE	192.168.2.1
Router 2	BHM	192.168.3.1	DTE	192.168.2.2

The enable secret password for both routers is **class**.

The enable, vty, and console passwords for both routers are **cisco**.

The subnet mask for both interfaces on both routers is 255.255.255.0.

Objective

- Use the **show ip route** and **show ip protocol** commands to diagnose a routing configuration problem.

Background/Preparation

Cable a network similar to the one in Figure 9-9. You can use any router that meets the interface requirements in Figure 9-9 (that is, 800, 1600, 1700, 2500, and 2600 routers or a combination). Refer to the information in Appendix B, "Router Interface Summary," to correctly specify the interface identifiers based on the equipment in your lab. The 1721 Series routers produced the configuration output in this lab. Any other router might produce slightly different output. You should execute the following tasks on each router unless specifically instructed otherwise.

Start a HyperTerminal session as you did in Lab 2-2.

Implement the procedure documented in Appendix C, "Erasing and Reloading the Router," before continuing with this lab.

Task 1: Configure the Hostname, Passwords, and Interfaces on the GAD Router

On the GAD router, enter global configuration mode and configure the router name as shown in Table 9-12. Then, configure the console, vty, and enable passwords. If you have trouble doing so, refer to Lab 3-2. Configure interfaces as shown in Table 9-12.

Task 2: Configure the Routing Protocol on the GAD Router

Go to the proper command mode and enter the following:

```
GAD(config)#router rip
GAD(config-router)#network 192.168.1.0
GAD(config-router)#network 192.168.2.0
GAD(config-router)#exit
GAD(config)#exit
```

Task 3: Save the GAD Router Configuration

To save the GAD router configuration, enter the following:

```
GAD#copy running-config startup-config
Destination filename [startup-config]?[Enter]
```

Task 4: Configure the Hostname, Passwords, and Interfaces on the BHM Router

On the BHM router, enter global configuration mode and configure the hostname as shown in Table 9-10. Then, configure the console, vty, and enable passwords. Finally, configure the interfaces.

Task 5: Configure the Routing Protocol on the BHM Router

Go to the proper command mode and enter the following:

```
BHM(config)#router rip
BHM(config-router)#network  192.168.2.0
BHM(config-router)#network  192.168.1.0
BHM(config-router)#exit
BHM(config)#exit
```

Task 6: Save the BHM Router Configuration

To save the BHM router configuration, enter the following:

```
BHM#copy running-config startup-config
Destination filename [startup-config]?[Enter]
```

Task 7: Verify That the Internetwork Is Functioning by Pinging the FastEthernet Interface of the Other Router

Step 1. From GAD, can you ping the BHM router's FastEthernet interface? ____________________

Step 2. From BHM, can you ping the GAD router's FastEthernet interface? ____________________

Task 8: Examine the Routing Table

After an unsuccessful ping, you need to check the routing table with the **show ip route** command. From the GAD router, enter the following:

```
GAD#show ip route
```

Is there a route to the BHM Ethernet LAN? ____

Task 9: Examine the Routing Protocol Status

After examining the routing tables, you discover that there is no route to the BHM Ethernet LAN. So you use the **show ip protocols** command to view the routing protocol status. From the BHM router, enter the following:

```
BHM#show ip protocols
```

What networks is RIP routing? ____

Are these the correct networks? ____

Task 10: Change the Configuration to Route the Correct Networks

After examining the **show ip protocols** command results, you notice that the network on the Ethernet LAN is not being routed. After examining it further, you also find that a network that does not belong has been configured to be advertised. You decide this is a typo and you need to correct it. You enter the router RIP configuration mode and make the appropriate changes. From the BHM router, enter the following:

```
BHM#configure terminal
BHM(config)#router rip
BHM(config-router)#no network 192.168.1.0
BHM(config-router)#network 192.168.3.0
BHM(config-router)#^Z
```

Task 11: Confirm That RIP Is Routing the Correct Networks

Confirm that the new statement corrected the RIP configuration problem. Again enter the **show ip protocols** command to observe what networks are being routed. From the BHM router, enter the following:

```
BHM#show ip protocols
```

What networks is RIP routing? ____________________

Are these the correct networks? ____________________

Task 12: Verify the Routing Table

Having confirmed that you corrected the configuration problem, verify that the proper routes are now in the routing table. Again issue the **show ip route** command to verify that the router now has the proper route. From the GAD router, enter the following:

```
GAD#show ip route
```

Is there a route to the BHM LAN? ____________________

Task 13: Verify Connectivity Between the GAD Router and the Host in BHM

Step 1. Use the **ping** command to verify connectivity from the GAD router to a host in BHM. From the GAD router, enter the following:

```
GAD#ping host-ip
```

For example, for a host with an IP address, enter the following:

```
GAD#ping 192.168.3.2
```

Was the ping successful? ____________________

Step 2. When you finish these tasks, log off (by typing **exit**) and turn off the router.

Lab 9-7: Troubleshooting Routing Issues with debug (9.3.7)

Figure 9-10 Topology for Lab 9-7

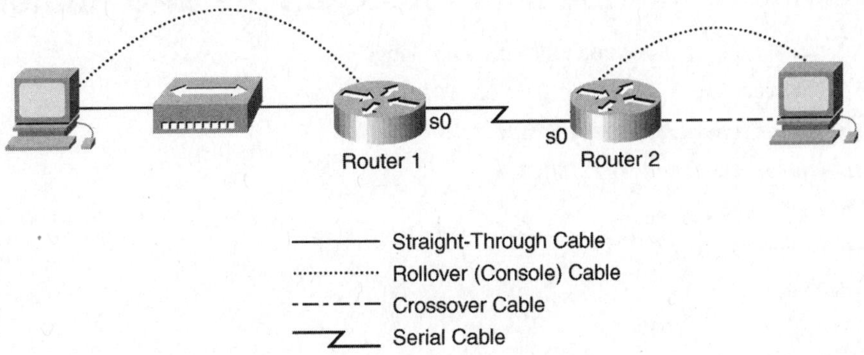

Table 9-13 Lab Equipment Configuration

Router Designation	Router Name	FastEthernet 0 Address	Interface Type Serial 0	Serial 0 Address
Router 1	GAD	192.168.1.1	DCE	192.168.2.1
Router 2	BHM	192.168.3.1	DTE	192.168.2.2

The enable secret password for both routers is **class**.

The enable, vty, and console passwords for both routers are **cisco**.

The subnet mask for both interfaces on both routers is 255.255.255.0.

Objectives

- Use a systematic OSI troubleshooting process to diagnose routing problems.
- Use various **show** commands to gather information.
- Use **debug** commands and logging.

Background/Preparation

Cable a network similar to the one in Figure 9-10. You can use any router that meets the interface requirements in Figure 9-10 (that is, 800, 1600, 1700, 2500, and 2600 routers or a combination). Refer to the information in Appendix B, "Router Interface Summary," to correctly specify the interface identifiers based on the equipment in your lab. The 1721 Series routers produced the configuration output in this lab. Any other router might produce slightly different output. You should execute the following tasks on each router unless specifically instructed otherwise.

Start a HyperTerminal session as you did in Lab 2-2.

Implement the procedure documented in Appendix C, "Erasing and Reloading the Router," before continuing with this lab.

Task 1: Configure the Hostname, Passwords, and Interfaces on the GAD Router

On the GAD router, enter global configuration mode and configure the router name as shown in Table 9-13. Then, configure the console, vty, and enable passwords. If you have trouble doing so, refer to Lab 3-2. Configure the interfaces as shown in Table 9-13.

Task 2: Configure the Routing Protocol on the GAD Router

Go to the proper command mode and enter the following:

```
GAD(config)#router rip
GAD(config-router)#network 192.168.1.0
GAD(config-router)#network 192.168.2.0
GAD(config-router)#version 2
GAD(config-router)#exit
GAD(config)#exit
```

Task 3: Save the GAD Router Configuration

To save the GAD router configuration, enter the following:

```
GAD#copy running-config startup-config
Destination filename [startup-config]?[Enter]
```

Task 4: Configure the Hostname, Passwords, and Interfaces on the BHM Router

On the BHM router, enter global configuration mode and configure the hostname as shown in Table 9-11. Then, configure the console, vty, and enable passwords. Finally, configure the interfaces.

Task 5: Configure the Routing Protocol on the BHM Router

Go to the proper command mode and enter the following:

```
BHM(config)#router rip
BHM(config-router)#network 192.168.2.0
BHM(config-router)#network 192.168.1.0
BHM(config-router)#version 1
BHM(config-router)#exit
BHM(config)#exit
```

Task 6: Save the BHM Router Configuration

To save the BHM router configuration, enter the following:

```
BHM#copy running-config startup-config
Destination filename [startup-config]?[Enter]
```

Task 7: Gather Facts—Ask and Listen

After asking around, you are told that a network associate on the night shift changed some of the routing parameters on the routers for a circuit between the GAD office and the BHM office. Unfortunately, he did not follow the proper procedure, and there is no documentation on these changes.

Task 8: Gather Facts—Test Basic Functionality

Verify that the internetwork is not functioning by pinging the LAN interfaces.

From GAD, can you ping the BHM router's FastEthernet interface? ______________________________

From BHM, can you ping the GAD router's FastEthernet interface? ______________________________

Task 9: Gather Facts—Start Testing to Isolate the Problem

You know that there is no communication between GAD and BHM. Even though you suspect a routing issue, you resist the temptation to directly begin testing the routing. Instead, you follow a scientific troubleshooting method.

Step 1. Start at the physical layer; confirm that the WAN link circuit is up. From the GAD router, issue the **show interfaces serial 0** command to confirm that the line and protocol are up.

Are they both up? ______________________________

Step 2. Now that you know that the line and protocol are both up, test the data link layer. From the GAD router, issue the **show CDP neighbors** command to confirm that the BHM router is a neighbor to the GAD router Serial 0 interface.

Do you see BHM as a neighbor on interface Serial 0? ______________________________

Task 10: Examine the Routing Table

It looks like the data link layer is good. It's time to move up and examine the network layer. Check the GAD routing table to see whether there is a route to the BHM LAN. To do this, issue the **show ip route** command on the GAD router.

Is the route there? ______________________________

Are there any RIP routes? ______________________________

Task 11: Examine the Routing Protocol Status

After examining the routing tables, you discover that there is no route to the BHM Ethernet LAN. You use the **show ip protocols** command to view the routing protocol status. From the GAD router, enter the following:

```
GAD#show ip protocols
```

What networks is RIP routing? ______________________________

Are these the correct networks? ______________________________

Task 12: Gather Facts—Identify the Exact Problem

Now that you have confirmed a routing issue, you must discover the exact source of the routing problem so that you can correct it. To observe the routing exchange between the routers, you will use the **debug ip rip** command.

Step 1. From a GAD console, enter the **debug ip packet** command and watch the output for a minute or two.

Record a sample of output from GAD or BHM.

Are routing updates being passed? ______________________________

What is happening to the routing updates from BHM?

____

Step 2. Enter **undebug all** to stop the output.

Task 13: Consider the Possibilities

From the information you have discovered through the troubleshooting process, what are the possible problems?

____

____

Task 14: Create an Action Plan

How will you correct the problem?

____

Task 15: Implement the Action Plan

Try the solution that you proposed in the preceding task.

Task 16: Observe the Results

You need to confirm that your plan has solved the problem. You do so by reversing the tests that you previously performed.

Step 1. Observe the routing exchange between the routers using the **debug ip rip** command, and watch the output for a minute or two.

Step 2. Enter **undebug all** to stop the output.

Check the GAD routing table to see if there is a route to BHM by using **show ip route**.

Are there any IP routes? ______________________________

Is the route to BHM there? ______________________________

Step 3. To confirm that everything is working, from the GAD router ping the LAN interface of the BHM router. Was it successful? ______________________________

Step 4. If your plan did not correct the problem, you need to repeat the process.

Step 5. If the tests were successful, you need to document the changes and back up the configuration.

Step 6. When you finish these tasks, log off (by typing **exit**) and turn off the router.

Challenge Lab 9-8: Basic Routing Troubleshooting

Figure 9-11 Basic Routing Troubleshooting

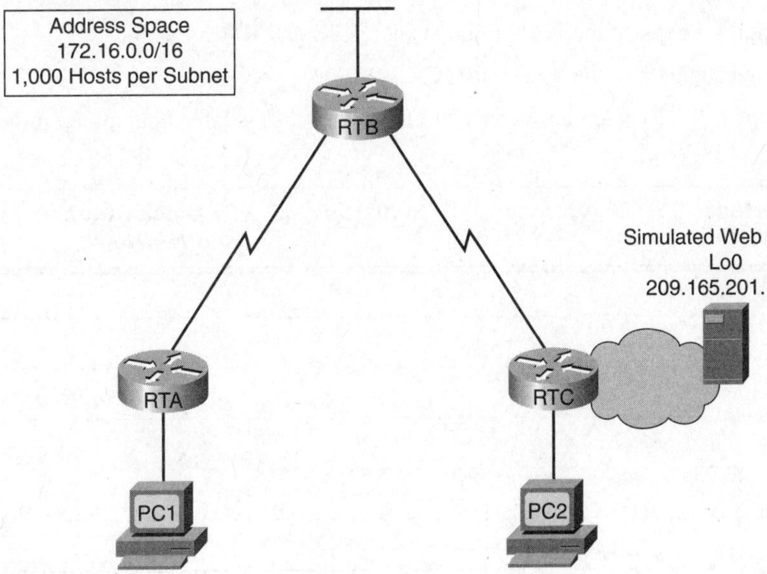

Objectives

- Implement a Class B addressing scheme.
- Configure RIP routing.
- Configure default routing.
- Use commands to verify and troubleshoot your configurations.

Equipment

This lab can be done with any combination of 1700, 2500, and 2600 Series routers.

NetLab Compatibility Notes

This lab can be completed using NetLab. If you are using the three-router pod version 2, you can also configure the workstations.

Task 1: Cable the Lab

Step 1. Cable the lab as shown in Figure 9-11.

Step 2. Label the topology with the correct interface designations for the equipment you have chosen (for example, Fa0/0, S0/0, and so on).

Task 2: Determine an Appropriate Addressing Scheme

Step 1. Subnet the network 172.16.0.0/16 to provide enough addresses for 1000 hosts per subnet. Assign subnets to the topology according to the following specifications:

- Assign subnet 1 to the LAN on RTA.
- Assign subnet 2 to the WAN link between RTA and RTB.
- Assign subnet 3 to the LAN on RTB.
- Assign subnet 4 to the WAN link between RTB and RTC.
- Assign subnet 5 to the LAN on RTC.

Step 2. Label the topology with the subnets and fill in the address table with all the missing information.

Router	Interface Type	IP Address	Subnet Mask	Clock Rate? (Yes/No)	Default Gateway
RTA					N/A
					N/A
RTB					N/A
					N/A
					N/A
RTC					N/A
					N/A
	Lo0	209.165.201.1	255.255.255.255	N/A	N/A
PC1	N/A			N/A	
PC2	N/A			N/A	

Task 3: Router, Routing, and PC Configuration

You might need to refer to your notes and labs from previous chapters to complete this section.

Step 1. Configure all routers with basic configurations according to your instructor's requirements, such as:

- Hostname
- Line configurations
- Global passwords
- Host tables
- Banner
- Other instructor-required global configurations

Step 2. Configure and activate all the necessary interfaces.

Step 3. Configure dynamic routing using RIP. Do not configure the simulated web server as part of RIP.

Step 4. Configure RTB with a default "quad-zero" route pointing to **null 0** as the outbound interface.

Note: Because RTC does not have a default route (for example, an ISP connection), use the null interface to simulate a default route. You must use a null interface because Cisco IOS software does not redistribute a default route that points to a loopback interface.

Step 5. Configure RTB to distribute the default route in the RIP routing process.

Step 6. Configure PC1 and PC3 with appropriate addressing.

Task 4: Verify and Troubleshoot Your Network Configuration

Step 1. Display the routing table on each router. What command did you use?

____

Step 2. Check off the following to verify your routing configuration:

- RTA has six routes: two directly connected routes, three RIP routes, and one RIP default route.
- RTB has six routes: three directly connected routes, two RIP routes, and one RIP default route.
- RTC has seven routes: three directly connected routes, three RIP routes, and one static default route.

Step 3. If one or more of your routing tables is incomplete, the first step is to check the status of all your interfaces. Display a summary of the interfaces on each router. What command did you use?

____

Step 4. Check off the following to verify that the necessary interfaces are in the "up and up" state:

- RTA has two interfaces correctly addressed and active.
- RTB has three interfaces correctly addressed and active.
- RTC has three interfaces correctly addressed and active.

Step 5. If all the necessary interfaces are active ("up and up"), you probably have a routing problem. Display detailed information about the routing process. What command did you use?

____

Step 6. Check off the following to verify that routing is configured correctly on each router:

- RTA is advertising the 172.16.0.0 network and is receiving updates from RTB. RTB's IP address should be listed under Routing Information Sources.
- RTB is advertising the 172.16.0.0 network and is receiving updates for RTA and RTC. Both RTA and RTC IP addresses are listed under Routing Information Sources.
- RTC is advertising the 172.16.0.0 network and is receiving updates from RTB. RTB's IP address should be listed under Routing Information Sources.

Step 7. If any router is missing the default route, make sure that RTC is correctly configured with a "quad-zero" default route pointing to **null 0** and that RTC is distributing that default route within the RIP routing process.

Step 8. Your final test is to verify that PC1 can ping PC2 and the simulated web server.

- Ping from PC1 to PC2 is successful.
- Ping from PC1 to simulated web server is successful.

Step 9. If any of your pings failed, verify that your PC IP address configurations are correct. You must have an IP address, subnet mask, and default gateway that belongs to the same network to which the PC is attached. You can also use the **tracert** command to see where the ping is failing.

CHAPTER 10

Intermediate TCP/IP

The Study Guide portion of this chapter uses a combination of fill-in-the-blank and open-ended questions and unique custom exercises to test your knowledge of the theory of TCP/IP.

The Lab Exercises portion of this chapter includes all the online curriculum labs to ensure that you have mastered the practical, hands-on skills of TCP/IP for this chapter.

Study Guide

TCP and UDP Operation

You have already studied the Transport layer and its two protocols, TCP and UDP, in Chapter 11 of the CCNA 1 curriculum. The exercises in this section are meant as a review of that material. Understanding TCP and UDP operation is a prerequisite to configuring security with access control lists, which are covered in the next chapter.

Vocabulary Exercise: Completion

Complete the paragraphs that follow by filling in appropriate words and phrases.

The TCP/IP layer includes the ______________________________ (TCP) and the ____________________ (UDP). TCP is a __________________-oriented protocol, and UDP is a ____________________ protocol. This means that TCP establishes communications with the destination before data is transferred, whereas UDP does not establish communications. UDP simply sends the data.

TCP uses a process called a ______________________ to create a new TCP connection and to initialize the various numbers that control and manage a TCP connection. Three segments are sent between the sending and receiving hosts. In the first segment, the host that wants to synchronize a connection can set the ___________ bit in the TCP header. The replying host acknowledges the first segment by setting the ___________ bit in the second segment. In addition, the replying host sets its own ___________ bit, requesting an acknowledgment from the originating host. The third segment is sent by the originating host back to the second host, acknowledging the reverse synchronization request by setting the ___________ bit. During this process of connection establishment, the two hosts also negotiate other parameters of the connection, including window size.

While hosts are sending data using TCP, the receiving host can control how fast each TCP sender sends the data over time. This process is called __________. The receiver tells the sending host how many _______ the sending host can send before the receiving host sends an ______________. The number of _______ the sending host can send is called the ___________ size.

TCP uses two TCP header fields—the _________________ and ____________________ fields—to signal the other computer as to whether a segment was received.

A ______________________ (DoS) attack is a malicious attack with one purpose: to reduce or eliminate the target's ability to process legitimate traffic. One of the most common DoS attacks is a _____________, which occurs when a hacker sends numerous TCP segments to a server, with each segment looking like a new request for a new TCP connection. The server reserves memory for the connection, sends back an ACK, and waits for the third handshake segment.

TCP Segment Format Exercise

Refer to Figure 10-1. Write in the missing field names.

Figure 10-1 TCP Segment

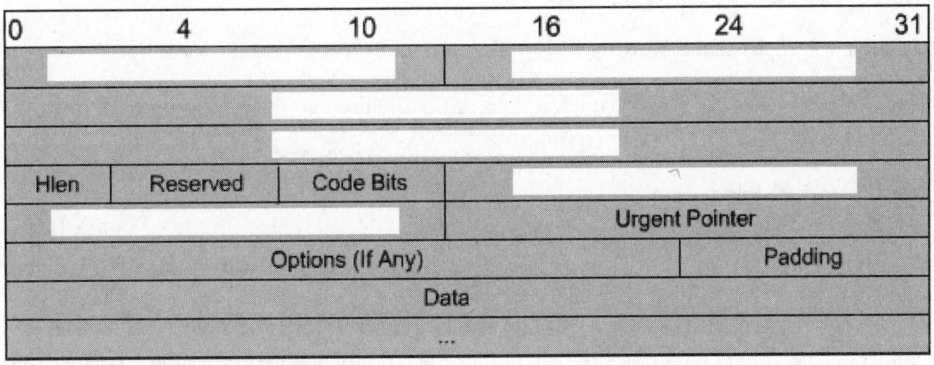

UDP Segment Format Exercise

Refer to Figure 10-2. Write in the missing field names. Notice how sparse the UDP segment format is compared to the TCP segment format.

Figure 10-2 UDP Segment

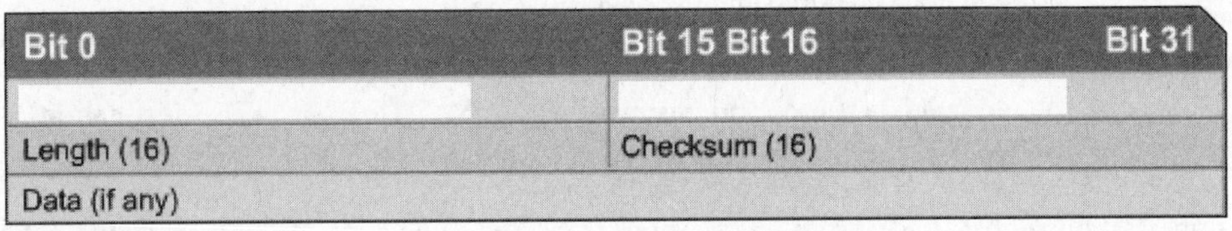

Bit 0
Bit 15 Bit 16
Bit 31
Length (16)
Checksum (16)
Data (if any)

Concept Questions

1. Compare TCP and UDP by listing the features TCP provides.

____

____

____

____

____

____

2. What two measures can be taken on a server to defend it against a SYN flood DoS attack?

____

____

____

3. Explain what Positive Acknowledgement with Retransmission (PAR) means.

____

____

____

Operation of Transport Layer Ports

The exercises in this section focus your attention on the port numbers used at the Transport layer.

Vocabulary Exercise: Completion

Complete the paragraphs that follow by filling in appropriate words and phrases.

When your PC receives an IP packet, it must determine to which application process it must give the data. To make this determination, TCP and UDP use ________________. To allow servers to work well, TCP/IP defines one or more __________________, each reserved for use by a specific application protocol. These are the ports that a client application inserts in the ________________ field in the TCP or UDP segment header. The value of the ________________ field is determined dynamically by picking a random number between __________ and __________.

Before a host can send data using TCP/IP to another host, the originating host must first encapsulate the data with three addresses or port numbers:

- At the ________________ layer, the originating host ______________ the data and adds a source and destination ________________. The source ______________ is generated dynamically. The destination ________________ matches the application that the host is attempting to access.
- At the ________________ layer, the originating host encapsulates the ______________ into ______________ and adds a source and destination ________________.
- At the __________________ layer, the originating host encapsulates the ______________ into ______________ and adds a source and destination ________________. The destination ____________ is the ________________ of the default gateway.

Port numbers allow a host to have multiple sessions using the same application. For example, you can have multiple web pages open at the same time. The destination port number for the web pages is _________ for all sessions, but the source port number is different for each instance of a web page. To see how many TCP sessions are currently open, you can use the Windows **netstat** command. Enter the command, a space, and then a question mark (**?**) to see all the options available.

TCP and UDP Port Numbers Exercise

In the following table, indicate which protocol is used (TCP, UDP, or both) and the well-known port number.

Application	Protocol	Port Number
FTP data		
FTP control		
Telnet		
SMTP		
DNS		
TFTP		
HTTP (WWW)		
POP3		
SNMP		

Comparing Layer 2, Layer 3, and Layer 4 Addresses

Refer to Figure 10-3, which shows the Layer 2 and Layer 3 addresses. For Frame Relay, the Layer 2 address is the data-link connection identifier (DLCI). For the PPP WAN protocol, the Layer 2 address field has no meaning because it uses a direct link between two devices. Therefore, the address field is always filled with eight 1 bits (11111111, 0xFF, 255).

Figure 10-3 Topology of Layer 2, 3, and 4 Addresses

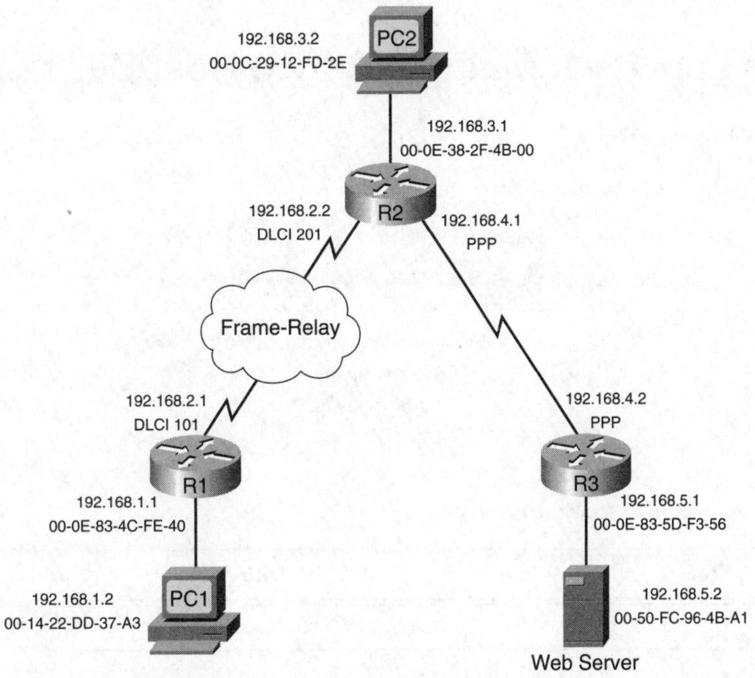

PC1 is requesting a web page from the web server. Fill in the following table with the correct Layer 2 and Layer 3 addresses, as well as the Layer 4 port numbers at each stage as a packet travels from PC1 to the web server. Remember that the source generates a random port number.

Stage	Destination (Layer 2)	Source (Layer 2)	Source (Layer 3)	Destination (Layer 3)	Source (Layer 4)	Destination (Layer 4)
PC1 to R1						
R1 to R2						
R2 to R3						
R3 to web server						

Lab Exercises

Command Reference

There are no commands for this chapter.

Curriculum Lab 10-1: Multiple Active Host Sessions (10.1.6)

Figure 10-4 Topology for Lab 10-1

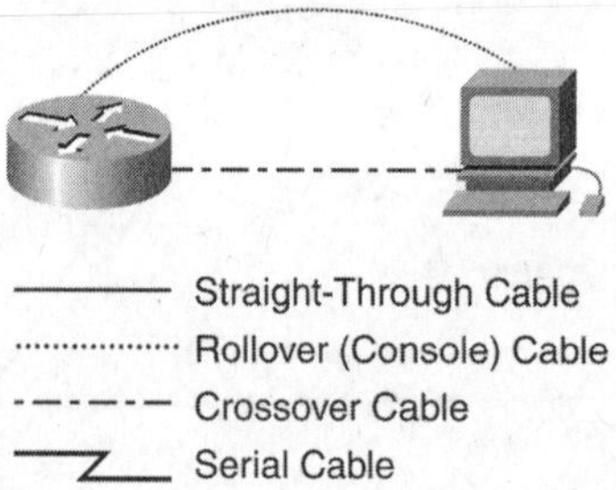

Table 10-1 Lab Equipment Configuration

Router Designation	Router Name	FA0/0 Address	Subnet Mask
Router 1	GAD	192.168.14.1	255.255.255.0

The enable secret password is **class**.

The enable/vty/console password is **cisco**.

Objectives:

This lab contains the following objectives:

- Enable HTTP services on a router
- Observe multiple HTTP and Telnet sessions on a single host using **netstat**

Background/Preparation:

Cable a network similar to the one shown in Figure 10-4. You can use any router that meets the interface requirements in Figure 10-4 (that is, 800, 1600, 1700, 2500, or 2600 routers, or a combination). Refer to the information in Appendix B, "Router Interface Summary," to correctly specify the interface identifiers based on the equipment in your lab. The 1721 Series routers produced the configuration output in this lab. Any other router might produce slightly different output. You should execute the following steps on each router unless specifically instructed otherwise:

Step 1. Start a HyperTerminal session as you did in Lab 2-2, "Establishing a Console Session with HyperTerminal."

Step 2. Implement the procedure documented in Appendix C, "Erasing and Reloading the Router," before continuing with this lab.

Task 1: Configure the Hostname, Passwords, and Interface on the GAD Router

On the GAD router, enter global configuration mode and configure the router name as shown in Table 10-1. Then, configure the console, virtual terminal, and enable passwords. Configure the Ethernet interface.

Task 2: Save the Configuration Information from Privileged EXEC Command Mode

Use the following command:

```
GAD#copy running-config startup-config
```

Task 3: Configure the Host

Configure the host with the proper IP address, subnet mask, and default gateway.

Task 4: Allow HTTP Access to the Router

Allow HTTP access by issuing the **ip http server** command in global configuration mode.

Task 5: Use the Workstation Browser to Access the Router

Open a browser on host 1 and type **http://***ip-address-of-Router-GAD*. You are then prompted for a username and the enable password of the router. The username can be left blank; only the password is required.

Task 6: Telnet to the Ethernet Interface on the Router from the Host

Open a command prompt and Telnet to the Ethernet interface, as follows:

```
Microsoft Windows XP [Version 5.1.2600]
(C) Copyright 1985-2001 Microsoft Corp.

C:\>telnet 192.168.14.1
```

Task 7: Start a Second Telnet Session to the Router

Open another command prompt and Telnet to the Ethernet interface, as follows:

```
Microsoft Windows XP [Version 5.1.2600]
(C) Copyright 1985-2001 Microsoft Corp.

C:\>telnet 192.168.14.1
```

Task 8: Check the Sessions on the Host

Step 1. Enter the **netstat** command from the command or MS-DOS prompt.

How many sessions are running on the host? ______________________________

Why isn't the web browser listed as an active session? ______________________________

Step 2. Log off (by typing **exit**) and turn off the router.

Curriculum Lab 10-2: Well-Known Port Numbers and Multiple Sessions (10.2.5)

Figure 10-5 Topology for Lab 10-2

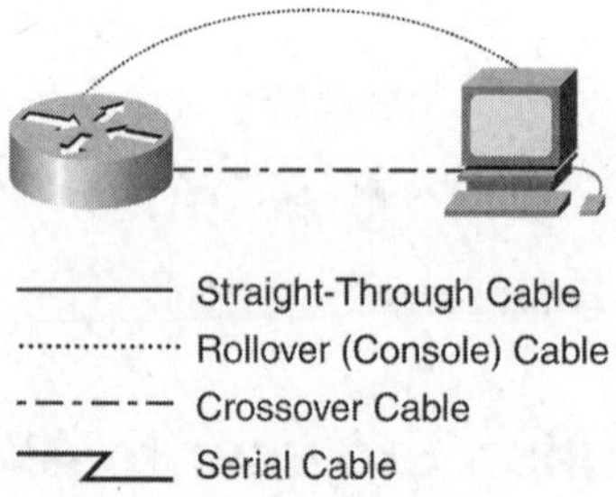

Table 10-2 Lab Equipment Configuration

Router Designation	Router Name	FA0/0 Address	Subnet Mask
Router 1	GAD	192.168.14.1	255.255.255.0

The enable secret password is **class**.

The enable/vty/console password is **cisco**.

Objectives:

This lab contains the following objectives:

- Enable HTTP services on a router
- Show multiple HTTP and Telnet sessions on a single host
- Observe well-known TCP port numbers on the host and router

Background/Preparation:

Cable a network similar to the one shown in Figure 10-5. You can use any router that meets the interface requirements in Figure 10-5 (that is, 800, 1600, 1700, 2500, or 2600 routers, or a combination). Refer to the information in Appendix B, "Router Interface Summary," to correctly specify the interface identifiers based on the equipment in your lab. The 1721 Series routers produced the configuration output in this lab. Any other router might produce slightly different output. You should execute the following steps on each router unless specifically instructed otherwise:

Step 1. Start a HyperTerminal session as you did in Lab 2-2.

Step 2. Implement the procedure documented in Appendix C before continuing with this lab.

Task 1: Configure the Hostname, Passwords, and Interface on the GAD Router

On the GAD router, enter global configuration mode and configure the router name as shown in Table 10-2. Then, configure the console, virtual terminal, and enable passwords. Configure the Ethernet interface.

Task 2: Save the Configuration Information from Privileged EXEC Command Mode

Use the following command:

```
GAD#copy running-config startup-config
```

Task 3: Configure the Host

Configure the host with the proper IP address, subnet mask, and default gateway.

Task 4: Allow HTTP Access to the Router

Allow HTTP access by issuing the **ip http server** command in global configuration mode.

Task 5: Use the Workstation Browser to Access the Router

Step 1. Open a browser on host 1 and type **http://***ip-address-of-Router-GAD*.

Step 2. You are then prompted for a username and the enable password of the router. The username can be left blank; only the password is required.

Task 6: Telnet to the Ethernet Interface on the Router from the Host

Open a command prompt and Telnet to the Ethernet interface, as follows:

```
Microsoft Windows XP [Version 5.1.2600]
(C) Copyright 1985-2001 Microsoft Corp.

C:\>telnet 192.168.14.1
```

Task 7: Start a Second Telnet Session to the Router

Open a second command prompt and Telnet to the Ethernet interface, as follows:

```
Microsoft Windows XP [Version 5.1.2600]
(C) Copyright 1985-2001 Microsoft Corp.

C:\>telnet 192.168.14.1
```

Task 8: Start a Third Telnet Session to the Router

Open a third command prompt and Telnet to the Ethernet interface, as follows:

```
Microsoft Windows XP [Version 5.1.2600]
(C) Copyright 1985-2001 Microsoft Corp.

C:\>telnet 192.168.14.1
```

Task 9: Start a Fourth Telnet Session to the Router

Open a fourth command prompt and Telnet to the Ethernet interface, as follows:

```
Microsoft Windows XP [Version 5.1.2600]
(C) Copyright 1985-2001 Microsoft Corp.

C:\>telnet 192.168.14.1
```

Task 10: Check the Number of Sessions on the Host

Step 1. Open another, fifth command prompt on the host and type **netstat /?** at the DOS prompt.

What options are available for the **netstat** command, and what information does this command and its options provide?

____

____

____

____

-a ____

-b

____

-e ____

-n ____

-o ____

-p *proto*

____

-r ____

-s

____

-v

____

interval

____

Step 2. Type **netstat -n**.

How many open sessions exist? ______________________

What are the open sessions? ______________________

What are the port numbers? ______________________

Task 11: Check the Number of Sessions on the Router

Step 1. In privileged EXEC mode, type **show tcp**.

How many open sessions exist? ______________________

What are the open sessions? ______________________

What are the port numbers on the sessions? ______________________

Why can all the sessions use port 23 (under Foreign Address)?

____

____

List some of the Local Address port numbers (the number after the colon following the IP address).

____

Why are all the Local Address port numbers different?

____

____

____

____

____

Step 2. Log off (by typing **exit**) and turn off the router.

CHAPTER 11

Access Control Lists (ACLs)

The Study Guide portion of this chapter uses a combination of fill-in-the-blank, open-ended questions, and unique custom exercises to test your knowledge of the theory of access control lists.

The Lab Exercises portion of this chapter includes all the online curriculum labs as well as a challenge lab to ensure that you have mastered the practical, hands-on skills needed for access control lists.

Study Guide

Access Control List Fundamentals

Up to this point in your studies, you have learned how to configure a basic network with IP addressing and routing. You have verified your configurations by making sure that all devices attached to the network can access any other device attached to the same network. With this chapter, you begin your journey into the field of network security. In production networks, it is more common to ask, "What services does this set of users need to access?" After that question is answered, you would configure your network to allow these services. Sometimes, it is easier to ask the inverse question: "What services do these users *not* need?" Then you would configure the network to block these services. Of course, your security policy can be formulated by answering a combination of these two basic questions: "What services does the user need, and what services does the user *not* need?"

This chapter focuses on one method to control user access in a network—access control lists. A basic understanding of how access control works in the Cisco IOS software is fundamental to your CCNA studies. Therefore, you spend a great deal of time in this section learning the rules of ACLs and their syntax, and how to calculate a wildcard mask.

Basic ACL Concepts and Rules Exercises

Complete the following list of ACL concepts and rules:

- ACLs can be written to filter packets based on _______ address, _________ address, _________, and ______ number.
- One access list exists per _________, per interface, per direction.
- Standard access lists should be applied as close to the _________ as possible.
- Extended access lists should be applied as close to the _________ as possible.
- Statements are processed sequentially from the top of list to the bottom until a match is found. If no match is found, the packet is ____________________________________.
- An _________ deny any command is found at the end of all access lists. This does not appear in the configuration listing.
- Access list entries should filter in order, from more _________ traffic to more _________ traffic.
- New lines are always added to the ___ of the access list.
- The _____________ command removes the entire list.
- You cannot selectively add and remove lines with ____________ ACLs.
- An IP access list sends an ____________________________ message to the sender of the rejected packet.
- ACLs do not affect traffic originating from the _______ router.

Refer to Figure 11-1. How many ACLs can be configured and actively applied to the router's interfaces?

Figure 11-1 How Many ACLs?

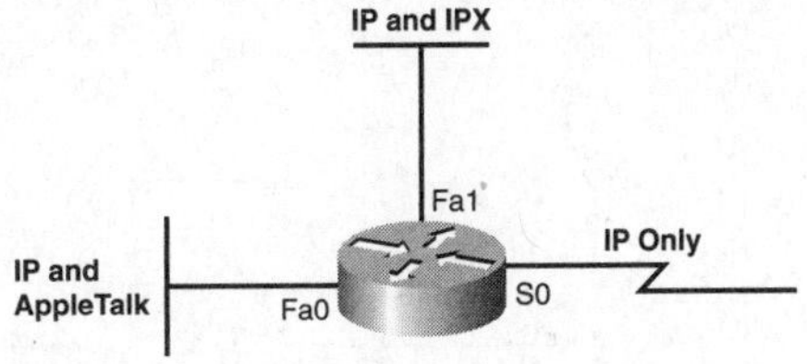

ACL Flow Chart Exercise

Refer to Figure 11-2. The flow chart shows the basic steps in the decision process used by a router to accept, filter, and then forward traffic. Fill in the missing parts of the flow chart with one of the following possible steps, most of which can be used twice:

- Permit
- Check next entry
- Packet routable?
- More conditions?
- Deny (send ICMP message)
- Match condition?

Standard ACL Syntax Exercise

1. What is the command syntax to configure a standard ACL? Include the router prompt and all command arguments in your answer.

2. What is the command syntax to apply a standard ACL to an interface?

3. Fill in the missing information in the following table to indicate the correct range of access list numbers for the listed protocol. For IP, include the expanded ranges.

Protocol	Range
Standard IP	
Extended IP	
AppleTalk	
Standard Internetwork Packet Exchange (IPX)	
Extended IPX	

Figure 11-2 ACL Flow Chart (Answer)

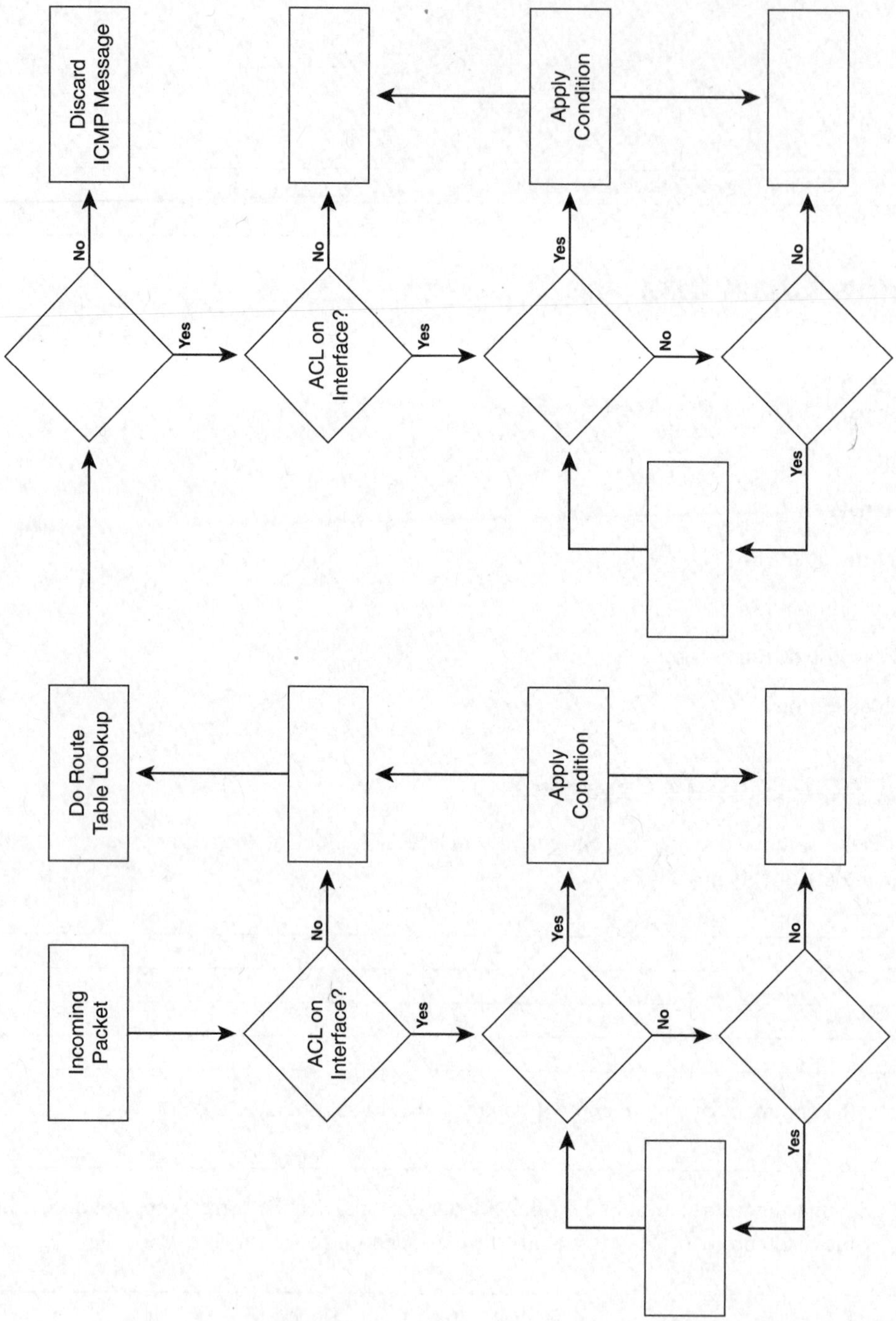

Determine the Wildcard Mask Exercise

In the following table, the first column lists a network/subnet mask pair that describes an address space for a range of addresses. All addresses in this range are to be filtered based on the requirement stated in the first column (for example, entire network, first half of subnet, and so on). To determine which bits are to be checked, IOS compares the prefix address to the wildcard mask. In the second and third columns, record the correct prefix address and wildcard masks. Caution: The prefix address might not be the same as the network address shown in the first column.

Filter Requirement	Prefix Address	Wildcard Mask
The entire 192.168.1.0/24 network		
The entire 172.16.0.0/16 network		
The entire 10.0.0.0/8 network		
All traffic using the long form		
All traffic using the shortcut keyword	N/A	
Only host 192.168.1.35 using the long form		
Only host 192.168.1.35 using the shortcut keyword		
The entire 192.168.1.96/27 subnet		
The entire 172.16.16.0/20 subnet		
The entire 10.2.0.0/15 subnet		
The second half of the 192.168.1.0/24 network		
The first half of the 172.16.0.0/16 network		
The second half of the 10.0.0.0/8 network		
The first half of the 192.168.1.192/26 subnet		
The second half of the 172.16.48.0/21 subnet		
The first four addresses in the 192.168.1.64/29 subnet		
The last eight addresses in the 192.168.1.224/27 subnet		
Only even-numbered IP addresses from the 192.168.1.0/24 network		
Only odd-numbered IP addresses from the 192.168.1.0/24 network		

Concept Questions

1. If an ACL is *not* configured on an interface, what happens to all routable traffic entering or exiting that interface? Why does this happen?

2. A packet is evaluated against the statements in an ACL. It matches none of the statements. What happens to the packet? Why does this happen?

3. What are the two major steps to implement ACLs to filter inbound and/or outbound traffic?

4. You have already configured a numbered ACL. Upon further inspection, you realize that some traffic is still being allowed through. Another statement needs to be inserted into the existing numbered ACL. Describe the steps you would go through to make the change.

5. After configuring the numbered ACL from the previous question, you discover that another statement is not necessary and must be removed. What can you do to fix this problem?

6. What three commands can be used to verify your ACL configuration and implementation?

Access Control Configuration

In the previous section, you worked through some exercises geared toward helping you gain an understanding of the basic concepts, rules, and configuration syntax of ACLs. This section focuses your attention on specific configuration scenarios. You start with simple configurations. Each scenario is increasingly more difficult than the previous scenario. In addition, all these scenarios can be implemented on your lab routers.

Standard ACL Configuration Exercises

1. Record the command(s) to configure a standard access list that stops all traffic from the 192.168.1.0/24 network, but permits all other traffic.

Record the commands to apply the previous ACL to outbound traffic on E0.

____

____

2. Record the command(s) to configure a standard access list to stop all traffic from the 192.168.1.64/28 subnet, but permits all other traffic.

____

____

Record the commands to apply the previous ACL to inbound traffic on E0.

____

____

3. Record the command(s) to configure a standard access list that allows traffic from the second half of the 192.168.1.0/24 subnet, but blocks all other traffic.

____

____

Record the commands to apply the previous ACL to outbound traffic on S0.

____

____

4. Record the command(s) to configure a standard access list that blocks traffic from host 192.168.1.177 and the first half of the 192.168.1.128/26 subnet, but allows all other traffic.

____

____

____

Record the commands to apply the previous ACL to inbound traffic on E1.

____

____

Standard ACL Scenario 1

Refer to Figure 11-3. Use a standard ACL to implement the following security policy: Stop only the users on the RTB LAN from accessing the Internet.

Figure 11-3 Standard ACL Scenario Topology

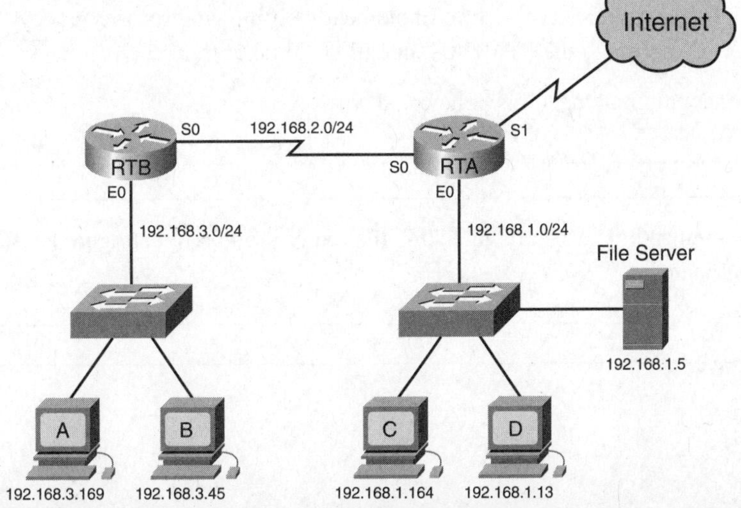

1. What router should implement this policy, and why?

2. Record the command(s) necessary, including the router prompt, to configure an ACL to meet the policy requirements.

3. Record the commands necessary, including the router prompt, to apply the ACL to the correct interface in the correct direction.

Standard ACL Scenario 2

Refer to Figure 11-3. Use a standard ACL to implement the following security policy: Stop all users on the RTA LAN from accessing hosts attached to the RTB LAN.

1. What router should implement this policy, and why?

2. Record the command(s) necessary, including the router prompt, to configure an ACL to meet the policy requirements.

3. Record the commands necessary, including the router prompt, to apply the ACL to the correct interface in the correct direction.

Standard ACL Scenario 3

Refer to Figure 11-3. Use a standard ACL to implement the following security policy: Block the second half of the RTB LAN access to the RTA LAN, but allow all other traffic.

1. What router should implement this policy, and why?

2. Record the command(s) necessary, including the router prompt, to configure an ACL to meet the policy requirements.

3. Record the commands necessary, including the router prompt, to apply the ACL to the correct interface in the correct direction.

Extended ACL Scenario 1

Refer to Figure 11-4. Use an extended ACL to implement the following security policy:

Stop all traffic from the RTB LAN from accessing the RTA LAN. However, the RTB hosts still need to be able to access the file server at 172.17.10.130. All other traffic should be allowed.

Figure 11-4 Extended ACL Scenario 1

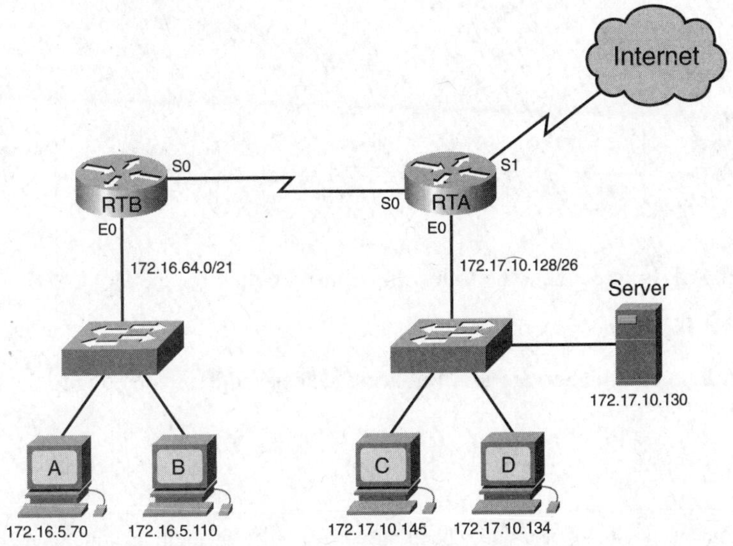

1. What router should implement this policy, and why?

2. Record the command(s) necessary, including the router prompt, to configure an ACL to meet the policy requirements.

3. Record the commands necessary, including the router prompt, to apply the ACL to the correct interface in the correct direction.

Extended ACL Scenario 2

Refer to Figure 11-5 for the next four extended ACL scenarios.

Figure 11-5 Extended ACL Scenarios

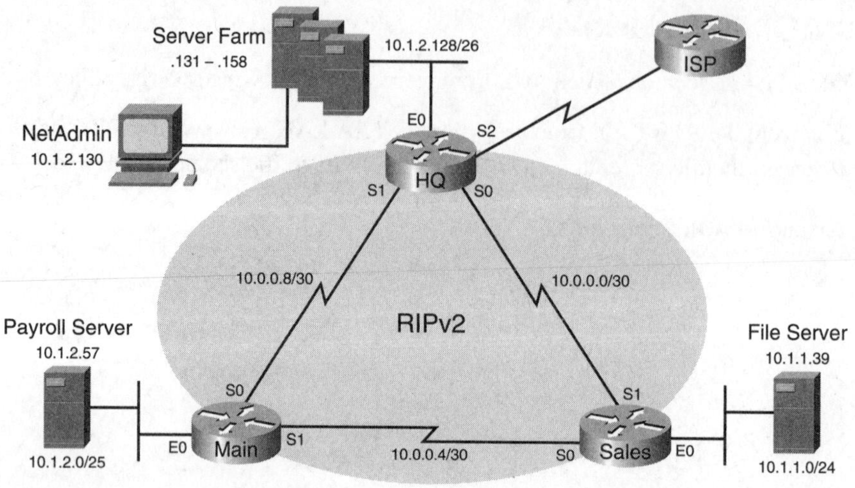

Use an extended ACL to implement the following security policy for the HQ LAN:

- Deny the user PCs Telnet access.
- Allow NetAdmin and the Server Farm full access. These addresses belong to the first half of the subnet 10.1.2.128/26.
- Permit all other traffic.

Note: The requirements might not necessarily be in the correct order. In addition, you might not find a one-requirement/one-statement relationship. Some requirements might require multiple statements to implement.

---

1. Record the command(s) necessary, including the router prompt, to configure an ACL to meet the requirements.

____

____

____

2. Record the commands necessary, including the router prompt, to apply the ACL to the correct interface in the correct direction.

____

____

Extended ACL Scenario 3

Refer to Figure 11-5. Use an extended ACL to implement the following security policy for the SALES LAN:

- Allow only web access to all outside (Internet) destinations.
- Allow access to all interior hosts except the Payroll server. Use the 10.0.0.0/8 address space to define "all interior hosts."

Note: The requirements might not necessarily be in the correct order. In addition, you might not find a one-requirement/one-statement relationship. Some requirements might require multiple statements to implement.

---

1. Record the command(s) necessary, including the router prompt, to configure an ACL to meet the requirements.

____

____

____

2. Record the commands necessary, including the router prompt, to apply the ACL to the correct interface in the correct direction.

____

____

Extended ACL Scenario 4

Refer to Figure 11-5. Use an extended ACL to implement the following security policy for the MAIN LAN:

- Allow Payroll Server full access.
- Allow PCs full Internet Control Message Protocol (ICMP) access.
- Allow PCs access to HTTP, FTP, and Domain Name System (DNS).

Note: The requirements might not necessarily be in the correct order. In addition, you might not find a one-requirement/one-statement relationship. Some requirements might require multiple statements to implement.

---

1. Record the command(s) necessary, including the router prompt, to configure an ACL to meet the requirements.

____

____

____

____

____

____

____

____

2. Record the commands necessary, including the router prompt, to apply the ACL to the correct interface in the correct direction.

____

____

Extended Named ACL Scenario

Refer to Figure 11-5. Use a named ACL called FIREWALL to implement the following security policy for Internet access:

- Allow pings sourced from inside to return from the Internet.
- Allow all unreachable error messages to return from the Internet.
- Allow an established TCP session from the Internet.

Note: Use the Cisco IOS help facility to find the correct parameter to allow unreachable error messages to return from the Internet. If you do not remember the codes, review Chapter 8, "TCP/IP Suite Error and Control Messages."

---

1. Record the command(s) necessary, including the router prompt, to configure an ACL to meet the requirements.

____

____

____

____

____

____

2. Record the commands necessary, including the router prompt, to apply the ACL to the correct interface in the correct direction.

____

____

Restricting vty and HTTP Access

If you have a Telnet password configured and then allow access through the **login** command, anyone can access the vty lines and attempt to break the password. A more secure solution is to configure which IP address or addresses should be allowed access. In Figure 11-5, the only host that needs Telnet access to the routers is NetAdmin. Access should be configured on all three routers. Record the commands necessary, including the router prompt, to allow only NetAdmin access to the Telnet lines.

____

____

____

____

____

In addition, in newer versions of IOS, the HTTP server feature is on by default. The HTTP server allows access to the router through a web-browser interface. What command, including the router prompt, turns off the HTTP server?

____

If you want to keep the HTTP feature active, you should configure an access list specifying which users are allowed access. For this scenario, you will use the ACL you configured for the Telnet lines. Access should be configured on all three routers. Record the commands necessary to apply the ACL to the HTTP server.

____

Lab Exercises

Command Reference

In the table that follows, record the command, *including the correct router prompt,* that fits the description. Fill in any blanks with the appropriate missing information.

Command or Keyword	Description
	Used in place of 0.0.0.0 255.255.255.255; can match any address that it is compared against
	Used in place of 0.0.0.0 in the wildcard mask; can match only one specific address
	Creates a standard ACL to permit all hosts on the 172.16.0.0/16 network
	Applies the previous ACL to an interface in the outbound direction
	Applies the previous ACL to the inbound Telnet lines
	Applies the previous ACL to the HTTP server
	Removes the previous ACL from the configuration
	Creates an extended ACL to permit all hosts on the 172.16.0.0/16 network HTTP access to all hosts on the 192.168.100.0/24 network
	Creates a named extended ACL with the name MY_ACL
	Adds a statement to permit all HTTP access to the named MY_ACL
	Shows all the ACLs currently configured on the router, as well as how many matches have occurred

Lab 11-1: Configuring Standard Access Lists (11.2.1a)

Figure 11-6 Topology for Lab 11-1

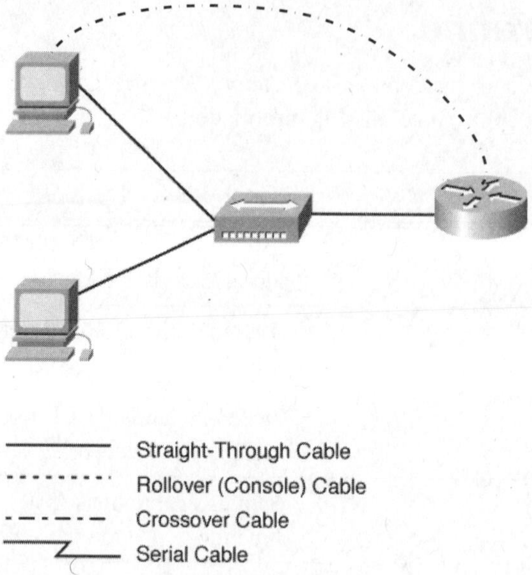

Table 11-1 Lab Equipment Configuration

Router Designation	Router Name	FA0/0 Address	Subnet Mask	Enable Secret Password	Enable/vty/ Console Passwords
Router 1	GAD	192.168.14.1	255.255.255.0	class	cisco

Objectives

- Configure and apply a standard access control list (ACL) to permit or deny specific traffic.
- Test the ACL to determine whether you achieved the desired results.

Background/Preparation

Cable a network similar to the one in Figure 11-6. You can use any router that meets the interface requirements in Figure 11-6 (that is, 800, 1600, 1700, 2500, and 2600 routers or a combination). Refer to the information in Appendix B, "Router Interface Summary," to correctly specify the interface identifiers based on the equipment in your lab. The 1721 Series routers produced the configuration output in this lab. Any other router might produce slightly different output. You should execute the following tasks on each router unless specifically instructed otherwise.

Start a HyperTerminal session as you did in Lab 2-2, "Establishing a Console Session with HyperTerminal."

Implement the procedure documented in Appendix C, "Erasing and Reloading the Router," before continuing with this lab.

Task 1: Configure the Hostname and Passwords on the GAD Router

On the GAD router, enter global configuration mode and configure the router name as shown in Table 11-1. Then, configure the console, virtual terminal, and enable passwords. Configure the FastEthernet interface on the router according to Table 11-1.

Task 2: Configure the Hosts on the Ethernet Segment

Step 1. For Host 1, configure the following:

IP address: 192.168.14.2

Subnet mask: 255.255.255.0

Default gateway: 192.168.14.1

Step 2. For Host 2, configure the following:

IP address: 192.168.14.3

Subnet mask: 255.255.255.0

Default gateway: 192.168.14.1

Task 3: Save the Configuration Information from Privileged EXEC Command Mode

To save the GAD router configuration information, enter the following command:

```
GAD#copy running-config startup-config
```

Task 4: Confirm Connectivity by Pinging the Default Gateway from Both Hosts

If the pings are not successful, correct your configuration and repeat until they are successful.

Task 5: Prevent Access to the Ethernet Interface from the Hosts

Create an ACL that will prevent access to FastEthernet 0 from the 192.168.14.0 network. At the router configuration prompt, enter the following command:

```
GAD(config)#access-list 1 deny 192.168.14.0 0.0.0.255
GAD(config)#access-list 1 permit any
```

Why do you need the second statement?

____

Task 6: Ping the Router from the Hosts

Were these pings successful? ____

Why or why not?

____

Task 7: Apply the ACL to the Interface

At the FastEthernet 0 interface mode prompt, enter the following:

```
GAD(config-if)#ip access-group 1 in
```

Task 8: Ping the Router from the Hosts

Were these pings successful? ______________________________

Why or why not?

____

Task 9: Create a New ACL

Create an ACL that will not allow the even-numbered hosts to ping but that permits the odd-numbered hosts to ping. What does that ACL look like? Finish this command with an appropriate comparison IP address (*aaa.aaa.aaa.aaa*) and wildcard mask (*www.www.www.www*):

```
access-list 2 permit  aaa.aaa.aaa.aaa  www.www.www.www
```

____

Why didn't you need the **permit any** statement at the end this time?

____

Task 10: Apply the ACL to the Proper Router Interface

Step 1. Remove the old ACL application by entering **no ip access-group 1 in** in interface configuration mode.

Step 2. Apply the new ACL by entering **ip access-group 2 in.**

Task 11: Ping the Router from Each Host

Was the ping from Host 1 successful? ______________________________

Why or why not?

____

Was the ping from Host 2 successful? ______________________________

Why or why not?

____

When you finish the preceding tasks, log off (by typing **exit**) and turn off the router.

Lab 11-2: Standard ACLs (11.2.1b)

Figure 11-7 Topology for Lab 11-2

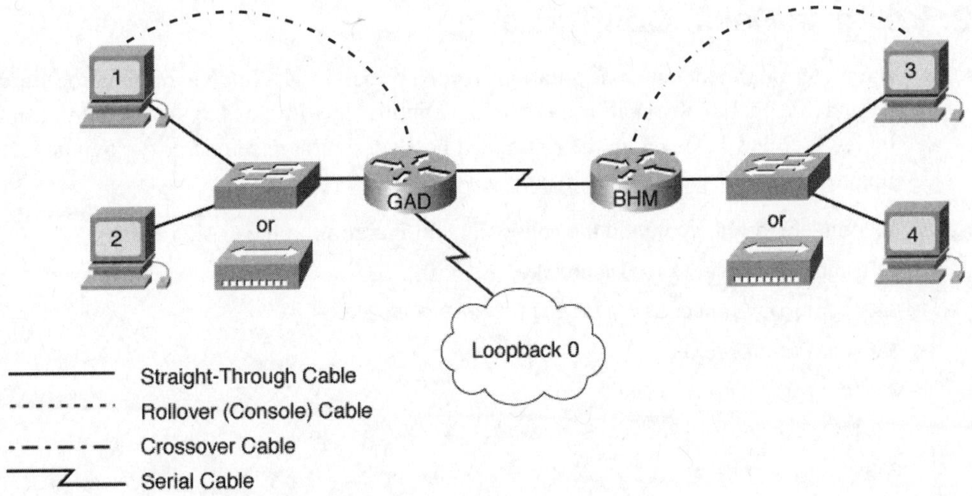

Table 11-2 Lab Equipment Configuration

Router Name	FA0/0 Address	S0/0 Address	LO0 Address
GAD	192.168.1.1/24	192.168.2.1/24	172.16.1.1/24
BHM	192.168.3.1/24	192.168.2.2/24	N/A

The enable password for both routers is **cisco**.

The vty password for both routers is **class**.

The routing protocol for both routers is RIP.

Table 11-3 Host IP Address, Subnet Mask, and Gateway Configuration

Host	IP Address	Subnet Mask	Gateway
1	192.168.1.2	255.255.255.0	192.168.1.1
2	192.168.1.3	255.255.255.0	192.168.1.1
3	192.168.3.2	255.255.255.0	192.168.3.1
4	192.168.3.3	255.255.255.0	192.168.3.1

Objectives

- Plan, configure, and apply a standard ACL to permit or deny specific traffic.
- Test the ACL to determine whether it achieved the desired results.

Background/Preparation

The company's home office in Gadsden (GAD) provides services to branch offices such as the Birmingham (BHM) office. These offices have some minor security and performance concerns. You will implement standard ACLs as a simple and effective tool to control traffic based on the following assumptions:

- Host 3 represents the kiosk station that needs its access limited to the local network.
- Host 4 represents another host in the BHM office.
- The Loopback 0 interface on the GAD router represents the Internet.

Task 1: Perform Basic Router Interconnection

Interconnect the routers as shown in Figure 11-7.

Task 2: Perform Basic Configuration

Step 1. The router might contain configurations from a previous use. Implement the procedure documented in Appendix C on all routers before continuing with this lab. Using the information in Tables 11-2 and 11-3, set up the router and host configurations and verify communications by pinging all systems and routers from each system.

Step 2. To simulate the Internet, add the following configuration to the GAD router:

```
GAD(config)#interface loopback0
GAD(config-if)#address 172.16.1.1 255.255.255.0
GAD(config-if)#exit
GAD(config)#router rip
GAD(config-router)#network 172.16.0.0
GAD(config-if)#^z
```

Task 3: Establish Access List Requirements

The kiosk station (Host 3) needs its access limited to the local network. You must create a standard access list to prevent traffic from this host from reaching any other networks. The ACL should block traffic from this host and not affect other traffic from this network. A standard IP ACL satisfies this requirement because it filters based on the source address to any destination.

What is the source address of the kiosk? ______________________________

Task 4: Plan the Access List Requirements

As with any project, the most important part of the process is the planning. First, you must define the information you need to create the ACL. An access list consists of a series of ACL statements. Because the list will consist of more than one statement, you must carefully plan the order of the statements. Each of these statements is performed in sequence as the ACL is processed.

Step 1. This ACL requires two logical steps. You can accomplish these steps with one statement each. For a planning tool, you can use a text editor such as Notepad to organize the logic and then write the list. In the text editor, enter the logic by typing the following:

```
! stop traffic from host 3
! permit all other traffic
```

From this logic, you will write the actual ACL.

Step 2. Using Table 11-4, document the information for each statement.

Table 11-4 Recording Information to Deny or Permit Traffic

Stop Traffic from Host 3

List Number	Permit or Deny	Source Address	Wildcard Mask

Permit All Other Traffic			
List Number	**Permit or Deny**	**Source Address**	**Wildcard Mask**

What would be the result of not including a statement to permit all other source addresses?

What would be the result of reversing the order of the two statements in the list?

Why do both statements use the same ACL number?

Step 3. The final step in the planning process is to determine the best location (interface) for the access list and the direction in which you should apply the list. Examine the internetwork diagram and choose the appropriate interface and direction. Document this information in Table 11-5.

Table 11-5 Selecting an Interface and Direction for Applying an ACL

Router	Interface	Direction

Task 5: Write and Apply the ACL

Step 1. Using the previously constructed logic and information, complete the commands in the text editor. Comments are entered into the ACL by using an exclamation mark as the first character of a line. This makes it easier to understand the function of the statements. The list syntax should look similar to the following:

```
! stop traffic from host 3
access-list # deny address wildcard
! permit all other traffic
access-list # permit address wildcard
```

Step 2. Add to this text file the configuration statements to apply the list. The configuration statements take the following form:

```
interface type #/#
ip access-group # {in, out}
```

Step 3. Now you must apply the text-file configuration to the router. Enter configuration mode on the appropriate router, and copy and paste the configuration. Observe the command-line interface (CLI) display to ensure that no errors appeared.

Task 6: Verify the ACL

Now you must confirm and test the ACL.

Step 1. The first step is to check the list to see whether it was configured properly in the router. To check the ACL logic, use the **show ip access-lists** command. Record the output:

____

____

____

____

Step 2. Verify that the access list was applied to the proper interface and in the correct direction. To do so, examine the interface with the **show ip interface** command. Look at the output from each interface, and record the lists applied to the interface.

Interface:____________________________________

Outgoing access list is ______________________________

Inbound access list is ______________________________

Step 3. Test the functionality of the ACL by trying to send packets from the source host, and verify that the packet is permitted or denied as appropriate. In this case, you use ping for the test.

Step 4. Verify that Host 3 can ping Host 4.

Step 5. Verify that Host 3 cannot ping Host 1.

Step 6. Verify that Host 3 cannot ping Host 2.

Step 7. Verify that Host 3 cannot ping GAD Fa0/0.

Step 8. Verify that Host 3 cannot ping GAD LO0.

Step 9. Verify that Host 4 can ping Host 1.

Step 10. Verify that Host 4 can ping Host 2.

Step 11. Verify that Host 4 can ping GAD Fa0/0.

Step 12. Verify that Host 4 can ping GAD LO0.

Task 7: Document the ACL

Step 1. As a part of all network management, you need to create documentation. The first step in documentation is to add comments to the ACL, as shown in Task 5. Using the text file created for the configuration, add comments as necessary to describe the ACL's purpose and application. This file should also contain output from the **show access-lists** and **show ip interface** commands.

Step 2. Save the file with other network documentation. The filenaming convention should reflect the function of the file and the date of implementation.

Step 3. When you finish with Step 2, log off (by typing **exit**) and turn off the routers.

Lab 11-3: Configuring Extended Access Lists (11.2.2a)

Figure 11-8 Topology for Lab 11-3

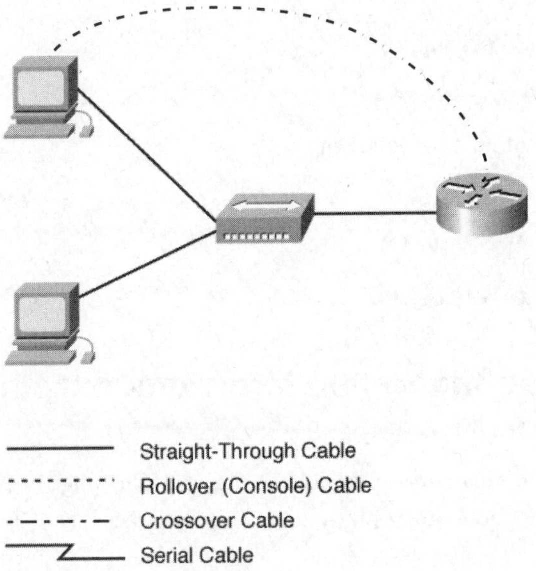

Table 11-6 Lab Equipment Configuration

Router Designation	Router Name	FA0/0 Address	Subnet Mask	Enable Secret Password	Enable/vty/ Console Passwords
Router 1	GAD	192.168.14.1	255.255.255.0	class	cisco

Objectives:

- Configure and apply an extended ACL to permit or deny specific traffic.
- Test the ACL to determine whether you achieved the desired results.

Background/Preparation

Cable a network similar to the one in Figure 11-8. You can use any router that meets the interface requirements in Figure 11-8 (that is, 800, 1600, 1700, 2500, and 2600 routers or a combination). Refer to the information in Appendix B, "Router Interface Summary," to correctly specify the interface identifiers based on the equipment in your lab. The 1721 series routers produced the configuration output in this lab. Any other router might produce slightly different output. You should execute the following tasks on each router unless specifically instructed otherwise.

Start a HyperTerminal session as you did in Lab 11-2.

Implement the procedure documented in Appendix C, "Erasing and Reloading the Router," before continuing with this lab.

Task 1: Configure the Hostname and Passwords on the GAD Router

Step 1. On the GAD router, enter global configuration mode and configure the router name as shown in Table 11-6. Then, configure the console, virtual terminal, and enable passwords. Configure the FastEthernet interface on the router according to the table.

Step 2. Allow HTTP access by issuing the **ip http server** command in global configuration mode.

Task 2: Configure the Hosts on the Ethernet Segment

Step 1. For Host 1, configure the following:

IP address: 192.168.14.2

Subnet mask: 255.255.255.0

Default gateway: 192.168.14.1

Step 2. For Host 2, configure the following:

IP address: 192.168.14.3

Subnet mask: 255.255.255.0

Default gateway: 192.168.14.1

Task 3: Save the Configuration Information from Privileged EXEC Command Mode

To save the GAD router configuration information, enter the following:

```
GAD#copy running-config startup-config
```

Task 4: Confirm Connectivity by Pinging the Default Gateway from Both Hosts

If the pings are not successful, correct your configuration and repeat until they are successful.

Task 5: Connect to the Router Using the Web Browser

From a host, connect to the router using a web browser to ensure that the web server function is active.

Task 6: Prevent Access to HTTP (Port 80) from the Ethernet Interface Hosts

Create an ACL that prevents web-browsing access to FastEthernet 0 from the 192.168.14.0 network. At the router configuration prompt, enter the following commands:

```
GAD(config)#access-list 101 deny tcp 192.168.14.0  0.0.0.255 any eq 80
GAD(config)#access-list 101 permit ip any any
```

Why do you need the second statement?

____

Task 7: Apply the ACL to the Interface

At the FastEthernet 0 interface mode prompt, enter the following:

```
GAD(config-if)#ip access-group 101 in
```

Task 8: Ping the Router from the Hosts

Were these pings successful? ____

If they were, why? ____

Task 9: Connect to the Router Using the Web Browser

Was the browser able to connect?

____

Task 10: Telnet to the Router from the Hosts

Were you able to Telnet successfully? ______________________________

Why or why not?

____

____

When you finish these tasks, log off (by typing **exit**) and turn off the router.

Lab 11-4: Simple Extended Access Lists (11.2.2b)

Figure 11-9 Topology for Lab 11-4

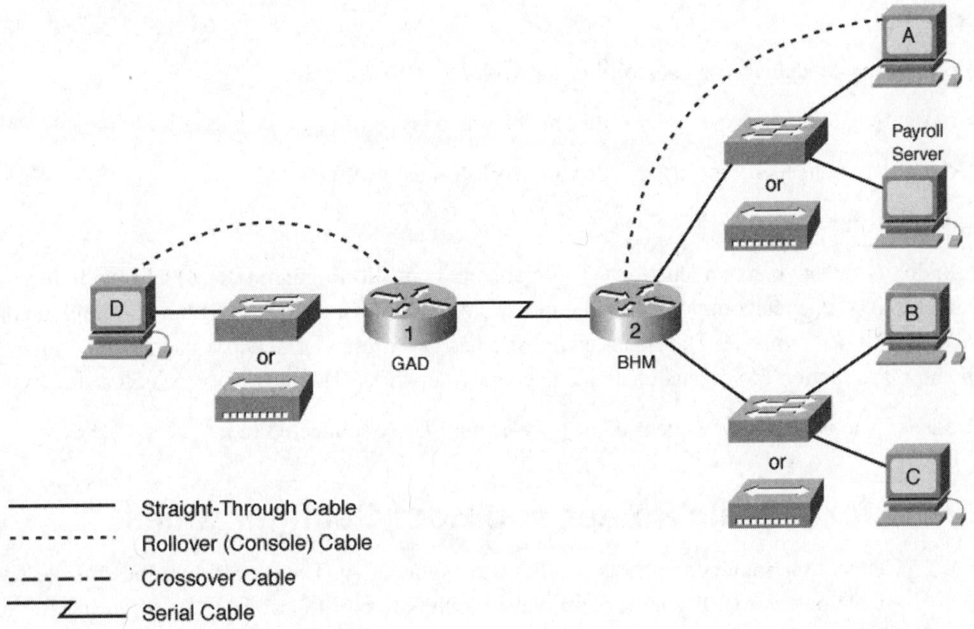

Table 11-7 Lab Equipment Configuration: Part I

Router Designation	Router Name	Routing Protocol	RIP Network Statements
Router 1	GAD	RIP	172.16.0.0
Router 2	BHM	RIP	192.168.1.0
			172.16.0.0

The enable secret password for both routers is **class**.

The enable, vty, and console passwords for both routers are **cisco**.

Table 11-8 Lab Equipment Configuration: Part II

Router Designation	FastEthernet 0 Address	Interface Type Serial 0	Serial 0 Address	FastEthernet 1 Address	IP Host Table Entry
Router 1	172.16.2.1/24	DTE	172.16.1.1/24	N/A	BHM
Router 2	192.168.1.17/28	DCE	172.16.1.2/24	192.168.1.33/28	GAD

Table 11-9 Host IP Address, Subnet Mask, and Gateway Configuration

Host	IP Address	Subnet Mask	Gateway
Payroll server	192.168.1.18	255.255.255.240	192.168.1.17
A	192.168.1.19	255.255.255.240	192.168.1.17
B	192.168.1.34	255.255.255.240	192.168.1.33
C	192.168.1.35	255.255.255.240	192.168.1.33
D	172.16.2.2	255.255.255.0	172.16.2.1

Objectives

- Configure extended access lists to filter network-to-network traffic.
- Configure extended access lists to filter host-to-network traffic.
- Configure extended access lists to filter network-to-host traffic.

Background/Preparation

A marketing company has two locations. The main site is in Birmingham (BHM) and the branch site is in Gadsden (GAD). The telecommunication administrator for both sites needs to plan and implement ACLs for security and performance. The Birmingham site has two groups of network users, an Administrative group and a Production group, and each is on separate networks. The networks are connected by routers.

The Gadsden site is a stub network and has only a small LAN connected to it.

Task 1: Perform Basic Router and Host Configurations

Step 1. Connect the routers and hosts as shown in Figure 11-9. Then, configure the console, vty, and enable passwords. If you have problems doing so, refer to Lab 3-2, "Configuring Router Passwords." Next, configure the interfaces and routing according to Tables 11-7 and 11-8. If you have problems doing so, refer to Lab 3-9, "Configuring Host Tables," and Lab 7-1, "Configuring RIP."

Note: The BHM router requires two Ethernet interfaces.

Step 2. Configure each router as follows:

```
BHM#show running-config

<Output Omitted>

hostname BHM
!
enable secret class
```

```
!
interface FastEthernet0
 ip address 192.168.1.17 255.255.255.240
!
interface Serial0
 ip address 172.16.1.2 255.255.255.0
 clock rate 56000
!
interface FastEthernet0/1
 ip address 192.168.1.33 255.255.255.240
!
router rip
 network 172.16.0.0
 network 192.168.1.0
!
line vty 0 4
 password cisco
 login
!
end

BHM#
```

```
GAD#show running-config

<Output Omitted>
!
hostname GAD
!
enable password class
!
interface FastEthernet0
 ip address 172.16.2.1 255.255.255.0
!
interface Serial0
 ip address 172.16.1.1 255.255.255.0
!
router rip
 network 172.16.0.0
!
line vty 0 4
 password cisco
 login
!
no scheduler allocate end

GAD#
```

Step 3. Configure each host IP address, subnet mask, and gateway according to Table 11-9.

Step 4. Before applying any type of access list, it is important to verify communications by pinging all systems and routers from each system.

All hosts should be able to ping each other and the router interfaces. If the pings to some interfaces are not successful, you must locate and correct the problem.

Always verify the physical layer connections, because they are a common source of connectivity problems.

Step 5. Verify the router interfaces. Make sure that they are not shut down or improperly configured and that RIP is correctly configured.

Step 6. Remember that along with valid IP addresses, hosts must also have default gateways specified. Now that the infrastructure is in place, it is time to begin securing the internetwork.

Task 2: Prevent the Production Users from Accessing the Gadsden Network

Company policy specifies that only the Administrative group should have access to the Gadsden site. You should restrict the Production group from accessing that network.

Configure an extended access list to allow the Administrative group access to the Gadsden site. The Production group should not have access to the Gadsden site.

Step 1. Careful analysis dictates that it would be best to use an extended access list and apply it to the outgoing Serial 0 interface on the BHM router.

Note: Remember when you configure the access list that the router processes each statement in the list in the order you create it. It is not possible to reorder an access list, skip statements, edit statements, or delete statements from a numbered access list. For this reason, create the access list in a text editor such as Notepad and then paste the commands to the router, instead of entering them directly on a router.

Enter the following:

```
BHM#config terminal
```

Enter configuration commands, one per line. End with **Crtl-Z**.

```
BHM(config)#access-list 100 deny ip 192.168.1.32 0.0.0.15 172.16.2.0 0.0.0.255
```

This statement defines an extended access list called **100**. It will deny **ip** access for any users on the 192.168.1.32/28 network who are trying to access network 172.16.2.0/24. Although you could define a less-specific access list, this access list could allow the Production users to access other sites (if available) through the Serial 0 interface. Remember that there is an implicit deny all at the end of every access list.

Step 2. You must now give the Administrative group access the Gadsden network. Although you could be more restrictive, you will simply let any other traffic through. Enter the following statement:

```
BHM(config)#access-list 100 permit ip any any
```

Step 3. You need to apply the access list to an interface. You could apply the list to any incoming traffic going to the Production network's Fa0/1 interface. However, for traffic between the Administrative network and the Production network, the router must check every packet. You can avoid adding this unwanted overhead to the router. Apply the access list to the outgoing traffic through the BHM router's S0 interface.

Enter the following:

```
BHM(config)#interface s0
BHM(config-if)#ip access-group 100 out
```

Step 4. Verify the syntax of the access list with the **show running-config** command. The following lists the valid statements that should appear in the configuration:

```
interface Serial0
 ip access-group 100 out

<Output Omitted>

access-list 100 deny ip 192.168.1.32 0.0.0.15 172.16.2.0 0.0.0.255
access-list 100 permit ip any any
```

Another valuable command is the **show access-lists** command. The following is sample output:

```
BHM#show access-lists
Extended IP access list 100
    deny ip 192.168.1.32 0.0.0.15 172.16.2.0 0.0.0.255
    permit ip any any
```

The **show access-lists** command also displays counters indicating how many times the router used the list. No counters appear here because you haven't attempted to verify the list yet.

Note: Use the **clear access-list counters** command to restart the access list counters.

Step 5. Test the access list by verifying communications with the Gadsden network on the Administrative and Production hosts.

Can Production Host B ping Gadsden Host D? ______________________________

Can Production Host C ping Gadsden Host D? ______________________________

Can Administrative Host A ping Gadsden Host D?

____

Can Production Host B ping Administrative Host A? ______________________________

Can Production Host B ping Gadsden router's serial interface? ______________________

Production Hosts B and C should be able to ping Administrative Host A and the Gadsden router's serial interface. However, they should not be able to ping Gadsden Host D. The router should return a reply message to the host, "Destination net unreachable."

Step 6. Issue the **show access-lists** command. How many matches are there?

____

____

____

____

Note: The **show access-lists** command displays the number of matches per line. Therefore, the number of deny matches might seem odd until you realize that the pings match the **deny** statement and the **permit** statement.

Step 7. To understand how the access list is operating, keep periodically issuing the **show access-lists** command.

Task 3: Allow a Production User Access to the Gadsden Network

A user in Production Group B is responsible for exchanging certain files between the Production network and the Gadsden network. You must alter the extended access list to give him access to the Gadsden network while denying everyone else on the Production network.

In this task, you need to configure an extended access list to give that user access to Gadsden.

Step 1. Unfortunately, it is not possible to reorder an access list, skip statements, edit statements, or delete statements from a numbered access list. With numbered access lists, any attempt to delete a single statement results in the entire list's deletion.

You must delete the initial extended access list and create a new one. To delete **access-list 100**, enter the following:

```
BHM#conf t
```

Enter configuration commands, one per line. End with **Ctrl-Z**.

```
BHM(config)#no access-list 100
```

Step 2. Verify that the list has been deleted with the **show access-lists** command.

Step 3. Create a new extended access list. Always filter from the most specific to the most generic. The first line of the access list should allow the Production Host B access to the Gadsden network. The remainder of the access list should be the same as the previous you entered.

To filter the Production Host B, the first line of the access list should appear as follows:

```
BHM(config)#access-list 100 permit ip host 192.168.1.34 172.16.2.0  0.0.0.255
```

Step 4. Deny all the remaining Production hosts access to the Gadsden network and permit anyone else. Refer to Task 2 for the next two lines of the configuration.

Step 5. The **show access-lists** command displays output similar to the following:

```
BHM#show access-lists
Extended IP access list 100
    permit ip host 192.168.1.34 172.16.2.0 0.0.0.255
    deny ip 192.168.1.32 0.0.0.15 172.16.2.0 0.0.0.255
    permit ip any any
BHM#
```

Step 6. Test the access list by verifying communications with the Gadsden network on the Administrative and Production hosts.

Can Production Host B ping Gadsden Host D? ______________________

Can Production Host C ping Gadsden Host D? ______________________

Production Host B should now be able to ping Gadsden Host D. However, all other Production hosts should not be able to ping Gadsden Host D. Again, the router should return a reply message to the host, "Destination net unreachable," for Host C.

Task 4: Allow Gadsden Users Access to the Administration Payroll Server

The Administrative group houses the payroll server. Users from the Gadsden site need FTP and HTTP access to the payroll server from time to time to upload and download payroll reports.

Configure an extended access list to give users from the Gadsden site FTP and HTTP access to the payroll server only. Also allow Internet Control Message Protocol (ICMP) access so they can ping the server. Gadsden users should not be able to ping any other host on the Administrative network.

You do not want unnecessary traffic between the sites, so configure an extended access list on the Gadsden router.

Step 1. Because someone anticipated that you might need privileged EXEC access to the Gadsden router, she configured Telnet access to it. Otherwise, you would have to travel to the Gadsden site to configure it.

Telnet to the Gadsden router from the Birmingham router and enter enable mode. Troubleshoot as necessary.

Note: A common pitfall when configuring access lists on remote routers is inadvertently "locking yourself out." This pitfall is not a big problem when the router is local. However, it can be a huge problem if the router is physically located in another geographic area.

For this reason, it is strongly suggested that you issue the **reload in 30** command on the remote router. This command automatically reload, the remote router in 30 minutes. Therefore, if you get locked out, the router eventually reloads to the previous configuration, allowing access again. Use the **reload cancel** command to deactivate the pending reload.

Step 2. Configure an extended access list to allow FTP access to the Payroll server. The access list statement should be similar to the following:

```
GAD(config)#access-list 110 permit tcp any host 192.168.1.18 eq ftp
```

This line will give any host from the Gadsden network FTP access to the payroll server at address 192.168.1.18.

What could you define instead of using the keyword **any**?

____

What could you define instead of using the keyword **host**? ____________________

What could you define instead of using the keyword **ftp**? ____________________

Step 3. Configure the next line of the access list to permit HTTP access to the payroll server. The access list statement should be similar to the following:

```
GAD(config)#access-list 110 permit tcp any host 192.168.1.18 eq www
```

This line gives any host from the Gadsden network HTTP access to the payroll server at address 192.168.1.18.

What else could you define instead of using the keyword **www?**

____

Step 4. Configure the next line of the access list to permit ICMP access to the Payroll server. The access list statement should be similar to the following:

```
GAD(config)#access-list 110 permit icmp any host 192.168.1.18
```

This line permits any host from the Gadsden network to ping the payroll server at address 192.168.1.18.

Step 5. No Gadsden user should be able to access any other host on the Administrative network. Although it is not required, it is always a good idea to include a **deny** statement. The statement serves as a reminder and makes it easier to "read" the access list. The access list statement should be similar to the following:

```
GAD(config)#access-list 110 deny ip any 192.168.1.16 0.0.0.15
```

Step 6. You need to apply the access list to an interface. To reduce unwanted WAN traffic, apply the access list to the outgoing traffic through the Gadsden router's S0 interface.

Enter the following:

```
GAD(config)#interface s0
GAD(config-if)#ip access-group 110 out
```

Step 7. Test the access list by verifying communications with the Payroll server on Gadsden Host D.

Can Gadsden Host D ping the payroll server? ______________________

Can Gadsden Host D ping Host A? ______________________

The Gadsden host should be able to ping the payroll server only. The router should return "Destination net unreachable" when it tries to ping Administrative Host D.

Task 5: Document the ACL

Step 1. As a part of all network management, you should create documentation. Using the text file created for the configuration, add your comments. This file should also contain output from the **show access-lists** and **show ip interface** commands.

Step 2. Save the file with other network documentation. The filenaming convention should reflect the files function and the date of implementation.

Step 3. When you finish this last step, log off (by typing **exit**) and turn off the routers.

Lab 11-5: Configuring a Named Access List (11.2.3a)

Figure 11-10 Topology for Lab 11-5

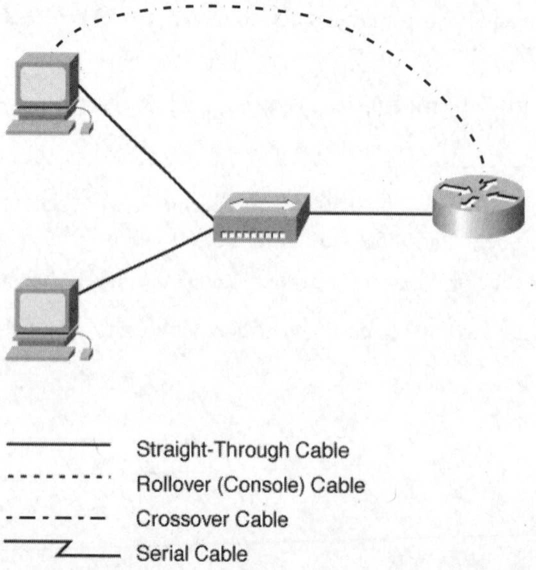

Table 11-10 Lab Equipment Configuration

Router Designation	Router Name	FA0/0 Address	Subnet Mask	Enable Secret Password	Enable/vty/Console Passwords
Router 1	GAD	192.168.14.1	255.255.255.0	class	cisco

Objectives

- Create a named ACL to permit or deny specific traffic.
- Test the ACL to determine whether you achieved the desired results.

Background/Preparation

Cable a network similar to the one in Figure 11-10. You can use any router that meets the interface requirements in Figure 11-10 (that is, 800, 1600, 1700, 2500, and 2600 routers or a combination). Refer to the information in Appendix B, "Router Interface Summary," to correctly specify the interface identifiers based on the equipment in your lab. The 1721 Series routers produced the configuration output in this lab. Any other router might produce slightly different output. You should execute the following tasks on each router unless specifically instructed otherwise.

Start a HyperTerminal session as you did in Lab 2-2.

Implement the procedure documented in Appendix C, "Erasing and Reloading the Router," before continuing with this lab.

Task 1: Configure the Hostname and Passwords on the GAD Router

On the GAD router, enter global configuration mode and configure the router name as shown in Table 11-10. Then, configure the console, virtual terminal, and enable passwords. Configure the FastEthernet interface on the router according to Table 11-10.

Task 2: Configure the Hosts on the Ethernet Segment

Step 1. For Host 1, configure the following:

IP address: 192.168.14.2

Subnet mask: 255.255.255.0

Default gateway: 192.168.14.1

Step 2. For Host 2, configure the following:

IP address: 192.168.14.3

Subnet mask: 255.255.255.0

Default gateway: 192.168.14.1

Task 3: Save the Configuration Information from Privileged EXEC Command Mode

To save the GAD router configuration information, enter the following:

```
GAD#copy running-config startup-config
```

Task 4: Confirm Connectivity by Pinging the Default Gateway from Both Hosts

If the pings are not successful, correct your configuration and repeat until they are successful.

Task 5: Prevent Access to the Ethernet Interface from the Hosts

Create a named ACL that prevents access to FastEthernet 0 from the 192.168.14.0 network. At the configuration prompt, type the following command sequence:

```
GAD(config)#ip access-list standard no_access
GAD(config-std-nacl)#deny 192.168.14.0 0.0.0.255
GAD(config-std-nacl)#permit any
```

Why do you need the third statement?

____

____

Task 6: Ping the router from the Hosts

Were these pings successful?

____

If they were, why?

____

Task 7: Apply the ACL to the Interface

At the FastEthernet interface mode prompt, enter the following:

```
GAD(config-if)#ip access-group no_access in
```

Task 8: Ping the Router from the Hosts

Were these pings successful? ____

Why or why not?

____

When you finish these tasks, log off (by typing **exit**) and turn off the router.

Lab 11-6: Simple DMZ Extended Access Lists (11.2.3b)

Figure 11-11 Topology for Lab 11-6

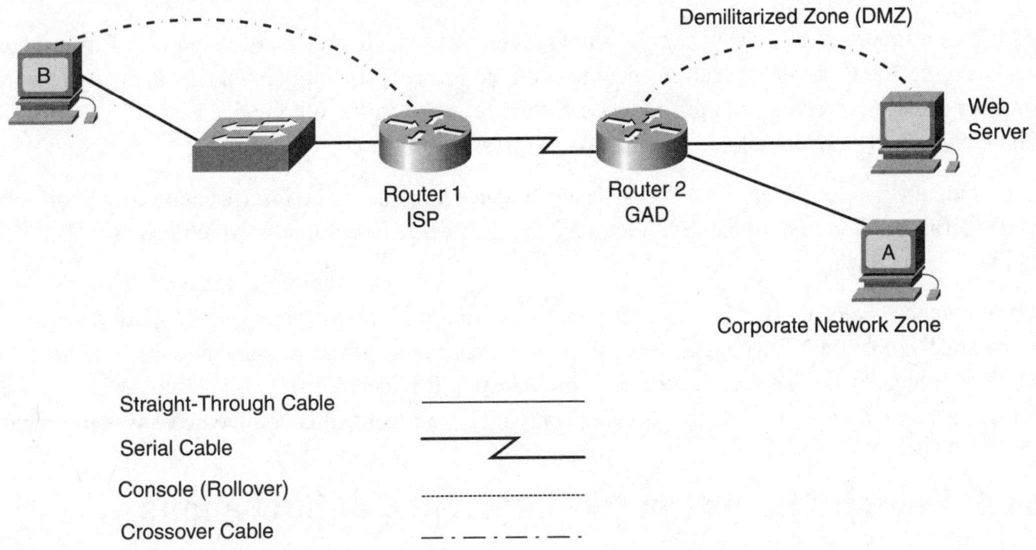

Table 11-11 Lab Equipment Configuration: Part I

Router Designation	Router Name	Routing Protocol	RIP Network Statements
Router 1	ISP	RIP	172.16.0.0
Router 2	GAD	RIP	10.0.0.0
			172.16.0.0

The enable secret password for both routers is **class**.

The enable, vty, and console passwords for both routers are **cisco**.

Table 11-12 Lab Equipment Configuration: Part II

Router Designation	FastEthernet 0 Address	Interface Type Serial 0	Serial 0 Address	FastEthernet 1 Address	IP Host-names
Router 1	172.16.2.1/24	DTE	172.16.1.1/24	N/A	ISP
Router 2	10.1.1.1/24	DCE	172.16.1.2/24	10.10.10.1/24	GAD

Table 11-13 Host IP Address, Subnet Mask, and Gateway Configuration

Host	IP Address	Subnet Mask	Gateway
Web server	10.1.1.10	255.255.255.0	10.1.1.1
A	10.10.10.10	255.255.255.0	10.10.10.1
B	172.16.2.10	255.255.255.0	172.16.2.1

Objective

- Use extended access lists to create a simple demilitarized zone (DMZ).

Background/Preparation

BMTC is a small manufacturing company in Gadsden. It wants to create an awareness of its products over the Internet. The immediate requirement is to promote its products to potential customers by providing product overviews, reports, and testimonials. Future requirements could include e-mail, FTP, Domain Name System (DNS), and online e-commerce services.

The company has contracted with you to design and configure a secure infrastructure to support its internal and external network requirements while maintaining fiscal responsibility—which means, "Make it secure but keep costs down."

Careful analysis dictates that you will create a two-tier security architecture consisting of a corporate network zone and a DMZ. The corporate network zone will house private servers and internal clients. The DMZ will house only one external server to provide World Wide Web services. Although the one server creates a single point of failure, the service is only informational and is not deemed mission-critical.

Task 1: Perform Basic Router and Host Configurations

Step 1. Connect the routers and hosts as shown in Figure 11-11.

Step 2. Configure all router basics such as hostname, router interfaces, and routing protocol using the preceding tables for reference. The configurations on each router should be similar to the following:

```
GAD#show running-config

<Output Omitted>

!
hostname GAD
!
interface FastEthernet0
 ip address 10.1.1.1 255.255.255.0
!
interface Serial0
 ip address 172.16.1.2 255.255.255.0
clock rate 56000
!
interface FastEthernet1
 ip address 10.10.10.1 255.255.255.0
!
router rip
 network 10.0.0.0
 network 172.16.0.0
! GAD#
```

```
ISP#show running-config

<Output Omitted>
```

```
!
hostname ISP
!
interface FastEthernet0
 ip address 172.16.2.1 255.255.255.0
!
interface Serial0
ip address 172.16.1.1 255.255.255.0
!
router rip
 network 172.16.0.0
!

ISP#
```

Step 3. Configure the hosts' IP address, subnet mask, and gateway according to Table 11-13 with the appropriate information.

Step 4. To make the lab more realistic, install web server software on the web server host. Examples include Microsoft IIS and Microsoft Personal Web Server (Windows 98). You can use third-party software such as TinyWeb Server (http://www.ritlabs.com/tinyweb/). If you use TinyWeb Server, also install TinyBox (http://people.freenet.de/ralph.becker/tinybox/), which is a GUI front end for TinyWeb Server.

Step 5. Create a default index.html page. The web page should include a message such as "Hello World." Save the page as instructed by the web-server software.

Step 6. Before applying any type of access list, verify communications between the systems by pinging all the systems and routers from each system.

Can Host A ping Host B? ______________________________

Can Host A ping the web server?

____

Can Host B ping Host A? ______________________________

Can Host B ping the web server? ______________________________

Step 7. All hosts should be able to ping each other. Troubleshoot if ping is not successful to some interfaces.

Step 8. Always verify the physical layer connections, because they are a common source of connectivity problems.

Step 9. Verify the router interfaces. Make sure that they are not shut down or improperly configured and that RIP is correctly configured.

Step 10. Along with valid IP addresses, hosts must also have default gateways specified. On Host A, open a web browser such as Windows Explorer or Netscape Navigator. Enter the address of the web server to verify that each host has web access to the web server.

Can Host A view the index.html page? ______________________________

Can Host B view the index.html page? ______________________________

Step 11. Both hosts should be able to view the index.html page in the web browser. Troubleshoot as necessary.

Now that the infrastructure is in place, it is time to begin securing the internetwork.

Task 2: Protect the Corporate Network

The corporate network zone houses private servers and internal clients. No other network should be able to access it.

Step 1. Configure an extended access list to protect the corporate network. Protecting a corporate network begins by specifying which traffic can exit the network. Although this step might initially sound strange, realize that the most damage results from hackers who are internal employees. The first access list will specify which traffic can exit the network. Enter the following:

```
GAD#conf terminal
```

Enter configuration commands, one per line. End with **Ctrl-Z**:

```
GAD(config)#access-list 101 permit ip 10.10.10.0 0.0.0.255 any
GAD(config)#access-list 101 deny ip any any
```

The first line defines that access list **101** will let only valid corporate users on network 10.10.10.0 into the router. The second line is not really required because of the implicit **deny all**, but it improves code readability.

Step 2. You need to apply the access list to the corporate network interface. Enter the following:

```
GAD(config)#interface fa1
GAD(config-if)#ip access-group 101 in
```

Step 3. Test the access lists by pinging all the systems and routers from each system.

Can Host A ping the web server?

____

Can Host A ping Host B? ____

Can Host B ping the web server? ____

Can Host B ping Host A? ____

All hosts should be able to ping any location.

Step 4. Configure an outbound extended access list on the corporate network interface. Traffic entering the corporate network will be coming from either the Internet or the DMZ. For this reason, you must limit which traffic is allowed into the corporate network.

First, make sure that only traffic that originates from the corporate network can return to that network. Enter the following:

```
GAD(config)#access-list 102 permit tcp any any established
```

The keyword **established** in this line permits only TCP traffic that originates from the 10.10.10.0 network.

Step 5. To make network management and troubleshooting easier, you will permit ICMP traffic into the network. This step will allow the internal hosts to receive ICMP messages (ping messages).

Enter the following:

```
GAD(config)#access-list 102 permit icmp any any echo-reply
GAD(config)#access-list 102 permit icmp any anunreachable
```

The first line allows only successful pings back into the corporate network. The second line allows unsuccessful ping messages to appear.

Step 6. At this time, you want to allow no other traffic into the corporate network. Therefore, enter the following:

```
GAD(config)#access-list 102 deny ip any any
```

Step 7. You must apply the access list to the corporate network FastEthernet port:

```
GAD(config)#interface fa1
GAD(config-if)#ip access-group 102 out
```

Step 8. Remember that an interface can support one incoming and one outgoing access list. Use the **show ip interface fa1** command to confirm that the outgoing access list is 102 and that the inbound access list is 101.

Step 9. Use the **show access-lists** command to verify the syntax of the access lists. The output should be similar to the following:

```
GAD#show access-lists
Extended IP access list 101
    permit ip 10.10.10.0 0.0.0.255 any
    deny ip any any

Extended IP access list 102
    permit tcp any any established
    permit icmp any any echo-reply
    permit icmp any any unreachable
    deny ip any any
```

Step 10. You might have to delete and re-enter access lists if you spot any discrepancy between the preceding output and the configuration.

Step 11. It's time to test the access lists.

Verify communications by pinging all the systems and routers from each system.

Can Host A ping the web server?

____

Can Host A ping Host B? ______________________________

Can Host B ping the web server? ______________________________

Can Host B ping Host A? ______________________________

Host A should be able to ping all locations. However, no external host should be able to ping Host A.

Step 12. On Host A, open a web browser and enter the address of the web server.

Can Host A view the index.html page? ______________________________

Host A should still be able to view the index.html page in the web browser. Troubleshoot as necessary.

The internal corporate network is now secure. Next, you need to secure the DMZ network.

Task 3: Protect the DMZ Network

The DMZ network will house only one external server, which will provide World Wide Web services. The company will add other services such as e-mail, FTP, and DNS at a later time. Although the one server creates a single point of failure, the service is only informational and is not considered mission-critical.

Step 1. Configure an extended access list to protect the DMZ network. As with the corporate network, specify which traffic can exit the network, and apply it to the interface.

Enter the following:

```
GAD#conf terminal
```

Enter configuration commands, one per line. End with **Ctrl-Z**.

```
GAD(config)#access-list 111 permit ip 10.1.1.0 0.0.0.255 any
GAD(config)#access-list 111 deny ip any any

GAD(config)#interface fa0
GAD(config-if)#ip access-group 111 in
```

Step 2. Test the new access lists by pinging all the systems and routers from each system.

Can Host A ping the web server?

____

Can Host A ping Host B? ____

Can Host B ping the web server? ____

Can Host B ping Host A? ____

Host A should be able to ping all locations. However, no external host should be able to ping Host A.

Step 3. You need an outbound extended access list to specify which traffic can enter the DMZ network. Traffic entering the DMZ network will come from either the Internet or the corporate network requesting World Wide Web services. Configure an outbound extended access list specifying that World Wide Web requests be allowed into the network.

Enter the following:

```
GAD(config)#access-list 112 permit tcp any host 10.1.1.10 eq www
```

This line will allow World Wide Web (HTTP) service requests destined for the web server into the DMZ network.

What command would you enter to allow DNS requests into the DMZ?

____

What command would you enter to allow e-mail requests into the DMZ?

____

What command would you enter to allow FTP requests into the DMZ?

____

Step 4. For management purposes, it would be useful to let corporate users ping the web server. However, Internet users should not get the same privilege. Add a line to the access list to give only corporate users ICMP access into the DMZ network.

Enter the following:

```
GAD(config)#access-list 112 permit icmp 10.10.10.0 0.0.0.255 host 10.1.1.10
```

This line allows only hosts on the corporate network to ping the web server. Although the configuration could be more restrictive with the ICMP options, the company does not view it as necessary.

Step 5. You could permit other services into the DMZ network in the future. However, at this time, you want no other traffic permitted into the DMZ network. Therefore, enter the following:

```
GAD(config)#access-list 112 deny ip any any
```

Step 6. Apply the outbound access list to the DMZ network FastEthernet port:

```
GAD(config)#interface fa0
GAD(config-if)#ip access-group 112 out
```

Step 7. To verify the syntax of the access lists, use the **show access-lists** command. The output should be similar to the following:

```
GAD#show  access-lists
Extended IP access list 101
    permit ip 10.10.10.0 0.0.0.255 any (70 matches)
    deny ip any any
Extended IP access list 102
    permit tcp any any established (8 matches)
    permit icmp any any echo-reply (12 matches)
    permit icmp any any unreachable
    deny ip any any (4 matches) Extended IP access list 111
    permit ip 10.1.1.0 0.0.0.255 any (59 matches)
    deny ip any any
Extended IP access list 112
    permit tcp any host 10.1.1.10 eq www (29 matches)
    permit icmp 10.10.10.0 0.0.0.255 host 10.1.1.10 (4 matches)
    deny ip any any (14 matches)
```

You might have to delete and re-enter the access lists if you spot any discrepancy between the preceding output and the configuration.

Step 8. Test the access lists by pinging all the systems and routers from each system.

Can Host A ping the web server?

____

Can Host A ping Host B? ____

Can Host B ping the web server? ____

Can Host B ping Host A? ____

Only Host A should be able to ping all locations.

Step 9. Use a web browser on each host, and enter the address of the web server to verify that the hosts still have web access to the web server.

Can Host A view the index.html page? ____

Can Host B view the index.html page? ____

Both hosts should still be able to view the index.html page in the web browser. Troubleshoot as necessary.

The DMZ network is now secure. Next, you need to configure your external interface to deter spoofing and hacking practices.

Task 4: Deter Spoofing

Networks are prone to attacks from outside users. Hackers, crackers, and script kiddies are names for various individuals who maliciously break into networks or render networks incapable of responding to legitimate requests (denial-of-service [DoS] attacks). Such attacks are troublesome for the Internet community.

You are well aware of the practices that some of these hackers use. A common method they employ is to forge a valid internal source IP address, a practice commonly known as *spoofing*.

To deter spoofing, you will configure an access list so that Internet hosts cannot easily spoof an internal network address. Three common source IP addresses that hackers attempt to forge are valid internal addresses (for example, 10.10.10.0), loopback addresses (that is, 127.*x.x.x*), and multicast addresses (that is, 224.*x.x.x* through 239.*x.x.x*).

Step 1. Configure an inbound access list that will make it difficult for outside users to spoof internal addresses, and apply it to the Serial 0 interface.

Enter the following:

```
GAD(config)#access-list 121 deny ip 10.10.10.0 0.0.0.255 any
GAD(config)#access-list 121 deny ip 127.0.0.0 0.255.255.255 any
GAD(config)#access-list 121 deny ip 224.0.0.0 31.255.255.255 any
GAD(config)#access-list 121 permit ip any any

GAD(config)#interface serial 0
GAD(config-if)#ip access-group 121 in
```

The first line stops outside users from forging a valid source IP address. The second line stops them from using the loopback address range. The third line stops hackers from using the multicast range of addresses (that is, 224.0.0.0 through 239.255.255.255) to create unnecessary internal traffic.

Step 2. Verify the syntax of the access lists with the **show access-lists** command. The output should be similar to the following:

```
GAD#show access-lists
Extended IP access list 101
    permit ip 10.10.10.0 0.0.0.255 any (168 matches)
    deny ip any any
Extended IP access list 102
    permit tcp any any established (24 matches)
    permit icmp any any echo-reply (28 matches)
    permit icmp any any unreachable
    deny ip any any (12 matches) Extended IP access list 111
    permit ip 10.1.1.0 0.0.0.255 any (122 matches)
    deny ip any any
Extended IP access list 112
    permit tcp any host 10.1.1.10 eq www (69 matches)
    permit icmp 10.10.10.0 0.0.0.255 host 10.1.1.10 (12 matches)
    deny ip any any (22 matches) Extended IP access list 121
    deny ip 10.10.10.0 0.0.0.255 any
    deny ip 127.0.0.0 0.255.255.255 any
    deny ip 224.0.0.0 31.255.255.255 any
    permit ip any any (47 matches)
```

You might have to delete and re-enter the access lists if you spot any discrepancy between the preceding output and the configuration.

Step 3. Test whether connectivity still exists by pinging all the systems and routers from each system.

Can Host A ping the web server?

____

Can Host A ping Host B? ____

Can Host B ping the web server? ____

Can Host B ping Host ?____

Only Host A should be able to ping all locations.

Step 4. Use a web browser on each host and enter the address of the web server to verify that the hosts still have web access to the web server.

Can Host A view the index.html page? ______________________________

Can Host B view the index.html page? ______________________________

Both hosts should still be able to view the index.html page in the web browser.

Troubleshoot as necessary.

The BMTC network is now secure.

Note: This lab provides a basic solution to providing a secure network. It is by no means a complete solution.

To properly protect enterprise networks, you should implement dedicated network devices such as Cisco PIX or ASA devices. As well, it is strongly recommended that you use advanced features such as Network Address Translation (NAT) and advanced access list options such as reflexive access lists and Context-Based Access Control (CBAC). These topics are beyond the scope of CCNA certification. Finally, network administrators should maintain strong relationships with their service providers to help when network security is compromised.

Task 5: Document the ACL

As a part of all network management, you should create documentation. Using the text file you created for the configuration, add your comments. This file should also contain output from the **show access-list** and **show ip interface** commands. Save the file with other network documentation. The filenaming convention should reflect the files function and the date of implementation.

When you finish the preceding tasks, log off (by typing **exit**) and turn off the routers.

Lab 11-7: Multiple Access Lists Functions (11.2.3c)

Figure 11-12 Topology for Lab 11-7

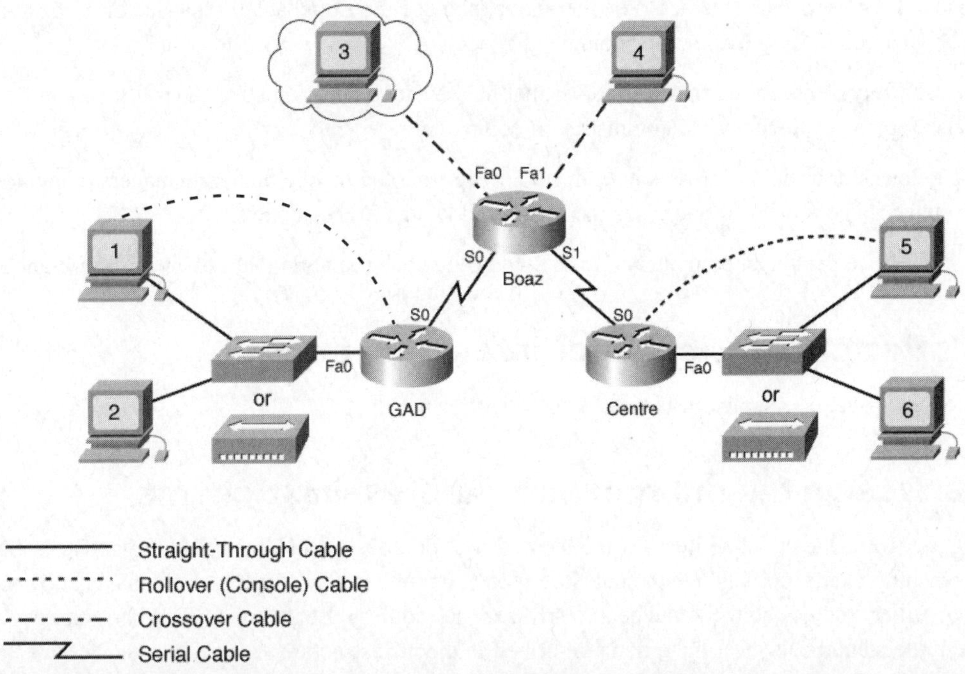

Table 11-14 Lab Equipment Configuration

Router Name	Router Type	FA0 Address	FA1 Address	S0 Address	S1 Address	Subnet Mask	Routing	Enable Password	vty Password

Table 11-15 Host IP Address, Subnet Mask, and Gateway Configuration

Host	IP Address	Subnet Mask	Gateway

Objective

- Configure and apply an extended ACL to control Internet traffic using one or more routers.

Background/Preparation

The company has a regional office (Boaz) that provides services to two branch offices (Gaston and Centre). These offices each have a branch manager and several people responsible for providing customer service. The service department has experienced a significant amount of turnover. A security audit has revealed that the computers that the service personnel use have no network restrictions.

The network infrastructure team leader wants a plan to enforce network security to prevent access. The criteria for this infrastructure follow:

- Host 3 represents the Internet. (An alternative is to use the Loopback 0 interface on Boaz and issue the Boaz(config)#**ip http server** command.)
- Host 4 represents an internal web server that has sensitive personnel and payroll information. Host 4 also represents the network administration computer.
- The lowest four host addresses in each subnet are reserved for the branch managers' computers (Hosts 1 and 5). The router interfaces use the highest addresses in the subnets.
- The service personnel computers (Hosts 2 and 6) use the remaining addresses in each branch's subnet.

Task 1: Perform Basic Router Interconnection

Connect the routers as shown in Figure 11-12.

Task 2: Design the Internetwork Addressing Scheme

Using a private Class C IP address for the internal network, design and document the network. Complete the preceding charts, and include the interface type and number, IP address, subnet mask, and cable type. The "Internet" (cloud) network can be any private space address. Be sure that the address ranges assigned to the routers and hosts meet the criteria described in the infrastructure section.

Task 3: Perform Basic Router Configuration

The router might contain configurations from previous use. Implement the procedure in Appendix C on all routers before continuing with this lab. Using the information previously created, set up the router configurations using RIP or Interior Gateway Routing Protocol (IGRP), and verify communications by pinging all the systems and routers from each system.

Step 1. To simulate specific locations on the Internet, add the following configuration to the Boaz router:

```
Boaz(config)#interface loopback 1
Boaz(config-if)#ip address 192.168.255.1 255.255.255.255
Boaz(config-if)#exit
Boaz(config)#interface loopback 2
Boaz(config-if)#ip address 192.168.255.2 255.255.255.255
Boaz(config-if)#exit
Boaz(config)#interface loopback 3
Boaz(config-if)#ip address 192.168.255.3 255.255.255.255
Boaz(config-if)#exit
Boaz(config)#interface loopback 4
Boaz(config-if)#ip address 192.168.255.4 255.255.255.255
Boaz(config-if)#exit
Boaz(config)#interface loopback 5
Boaz(config-if)#ip address 192.168.255.5 255.255.255.255
Boaz(config-if)#exit
Boaz(config)#interface loopback 6
Boaz(config-if)#ip address 192.168.255.6 255.255.255.255
Boaz(config-if)#exit
Boaz(config)#interface loopback 7
Boaz(config-if)#ip address 192.168.255.7 255.255.255.255
Boaz(config-if)#exit
Boaz(config)#interface loopback 8
Boaz(config-if)#ip address 192.168.255.8 255.255.255.255
Boaz(config-if)#exit
Boaz(config)#interface loopback 9
Boaz(config-if)#ip address 192.168.255.9 255.255.255.255
Boaz(config-if)#exit
Boaz(config)#interface loopback 10
Boaz(config-if)#ip address 192.168.255.10 255.255.255.255
Boaz(config-if)#exit
```

Step 2. Add a **network** statement to the Boaz routing protocol to advertise this network:

```
Boaz(config-router)#network 192.168.255.0
```

Task 4: Configre the Clients

Configure the hosts with the appropriate information using the information previously defined.

Step 1. Verify communications by pinging all the systems and routers from each system.

Step 2. On Hosts 3 and 4, install and configure a web server such as TinyWeb (http://www.simtel.net/pub/pd/13103.html). Host 3 represents the Internet. Host 4 represents an internal web server that has sensitive personnel and payroll information. Host 4 can be the loopback of the Boaz router.

Step 3. Verify that all systems can use a web browser to access the web pages of both the intranet server (Host 4) and the Internet server (Host 3).

Step 4. On Host 3, install and configure a Telnet server such as TelnetXQ (http://www.datawizard.net/Free_Software/TelnetXQ_Free/telnetxq_free.htm).

Step 5. Verify that all systems can telnet to the Internet (Host 3).

Now that the infrastructure is in place, it is time to begin securing the internetwork.

Task 5: Secure the Intranet Server

Host 4 represents an internal web server that has sensitive personnel and payroll information. The information on this server should be accessible only to the branch managers. Create ACLs to secure this server so that only branch managers' machines have web access (HTTP) to this internal server.

How many ACLs will you use? ______________________________

Where will you apply the ACLs?

____

In which direction will you apply the ACLs?

____

For what reasons might it be better to use multiple ACLs?

____

For what reasons might it be better to use a single ACL?

____

____

Step 1. Using a text editor, such as Notepad, construct the logic of the access lists and then enter the proper commands. After you properly construct the list, paste it into the router's configuration, and apply it to the appropriate interface(s). Confirm that the ACL is functioning properly.

Step 2. Verify communications by pinging all the systems and routers from each system.

Step 3. Verify that all the computers' systems can use a web browser to access the web pages on the Internet (anywhere except the internal web server).

Step 4. Verify that the service personnel computers cannot use a web browser to access (HTTP) the intranet server.

Step 5. Verify that the computers from the Internet (Host 3) cannot use a web browser to access (HTTP) the intranet server.

Task 6: Secure the Intranet Documents

There is concern that internal policy and procedures documents are available outside of the company. To ensure that users in the internetwork cannot forward these documents, do not allow any Telnet or FTP access to the Internet.

Will you create new ACLs or modify the current lists?

____

If you create new lists:

How many new ACLs will you create? ____

In which direction will you apply the new ACLs? ____

Step 1. Again, use a text editor, such as Notepad, to construct the logic of the access lists and enter the proper commands. After you properly construct the list, paste it into the routers and apply it to the appropriate interfaces. Confirm that the ACL is functioning properly.

Step 2. Verify communications by pinging all the systems and routers from each system.

Step 3. Verify that all the computers' systems can use a web browser to access the web pages on the Internet (anywhere except the internal web server).

Step 4. Verify that the service personnel computers cannot use a web browser to access (HTTP) the intranet server.

Step 5. Verify that computers from the Internet (Host 3) cannot use a web browser to access (HTTP) the intranet server.

Step 6. Verify that the computers cannot telnet to the Internet (Host 3 and loopback interfaces on Boaz) but can telnet to the routers.

Task 7: Deter Internet Abuse

There have also been some complaints that employees are abusing Internet access. They have been accessing sites with questionable content. To help stop this practice, do not allow any IP traffic from the internetwork to the following sites:

- 192.168.255.1
- 192.168.255.4
- 192.168.255.8
- 192.168.255.9

Will you create new ACLs or modify the current lists?

____

____

____

If you create new lists:

How many new ACLs will you create?

____

Where will you apply the new ACLs?

____

In which direction will you apply the new ACLs?

____

Step 1. Again, use a text editor, such as Notepad, to construct the logic of the access lists, and enter the proper commands.

Step 2. After you properly construct the list, paste it into the routers and apply it to the appropriate interfaces. Confirm that the ACL is functioning properly.

Step 3. Verify that the service personnel computers cannot use a web browser to access (HTTP) the intranet server.

Step 4. Verify that the computers from the Internet (Host 3) cannot use a web browser to access (HTTP) the intranet server.

Step 5. Verify that the computers cannot telnet to the Internet (Host 3 and loopback interfaces on Boaz) but can telnet to the routers.

Step 6. Verify that the computers cannot telnet to, use a web browser to access, or ping 192.168.255.1.

Step 7. Verify that the computers cannot telnet to, use a web browser to access, or ping 192.168.255.4.

Step 8. Verify that the computers cannot telnet to, use a web browser to access, or ping 192.168.255.8.

Step 9. Verify that the computers cannot telnet to, use a web browser to access, or ping 192.168.255.9.

Step 10. Verify communications by pinging all the other systems and routers from each system.

Step 11. Verify that all the computer systems can use a web browser to access the other web pages on the Internet (Host 3 and loopback interfaces on Boaz).

Task 8: Deter DoS Attacks

In the last few weeks, the company's internetwork has been the subject of numerous Denial of Service (DoS) attacks. Most have had the form of the "ping of death" (oversized ICMP echo packets) or directed broadcasts (*x.x.x*.255). To help stop ping-of-death attacks, do not allow any ICMP echo packets into the internetwork. To stop directed broadcasts, stop all IP packets addressed to the directed broadcast address from entering the internetwork.

Will you create new ACLs or modify the current lists?

____

If new list(s):

How many new ACLs will you create?

____

Where will you apply the new ACLs?

____

In which direction will you apply the new ACLs? ____________________

Step 1. Use a text editor, such as Notepad, to construct the logic of the access lists and enter the proper commands. After you properly construct the list, paste it into the routers and apply it to the appropriate interfaces. Confirm that the ACL is functioning properly.

Step 2. Verify that the service personnel computers cannot use a web browser to access (HTTP) the intranet server.

Step 3. Verify that the computers from the Internet (Host 3) cannot use a web browser to access (HTTP) the intranet server.

Step 4. Verify that the computers cannot telnet to the Internet (Host 3 and loopback interfaces on Boaz) but can telnet to the routers.

Step 5. Verify that the computers cannot telnet to, use a web browser to access, or ping 192.168.255.1.

Step 6. Verify that the computers cannot telnet to, use a web browser to access, or ping 192.168.255.4.

Step 7. Verify that the computers cannot telnet to, use a web browser to access, or ping 192.168.255.8.

Step 8. Verify that the computers cannot telnet to, use a web browser to access, or ping 192.168.255.9.

Step 9. Verify that all the computer systems can use a web browser to access the other web pages on the Internet (Host 3 and loopback interfaces on Boaz).

Step 10. Verify that Host 3 cannot successfully ping anything in the internetwork.

Step 11. Verify that the systems can successfully ping the other Internet hosts.

Step 12. Verify communications by pinging all the other systems and routers from each system.

Task 9: Stop Telnet into the Routers

There have been some attempts to telnet into the routers both inside and outside the internetwork. The only host that should have Telnet access to the routers is the network administration computer. To stop Telnet access to the routers, create an ACL and apply it to the vty lines of the routers that will permit only the network administration computer to telnet.

What type of access list will you use? ______________________________

What command will you use to apply the list to the vty lines? ______________________________

Step 1. Use a text editor, such as Notepad, to construct the logic of the access lists and enter the proper commands. After you properly construct the list, paste it to the routers and apply it to the vty lines.

Step 2. Confirm that the ACL is functioning properly.

Step 3. Verify that the service personnel computers cannot use a web browser to access (HTTP) the intranet server.

Step 4. Verify that the computers from the Internet (Host 3) cannot use a web browser to access (HTTP) the intranet server.

Step 5. Verify that the computers cannot telnet to the Internet (Host 3 and loopback interfaces on Boaz) but can telnet to the routers.

Step 6. Verify that the computers cannot telnet, to use a web browser to access, or ping 192.168.255.1.

Step 7. Verify that the computers cannot telnet to, use a web browser to access, or ping 192.168.255.4.

Step 8. Verify that the computers cannot telnet to, use a web browser to access, or ping 192.168.255.8.

Step 9. Verify that the computers cannot telnet to, use a web browser to access, or ping 192.168.255.9.

Step 10. Verify that all the computer systems can use a web browser to access the other web pages on the Internet (Host 3 and loopback interfaces on Boaz).

Step 11. Verify that Host 3 cannot successfully ping anything in the internetwork.

Step 12. Verify that the systems can successfully ping the other Internet hosts.

Step 13. Verify that the systems can successfully ping Host 3.

Step 14. Verify that the network administration computer (Host 4) can telnet to all the routers.

Step 15. Verify that the other internal computers cannot telnet to any of the routers.

Step 16. Verify that the other external computers (Host 3) cannot Telnet to any of the routers.

Task 10: Verify the Access Lists

After you apply the access lists, you need to verify them.

Step 1. First, verify what lists you have defined. From a CLI session on one of the routers with access lists, display the access lists with the Boaz#**show ip access-lists** command. Record the information about one of the access lists:

What does the **(# matches)** in the output represent?

____

Step 2. Confirm which access list is applied to each interface. You do so from the terminal session of one of the routers with access lists, with the Boaz#**show ip interface** command. Look at the output from each interface and record the lists applied to each interface:

Interface: ______________________________

Outgoing access list is ______________________________

Inbound access list is ______________________________

Interface: ______________________________

Outgoing access list is ______________________________

Inbound access list is ______________________________

Interface: ______________________________

Outgoing access list is ______________________________

Inbound access list is ______________________________

Interface: ______________________________

Outgoing access list is ______________________________

Inbound access list is ______________________________

When you finish the preceding steps, log off (by typing **exit**) and turn off the routers.

Lab 11-8: VTY Restriction (11.2.6)

Figure 11-13 Topology for Lab 11-8

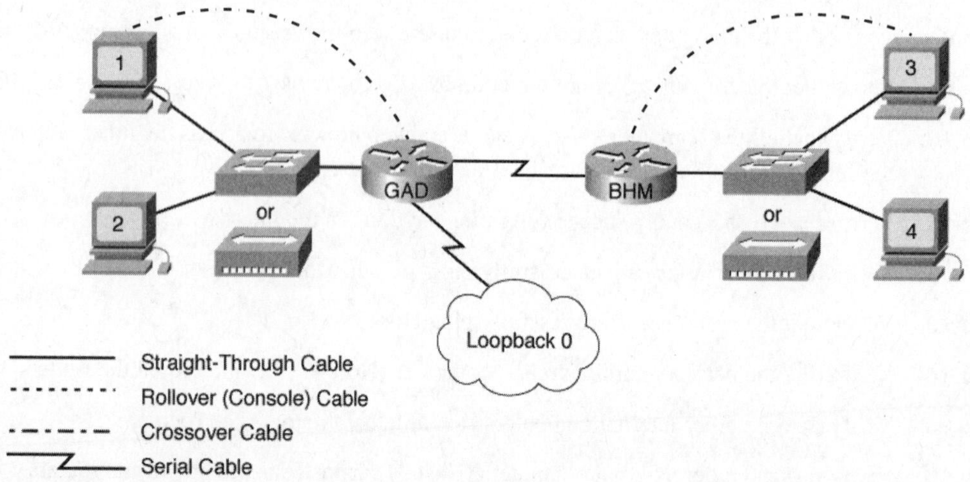

Table 11-16 Lab Equipment Configuration

Router Name	FA0 Address	S0 Address
GAD	192.168.1.1/24	192.168.2.1/24
BHM	192.168.3.1/24	192.168.2.2/24

The enable password for both routers is **cisco**.

The vty password for both routers is **class**.

The routing protocol for both routers is RIP.

Table 11-17 Host IP Address, Subnet Mask, and Gateway Configuration

Host	IP Address	Subnet Mask	Gateway
1	192.168.1.2	255.255.255.0	192.168.1.1
2	192.168.1.3	255.255.255.0	192.168.1.1
3	192.168.3.2	255.255.255.0	192.168.3.1
4	192.168.3.3	255.255.255.0	192.168.3.1

Objective

- Use the **access-class** and **line** commands to control Telnet access to the router.

Background/Preparation

The company's home office in Gadsden (GAD) provides services to branch offices such as the Birmingham (BHM) office. Only systems within the local network should be able to telnet to the router. You will create a standard access list that will permit users on the local network to telnet to the local router. You will then apply the access list to the virtual terminal lines (vty).

Task 1: Perform Basic Router Interconnection

Connect the routers as shown in Figure 11-13.

Task 2: Perform Basic Configuration

Step 1. The router might contain configurations from a previous use. Implement the procedure in Appendix C on all routers before continuing with this lab. Using the information in Tables 11-16 and 11-17, set up the router and host configurations and verify communications by pinging all systems and routers from each system.

Step 2. Telnet from the hosts to both the local router and the remote router.

Task 3: Create the Access List That Represents the Gadsden LAN

The LAN in Gadsden has a network address of 192.168.1.0 /24. To create the access list, use the following command:

```
GAD(config)#access-list 1 permit 192.168.1.0 0.0.0.255
```

Task 4: Apply the Access List to Permit Only the Gadsden LAN

After you create the list to represent traffic, you must apply it to the vty lines. This will restrict any Telnet access to the router. Although you could apply it separately to each interface, it is easier to apply the list to all vty lines in one statement. Enter interface mode for all five lines with the global configuration command **line vty 0 4**.

For the GAD router, enter the following:

```
GAD(config)#line vty 0 4
GAD(config-line)#access-class 1 in
GAD(config-line)#^Z
```

Task 5: Test the Restriction

Test the ACL's functionality by trying to telnet from the hosts, and verify that the access list is working correctly.

Step 1. Verify that Host 1 can telnet to GAD.

Step 2. Verify that Host 2 can telnet to GAD.

Step 3. Verify that Host 3 cannot telnet to GAD.

Step 4. Verify that Host 4 cannot telnet to GAD.

Task 6: Create the Restrictions for the BHM Router

Step 1. Repeat Tasks 3, 4, and 5 to restrict Telnet access to BHM. The restriction should allow only hosts in the Birmingham LAN to Telnet to BHM.

Step 2. Test the ACL's functionality by trying to telnet from the hosts, and verify that the access list is working correctly.

Step 3. Verify that Host 1 cannot telnet to BHM.

Step 4. Verify that Host 2 cannot telnet to BHM.

Step 5. Verify that Host 3 can telnet to BHM.

Step 6. Verify that Host 4 can telnet to BHM.

Task 7: Document the ACL

Step 1. As a part of all network management, you should create documentation. Capture a copy of the configuration, and add your comments to explain the purpose of the ACL code.

Step 2. Save the file with other network documentation. The filenaming convention should reflect the file's function and the date of implementation.

Step 3. When you finish these steps, log off (by typing **exit**) and turn off the routers.

Comprehensive Lab 11-9: Standard, Extended, and Named ACLs

Figure 11-14 Standard, Extended, and Named ACL Topology

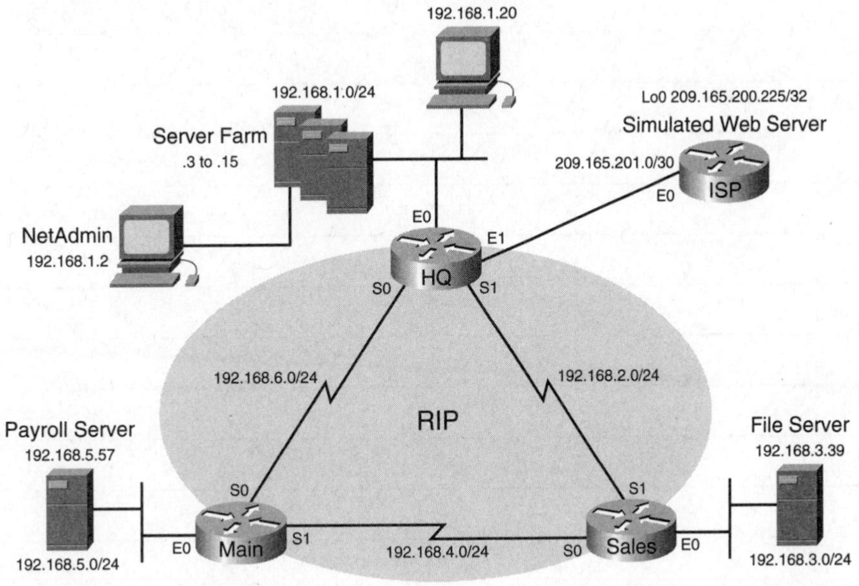

Objectives

This lab contains the following objectives:

- Cable and configure routers with basic configuration.
- Configure Routing Information Protocol (RIP) routing.
- Implement multiple ACL security policies.
- Verify ACL configurations.

Equipment

This lab can be done with any combination of 1700, 2500, and 2600 routers. You need at least one router with four interfaces for HQ. If you do not have a router with four interfaces, you will simulate the link to ISP with a loopback address.

NetLab Compatibility Notes

This lab can be completed using NetLab. However, you cannot effectively test your access control lists.

Task 1: Cable and Document the Lab

Step 1. Cable the lab as shown in Figure 11-14.

Step 2. If you use different interface designations, change the topology labels accordingly.

Step 3. Complete the table that follows with the addresses you are using for each device.

Device	Interface	IP Address	Subnet Mask
ISP			
HQ			
Sales			
Main			
NetAdmin			
HQ PC			
File server			
Payroll server			

Task 2: Router, Routing, and PC Configuration

You might need to refer to your notes and labs from previous chapters to complete this task.

Step 1. Configure all routers with the following basic configurations according to your instructor's requirements:

- Hostname
- Line configurations
- Global passwords
- Host tables
- Banner
- Other instructor-required global configurations

Step 2. Configure and activate all the necessary interfaces.

Step 3. Configure dynamic routing using RIP. *Do not* advertise the 209.165.201.0/30 link within the RIP routing process. *Do not* configure ISP with RIP routing.

Step 4. Configure static routing between ISP and HQ. HQ redistributes a default route to Main and Sales. Use the following commands:

```
HQ(config)#ip route 0.0.0.0 0.0.0.0 209.165.201.1
HQ(config)#router rip
HQ(config)#default-information originate

ISP(config)#ip route 192.168.0.0 255.255.248.0 209.165.201.2
```

Step 5. Configure PCs with appropriate addressing.

Task 3: Verify and Troubleshoot Your Network Configuration

Each router should have complete routing tables similar to the following:

```
ISP>show ip route
! Codes omitted for brevity

Gateway of last resort is not set

     209.165.200.0/32 is subnetted, 1 subnets
C       209.165.200.225 is directly connected, Loopback0
     209.165.201.0/30 is subnetted, 1 subnets
C       209.165.201.0 is directly connected, Ethernet0
S    192.168.0.0/21 [1/0] via 209.165.201.2
```

```
HQ>show ip route
! Codes omitted for brevity

Gateway of last resort is 0.0.0.0 to network 0.0.0.0

R    192.168.4.0/24 [120/1] via 192.168.2.2, 00:00:22, Serial1
                    [120/1] via 192.168.6.1, 00:00:03, Serial0
     209.165.201.0/30 is subnetted, 1 subnets
C       209.165.201.0 is directly connected, Ethernet1
R    192.168.5.0/24 [120/1] via 192.168.6.1, 00:00:03, Serial0
C    192.168.6.0/24 is directly connected, Serial0
C    192.168.1.0/24 is directly connected, Ethernet0
C    192.168.2.0/24 is directly connected, Serial1
R    192.168.3.0/24 [120/1] via 192.168.2.2, 00:00:22, Serial1
S*   0.0.0.0/0 is directly connected, Ethernet1
```

```
SALES>show ip route
! Codes omitted for brevity

Gateway of last resort is 192.168.2.1 to network 0.0.0.0

C    192.168.4.0/24 is directly connected, Serial0
R    192.168.5.0/24 [120/1] via 192.168.4.2, 00:00:14, Serial0
R    192.168.6.0/24 [120/1] via 192.168.4.2, 00:00:14, Serial0
                    [120/1] via 192.168.2.1, 00:00:26, Serial1
R    192.168.1.0/24 [120/1] via 192.168.2.1, 00:00:26, Serial1
C    192.168.2.0/24 is directly connected, Serial1
C    192.168.3.0/24 is directly connected, Ethernet0
R*   0.0.0.0/0 [120/1] via 192.168.2.1, 00:00:26, Serial1
```

```
MAIN>show ip route
! Codes omitted for brevity
```

```
Gateway of last resort is 192.168.6.2 to network 0.0.0.0

C     192.168.4.0/24 is directly connected, Serial1
C     192.168.5.0/24 is directly connected, Ethernet0
C     192.168.6.0/24 is directly connected, Serial0
R     192.168.1.0/24 [120/1] via 192.168.6.2, 00:00:16, Serial0
R     192.168.2.0/24 [120/1] via 192.168.4.1, 00:00:22, Serial1
                     [120/1] via 192.168.6.2, 00:00:16, Serial0
R     192.168.3.0/24 [120/1] via 192.168.4.1, 00:00:22, Serial1
R*    0.0.0.0/0 [120/1] via 192.168.6.2, 00:00:16, Serial0
```

Use the **ping** command to test connectivity throughout the network. Make sure that all LANs are reachable and that all devices can reach all destinations before configuring access control lists in the next task.

Task 4: Configure and Verify Access Control Lists

Use the space provided following each step of each security policy to write out the access control list or required access list statement.

Security Policy #1

On HQ, implement the following policy:

- Deny user PCs Telnet access.
- Allow NetAdmin and Server Farm full access.
- Permit all other traffic.

Step 1. The first statement should be to permit addresses 192.168.1.2 through 192.168.1.15 full access:

```
HQ(config)#access-list 100 permit ip 192.168.1.0 0.0.0.15 any
```

Step 2. Now you can safely deny Telnet access to the entire subnet. NetAdmin and Server Farm Telnet sessions are permitted by the first statement:

```
HQ(config)#access-list 100 deny tcp 192.168.1.0 0.0.0.255 any eq 23
```

Step 3. The third statement is to permit everything else:

```
HQ(config)#access-list 100 permit ip any any
```

Step 4. Apply the ACL to the first interface that the filtered traffic hits, and specify inbound as the direction:

```
HQ(config)#interface e0
HQ(config-if)#ip access-group 100 in
```

Verify Security Policy #1

The NetAdmin PC should be able to telnet anywhere in the network. The other HQ PC with the 192.168.1.20 address should not be able to telnet, but should be able to ping anywhere.

Security Policy #2

On SALES, implement the following policy:

- Allow only web access to all outside (Internet) destinations.
- Allow access to all interior hosts except the payroll server.

Step 1. Deny access to the payroll server:

```
SALES(config)#access-list 110 deny ip 192.168.3.0 0.0.0.255 host 192.168.5.57
```

Step 2. Permit full access to interior hosts only. To do this in one statement, you find the common bit boundary that covers all the 192.168 networks in one wildcard mask:

	00000000
192.168.1.0	00000001
192.168.2.0	00000010
192.168.3.0	00000011
192.168.4.0	00000100
192.168.5.0	00000101
192.168.6.0	00000110
	00000111

Because all the interior networks share the first 5 bits in the third octet, check these bits and ignore the last 3 bits in the third octet:

```
SALES(config)#access-list 110 permit ip 192.168.3.0 0.0.0.255 192.168.0.0 0.0.7.255
```

Step 3. Permit web access to all other sites. This allows web access to the Internet:

```
SALES(config)#access-list 110 permit tcp 192.168.3.0 0.0.0.255 any eq 80
```

Step 4. Apply the ACL to the Ethernet interface on Sales:

```
SALES(config)#interface e0
SALES(config)#ip access-group 110 in
```

Verify Security Policy #2

Pings from any host on Sales to the Payroll server should fail. Hosts on Sales should be able to ping any inside host. Pings to the web server should fail. However, web access to the simulated web server should succeed if you have the **ip http server** command configured on ISP.

Security Policy #3

On Main, implement the following policy:

- Allow the Payroll server full access.
- Allow PCs full ICMP access.
- Allow PCs access to FTP, DNS, and HTTP services.

Step 1. Allow the Payroll server full access to anywhere:

```
MAIN(config)#access-list 120 permit ip host 192.168.5.57 any
```

Step 2. The following statement allows full ICMP access. You do this by specifying **icmp** as the protocol:

```
MAIN(config)#access-list 120 permit icmp any any
```

Step 3. Permit all the allowed services: FTP, DNS, and HTTP. For FTP, you must allow two ports. For DNS, change the protocol to **udp** because hosts use the User Datagram Protocol (UDP) port to send DNS requests to a DNS server:

```
MAIN(config)#access-list 120 permit tcp 192.168.5.0 0.0.0.255 any eq 20
!or keyword "ftp-data"
MAIN(config)#access-list 120 permit tcp 192.168.5.0 0.0.0.255 any eq 21
! or keyword "ftp"
MAIN(config)#access-list 120 permit udp 192.168.5.0 0.0.0.255 any eq 53
! or keyword "domain"
MAIN(config)#access-list 120 permit tcp 192.168.5.0 0.0.0.255 any eq 80
! or keyword "www"
```

Step 4. Apply the ACL to the Ethernet interface on Main:

```
MAIN(config)#interface e0
MAIN(config-if)#ip access-group 120 in
```

Verify Security Policy #3

The Payroll server should be able to telnet anywhere. However, no other devices on the LAN can telnet. To test this, attach a PC to Main's LAN and configure it with an IP address from the 192.168.5.0 network. Make sure that HTTP and pings are allowed. However, Telnet should be denied.

Security Policy #4

On HQ, use the named ACL, FIREWALL, to implement the following policy:

- Allow pings sourced from inside to return from the Internet.
- Allow "Destination Unreachable" error messages to return from the Internet.
- Allow established TCP sessions from the Internet.

Step 1. Specify an extended ACL with the name FIREWALL:

```
HQ(config)#ip access-list extended FIREWALL
```

Step 2. Only allow echo replies to return to the sourcing hosts inside the network:

```
HQ(config-ext-nacl)#permit icmp any any echo-reply
```

Step 3. To allow "Destination Unreachable" error messages to return, use the argument **3** to cover all codes for this message type:

```
HQ(config-ext-nacl)#permit icmp any any 3
```

Step 4. For established TCP connections, simply use the argument **established**. This prevents outside destinations from successfully initiating a TCP session with inside hosts:

```
HQ(config-ext-nacl)#permit tcp any any established
```

Step 5. Apply the ACL to the Ethernet interface on MAIN:

```
HQ(config)#interface e1
HQ(config-if)#ip access-group FIREWALL in
```

Verify Security Policy #4

Inside hosts should be able to ping ISP and the simulated web server. However, ISP should only be able to ping the 209.165.201.2 address on HQ. All other pings from ISP to inside hosts should fail.

Security Policy #5

NetAdmin should be allowed Telnet and HTTP access to the routers HQ, Sales, and Main. In addition, HQ, Sales, and Main should be allowed to telnet into each other. Enforce this policy on all three routers. The following steps show how to write and apply the policy on HQ. Modify the policy where necessary when applying it to Sales and Main.

Step 1. Allow NetAdmin access:

```
HQ(config)#access-list 10 permit host 192.168.1.2
```

Step 2. Allow Telnet from any IP address on Sales or Main:

```
HQ(config)#access-list 10 permit host 192.168.2.2
HQ(config)#access-list 10 permit host 192.168.3.1
HQ(config)#access-list 10 permit host 192.168.4.1
HQ(config)#access-list 10 permit host 192.168.4.2
HQ(config)#access-list 10 permit host 192.168.5.1
HQ(config)#access-list 10 permit host 192.168.6.1
```

Step 3. Deny all other access explicitly. This allows you to monitor the number of attempts that were denied with the **show ip access-list** command:

```
HQ(config)#access-list 10 deny any
```

Step 4. Apply the ACL to HTTP access:

```
HQ(config)#ip http access-class 10
```

Step 5. Apply the ACL to Telnet lines:

```
HQ(config)#line vty 0 4
HQ(config-line)#access-class 10 in
```

Challenge Lab 11-10a: Three Routers with Multiple ACL Configurations (Form A)

Figure 11-15 Three-Router ACL Configuration Topology (Form A)

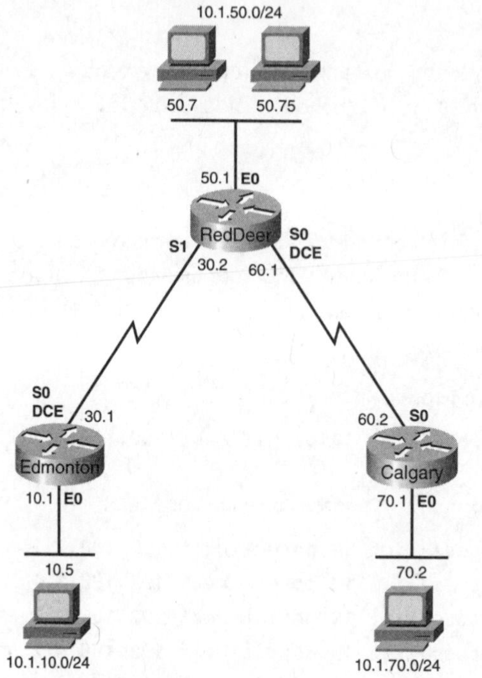

Objectives

- Cable and configure routers with basic configuration.
- Configure RIP routing.
- Implement multiple ACL security policies.
- Verify ACL configurations.

Equipment

This lab can be done with any combination of 1700, 2500, and 2600 routers. However, if you have at least three routers with two Ethernet or Fast Ethernet interfaces each, consider completing "Challenge Lab 11-10b: Three Routers with Multiple ACL Configurations (Form B)". The security requirements for the two forms of this lab are similar. The tasks are adjusted to fit routers with two Ethernet or Fast Ethernet interfaces.

Although the topology shows seven PCS, you need only two each time you test an ACL. This can be achieved by moving PCs from LAN to LAN and changing the IP addressing.

NetLab Compatibility Notes

This lab can be completed using NetLab. However, you cannot effectively test your access control lists.

Task 1: Cable the Lab

Step 1. Cable the lab as shown in Figure 11-15.

Step 2. If you use different interface designations, change the topology labels accordingly.

Task 2: Router, Routing, and PC Configuration

You might need to refer to your notes and labs from previous chapters to complete this section.

Step 1. Configure all routers with basic configurations according to your instructor's requirements, such as:

- Hostname
- Line configurations
- Global passwords
- Host tables
- Banner
- Other instructor-required global configurations

Step 2. Configure and activate all the necessary interfaces.

Step 3. Configure dynamic routing using RIP.

Step 4. Configure PCs with appropriate addressing.

Task 3: Verify and Troubleshoot Your Network Configuration

Each router should have five routes. The routing table for RED_DEER is shown here.

```
RED_DEER#show ip route
!Codes omitted for brevity
     10.0.0.0/24 is subnetted, 5 subnets
R       10.1.10.0 [120/1] via 10.1.30.1, 00:00:00, Serial1
C       10.1.30.0 is directly connected, Serial1
C       10.1.60.0 is directly connected, Serial0
C       10.1.50.0 is directly connected, Ethernet0
R       10.1.70.0 [120/1] via 10.1.60.2, 00:00:21, Serial0
```

Use ping to test connectivity throughout the network. Make sure that all LANs are reachable before configuring access control lists in the next step.

Task 4: Configure and Verify Access Control Lists

Use the space that follows each security policy to write out the access control list.

Security Policy #1

Host 10.1.10.5 is not allowed to access host 10.1.50.7. All other hosts are allowed to access 10.1.50.7.

- Standard or extended? ______________________________
- Router? ______________________________
- Interface? ______________________________
- Direction? ______________________________

____

____

____

____

Verify Security Policy #1

Host 10.1.10.5 should not be able to ping 10.1.50.7. All other addresses should be able to ping 10.1.50.7. Host 10.1.10.5 should be able to ping 10.1.50.75 and the 10.1.50.1 interface.

Security Policy #2

Host 10.1.70.2 is allowed Telnet access to the RED_DEER router. In addition, the EDMONTON and CALGARY routers should be able to Telnet to the RED_DEER router. All other Telnet access to RED_DEER is blocked.

Tip: The IP address that EDMONTON uses to Telnet to RED_DEER is 10.1.30.1. The IP address that CALGARY uses to Telnet to RED_DEER is 10.1.60.2.

- Standard or extended? ______________________________
- Router? ______________________________
- Interface or line? ______________________________
- Direction? ______________________________

____

____

____

____

____

Verify Security Policy #2

You need only one PC to test this policy. From a command prompt on host 10.1.10.5, you should be able to Telnet to any address on RED_DEER. All other hosts and routers should *not* be able to telnet to RED_DEER.

Security Policy #3

Hosts 10.1.50.1 through 10.1.50.63 are not allowed web access to 10.1.70.2. All other hosts are allowed web access to 10.1.70.2. All other access is allowed.

Tip: To test web access to a host, you can install a web server or simulated web server on host 10.1.70.2. Use your favorite search engine to find a freeware web server or simulator you can install. For example, ServTerm 1.0, at http://www.pc-tools.net/win32/servterm/, can simulate any port number you want to test.

- Standard or xtended? ______________________________
- Router? ______________________________
- Interface? ______________________________
- Direction? ______________________________

____

____

____

____

Verify Security Policy #3

To test this policy, you need a web server installed and running on host 10.1.70.2. You can use ServTerm 1.0 to simulate a web server, or you can download and install one of the many freeware web servers available on the Internet. Web access from host 10.1.50.7 to host 10.1.70.2 should be blocked. All other hosts should have web access to 10.1.70.2. Also, test to make sure that 10.1.50.7 has web access to other destinations. For example, 10.1.50.7 should be able to open a web page from one of the three routers as long as the routers have the HTTP service active.

Security Policy #4

Only hosts from the 10.1.50.0/24 LAN should be allowed to access the HTTP service on the CALGARY router. Make sure that HTTP is enabled on CALGARY with the **ip http server** command. All other hosts should be denied this access.

- Standard or extended? ______________________________
- Router? ______________________________

____

____

Verify Security Policy #4

A host from the 10.1.50.0/24 LAN should be able to open a web browser to any valid address on the CALGARY router. No other host should be able to gain access to CALGARY through a web browser.

Security Policy #5

Use the name NOPINGS to configure a named ACL that stops all pings from the 10.1.70.0/24 network from reaching hosts on the 10.1.10.0/24 network. All other access should be allowed.

- Router? ______________________________
- Interface? ______________________________
- Direction? ______________________________

____

____

____

____

____

Verify Security Policy #5

Host 10.1.70.2 should not be able to ping host 10.1.10.5. However, host 10.1.70.2 should be able to ping all other addresses. All other hosts should be able to ping 10.1.10.5.

Challenge Lab 11-10b: Three Routers with Multiple ACL Configurations (Form B)

Figure 11-16 Three-Router ACL Configuration Topology (Form B)

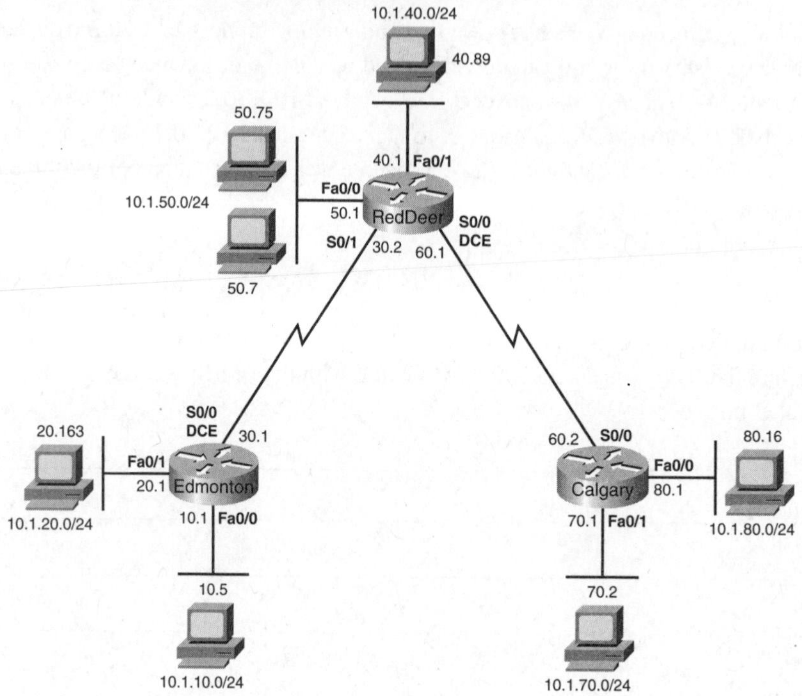

Objectives

- Cable and configure routers with basic configuration.
- Configure RIP routing.
- Implement multiple ACL security policies.
- Verify ACL configurations.

Equipment

This lab can be done with any combination of routers. However, all routers must have at least two Ethernet or Fast Ethernet interfaces. If your lab equipment does not support this lab, complete "Challenge Lab 11-10a: Three Routers with Multiple ACL Configurations (Form A). The security requirements for the two forms of this lab are similar. The tasks are adjusted to fit routers with only one Ethernet or Fast Ethernet interface.

Although the topology shows seven PCS, you need only two each time you test an ACL. This can be achieved by moving PCs from LAN to LAN and changing the IP addressing.

NetLab Compatibility Notes

This lab can be completed using NetLab. However, you cannot effectively test your access control lists.

Task 1: Cable the Lab

Step 1. Cable the lab as shown in Figure 11-16.

Step 2. If you use different interface designations, change the topology labels accordingly.

Task 2: Router, Routing, and PC Configuration

You might need to refer to your notes and labs from previous chapters to complete this section.

Step 1. Configure all routers with basic configurations according to your instructor's requirements, such as:

- Hostname
- Line configurations
- Global passwords
- Host tables
- Banner
- Other instructor-required global configurations

Step 2. Configure and activate all the necessary interfaces.

Step 3. Configure dynamic routing using RIP.

Step 4. Configure PCs with appropriate addressing.

Task 3: Verify and Troubleshoot Your Network Configuration

Each router should have eight routes. The routing table for RED_DEER is shown here.

```
RED_DEER#show ip route
!Codes omitted for brevity
     10.0.0.0/24 is subnetted, 8 subnets
R       10.1.10.0 [120/1] via 10.1.30.1, 00:00:09, Serial0/1
C       10.1.30.0 is directly connected, Serial0/1
R       10.1.20.0 [120/1] via 10.1.30.1, 00:00:09, Serial0/1
C       10.1.40.0 is directly connected, FastEthernet0/1
C       10.1.60.0 is directly connected, Serial0/0
C       10.1.50.0 is directly connected, FastEthernet0/0
R       10.1.70.0 [120/1] via 10.1.60.2, 00:00:17, Serial0/0
R       10.1.80.0 [120/1] via 10.1.60.2, 00:00:22, Serial0/0
```

Use the **ping** command to test connectivity throughout the network. Make sure that all LANs are reachable before configuring access control lists in the next step.

Task 4: Configure and Verify Access Control Lists

Use the space that follows each security policy to write out the access control list.

Security Policy #1

Block the 10.1.10.0 network from accessing the 10.1.40.0 network. All other access to 10.1.40.0 is allowed.

- Standard or extended? ______________________________
- Router? ______________________________
- Interface? ______________________________

- Direction? ______________________________

____

____

____

____

Verify Security Policy #1

For this policy, you need only the 10.1.40.89 host configured. You can use extended ping from the EDMONTON router, specifying the 10.1.10.1 interface address as the source address. The ping should fail. A regular ping from the EDMONTON router, as well as pings from any other destination, should succeed.

Security Policy #2

Host 10.1.10.5 is not allowed to access host 10.1.50.7. All other hosts are allowed to access 10.1.50.7.

- Standard or extended? ______________________________
- Router? ______________________________
- Interface? ______________________________
- Direction? ______________________________

____

____

____

____

Verify Security Policy #2

Host 10.1.10.5 should not be able to ping 10.1.50.7. All other addresses should be able to ping 10.1.50.7. Host 10.1.10.5 should be able to ping 10.1.50.75 and the 10.1.50.1 interface.

Security Policy #3

Host 10.1.70.2 is allowed Telnet access to the RED_DEER router. In addition, the EDMONTON and CALGARY routers should be able to telnet to the RED_DEER router. All other Telnet access to RED_DEER is blocked.

Tip: The IP address that EDMONTON uses to telnet to RED_DEER is 10.1.30.1. The IP address that CALGARY uses to telnet to RED_DEER is 10.1.60.2.

- Standard or extended?______________________________
  Router? ______________________________
- Interface or line? ______________________________
- Direction? ______________________________

____

Verify Security Policy #3

You need only one PC to test this policy. From a command prompt on host 10.1.70.2, you should be able to telnet to any address on RED_DEER. You should also be able to telnet from either router. All other hosts should *not* be able to telnet to RED_DEER.

Security Policy #4

Host 10.1.20.163 is allowed to telnet to host 10.1.70.2. No other host on the 10.1.20.0/24 network should be allowed Telnet access to 10.1.70.2. All other access is allowed.

Tip: To test Telnet access to a host, you can install a Telnet server or simulated Telnet server on host 10.1.70.2. Use your favorite search engine to find a freeware Telnet server or simulator you can install. For example, ServTerm 1.0, at http://www.pc-tools.net/win32/servterm/, can simulate any port number you want to test. So it can also be used to simulate a web server, mail server, or file server.

- Standard or extended? ______
- Router? ______
- Interface? ______
- Direction? ______

Verify Security Policy #4

Host 10.1.20.163 should be allowed to telnet to 10.1.70.2. Configure the workstation with a different IP address from the 10.1.20.0/24 network to test that Telnet access is denied.

Security Policy #5

Hosts 10.1.50.1 through 10.1.50.63 are not allowed web access to 10.1.80.16. All other hosts are allowed web access to 10.1.80.16. All other access is allowed.

- Standard or extended? ______
- Router? ______
- Interface? ______
- Direction? ______

Verify Security Policy #5

To test this policy, you need a web server installed and running on host 10.1.80.16. You can use ServTerm 1.0 to simulate a web server, or you can download and install one of the many freeware web servers available on the Internet. Web access from host 10.1.50.7 to host 10.1.80.16 should be blocked. All other hosts should have web access to 10.1.80.16. Also, test to make sure that 10.1.50.7 has web access to other destinations. For example, 10.1.50.7 should be able to open a web page from one of the three routers as long as the routers have the HTTP service active.

Security Policy #6

Only hosts from the 10.1.50.0/24 LAN should be allowed to access the HTTP service on the CALGARY router. Make sure that HTTP is enabled on CALGARY with the **ip http server** command. All other hosts should be denied this access.

- Standard or extended? ______
- Router? ______

Verify Security Policy #6

A host from the 10.1.50.0/24 LAN should be able to open a web browser to any valid address on the CALGARY router. No other host should be able to gain access to CALGARY through a web browser.

Security Policy #7

Use the name NOPINGS to configure a named ACL that stops all pings from the 10.1.70.0/24 network from reaching hosts on the 10.1.10.0/24 network. All other access should be allowed.

- Router? ______
- Interface? ______
- Direction? ______

Verify Security Policy #7

Host 10.1.70.2 should not be able to ping host 10.1.10.5. However, host 10.1.70.2 should be able to ping all other addresses. All other hosts should be able to ping 10.1.10.5.

APPENDIX A

CCNA 2 Skills-Based Assessment Practice

Figure A-1 **CCNA 2 Skills-Based Assessment Topology**

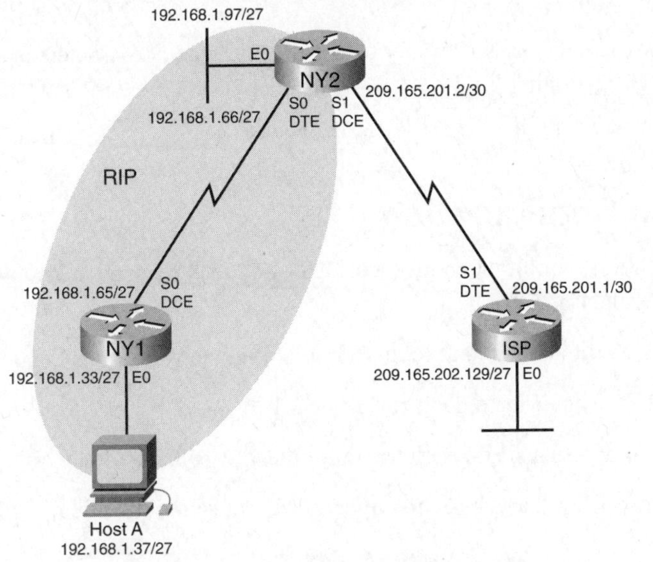

Objectives:

This assessment contains the following objectives:

- Basic router configuration
- Routing configuration
- Security—Access control list (ACL) configuration

Equipment:

Depending on the router model, the interfaces can differ. For example, on your router, Serial0 might be Serial0/0 and Ethernet0 might be FastEthernet0/0.

NetLab Compatibility Notes:

This lab can be completed using NetLab. However, you cannot test all your access control lists.

Task 1: Basic Router Configuration

Step 1. Cable the lab as shown in Figure A-1.

Step 2. On all three routers, do the following:

- Configure host names for the routers according to the topology.
- Configure interfaces with IP addresses according to the topology.
- Enable the configured interfaces.
- Set the clock rate to 64000 bps on the required serial interfaces.
- Routers should log out of an unattended session after being idle for 5 minutes.

- Prevent console messages from interrupting command-line input.
- Prevent the routers from searching for a Domain Name System (DNS) server.
- Console and vty line passwords are **cisco**; encrypted privileged passwords are **class**.

Step 3. On NY2, do the following:

- Add the description "Connection to the Internet" to the serial 1 interface.
- Configure a message (banner), "Authorized Access Only", that the user will see when logging in to the router.
- Allow users on the NY2 router to ping the ISP and NY1 routers using the commands **ping ISP** and **ping NY1**.

Step 4. On ISP, make sure that the HTTP server is enabled.

Task 2: Routing Configuration

Step 1. Enable Routing Information Protocol (RIP) on the NY1 and NY2 routers to route for the 192.168.1.0/24 network.

Step 2. On NY2, configure a default route to forward unknown destinations to ISP.

Step 3. On NY2, propagate the default route to NY1.

Step 4. On ISP, configure a single static route for the 192.168.1.0/24 network pointing to NY2.

Step 5. Configure RIP so that the routing updates are not sent out the NY1 or NY2 LANs.

Task 3: Security—Named Access Control List Configuration

Step 1. Design a named access control list and apply it to only one interface with all of the following requirements:

- Restrict all hosts/networks except the NY1 LAN (192.168.1.32/27 network) from accessing the Internet through HTTP and Telnet.
- Allow all internal hosts/networks to send Internet Control Message Protocol (ICMP) traffic to any other hosts/networks inside or outside. All internal hosts should be able to ping any destination address.

Step 2. Design a named access control list and apply it to only one interface with all of the following requirements:

- Permit only the ICMP echo-reply traffic into the New York networks. (A ping sent from the inside of the network will get a response, but a ping sent from the ISP will be unreachable.)
- Permit only TCP traffic that left the New York network to return. (Only the traffic that was established on the New York network will be allowed to return to the network. Any traffic originating from the ISP will fail.)

Step 3. To test your ACLs, you should be able to do the following. (Remember that you *cannot* test from the router that you configured the ACLs on. All traffic must traverse the interfaces of the router to follow the ACLs.)

- Ping from any host or device on the New York network to the ISP router and get a successful response.

- Telnet from the NY1 LAN on the New York network and be able to log in to the ISP router. If you do not have a host on the NY1 LAN, you can test this by using the following command on the router. This command causes the router to source the Telnet traffic from the Ethernet or Fast Ethernet interface:

```
NY1#telnet 209.165.201.1 /source-interface fa0/0
```

- A ping from the ISP router to any host or device on the New York network should fail.
- A Telnet from the ISP router to any host or device on the New York network should fail.
- Host A should be able to open a web page using any IP address on the ISP router. However, a host attached to ISP should not be able to open a web page using an address from 192.168.1.0/24.

APPENDIX B

Router Interface Summary

For the majority of CCNA 2 labs, you need to examine the following chart to correctly reference the router interface identifiers to use in IOS commands. The correct identifier to use is based on the equipment in your lab.

Router Model	Ethernet Interface #1	Ethernet Interface #2	Serial Interface #1	Serial Interface #2
800 (806)	Ethernet 0 (E0)	Ethernet 1 (E1)		
1600	Ethernet 0 (E0)	Ethernet 1 (E1)	Serial 0 (S0)	Serial 1 (S1)
1700	FastEthernet 0 (FA0)	FastEthernet 1 (FA1)	Serial 0 (S0)	Serial 1 (S1)
2500	Ethernet 0 (E0)	Ethernet 1 (E1)	Serial 0 (S0)	Serial 1 (S1)
2600	FastEthernet 0/0 (FA0/0)	FastEthernet 0/1 (FA0/1)	Serial 0/0 (S0/0)	Serial 0/1 (S0/1)

To find out exactly how the router is configured, look at the interfaces and identify what type and how many interfaces the router has. There is no way to effectively list all of the combinations of configurations for each router class. What the chart provides are the identifiers for the possible combinations of interfaces in the device. This interface chart does not include any other type of interface even though a specific router might contain one. An example of this is an ISDN BRI interface. The string in parentheses is the legal abbreviation that you can use in Cisco IOS software commands to represent the interface.

Erasing and Reloading the Router

For the majority of CCNA2 labs, it is necessary to start with a basic unconfigured router; otherwise, the configuration parameters you enter might combine with previous ones and produce unpredictable results. The instructions here allow you to prepare router the before performing the lab so that previous configuration options do not interfere with your configurations.

The following is the procedure for clearing out previous configurations and starting with an unconfigured router:

1. Enter privileged EXEC mode by entering **enable**:

   ```
   Router>enable
   ```

   If prompted for a password, enter **class**. (If that does not work, ask your instructor.)

2. In privileged EXEC mode, enter the command **erase startup-config**:

   ```
   Router#erase startup-config
   ```

   The response from the router is

   ```
   Erasing the nvram filesystem will remove all files! Continue? [confirm]
   ```

3. Press **Enter** to confirm. The response is

   ```
   Erase of nvram: complete
   ```

4. In privileged EXEC mode, enter the command **reload**:

   ```
   Router# reload response:
   System configuration has been modified. Save? [yes/no]:
   ```

   Enter **n** and press **Enter**. The router responds with

   ```
   Proceed with reload? [confirm]
   ```

5. Press **Enter** to confirm.

   The first line of the response is

   ```
   Reload requested by console.
   ```

   After the router reloads, the prompt is

   ```
   Would you like to enter the initial configuration dialog? [yes/no]:
   ```

6. Enter **n** and press **Enter**. The responding prompt is

   ```
   Press RETURN to get started!
   ```

7. Press **Enter**.

   The router is ready for you to perform the assigned lab.

Notes

Notes

Notes